1971

THE ORPHIC VISION

THE ORPHIC VISION

Seer Poets from Novalis to Rimbaud

GWENDOLYN BAYS

University of Nebraska Press • Lincoln • 1964

The publication of this book was assisted
by a grant from the Ford Foundation.

Publishers on the Plains
UNP

Acknowledgments for the use of copyrighted
material begin on page 292

Library of Congress Catalog card number 63-14693

Manufactured in the United States of America

To my mother, Mary McKee

Preface

In the literature of Romanticism the theme of the poet as seer is not the large and all-embracing subject it might appear to be at first glance. It is, in fact, a small branch of a much larger current of thought known as Illuminism, which was extremely rich and complex and which affected, to a greater or lesser degree, the majority of writers from the middle of the eighteenth century to the end of the nineteenth. The purpose of this volume is not, therefore, to cover the entire current of Illuminist thought during those years, but merely to bring into sharper focus one of its branches which, although minor in comparison with the whole, had nevertheless a profound effect upon the literature of Romanticism. The intention is not to present an exhaustive study of any single author or movement mentioned, but to select that part of each author's work which is directly related to the idea of the poet as seer. Writers were chosen for scrutiny only if they had made a clear and precise statement of this idea in their works or, as in the case of E. T. A. Hoffmann and Balzac, if certain of their characters were seer poets and therefore incarnations of the idea. As the research progressed and it became increasingly likely that the idea of poet as seer grew out of the Illuminist thought of the Romantic period, the omission of such apparently visionary poets as Lamartine, Vigny, and Hölderlin seemed quite justified, since their primary inspiration came from other sources. All three possibly could be referred to as visionary, but they were not seers in the precise sense in which the Romantics used this word: one who possessed magic vision of the kind which could be found both in the wisdom of the ancient Magi and in the modern discovery of Mesmer. The experiments of the Austrian doctor made the phenomenon of voyance, or second sight, seem plausible to many and also stimulated re-examination and re-evaluation of the lore of the Egyptians and the Magi. The intellectual curiosity of the Romantics toward the phenomenon of voyance, it may be noted, has an exact parallel in present-day interest in such subjects as hypnosis, telepathy, and extrasensory perception.

Illuminism is a term eighteenth-century writers borrowed from the Renaissance to refer to the more transcendental aspects of these doctrines of the ancient world. It referred to white magic rather than black, and because one of its primary aims was the spiritual development of its adherents, most Romantics were unaware that it was philosophically incompatible with the tenets of Christianity. Since it was within this more idealistic side of Illuminism that the Romantics discovered the phenomenon of voyance, it has seemed appropriate to eliminate from this study works of the *roman noir* variety, such as Alexandre Dumas' *Joseph Balsamo,* some of the early works of Nodier, and Balzac's *Melmoth réconcilié.* Emphasizing the serious purpose of the Illuminists, Balzac objects to the use of the word magic to refer to their activities:

> To make gold was their point of departure, but . . . they were looking for something better, they wanted to find the essential molecule, they were looking for movement at its beginning. In the infinitely small they wanted to take by surprise the secrets of universal life, of which they perceived the play. The assembly of these sciences constitutes Magism; don't mistake it for Magic. Magism is the lofty science which seeks to discover the intimate meaning of things and which inquires by what unbound threads natural effects are connected with them.[1]

Although Balzac and Hugo discovered the phenomenon of voyance in greater detail than any of the other French Romantics, it was the young poet Arthur Rimbaud who perceived most clearly the creative possibilities of this interior vision and formulated it into an esthetic doctrine which has been translated and analyzed in the second part of this study. Rimbaud may not, of course, be considered the direct heir of all the German writers who preceded him, or in fact of any one of them, but the ideas which appear in the *Voyant* letters become clearer if they are placed in this perspective. Moreover, a more precise understanding of the *Voyant* letters sheds much light upon many of the enigmatic poems of Rimbaud's *Illuminations.*

The subject chosen for discussion here has, strangely enough, not been studied per se before by any other critic, although numerous references have been made here and there in their works to this well-known theory of Romanticism. Since it was therefore necessary to begin on completely untouched ground, some selection had to be made.

As an esthetic theory, the idea of the poet as seer is not one which passed away quickly in the nineteenth century. It has survived and has many modern adherents, who, although they state the theory in different terms, still hold to its essential tenet that art is not an end in itself but a valid means of arriving at new knowledge. As such, the doctrine lies midway between two extreme esthetic viewpoints of today. On the one hand are the purists who hold tenaciously to the doctrine of art for art's sake and do not want their literature contaminated with ideas; at the other extreme are the advocates of "committed art" who contend that serious art should ally itself with the political and social causes of the times. The first view tends to relegate the artist to the ivory tower where he can remain less affected by the events which take place around him and therefore more capable of producing "pure art"; the second view subjects the artist too much to the hue and cry of the masses. In its more extreme form, the latter view destroys both the artist and his art, when both must become the mouthpiece of a particular government. The conception of the poet as seer, which lies between these two extremes, neither separates the artist from the human lot nor subjects him to mob thinking for, like the priest, he has been in touch with something larger than individual existence, but is not for this reason exempt from the human condition. Translated into the modern philosophical terminology of F. S. C. Northrop, this larger existence would be best called "the esthetic continuum," with the meaning which he ascribes to it.[2] Rimbaud and the German Romantics called it the "World Soul" but, in any case, the creative process is conceived as a dynamic one, in that the role of the poet is passive as well as active and proceeds by an incoming as well as by an outgoing method. In his outgoing active capacity the poet is a "stealer of fire" in the Rimbaldian sense, whereas in his passive role he is an instrument for the reception of ideas from the Beyond. But it is the passive role of the artist which is usually overlooked, and this is the very one which must precede, for the poet cannot seize Eternity until Eternity has first seized him.

Contents

PART I

Historical Origins

CHAPTER 1

A Confusion of Ways

Poetry lies where the known
verges upon the unknown.
PRESCOTT, *The Poetic Mind*

The theory of the poet as seer, as prophet and interpreter of the gods, as one endowed with supernormal powers, may accurately be called the perennial philosophy of poetry, for in the history of esthetic conceptions it has had many rebirths. It has existed at one time or another in almost every ancient culture. In the Biblical world and in ancient Greece particularly, poetry and prophecy were one. Among the Greeks, Pindar first advanced the idea and Plato developed it in the *Ion* and the *Republic* as an attack upon the Homeric conception of the poet as sorcerer or entertainer. Homer and other poets whose art Plato admits he admires are reluctantly excluded from his ideal state on the grounds that their works have an injurious effect upon men. In Plato's opinion, Homeric poetry not only stirs the passions which blind men to truth, but also is treacherous because it possesses a power which may be compared with the forces of magic (*Republic,* Book X). Although today few would agree with Plato in his attack on Homer, his insight into the Homeric creative conception is precise and accurate. It is perhaps not without some semantic significance that the most frequent Homeric word for poet is *aiodos* (singer), while his song is referred to as *kēlēthmos* (enchantment), signifying that the poet's chief function is to charm his listeners. Only among later Greek writers was the word for poet replaced by *poiētēs,* having the connotation of craftsman. Similarly, among the Romans the word *vātes* was replaced by the word *poēta.*[1] Yet, in spite of the Platonic attack. the Homeric idea of the poet as entertainer seems to have persisted; the poet and grammarian Apollonius of Rhodes, writing a century and a half after Plato, uses the verb *thelgein* (to charm) in describing the process of writing poetry — the same word Homer chose to describe Hermes putting Odysseus' men to sleep in the episode of the sirens.

To the Homeric conception Plato, in the *Ion,* opposes his own theory of poetic creation as the result of divine possession and inspiration. The poet does not create by his own powers but, deprived of his senses, utters the prophecies of the gods:

> For the poet is a light and winged and holy thing, and there is no invention in him until he has been inspired and is out of his senses, and the mind is no longer in him: when he has not attained to this state, he is powerless and is unable to utter his oracles . . . for not by art does the poet sing, but by power divine. Had he learned by rules of art, he would have known how to speak not of one theme only, but of all; and therefore God takes away the minds of poets, and uses them as his ministers, as he also uses diviners and holy prophets, in order that we who hear them may know that they speak not of themselves who utter these priceless words in a state of unconsciousness, but that God is the speaker, and that through them he is conversing with us.[2]

The real significance of the Homeric as opposed to the Platonic theory of artistic creation, however, consists of more than the ancient world's way of expressing the opposition between the conception of art for art's sake (the Homeric theory) and the idea of art as a means of communicating truth (the Platonic theory). The Homeric conception implies that the poet is a magician whose chants have hypnotic effects, and the poetic process therefore involves a lowering of consciousness. The Platonic theory suggests the opposite. Instead of having soporific effects, the creative process is compared by Plato to a Bacchic frenzy. A heightening or quickening of the waking consciousness is suggested rather than a lowering or slowing-down process, as was the case in the Homeric idea.

Much importance was attached by the ancients to the "ecstatic" theory of artistic creation which appears again in Plotinus six centuries later, whereas after Plotinus the Homeric idea fell into a long oblivion. Attacking the Artistotelian conception of art as an imitation of nature, Plotinus maintains that the artist, instead of copying nature, must shape it as the sculptor does his marble in accordance with his own inner vision. Artistic excellence, in the Plotinian doctrine, depends upon the quality of the artist's vision, which improves only as he develops spiritually. In the sixth book of the *Enneads* Plotinus compares the mystic and the sculptor, both of whom must "cut away what is gross, straighten what is crooked, lighten what is too heavy" until the good "has been enthroned in a stainless shrine." The importance of the vision as a means of artistic creation is developed by Plotinus:

> I am vision-loving and I create by the vision-seeing faculty within me. . . . I gaze within and the figures of my material world take being as if they fell from my brooding. . . . All the failures among men, whether in being or doing, mark but the swervings of visionaries from the objects of contemplation.[3]

Plotinus described the nature of his numerous intimate experiences of union with the One in these terms:

> We may know we have had the vision when the Soul has suddenly taken light. This light is from the Supreme and is the Supreme. . . . He comes bringing light; the light is the proof of the advent. Thus the Soul unlit remains without vision; lit, it possesses what it sought. And this is the true end set before the Soul, to take that light, to see the Supreme by the Supreme . . . just as it is by the sun's own light that we see the sun.[4]

Thus, in the minds of the ancients there existed between these two kinds of seers a distinction which should be discussed at the beginning of this study. The experiences of the first, which will be referred to as the nocturnal, are related to the Freudian unconscious, while those of the second, called here the mystical, belong to another area of the human psyche and pertain to the Platonic-Plotinian experience later cultivated by medieval Christian mystics. In considering the basis on which such a distinction is made, the unconscious must be thought of as related to the past of an individual, being a vast repository containing all events. It must also be regarded as having various depth levels, the first of which contains events dating from the immediate past back to the time of birth. In this region the past is present; it is re-enacted on the screen of memory. (Thus, a writer like Proust, as he recalls his childhood, can speak of having the impression that he has overcome Time.) In a second and deeper stratum of the unconscious lie the ancestral and animal origins, those links by which man is bound to the evolutionary process, the region of his instincts and powerful drives. This is the primitive man, with his belief in magic, who lies dormant in us all. Finally, there is the third level, the most mysterious and the most difficult to reach, which Jung has called the collective unconscious. On this level, man the individual is linked with humanity or his racial consciousness. Both Freud and Jung agree that in comparison with the unconscious, the conscious waking psyche is a far more recent development and much more superficial than the vaster realms of the instinctual psyche. Whatever judgment one may wish to make of other aspects of Freudian psychology, this distinction between a waking consciousness and a sleeping or "unconscious" state has not been superseded and can hardly be denied, for it is within the direct experience of us all.

The existence of a barrier between the realms of sleep and waking was perceived by both Homer and Virgil, and both made a distinction between the two kinds of visionary experiences. In the celebrated imagery of the gates of ivory and the gates of horn they represented this fundamental poetic insight (*Odyssey* IX, 562-567; *Aeneid* VI, 893-896). Through the portal of horn, leading into the realm of the dead, came nothing but truth, whereas through the gate "of gleaming ivory" false dreams often came to men. Thus, the ancients wisely saw that dreams can be the bearers of both truth and error, for in the light of modern knowledge is it not true that mis-evaluations of the past can lead men to errors which are often embodied in their dreams? Or, conversely, that dreams may be representations of the highest truths?

Significantly, one of the chief problems of modern psychiatry concerns the barrier between the conscious and the unconscious. That these two states intermingle is easily perceived, the unconscious often shaping the course of daily actions, the events of every day entering freely into dreams. As Jung has written, "We know for certain today that the unconscious contains contents which would mean an immeasurable increase of knowledge if they could be released."[5]

Methods of treating the mentally ill and investigation of other pressing problems have left psychiatrists little time for exploration of positive and creative uses of the unconscious by the mentally healthy. Freud abandoned hypnosis because it established an unhealthy relationship between psychologist and patient. Since then the standard procedure among psychologists has been free association, which is time-consuming, expensive, and also difficult for many patients. During the last war doctors often resorted to the use of drugs like sodium pentathol as a short cut for cases requiring urgent and immediate treatment. Aware that a more effective means of penetrating the barrier was a fundamental psychological problem, Aldous Huxley published his experiments with the drug mescalin, which he claimed was nonhabit-forming and altogether harmless from a medical point of view.[6] In its report on Huxley's work, *Time* (June 28, 1954), citing the *London Journal of Medical Science,* declared that the best hypnotic drug known to the medical world was not mescalin but lysergic acid diethylamide, better known in medical circles at LSD 25. Although discovered in Switzerland as long ago as 1938, this drug, according to the *London Journal of Medical Science,* has been neglected until quite recently. Unlike sodium pentathol, LSD 25 enables the patient to re-experience his past without loss of consciousness, watching himself in the process: The importance of such discoveries is not limited to their usefulness in the treatment of mental illness, nor are they of interest only to readers of psychiatric journals. Because they contribute to man's understanding of himself, they are of vital significance to the humanities in general. Today, a safe crossing of the barrier — into a greatly enlarged area of self-awareness — seems possible.

Psychological data of this sort are particularly relevant here because many of the French Romantics with whom we are dealing — Nodier, Nerval, Gautier, Baudelaire, Verlaine, and Rimbaud — made free use of the drug hashish to "penetrate the Unknown," as Rimbaud expressed it. *Les Paradis artificiels* of Baudelaire, Nerval's *Aurélia,* and Rimbaud's *Voyant* letters, as well as many passages from *Les Illuminations* and *Une Saison en enfer,* contain much valuable information about the unconscious, anticipating the discoveries of scientists by some fifty to a hundred years. These poets not only succeeded in revolutionizing French poetry but also discovered a whole new area of the human psyche. Only partially aware of the original nature of their discoveries, they took hashish not so much to shock and scandalize, as many critics in the past have thought, but in order to explore this unknown world. In fact, Baudelaire's last words at the end of *Les Paradis artificiels* contains a plea for achieving, without the use of drugs, the extraordinary state of consciousness which he had experienced under hashish. Rimbaud, in particular, expressed in the *Voyant* letters his great urgency to find a technique, but he assumed, in accordance with the knowledge of his times, that the method could only be a destructive one. All of the above-mentioned poets are nocturnal seers, as defined here, because of the dark regions into which they delved at such a terrible price to their health and sanity; their vision may be more accurately termed the orphic vision to distinguish it from the mystic vision with which it has been so often confused.

Let us now consider the hypothesis that there may also exist a third area of the human psyche pertaining to the future, just as the unconscious is the repository of an individual's past and his waking consciousness is related to the present. To distinguish this third area from the Freudian concept of the superego, the censor which is unrelated to the conception under discussion here, we shall call it the *superconscious*. A realm of contingency and potential spiritual fulfillment, the superconscious may be said to contain the future as an acorn contains an oak. This realm of "ecstasy," which Plotinus describes in *The Enneads,* is the region of mystic vision which must be distinguished from the visions of the nocturnal seers.

But how can one be certain that the mystic's visions do not proceed from the unconscious, as do those of the poets mentioned above? Why must a separate area of consciousness be postulated to account for them? Three reasons may be given which would seem to indicate that the nature of the experience is different. The *first* is purely physical. We know that in a state of hypnosis or sleep the body metabolism and pulse are lower than they are in a state of waking. This can be accurately measured. To be sure, no one has ever taken the pulse or metabolism of a mystic in his trance, but in the descriptions which mystics have written of their experiences there is wide agreement. The moment of illumination is usually described as a state of great exaltation, of heightened awareness and "transport," to use the word of Saint Theresa. Among mystics the metaphor of fire or blinding light is most commonly used (e.g., the passage quoted above from Plotinus, St. Paul's experience on the road to Damascus, Pascal's *Mémorial,* etc.). Many examples could be given, but perhaps these two will suffice. The first is from the poem "Wonder" by Thomas Traherne, describing a state of heightened consciousness; the second is taken from Saint Theresa, who used the image of fire:

I

A native health and innocence
Within my bones did grow,
And while my God did all his glories show,
I felt a vigor in my sense
That was all Spirit. I within did flow
With seas of life, like wine;
I nothing in the world did know
But 'twas divine.[7]

II

What is intelligence? In what does it differ from the soul and the spirit? I do not rightly know; all that seems to me one and the same thing. What I do know is that the soul sometimes goes out of itself, like a bright fire which throws flames. The brilliance of this fire begins to increase violently, the flame rises very high, but it does not for this reason change its nature, it is still the flame of fire. . . .[8]

Second, we know that the aftereffects of a mystic's state of illumination differ greatly from those visionary states produced under hypnosis, drugs, and free association. Nervous depletion, exhaustion, or depression are generally reported to be the aftereffects of the methods mentioned above. Baudelaire referred to these states after taking hashish as "spleen," while extreme fatigue is experienced by patients after an hour of free association. Under hypnosis and drugs like sodium pentathol the patient cannot remember his experiences unless he is told to do so by the hypnotist. Mystics, on the other hand, remember their experiences vividly and insist that the aftereffects of their illuminative states are entirely beneficial and even invigorating (as in Traherne's poem). Saint Theresa writes: "This orison, however long it may be, is never harmful to the health; at least it has never been prejudicial to me. . . . I experienced on the contrary a very noticeable well-being."

A *third* and equally strong barrier, comparable to the one dividing the conscious from the unconscious psyche, exists between the conscious and the superconscious or mystical state. In its search for effective ways of treating the mentally ill, the medical world has been able to penetrate the barriers of the unconscious by means of drugs, but neither by drugs nor by hypnosis has anyone been able to induce a true mystical state. Such a drug would have to be one which produces opposite physical effects of those drugs now generally used on the mentally ill, not to mention the extraordinary trance states many mystics describe. Before man can be in full possession of himself this area as well as the unconscious must be explored. So far, the only way of entering this area is by means of the thorny road of spiritual development outlined by the mystics. Accounts given of the effects of drugs such as Huxley's mescalin or LSD 25 bear a much closer resemblance to Baudelaire's descriptions of the effects of hashish than to the experience of mystics, but this does not lessen their value. To travel mentally into one's past can have a highly beneficial effect on even the healthy, but it is not the same state as the Platonic-Plotinian-Christian mystical experience, and is never described in the same terms.

The unknown in man therefore extends not in one direction only, as Freudian psychologists believe, but in two. Value judgments of the three areas of consciousness would be erroneous; one of them is not superior to another as each has its own function which is equally vital to the whole man. Unconscious and superconscious must be explored before a man can be in complete possession of himself. Such an individual would be a true seer as Novalis has defined the word: "Man fully conscious is called a seer," he writes in the *Fragmente*.[9] In the same way, the Homeric and Platonic theories of poetry are equally valid, the one implying that the creative process involves a lowering of consciousness and the other a heightening. This is true because artistic creation depends vitally upon the poet's achieving a larger awareness than others, upon his extending his own knowledge of the human spirit. In a very particular sense, therefore, the quotation at the beginning of the chapter, "Poetry lies where the known verges upon the unknown," is fraught with a special meaning.

We have called the idea of the poet as seer or *vātes* a perennial philosophy of poetry. A brief glance at some of its recurrent manifestations in literary history prior to the Romantic period shows that before this time seer poets were inspired for the most part by the Plotinian-Christian tradition. This does not mean that the unconscious never entered into their poetry, but simply that until the Romantic era the idea of the poet as seer was connected primarily with the Plotinian-Christian mystical experience. Since beauty and truth were equivalent and mutually dependent in the conception of the ancients, no conflict existed between the two. It was then that the *vātes* idea flourished. In the Middle Ages, however, when beauty became subordinate to truth as the medieval mind conceived it, and art became the servant or handmaiden of religion, the idea of the poet as seer did not reappear. For men like St. Bernard, Ruysbroeck, Meister Eckhart, and other great writers of this period, the mystical experience was a completely absorbing end in itself. Among the medieval poets only Dante (and he, in point of time, stood on the threshold of the Renaissance) seemed to incarnate the conception of the poet as seer.

Significantly enough, it was only with the discovery of the ancient world by Renaissance humanists, and along with it the idea of beauty as a positive good, that the *vātes* conception reappeared. It was revived in France by the Pléiade; Du Bellay developed it at the end of his famous *Deffence et Illustration* (1549), and Ronsard also stated it as his poetic credo in his "Ode à Michel de l'Hôpital." In spite of their mythological erudition, Ronsard's *Hymnes* — especially one such as "Les Daimons" — in which the poet describes his descent into hell, have visionary and prophetic qualities which may be compared with the later works of Hugo. Mention should be made of three other great Renaissance visionaries whose influence reached far beyond the boundaries of their countries and times — the two Spanish mystics, St. Theresa of Avila and St. John of the Cross, and the German shoemaker of Görlitz, Jakob Boehme.

It is not surprising that the idea of the poet as seer does not appear in France or England during the classical era. The spirit of the times was Cartesian, and form and reason, it was thought, should dominate inspiration — doubtless a healthy reaction against some of the unleashed excesses of the Renaissance. Nevertheless, there were small groups of visionary dissenters, many of whom were disciples of either Plato and Plotinus or of St. Theresa: in France, Pascal, the Quietists, and a small group of recently discovered mystical poets, the best of whom were Chastenet, Lacépède, and Jean de Sponde; in England, the Cambridge Platonists and the "metaphysical poets."

The Quietist movement in France had Spanish origins, not only through its founder, Miguel de Molinos, but also through a relative of Malebranche's mother, Madame Acarie, who introduced the works of St. Theresa into France. Like the more controversial Jansenism, to which Pascal was attached, Quietism expressed the need of many to free themselves from the excesses of a bureaucratic religion and to cultivate their inner life with more freedom. Significantly, both movements were crushed, largely through the efforts of the Jesuits. Doubtless, the Jesuits were able to do this because the spirit of the times was hostile to individualism in religion; religious innovators had already brought too much suffering to France during the preceding century. Although the Jansenists may by no means be considered mystics in the sense that the Quietists were, they were indirectly descended from Plato through their acknowledged inspirer, St. Augustine. The two movements produced three mystical writers of the first order — Pascal (1623-1662), Malebranche (1638-1715), and Fénelon (1651-1715) — in whose works the Plotinian-Christian mystic tradition abounds.

Although greatly different in form and content and of much more limited influence, the Cambridge Platonists had two points in common with the Quietists and Jansenists: they hoped to evolve a philosophy to refute materialism (Hobbes) while freeing theology from the errors of scholasticism. This group, of whom Henry More (1614-

1687) and Ralph Cudworth (1617-1688) were leading figures, often met at Ragley in Warwickshire at the home of Lady Conway, one of More's pupils who became a Quaker and a personal friend of William Penn and the German occultist, Van Helmont. More summarized their philosophy, which claimed Platonism and Neoplatonism as its source of inspiration, in his best-known prose work, *Divine Dialogues* (1668). On the whole, the influence of the Cambridge Platonists was slight. The spirit of the times was opposed to such a philosophy; it was the era of Classicism, and the minds of the best thinkers did not go in the direction of Neoplatonism.

In the same tradition, visionary poetry had another brief flowering in the metaphysical poets—George Herbert (1593-1633), Richard Crashaw (1613?-1949), Henry Vaughan (1622-1695), and Thomas Traherne (1637?-1674). Crashaw, an Anglican converted to Catholicism at the age of thirty-three, was inspired in his early youth by St. Theresa. In a long poem, "A Hymn to the Name and Honor of the Admirable Sainte Teresa," he celebrates the Spanish mystic whom he admired so much. Vaughan and Traherne, whose poems were only recently discovered (1903), had turned to metaphysical poetry after reading George Herbert's poem, "The Temple," published posthumously in 1634. Among modern critics, there has been a recent tendency inspired by T. S. Eliot to exaggerate the contribution of these poets to English poetry as a whole. That they hold a unique place in any literary history is undeniable, but actually the number of poems which achieve real excellence is slight. Only too often their mystical inspiration, while fundamentally original, is stifled by knotty and bizarre figures of speech, spread out through an entire poem in intricate and often far-fetched detail. However, when they did succeed in overcoming these stylistic peculiarities, their success was spectacular. Poems such as Vaughan's "The World," "The Retreate," and "They are All Gone into the World of Light," Crashaw's poem to St. Theresa, and Traherne's "Wonder" and "The Vision" represent some of their best works.

In English literature a definite Platonic-Plotinian tradition of visionary poetry continues unbroken from the metaphysical poets to Blake, Wordsworth, Francis Thompson, Alice Meynell, and Evelyn Underhill. On the continent, however, this tradition, revived by the Pléiade, underwent a significant change toward the end of the eighteenth century. In the literature of French and German Romanticism, the poet is again a seer, but in a very different sense. The mystic has become a magician, an explorer of dreams and the night, an adept of Mesmer's "animal magnetism," making his way as intrepidly through the gates of horn as through the ivory gates of dream. The long-abandoned Homeric theory of the poetic process as a lowering of consciousness or the Virgilian descent into Avernus was rediscovered. (In the next two chapters the origin and development of this new non-Platonic seer concept in Germany and in France will be traced.) It was in the literature of Romanticism that the concept of the seer and of the poet as seer received their most elaborate treatment, and finally in the *Voyant* letters of Arthur Rimbaud that a theory of artistic creation based upon the idea was formulated.

In Germany, during the latter half of the eighteenth century, the revival of secret societies whose tenets were based on the main body of occult doctrine, the example and influence of Swedenborg and, finally, at the height of the *Sturm und Drang* period, the semi-scientific discoveries of Mesmer, awakened the curiosity of many German intellectuals to the phenomena of the unconscious and of second sight as both spiritual and scientific possibilities. The idea of the poet as seer was mentioned first by Hamann and developed most completely in the person and philosophic writings of Novalis, who was himself the epitome of a seer poet. The "Romantic physicists" — Franz von Baader, J. W. Ritter, Heinrich Steffens, and G. H. von Schubert — were disciples of Mesmer who in their scientific experiments explored the unconscious and wrote of its extraordinary visual powers. Exactly a hundred years before Freud, G. H. von Schubert wrote a *Traumdeutung* entitled *The Symbolism of the Dream* (*Die Symbolik des Traumes,* 1814), anticipating some of the chief Freudian theories about dreams as well as Jung's idea of the rapport between the dream and the myth. But in the excitement of their discovery of this new realm of the psyche, certain of the German Romantics — Achim von Arnim, G. H. von Schubert, and E. T. A. Hoffmann in particular — considered the unconscious and the dream world superior to the conscious realm of the psyche. Opium was used freely, in the initiation rites of the secret societies and by many writers to produce dream states. The most effective artistic results of this technique were achieved by E. T. A. Hoffmann, whose works more than those of any other writer across the Rhine served to popularize visionary literature in France.

The idea of the poet as seer took on particular significance in France, serving as opposition to the theory of art for art's sake in an esthetic battle which lasted during the entire nineteenth century. The history of the quarrel is well known and has been outlined in detail by A. Cassagne in *La Théorie de l'art pour l'art* (1906). By the end of the century events themselves had revealed to the partisans of each side some of their errors. Those who favored the doctrine of art for art's sake (which maintains that pleasure and not truth is the chief aim of poetry) witnessed the increasing tendency of many Parnassian poets to produce verse which was both trivial and artificial because it was detached from life. The defeat of 1870-1871 proved conclusively to them that the modern poet could not afford to isolate himself from society. Similarly, partisans of voyant poetry felt the temptation to write moralistic, utilitarian, and even propagandistic poetry. *Les Chants modernes* of Maxime du Camp, with its poems in praise of gas, electricity, and chloroform, caused this group of poets to reflect upon the extremes to which "engaged" literature could degenerate. Today, the error in this nineteenth-century esthetic dilemma seems clear enough: both poets and critics were attempting to divide form and content arbitrarily – as the philosophers had tried to divide mind and matter – rather than viewing them as the inseparables which they are.

The idea of the poet as seer, however, does not end with Rimbaud and Romanticism. In both the Symbolist and Surrealist movements, the late nineteenth and early twentieth centuries witnessed two further rebirths of this perennial philosophy. Brunetière, a contemporary critic of Symbolism, viewed this movement as a disaffection for Positivism and Naturalism and as a rediscovery of a sense of mystery by young men of letters of the late 1880's. More recently, Guy Michaud in his four-volume study of Symbolism, concludes that the real merit of this movement consists in two particular contributions: (1) the rediscovery of the essence of poetry in its affinity with mystical experience, and (2) the poet's consciousness of himself and his task, "la reprise de l'âme dans ses propres profondeurs."[10] Michaud's statement is of particular significance to this study, since we see the Symbolists' search for the Absolute (the Plotinian-Christian mystic experience) as their *theoretical* ideal, while in fact they erroneously sought to achieve this on the paths of occultism and the unconscious, as some of their statements show.

For example, in the manifesto, *La Littérature de tout à l'heure* (1889), which was the Symbolist movement's "Preface to Cromwell," Charles Morice proclaims the need his generation felt to unite beauty and truth in a new art, which would be a synthesis of esthetics and metaphysics: "Beauty is the radiance of Truth in symbols which have cast off the dryness of abstraction."[11] The new art will return to its true sources of inspiration — religion, legend, tradition, and philosophy. Pursuing this concept further, Morice insists upon the religious role of art and the artist. Art is not only a revealer of the infinite, he holds, but also the means whereby the poet is able to penetrate it: "Art has ceased to be a diversion; it is sacerdotal. . . . The true poem must emerge from Time and go beyond it." Other writers of manifestoes proclaimed much the same ideas as Morice. "The next literature will be mystic," said Rémy de Gourmont, while Vielé-Griffin defined the anguish of the modern poet as "the thirst for eternity, the need for the infinite." Saint-Pôl-Roux wrote: "The role of the Poet consists therefore in this: realizing God."[12] In short, the Symbolist poet was a Romantic who thought he ought to possess the erudition of a scholar. It was no longer enough to feel and to express his emotions; the Symbolist poet also had to have knowledge and to communicate it with accuracy and beauty of form.

While proclaiming the Plotinian ideal of artistic creation, the Symbolists turned nonetheless to the occult and the unconscious for their actual source of inspiration. Beneath all Symbolist *Weltanschauung* lay Baudelaire's Hermetic doctrine of correspondence, whereby objects of the material world are magically charged with life and meaning which the poet must decipher and communicate by the Mallarmean principle of suggestion. To evoke an object is to create it, Mallarmé says in effect as he comments in *Divagations* ("Magie") upon the "secret similarity of poetry and magic."[13] Amiel's famous statement that a landscape is *"un état de l'âme"* gives further evidence of the Symbolists' belief in the interior magic of the unconscious which has power to transform the material world. Finally, Laforgue formulated in philosophical terms the Symbolist doctrine that "esthetic production has its source in the unconscious" *(Mélanges posthumes)*.[14] In the same year Morice's manifesto appeared, Edouard Schuré published *Les grands Initiés* (1889), which served to formulate a philosophy of the occult for modern readers imbued with scientific rationalism. Both a poet and an occultist, Schuré moved freely in the world of letters and thus enjoyed a unique opportunity for influencing the Symbolists. If Morice had sought to reconcile beauty and truth, Schuré hoped to reconcile science and religion. In the introduction to his work he maintained that behind all the great religions, however widely they differ in outward form, lies an inner esoteric meaning which is the same in all. The prophets of the great religions were all initiates of this wisdom. Schuré held that modern scientific ideas such as energy, ether, evolution, magnetism, and somnambulism show how near to the ancient theosophical ideas research has led men. Schuré believed that only in this esoteric wisdom could science and religion, two equally valid needs of modern man, find true reconciliation and synthesis. One of the greatest contributions of Symbolism consists in the efforts of its followers to reconcile the numerous ideological conflicts which were increasingly dividing complex modern man against himself. Two other occult studies which also sought to reconcile science and religion through a return to and a reappraisal of the ancient wisdom, had preceded Schuré's work by a few years: Stanislas de Guaïta's *Au Seuil du Mystère* (1886) and Papus' (Dr. Encausse) *Traité élémentaire de science occulte* (1888), two works based on the Kabbala. What these two modern occultists sought primarily was to justify the ancient wisdom in the light of modern scientific discovery and to extend, if possible, the scientific horizon to recognize the existence of a non-material domain. Anatole France, in his Preface to Papus' *Traité,* described the preoccupation of his contemporaries with occult thought:

> A certain knowledge of occult science is becoming necessary to the understanding of a large number of literary works of these times. Magic occupies a large place in the imagination of our poets and our novelists. The vertigo of the invisible has seized them, the idea of the unknown haunts them and the times of Apuleius and Phlegon of Trailes has come.[15]

In this proposed synthesis of science and religion through esotericism, the Symbolist poet had the role of Orpheus, interpreter of the mysteries and messenger of the invisible. "All the great poets were either initiates or intuitives," wrote V. E. Michelet in *De l'Esotérisme dans l'art* (1891). A flurry of occult-inspired works followed these manifestoes, among which were: Villiers de l'Isle Adam's *Axël* (1890), the esoteric plays of Sâr Péladan, Dujardin's trilogy *La Légende d'Antonia* (1891-1893), Maeterlinck's *Trois petits Drames pour marionettes* (1894), and Mallarmé's Hermetic masterpiece, *Un Coup de Dés* (1897), intended as a part of a larger work which he called the "Orphic explanation of the Earth." But what did such a probing of the occult and an increasing awareness of the unconscious signify if not what Camille Mauclair suggested and Gide later developed: the myth of Narcissus, the poet who discovered his own image in the none-too-clear waters of the unconscious. In their insistence upon the synthesis of science and religion by means of the sacerdotalism of art, the Symbolists had set for themselves the Plotinian ideal and then proceeded in the opposite direction. It was no wonder they fell into preciosity, that is, they began to seek the symbol for its own sake. Preciosity is often the symptom of poets who have lost their source of inspiration. Within ten years after it began, Symbolism was already beginning to decline and, by 1905, critics were writing about it in the past tense.

The Surrealists did not make the mistake of confusing their experience with that of the Plotinian mystic tradition, but knew that they were dealing with the unconscious area of the human psyche. "Surrealist poetry . . . aims above all," said Raymond Queneau, "at creating a mysticism of a new kind."[16] This he called "*illumination surréaliste.*" Recognizing the connection which exists between the unconscious and magic, Artaud calls the surrealist vision "a new kind of magic."[17] The magic of the surrealist experience lies not only in the enlargement of the poet's vision, but also in the transformation of his personality. "The Surrealist discovers a new world, he becomes a new man," writes Eluard.[18] This change consists, according to Breton, in the poet's discovery of the lost equilibrium between dream and action, between his interpretation of the world and his ability to transform it. Alluding to Rimbaud's famous line, "*Changer la vie,*" Breton writes on the subject of surrealist magic:

> This rapport can pass for magic in this sense, that it consists in the unconscious immediate action of the internal on the external and that there slips easily into the summary analogy of such a notion the idea of a transcendent mediation which might be . . . more that of a demon than of a God.[19]

Although the Surrealists knew they were exploring the unconscious, they made an even greater error than the Symbolists, and with more serious effects upon their art: they attempted to eliminate altogether the role of the conscious in literary production. When André Breton formulated the surrealist doctrine in the 1920's, it was still necessary to attack the idea of art for art's sake, that last vestige of Parnassianism, and also the extremes of Symbolist estheticism. Declaring Rimbaud and Lautréamont to be the spiritual ancestors of the new movement, Breton said in *Les Pas perdus* (1922): "There roam in the world at present certain individuals for whom art has ceased to be an end in itself."[20] In his *Second Manifesto* (1929) he referred again to Rimbaud, this time to the *Voyant* letters in particular, and advocated that surrealist poets practice the "psychic automatism" which Rimbaud declared to be the basis of his esthetics.[21] But Breton read only half the Rimbaldian doctrine (as we shall see later when we examine it in more detail). Theoretically, as he insists in the *Voyant* letters, and in actual fact, Rimbaud was what he called himself, "the architect of my fantasies." For it is one thing to draw inspiration for literary production from the unconscious, and even to receive a *"dictée de la pensée"* (which Rimbaud advocates) but it is quite another to abandon the conscious altogether. A dream, however beautiful it may be, is not a poem or a story, and when literary form is given to the discovery of the unconscious, it must be done by the conscious – unless poets some day learn how to produce directly from the unconscious. Nevertheless, what Breton advocates in *Les Pas perdus* (1922) is quite feasible: by liberating and exploring the powerful forces of the unconscious and the dream, surrealist poets will be able to make a fuller, more conscious use of those powers only touched by poets in the past.[22] It was with this in mind that Breton encouraged automatic writing. Eluard also writes in favor of this practice: "It may be thought that automatic writing produces useless poems. No, it increases, merely develops the field of poetic examination of consciousness while enriching it. . . ."[23]

The Surrealists thus decided that all poetic vision and composition depended on direct inspiration from the unconscious. Since this type of inspiration is difficult to achieve without the use of drugs, they had set themselves a most elusive goal. Perhaps this explains their frenzied efforts.

Even more recently than the Surrealist movement, the phenomenon of the visionary in literature attracted the attention of psychiatrist Carl Jung. In an essay entitled "Psychology and Literature" (1933), Jung distinguished between two types of literature: "the psychological and the visionary."[24] The two are illustrated, he says, by the first and second parts of *Faust*. The first type, includes the vast majority of literary works and deals with the gamut of human experience, familiar to all men but treated with fresh insight and in new combinations – such is the love episode in the first part of *Faust*. In the second, the visionary type of literature, the artist attempts to see beyond everyday experience, to communicate something surpassing his own complete understanding and opening doors to the unknown. Visionary literature, different in purpose from psychological literature, should be judged in a different manner. Jung cites as examples of visionary literature, in addition to the second part of *Faust,* such works as *The Divine Comedy, Paradise Lost,* and Blake's *Prophetic Books.* Wisely, Jung does not maintain that visionary literature is superior to psychological, but merely that it is different in its purpose.

Until the mid-eighteenth century, visionary literature was inspired by the Platonic-Plotinian tradition. The discovery of a new area of the human psyche at the beginning of the nineteenth century, however, led the literary world to include in this classification literature originating from the visions of the unconscious. Thereby, many fell into the error of confusing two different types of experience.

In order to see more precisely the basis for the distinction which has been made here between the mystical and the nocturnal seers, let us examine briefly the type of experience and the symbols used to record it by three of the seer poets who took hashish—Nerval, Baudelaire, and Rimbaud. Since Nerval is not as well known as Baudelaire and will not be discussed later as fully as Rimbaud, a few preliminary remarks should be made about him.

Although born later than Hugo, Gérard de Nerval (1808-1855) was actually the pioneer in this lineage of nocturnal seers, Hugo having begun his discoveries only later in his life, a year before Nerval's death. The most erudite among the seer poets, Nerval, at the age of eighteen, translated *Faust.* Thus Nerval, along with Rimbaud, has some claim to literary precocity. Nerval made frequent journeys into Germany; among his contemporaries it was doubtless he who was most familiar with the Romantic movement beyond the Rhine. During the 1830's he published translations of many German poets—Heine, Klopstock, and Jean Paul Richter. In his uncle's library, Nerval pursued his other great interest in addition to literature, occultism, and esoteric religions. In his *Aurélia,* he mentions having read the Kabbala, Swedenborg, and the Egyptian Hermetic Books.[25] Before Hugo and Baudelaire, Nerval wrote in *Aurélia* on such subjects as correspondence, universal analogy, animism, and palingenesis. *La Phalange,* the Fourierist review, published Nerval's long article, "Isis," on the subject of the Egyptian goddess.[26] His interest in occultism also inspired him to a longer research work on eighteenth-century initiates of secret societies, such as Jacques Cazotte, Restif de la Bretonne, Quintus Aucler, Dom Pernéty of Avignon, Cagliostro, and Court de Gébelin. Their doctrines and stories relating to their lives were compiled in Nerval's book, *Les Illuminés ou les précurseurs du socialisme* (1852). Beneath his lifelong pursuit of occult and esoteric doctrines was the continually cherished hope that religious syncretism was possible and desirable in the modern world.

Nerval was a seer by temperament as well as by formation. Of the entire group of seer poets he was the most purely visionary, the one who lived most intimately with the world of dreams, and perceived the most clearly the subtle fusion of the visible with the invisible. It is the constant intrusion of the marvelous into everyday experience which makes *Aurélia* a work of sheer enchantment. Those glimpses into the unknown for which Baudelaire and Rimbaud must struggle, suffer, and revolt, seem to be taken for granted by Nerval in *Aurélia,* as if nothing could be more natural. "I could not doubt what I had seen so distinctly," he says, after having had the vision of his double.[27] Undoubtedly his malady, like the deafness of Beethoven or the blindness of Milton, aided him in his quest, in that it gave him freer access to the unconscious. Poetically and in Homeric metaphor, Nerval expressed his own intuition of the natural barrier between the conscious and the unconscious psyche: "The dream is a second life. I never could penetrate without trembling those ivory or horned gates which separate us from the invisible world."[28] Let us now examine this newly discovered terrain as our three seer poets recorded it.

Significantly, the seer poets chose the symbols water, darkness, and descent to describe their experiences — the exact opposites of those used by the mystics who spoke of theirs in terms of fire, light, and ascent. "The dark night of the soul," which Spanish mystics described, was a preliminary stage considered essential to illumination proper. In modern terms, this is the Spanish mystic's way of recording the necessity for coming face to face first with the unconscious before he can ever hope to attain illumination.

Access to the world of dreams is described by seer poets in metaphors implying descent into an abyss. Nerval uses the image of the staircase and summarizes his explorations at the end of *Aurélia* as "a descent into hell," while Rimbaud calls his hashish investigations "a season in hell."[29] In *Les Paradis artificiels,* Baudelaire uses two metaphors to describe the unconscious: the palimpsest and the abyss (*"le gouffre"*). In the first he compares the mind, as it appears to him under hashish, to an immense palimpsest (a medieval parchment manuscript) with innumerable layers of writings and illuminations, each covering up the other, but from which nothing is ever lost.[30] In the light of modern psychological knowledge the metaphor is remarkably accurate. Just as a sudden accident has been known to illuminate all the darkened layers or the forgotten incidents, so, Baudelaire continues, the drug brings back the past. The metaphor of the abyss, which he uses in *Les Fleurs du mal* to symbolize both death and sleep, represents in *Les Paradis artificiels* the plunge into the unconscious. One has the pleasant impression, he says, of plunging into an immense expanse of water ("*un gouffre limpide*") and of being pulled under "like the knight in the story of Ondine." Describing the effects of opium on De Quincey, Baudelaire writes: "It seemed to him, every night, that he was descending indefinitely into abysses without light, beyond all known depth, without hope of being able to climb back." In addition to darkness and the abyss, Baudelaire has the sensation of plunging through water: "Water became the obsessing element. We have already noted, in our work on hashish, this astonishing predilection of the brain for the liquid element and for its mysterious seductions."

Baudelaire's passages should be compared with the following excerpt from Nerval's *Aurélia,* in which the same experience of the abyss and the water is related:

> In the meantime the night was becoming slowly darker and appearances, sounds and the awareness of places were becoming confused in my somnolent spirit. *I thought that I fell into an abyss* which crossed the globe. I felt myself carried away without suffering by a current of melted metal, and a *thousand similar rivers,* the colors of which indicated chemical differences, were furrowing *the womb of the earth* like vessels and veins which wind among the lobes of the brain.[31]

The Freudian overtones of this passage, in which Nerval describes a moment before going to sleep, seem very obvious and even more suggestive of the birth process than those cited from Baudelaire. Descent, darkness, and water are all mentioned here just as they are in *Les Paradis artificiels.* Jung says of the metaphor of water: "Water is the commonest symbol for the unconscious."[32]

The successive psychosomatic effects of hashish are described by Baudelaire in great detail and are worthy of attention. The subject experiences first a state of hilarity and nervous expectation, which passes into a sensation of extreme coldness and numbness of the extremities. This state is followed by one of lassitude, stupor, and great fatigue accompanied by an excessive dryness of the mouth. At this point hallucinations gradually begin. Material objects change appearance: "they are deformed and transformed."[33] One perceives an extraordinary identity with material objects. If the subject smokes, he identifies himself with his pipe and has the strange sensation that he is himself going up in smoke and is smoking himself.[34] His own perception of space and time, like De Quincey's, which he describes, undergoes an unusual change – space becomes inflated and past becomes present. He returns to his childhood:

> Space became inflated, so to speak, to infinity. But the expansion of time became an even keener anguish; feelings and ideas which filled the duration of a night represented the length of a century. In addition the most common events of childhood, scenes long since forgotten, were reproduced in his brain, which was living a new life.[35]

De Quincey reports essentially the same extraordinary revelation of past events long forgotten by his conscious mind and adds:

> Of this, at least, I feel assured, that there is no such thing as ultimate *forgetting*; traces once impressed upon the memory are indestructible; a thousand accidents may and will interpose a veil between our present consciousness and the secret inscriptions on the mind. Accidents of the same sort will also rend away this veil. But alike, whether veiled or unveiled, the inscription remains forever.[36]

After their initial plunge into the unconscious, other seer poets also found themselves in the domain of childhood. Rimbaud identifies his childhood with Eden or the Golden Age after the Deluge and also with the Orient of the Magi in the poem, "Conte." Baudelaire devotes an entire chapter in *Les Paradis artificiels,* "Chagrins d'Enfance," to De Quincey's account of his childhood as seen under the influence of opium, and Nerval dreams of his ancestral past.

Because Rimbaud had not himself completely crossed the borderland between childhood and manhood, he could recreate more vividly the child's world in poems like "Après le déluge" and "Enfance." This technique of seizing impressions kaleidoscopically, as they appeared to him from the unconscious, was a totally new method at the time. This poetic technique might be compared with the most recent fictional method of Nathalie Sarraute in *Le Planétarium.* The method is similar to the painting technique of "collage" developed by the Surrealists, who claim Rimbaud as their ancestor. It is this which makes *Les Illuminations* difficult to read: they are not single but composite visions, remembered from hashish dreams. Fragments of childhood impressions and incidents are put together; past and present mingle and merge, as they do in dreams. This does not mean that the poems lack coherence, but merely that in order to be read correctly some understanding of the language of dreams is required.

The waters of the Deluge mentioned in the first poem of *Les Illuminations* are followed in the second poem by a cryptic reference to darkness in the symbol of the "idol with the dark eyes and yellow hair."[37] This image, which has not yet been explained by any of Rimbaud's critics, becomes clear if related to *Les Paradis artificiels* in which Baudelaire, quoting De Quincey, calls opium "the dark idol" and his taking the drug "a prostration before the dark idol" or the *Mater Tenebrarum.*[38] The word *crin,* which may be poetically translated "hair," actually means either "a horse's mane" or the fibrous stem of a plant such as hemp from which opium comes. In another poem, "Matinée d'Ivresse," Rimbaud makes it clear that he also took hashish. These key words in the second poem serve as a clue to *Les Illuminations* as a whole, making it reasonably certain that these are visions seen under the influence of drugs.

Other metaphors used by Baudelaire and Rimbaud which suggest the experience of the nocturnal seer as opposed to the mystical — the figure of descent into an abyss, water, darkness, and coldness — are discussed in Chapter 6 of this book. Here, it will suffice to mention two other ideas of Baudelaire on the effects of opium. In a passage which reminds us of some modern book on psychology, Baudelaire insists upon the powerful effect of childhood impressions and their enduring quality: "Passion and sickness do not have a chemistry powerful enough to burn out these immortal impressions."[39] As an example of the difference between ordinary power of recollection and the recall which takes place under opium, Baudelaire cites De Quincey's memory of his sister Elizabeth's death. As an elderly man, De Quincey relived these events in their entirety with all details present, even his own childish desire to join his sister who could not return to him. Baudelaire says:

> He relived the whole universe of his childhood, but with the poetic richness which a mind, already cultivated, subtle and in the habit of drawing the greatest pleasures from solitude and memory, would add to it now.[40]

Instead of his own past or childhood, Nerval seems to dream of his ancestors or his ancestral past. One is tempted to think he did so because he attained a deeper level of the unconscious than Baudelaire and Rimbaud. *Aurélia* contains three such visions in which the poet encounters or becomes aware of the presence within himself of dead relatives. In one dream he descends to a mysterious city peopled with faces which greatly resemble his own. "It seemed to me that my feet were sinking into the successive layers of the buildings of different ages,"[41] he says. At the gate of this underground city an old man dressed in white threatens him with a weapon to keep him from entering. When he finally gains admittance all the people gather around him, eagerly asking him whether there is a God. He replies "Yes" spontaneously delighted with his own new inner certitude. In a second vision of his ancestors, Nerval finds himself at a banquet table with a large group of persons he again recognizes as his dead relatives. Many of them are dressed in ancient costumes and wearing powdered wigs. One of them, who seems particularly lively and interested in him, turns out to be his dead uncle, with whom he had lived as a child. "Our past and our future are indissolubly linked," the uncle tells him. "We live in our race and our race lives in us."[42]

In this way, Nerval holds, all individual existence is linked from within, the ego to the nonego, the interior to the exterior, forming a chain of immanent consciousness. "I thought that between the external and the internal world there existed a link,"[43] Nerval writes after these visions of his ancestors. He feels great happiness at his discovery of this new identity with nature and the material world which he had not perceived before. "How could I have existed so long outside nature without identifying myself with it?" he asks.

This same realization of the linked existence of man with nature gives rise to one of Rimbaud's most joyous lines: "I have stretched cords from steeple to steeple, garlands from window to window, golden chains from star to star and I dance!"[44] The analysis of the poem "Enfance" in Chapter 6 contains a discussion of Rimbaud's perception of identity with others while under the influence of drugs.

A contradiction appears at the very outset in Baudelaire's attitude toward the feeling of identity with nature. On the one hand he attaches great importance to the Swedenborgian doctrine of correspondence (which certainly includes both man and nature in its hierarchy), while in many passages he expresses his loathing of nature: "Nature is ugly . . . this stupid worship of nature," he says, and—in two longer passages—"I have always thought that there was in nature something painful, hard, cruel. . . ."[45] In a letter to Fernand Desnoyers he writes: "You ask me for some verses on nature. . . . But you know indeed that I am incapable of becoming tender over vegetables."[46] Under hashish, however, Baudelaire expresses an altogether different opinion, since he then directly experiences identity with nature:

> the personality disappears, and objectivity, which is the particular quality of pantheistic poets, develops in you so abnormally that the contemplation of the exterior objects makes you forget your own existence and soon confuse yourself with them.[47]

Finally, Baudelaire even writes eloquently, as he said he could not, about his perception of identity with the vegetable world. Seeing a tree, he says, "First you lend the tree your passions, your desires or your melancholy; its sighs and its oscillations become yours and soon you are the tree."[48] From these passages in *Les Paradis artificiels,* it would seem safe to conclude that although Baudelaire's conscious, waking psyche makes fun of the idea of identity with nature, when the barrier of the unconscious has been overcome by means of the drug, his prejudice breaks down and he too has an experience of identity with the objects of the material world. His feeling of identity with nature is not, however, the "objective" experience which he thinks it is, but a subjective one.

On these lower levels of the unconscious the seer poets became aware of the primitive and the animal in themselves. Attacking the belief in progress, Baudelaire maintains that man conceals only slightly his true predatory nature: "Whether man ensnares his victim on the boulevard or pierces his prey in unknown forests, is he not always man, the eternal, the most perfect animal of prey?"[49] In *Une Saison en enfer,* Rimbaud deplores his barbaric Celtic ancestry: "It is quite clear to me," he says, "that I have always been of an inferior race. . . . My race never rose in rebellion except to pillage." This, he feels, accounts at least in part for his own savage nature. "I have never been a Christian. . . . Laws I have never understood. . . . I have no moral sense, I am a brute. . . . I am a beast, a Negro. But I can be saved."[50] This is only one of numerous indications in the *Saison* in which Rimbaud states his determination to break with his violent past. In one of the dreams related in *Aurélia,* Nerval tells of having been transported into a primordial world where huge monsters struggled with each other in mortal combat. At length, when they changed form and became more gigantic, he noticed that his own body was as strange as theirs and that he too was engaged in conflict with them. After a time the beasts became tamer and he noticed to his surprise that some of them had changed into men and women, while others remained beasts.[51]

The climax or ultimate stage of the effect of hashish, accompanied by the seer poet's realization of his identity with nature, is described by Baudelaire as a state of extraordinary inner harmony and absolute happiness. The subject has a feeling of his own divinity. "This new state is what Orientals call *kief,*" he explains. "It is a calm and immobile beatitude, a glorious resignation. For a long time you have not been your master, but you no longer bother yourself about it."[52] Aldous Huxley also describes this same sensation of beatitude, which he experienced under mescalin, and it suggests to him the old dispute between actives and contemplatives. There is no real conflict between the two, he concludes, for the way of Mary includes the way of Martha; the true contemplative would leave the seventh heaven to give a cup of water to his sick brother, as Meister Eckhart has pointed out.[53]

Baudelaire summarizes his hashish experiences by saying, wisely, that hashish "reveals nothing to the individual except the individual himself."[54] In other words, the experience is one of selfhood and duality. It is Narcissus gazing at himself in the pool. This is why Baudelaire's Eden, in contrast with Rimbaud's, is more static, more characterized by repose and resignation. Rimbaud is the magician who would control and dominate his world, refashioning it after his ideals; Baudelaire, on the contrary, does not want change, but protection and absolution from his feelings of guilt. "The sense of protection," he writes, "a feeling of ardent and devoted paternity, may be mixed with a guilty sensuality which hashish will always be able to excuse and absolve."

The seer poets thus describe their experiences not only in terms of descent, darkness, and water, but also in an accentuated sense of selfhood and individuality, whereas the mystics speak in metaphors which are exactly opposite — ascent, light, fire, and an impersonal sense resulting from self-naughting and *ekstasis.*

Taking man and the mysterious path of his unconscious as their point of departure, the seer poets have described a semicircle; that is, they have made their way back to the surface, to nature and the material world. Similarly, Wordsworth, proceeding in the opposite direction by taking nature as his point of departure, ended with man and "the still sad music of humanity." Both the seer poets and Wordsworth reported their encounter with a nonego, an immanent consciousness. Whether this experience is called a perception of the macrocosm in the microcosm (Baudelaire's "correspondence") or the collective unconscious (Jung's terminology), the important point is that the seer poets and later the psychological world believed that they had discovered within man a consciousness surpassing his own individual one. In so doing they added a third dimension, so to speak, to poetic experience and greatly enriched our knowledge of man himself.

In view of this, one would think that the seer poets, delighted at having discovered a new domain, might have forged ahead exhilarated at the prospect of further discoveries. Unfortunately, however, this was not the case. Instead, disillusionment abounds in their poetry, and in their personal lives each reached a serious spiritual impasse. The tragedy of the seer poets lies in the fact that they confused their very rich and significant discovery of the unconscious with the mystical experience, and were disillusioned when what they had found did not correspond with what they wanted to find. They were seeking with great intensity an experience of transcendence rather than of immanence, but were unable to achieve it or to progress in it with consistency. Another brief glance at the texts will make this point more precise.

Instead of the unitive experience of the mystic, a sense of duality and multiplicity oppressed them constantly. "Who among us is not *homo duplex?*" asks Baudelaire.[55] Instead of discovering that man was one, they found him to be legion. "Hashish," Baudelaire says, "is a means of multiplying the personality."[56] Later, in the *Journaux intimes,* he writes: "All is number. Number is in everything. Number is in the individual."[57] The last line of his famous poem, "Le Gouffre," in *Les Fleurs du mal* expresses his despair that he cannot escape the oppression of multiplicity: "Ah, never to escape from beings and numbers!"[58] What Baudelaire wants most is an experience of unity and transcendence. The very first chapter of *Les Paradis artificiels* is entitled "Le Goût pour l'infini," concerning which he says: "Man aspires always to lift himself toward the infinite."[59] Baudelaire records an intimation of this transcendence which, significantly, he experienced not under the influence of hashish but while listening to the overture to *Lohengrin.* The Plotinian metaphors of light and ecstasy appear in the passage in which Baudelaire says he experienced

> the sensation of a much more vivid clarity, of an intensity of light increasing with such rapidity that the nuances furnished by the dictionary would not suffice to express this over-increasing rebirth of ardor and whiteness. . . . Then I fully understood the idea of a soul moving in a luminous milieu, of an ecstasy composed of sensuousness and knowledge, and soaring above and very far from this natural world.[60]

At the height of his spiritual quest, Rimbaud believed he had overcome duality. The poem, "Eternité," which marks the summit of his experience, indicates that he caught a momentary glimpse of spiritual unity, but he was unable to maintain it. Later, in the *Saison,* he calls his illuminations "hallucinations" and, like Baudelaire, deplores the feeling of his own multiplicity. "All that [his hashish experiences] is the vision of Numbers," he says. "We are going toward Spirit. . . . What I am saying is oracular."[61] In the very next paragraph he adds his famous confession: "I am awaiting God greedily." Clearly, Rimbaud is contrasting his previous experience of multiplicity under hashish with the new direction toward Spirit and oneness which he intends to take in the future.

Similarly, Nerval, perplexed by the vision of his double and by the sense of multiplicity which the vision of his ancestors had produced in him, wonders how this may be reconciled with the idea of unity and universal harmony he thought he had discovered in his study of comparative religion. He even goes so far as to equate multiplicity with evil:

> An error had slipped into the general combination of numbers, according to my estimate, and from there came all the evils of humanity. . . . My role seemed to me to be the re-establishment of universal harmony through Kabbalistic art and the finding of a solution by evoking the occult forces of different religions.[62]

Finally, Nerval makes a prophecy regarding the synthesis of opposites which seems to be more charged with meaning for the twentieth century than for his own times:

> perhaps we are reaching a prophesied epoch in which science, having accomplished its entire circle of synthesis and analysis, of belief and of negation, will be able to purify itself and to build the marvelous city of the future . . . out of the disorder and the ruins.[63]

At length each of the seer poets arrived at the impasse of madness or the threat of madness. Baudelaire wrote in *Mon coeur mis à nu*:

"I have cultivated my hysteria with enjoyment and terror. Now I have vertigo constantly and today, the 23rd of January, 1862, I have experienced a singular warning; I have felt the wind of imbecility."[64] Nerval, who fared even worse, said: "I was put on a bed, and for a long time I lost the meaning and connection of the images which presented themselves to me. This state lasted for several days. I was transported to a sanitorium."[65] Rimbaud was also seized with terror: "My health was threatened," he writes in the *Saison*. "Terror came. I fell into a slumber of several days and on rising would go on with the same sad dreams. I was ripe for death and along a road of perils my weakness led me to the border of the world and of Cimmeria, land of whirlwinds and darkness."[66]

In one way or another each of these poets destroyed himself. Nerval hanged himself in the Rue de la Vieille-Lanterne where his body was found by Gautier. In his pockets were a few pages of the manuscript of *Aurélia*.[67] Baudelaire also destroyed himself quite as deliberately, although he did it gradually by means of his debauches. Having a healthier respect for the body, Rimbaud refused to destroy his, but chose to slay the poet in himself instead, to commit artistic suicide. In recording his last spiritual struggle in the rough draft of the *Saison,* he says: "Now I can say that art is folly." (*"Maintenant je puis dire que l'art est une sottise,"*).[68] In the same vein he writes in the final draft of the *Saison*: "Well, I must bury my imagination and my memories! An artist's and story-teller's precious fame flung away." These lines and others such as, "No more words . . . No hymns!" (*"Point de cantiques"*) and "Hold the ground gained" (*"tenir le pas gagné"*) leave no doubt as to his intentions of remaining firm in his purpose to renounce art.[69] The reasons which drove him to this regrettable decision and the nature of the spiritual victory which he believed he had won will be discussed in Part II of this book.

Two very different types of conclusions may be drawn from these experiences of the seer poets, depending upon one's own inner nature. It is possible to see in them an illustration of the fact that it is both dangerous and morbid to be preoccupied with such an unknown area of the psyche, especially when precise scientific knowledge has today progressed but little beyond these early efforts. Those who hold this point of view may say that the exploration of the unconscious is, in any case, the business of specialists. On the other hand, it is possible to conclude that the seer poets raised the curtain on the prelude of an important drama, that is, the awakening of man's consciousness.

One may decide that the personality of the individual can never develop and have strength unless he can make his own choices consciously, and that he cannot do this with true freedom if he remains blind to so large an area of his psyche. The fact that some who made the first efforts suffered reverses makes no more difference in this realm than it does in aviation, for example, where none would seriously advance the idea that, because planes have crashed and young men have been killed, all further attempts to fly should be abandoned. Nor can one honestly dismiss the whole matter as an affair for specialists only, since all must face daily the problem of inner personality growth or its stagnation. For the artist, this means not only a more authentic art, but also wider areas from which to draw.

The Romantic period, with its emphasis upon the intensely personal, contributed little to the development of the Plotinian experience, which had already declined greatly since the end of the seventeenth century. Even Wordsworth, whose works contain many passages indicating that during his youth he had known brief flashes of mystical experience, was unable to achieve anything permanent. In the *Prelude* he writes in the usual Plotinian metaphors:

> . . . in such visitings
> Of awful promise when the light of sense
> Goes out in flashes that have shown to us
> The invisible world.

But as he grew older, Wordsworth became more acutely aware that not only had he made no progress, he had actually retrogressed. In "Tintern Abbey" he asks himself in despair about his youthful visions: "Whither is it gone, the visionary dream?" He failed to develop his experience because, like the French seer poets, he was unaware of the conditions which would have to be fulfilled in order to achieve an experience of transcendence. Similarly, the seer poets enjoyed a few brief glimpses of that Canaan which none of them was ever able to enter. They mistook their exploration of the unconscious for the mystical experience. Nevertheless, theirs was a task of vast importance, for the treacherous descent into Avernus, "the dark night of the soul," must precede the arduous ascent of Carmel which leads up the steep hill of self-naughting, nonattachment, and charity.

CHAPTER 2

The Occult Way

The magician is a poet. . . .
The words of the poet are magic words.
NOVALIS, *Fragmente*

Literary critics have often written about the magic of poetry, but seldom have they had the opportunity to discover the poetry of magic. This is precisely what Romantic writers in Germany and France discovered in the rich symbolism of Eastern thought. The descent into the self so characteristic of the whole Romantic movement received at least some of its impetus from the large body of Eastern works translated in the late eighteenth century. Even Auguste Viatte in a work as monumental as *Les Sources occultes du romantisme* does not fully perceive the real extent of the intellectual fecundation produced by this literary meeting of East and West. Within the brief space of about thirty years (1771-1800) many of the important works of Hinduism and Zoroastrianism were made available to the literary and scholarly world through manuscripts brought from India; by 1840 the Buddhistic works were also available. The discovery and translation of Oriental manuscripts began almost simultaneously in France and England with the two scholars Anquétil du Perron (1731-1805) and Sir William Jones (1746-1794). After a period of study in India, the former returned to France with 180 manuscripts, among them the *Zend-Avesta* which he published in 1771 along with a life of Zoroaster and a collection of fragments attributed to the Persian prophet. It is not without historic irony that Anquétil du Perron's translation of fifty of the Upanishads appeared just as the goddess Reason was being crowned in front of Notre Dame. The same year, Sir William Jones published a grammar of Persian and, in 1772, a translation of poems from that language. These were followed by a commentary in Latin on six books of Asiatic poetry and finally in 1789 by translations of many of the important works from Sanskrit: the *Śakuntalá* of Kalidása, the *Hitopadeśa,* the *Gītāgovinda,* and the

Vedas. In Germany, August von Schlegel (1767-1845), professor of literature at Bonn, translated the *Bhagavad-Gītā,* the *Ramāyana,* and the *Hitopadeśa* into Latin. Schlegel did his work in collaboration with another German orientalist, Christian Lassen, who had studied in Paris with Eugène Burnouf (1801-1852), who translated the Buddhistic works into French in 1840 along with a commentary, *Introduction à l'histoire du bouddhisme.* The significance of the discovery and translation of these manuscripts cannot yet be fully evaluated, since they present a system built on premises radically different from those of Western culture. One can only compare it with the discovery of manuscripts of the ancient Greek and Roman world by Renaissance scholars.

This sudden appearance of so many Oriental masterpieces would undoubtedly have attracted much more attention in the literary world had it not been eclipsed by the political storm in France with which it had the misfortune to coincide. For the most part, attempts to evaluate these works were therefore delayed for some thirty years. In spite of the new sense of historical perspective achieved during the nineteenth century, critics and historians were even then incapable of quickly comprehending the mind of the Orient. For the naive, these works were simply records of the superstitions of "primitive" peoples who had not had the good fortune to be converted to Christianity. For scholars, as well as for countless pseudo-scholars — all inspired by Herder — the Oriental works, in that they originated among "primitive" and therefore "unspoiled" people, were "purer" than Christianity, since a stream of water is purer when nearer to its source. Intellectuals of an anticlerical bent hailed the new works because they saw in them the possibility of establishing a reformed, universal religion based on beliefs common to all. In Germany, this idea of syncretism was particularly cherished by the Schlegels, Fichte, Schelling, and Novalis; in France, Nerval, Balzac, Hugo, and Vigny all expressed their need for a new and more truly universal religion.

On the whole, the translations of Oriental manuscripts had two significant effects. First, they confronted Western scholars for the first time with a body of thought built upon assumptions differing completely from the rationalistic foundations of Western philosophy and, second, they stimulated interest in, and re-evaluation of, a more familiar body of Orientalism, the occult doctrines of the Middle East which had existed in Europe since the Middle Ages — Gnosticism, Kabbalism, and Neoplatonism. Lacking a proper background for understanding Hindu and Buddhistic works, but considering that Oriental thought should nevertheless be evaluated, some scholars began to examine the Middle Eastern systems with greater curiosity. These systems were not so unfamiliar to the Western mind and were therefore easier to grasp.

Such a scholar was Court de Gébelin (1725-1784), whose eight-volume work, *Le Monde primitif* (1772), not only secured him a reputation as the most profound scholar of his time, but also focused attention on Egyptian occultism. Born in Nîmes and educated in ancient religions and languages at Lausanne, he was among the first in France to develop the idea of the greater purity of Oriental religions. Before Creutzer, Gébelin had sought in *Le Monde primitif* to explain the symbolic meaning of myths. Since the ancients thought and wrote allegorically, he held that the key to understanding the myth is penetration of its allegorical significance. Through many tedious pages Court de Gébelin attempts to show the Egyptian origin of Greek mythology, maintaining that the understanding of allegory depends on the ability of scholars to decipher the Egyptian hieroglyphics in which the myths were originally written. Egyptian hieroglyphics, he believed, constitute the most ancient of existing languages and also the purest because the pictures are based directly on nature and natural objects. Behind the picture writing and beneath its literal meaning "all is allegory," and since "allegory is an essential key and a fundamental basis of antiquity," a key to the allegories is needed as well as one for the language itself.[1] (This remark is interesting in that it was written twenty-seven years before the discovery of the Rosetta Stone in 1799.)

Further speculations on the Egyptian language led Gébelin to theorize about a primitive language from which all other languages sprang. All alphabets too are descended from an "alphabet of nature," he held: "The primitive alphabet was taken from nature; each one of its elements painted a particular object; its pronunciation instantly caused the idea to be born in the one who heard it."[2] It should be noted that in the same year that *Le Monde primitif* appeared, Herder wrote a refutation of the idea of the divine origin of language (Über den Ursprung der Sprache) maintaining that languages sprang from a primitive language or *Ursprache.*

Although *Le Monde primitif* is a curiosity today, its influence in its time was considerable, and its ideas about a primitive language of nature may be found in writings of Novalis, Baudelaire, Rimbaud, and many others. It was cited with great respect by Saint-Martin, Fabre d'Olivet, and Pierre-Simon Ballanche. Bailly, inspired by it, wrote about "la sagesse première" of the Hindus; Ballanche believed that all religions originated in the Orient, "our cosmogonic and intellectual cradle, the eternal source of dogmas"; Jean Reynaud maintained that Buddhism was the source of Christianity; and Fabre d'Olivet traced the origin of religion to the god, Rama, of India whose three major prophets were Orpheus (Greece), Moses (Egypt), and Buddha (India).[3] Hugo, Nerval, Leconte de Lisle, and Rimbaud all thought the Oriental religions less corrupt and more profound than Christianity; none, in fact, seemed to suspect that the Oriental religions in their long history of development, might also have developed a few superstitions, errors, and false prophets.

In the discovery of the Oriental manuscripts, in the re-examination of the more familiar ideologies of the Middle East, and finally in its general ebullient spirit, the Romantic period was a second Renaissance. Court de Gébelin, whose eight-volume work had impressed many, became a precursor and high priest of the new esotericism, which in the final analysis was destined to affect literature more profoundly than the Far Eastern doctrines. A satisfactory classification of writers commonly referred to as "occult" is difficult to find. Professor Roos of the University of Strasbourg has arranged them according to their doctrines, pointing out their similarities and differences.[4] He correctly underscores the international character of the various groups, but his chapter on the sources of their inspiration omits certain basic works. Others, like Viatte, have listed the writers chronologically and according to their country of origin. In *The Holy Kabbalah* (*sic*), A. E. Waite has made a list of certain well-known literary figures who drew their inspiration from the Kabbala, but his list is incomplete. It would be possible to arrange them in order of their degree of influence in the literary world, but here it seems best to list (see below) first the basic source works from which they drew their inspiration, for they were all popularizers, from Boehme and Swedenborg to Eliphas Lévi and Edouard Schuré at the end of the nineteenth century. The popularizations differed, of course, in imagination, talent, and most of all in accuracy, but with the exception of the last two works mentioned here (*De planetarum influxu* and *Le Livre des Esprits*) the sources are all ancient and esoteric. The various traditions represented here are theosophical in that direct knowledge of a spiritual world is presumed to be intuitively accessible to man. Faith, therefore, does not have an important role. Second, they hold that finite man cannot know fully the Infinite or God; all attempts at definitions of God are therefore approximations and have only allegorical significance.

(1) *The Kabbala* was officially introduced into Europe during the Renaissance by Pico della Mirandola, who presented a copy to the Pope in the opinion that it contained proof that the ancient world knew symbolically the truth of Christianity. The Kabbala (the word in Hebrew means "that which has been handed down") consists of a series of books written at various periods in Jewish history, from the second century A.D. to the thirteenth. The earliest of the books were the *Sefer Yetzirah* (*Book of Creation*) and the Hekaloth books containing the *Book of Enoch.* The principal work of the Kabbala is the *Sepher ha Zohar* (*The Book of Splendor*), a mystical commentary on the Pentateuch. It is written partly in Aramaic and partly in Hebrew, and from this linguistic evidence scholars were able to determine that, although the central portion of the *Zohar* does contain the teachings of Simon ben Jochai, a rabbi of the second century A.D., large portions were later added by Kabbalists during the Middle Ages.[5] There has been a recent revival of interest in the Kabbala, particularly in Germany, where historically it had the most influence.[6]

(2) *The Corpus Hermeticum* is a collection of forty-two Egyptian Hermetic books dating from the third century A.D. and attributed to Hermes Trismegistus. Alchemical knowledge was first introduced into the Western world when the Arabs invaded Spain in the eighth century; Arabic manuscripts dating from the third and fourth centuries exist in the Leyden Museum, the Library of St. Mark's in Venice, and in the Bibliothèque Nationale in Paris. The first significant Latin translation of these works, Morienus' *Liber de compositione alchemicae,* dates from near the end of the twelfth century, while the oldest Greek manuscript, dating from the tenth century and now in the Library of St. Mark's, was translated by Marsilio Ficino in the latter part of the fifteenth century. These cryptic works, which were supposed to contain the "secrets of nature," that is, the formula for a universal medicine to cure all diseases and a technique for changing the baser metals into gold, also represented in allegorical form a process for the spiritual transformation and perfection of man.[7]

(3) *Gnostic, Manichean, and Pythagorean works*: These philosophies

of the ancient world were revived in the sixteenth and seventeenth centuries, in Spain and Germany in particular. Menéndez y Pelayo states that a group called the *Alumbrados* (*Illuminati*), whom he traces to Gnostic origins, existed in Spain at the end of the fifteenth century; many of their members were burned by the Inquisition.[8] A large number, who were undoubtedly Kabbalists, in the seventeenth century fled from Seville and Granada into southern France, where they established groups of followers. Molinos, the founder of Quietism, was definitely connected with these *Illuminati*.[9] In Germany, Rosicrucians and Freemasons attempted to preserve and hand down this lore of the ancient world. Members of all the secret societies preferred to consider the apostle St. John, patron of visionaries, as their head instead of St. Peter, patron of the ecclesiastical hierarchy. Herder, who was a Freemason, maintained that the Manichees, one of the largest of the Gnostic sects, were descendants of the Persian Magi, who attached particular importance to the symbolic worship of fire and light. This was undoubtedly the origin of the rituals of fire and light used by Rosicrucians and Freemasons in their rituals, and also the use of the title "Magus" to designate anyone who had become "illuminated."[10] Pythagorean number mysticism, also revived at the end of the eighteenth century in France, received a special impetus in the early nineteenth century from Fabre d'Olivet's translation of *Les Vers dorés de Pythagore* (1813).

(4) Two other works belonging to a later period, Mesmer's *De Planetarum influxu,* (1766), containing his doctrine of animal magnetism, and *Le Livre des Esprits* (1857) of Allan Kardec, who became chief of the French Spiritualists, inspired many parlor games among the people and resulted in a much wider popularization of occult doctrines.

During the last three decades of the eighteenth century, these doctrines of the ancient world were particularly cultivated by secret societies — Rosicrucians, Freemasons, and Martinists — which became increasingly numerous all over Europe, even as far east as Russia. They became most powerful, however, in Germany, where they received official recognition and support. An estimated thirty German princes were initiated during these years; the best known being Friedrich Wilhelm II of Prussia, Charles of Hesse, and Ferdinand of Brunswick. Charles of Hesse, who studied alchemy and was reputed to have discovered a magic elixir because of the advanced age (ninety-six) to which he lived, made an effort to unite a group of Masonic societies with a view toward forming a new church.[11] It was at his court that the exiled French Court of Saint-Germain spent his last years.

Mme de Staël in *De l'Allemagne* gives the following classification of various Illuminist groups within Germany at the end of the eighteenth century: (1) the mystical or religious Illuminists who drew their inspiration from Jakob Boehme and Saint-Martin; (2) the visionary Illuminists who stemmed from Swedenborg; and (3) the political Illuminists who proposed a reform of the social order.[12]

Although unmentioned in this classification by Mme de Staël, the Moravian Zinzendorf, leader of a Pietists group which attempted to restore the apostolic community of primitive Christianity, should be included in the first group. His aspirations for uniting the various Illuminist and mystical sects were even more ambitious than those of Charles of Hesse. Zinzendorf hoped for a second Reformation, which would be as radical as that of Luther. With the aid of the Pietist reform which was taking place in the Lutheran Church, his aim was to unite Lutherans of a mystical bent with Rosicrucians, Freemasons, and even Catholics into a vast society or "Order of Jesus." On Zinzendorf's estate in Saxony, Moravian refugees built the town, Herrnhut, based not on monastic but on family life. True Christianity, Zinzendorf thought, could be best promoted by such free associations of Christians which might grow into churches having no state connections. On this last point, the Moravians, spiritual descendents of John Huss, were insistent. It was from the Moravians that Schleiermacher learned his religion, and it was by them that John and Charles Wesley were converted. Novalis, whose father was a member of this sect, developing one of Zinzendorf's ideas in his *Fragmente,* opposes the "Inner Church" or mystical body of believers to the "Outer Church" or ecclesiastical hierarchy, and adds: "There is not yet any religion. We must begin by founding a lodge in which the true religion will be taught."[13] In this same connection, Jean-Paul Richter wrote *The Invisible Lodge,* while Benjamin Constant complained in his journals of Friedrich Schlegel: "He wants to found a religion."[14]

These statements reflect one of the fundamental tenets of Rosicrucianism and Freemasonry: all the great religions have an esoteric as well as an exoteric doctrine and their leaders are initiated into the former while the masses of believers are only able to attain the latter. The reform of man and society was also the special concern of the second category of Illuminists outlined by Mme de Staël. But these expected to accomplish their purpose chiefly through spiritual development fostered in the lodges and secret societies rather than in a church. Mme de Staël should have extended this group to include not only Swedenborg, but all those whose ideas originated from occult sources — Rosicrucians, Freemasons, and other groups of independent Illuminists. German Freemasons and Rosicrucians of the eighteenth century had much in common. Both hoped to continue the reforms begun by Luther and to combine the teachings of the Christian mystics with Gnostic and occult doctrines. Both made use of Egyptian initiation rites and, although Freemasonry had become officially rationalistic in the seventeenth century, the lodges were filled with occult thought. Mme de Staël says that German Freemasons were divided into two groups: the philosophic, primarily concerned with spiritual development, and the hermetic, descendants of the alchemists, seeking to penetrate the secrets of nature.[15]

A few brief remarks should be added here about the Rosicrucian movement, formerly thought to have begun officially in Kassel, Germany, in 1614, when it was proclaimed by Johann Andrea in his *Fama Fraternitatis Rosae-Crucis*. Recent research has shown, however, that the society was old even in the sixteenth century, and rare manuscripts in Cologne have established that the order existed as early as 1115. Michael Maier, an officer of the fraternity in the sixteenth century, states that its greatest revival occurred in the year 1414, while Paracelsus records his initiation into such a lodge in Basle in 1530.[16] At any rate, Andrea's proclamation in the early seventeenth century marked a significant revival of these secret societies. Two years after Andrea's *Fama,* Robert Fludd, friend of John Milton and founder of the English Rosicrucian society, published a pamphlet in its defense. Thomas Vaughan, the twin brother of the metaphysical poet Henry Vaughan, translated Andrea's *Fama* into English in 1625 under the pseudonym of Eugenius Philalethes, preserving his anonymity in accordance with Rosicrucian practices. In several articles about the Rosicrucians written for the *London Magazine* (Jan.-Feb., 1824), Thomas De Quincey maintained that Freemasonry in England originated from the English Rosicrucian Society and not vice versa as was commonly thought.[17] De Quincey says that Paracelsus was the real founder of the Rosicrucians but that the name Rosicrucian did not exist before the seventeenth century. This latter statement is correct, for before this time initiates of the society were called

Illuminati or "Brethren of the Light," the significance of which may be explained as follows.

The ritual of the Rosicrucians as well as of the Freemasons, as we have stated, was based on initiation rites practiced in Egypt in the worship of Osiris and Isis. As the sun (Osiris) is the lifegiver in the universe or macrocosm, the soul of man is the light of the microcosm. The secret societies sought to bring about illumination in the individual, the shining of the sun within or, as Paracelsus stated it: "As it is in the Inner, so must it be in the Outer; as it is in the Outer, so must it be in the Inner."[18] The initiation rites symbolized not only the regeneration of the individual but also the change of seasons, the progressive stages of agriculture, and the spiritual development of the race.

Among the political reformers included in Mme de Staël's third category of Illuminists, Freemasons should be mentioned. They aspired, however, to carry out their reforms slowly and by means of enlightenment of the people. Others, such as the *Illuminati* of Bavaria, expected to seize political power by more violent means. An attempt was made in 1782 by Weisshaupt of Ingolstadt and Baron von Knigge to graft the Bavarian *Illuminati* to Freemasonry, but when the Masons discovered the revolutionary aspirations of this group they denounced it to the Bavarian government.[19] The plot became evident at a congress of Freemasons held in Wilhelmsbad, at which forty delegates from various European countries assembled to discuss the possibility of uniting the French and German lodges. The conference took place as a result of the planning of Willermoz, chief of the Freemasons of Lyons, who had previously received as his guest the Baron von Plessen, special emissary of Ferdinand of Brunswick and Charles of Hesse. These two German princes acknowledged that the founder of their lodges, Haugwitz, was inspired by Martinist doctrines, but the congress ended in fiasco because of wide differences of opinion among the delegates or, as delegate Joseph de Maistre said, because of the "insufficiency of human deliberations."[20] Among those present were Saint-Martin, Lavater, Ferdinand of Brunswick, Charles of Hesse, and Haugwitz. The German delegates were divided between the Pietist sects of Zinzendorf in the North and the Rosicrucians in the South; the French delegates were also divided in their adherences. The opponents of the *Illuminés* of Lyons were the Elus Coëns of Paris, disciples of Martinez de Pasqually, who were more eclectic in their views and had succeeded in uniting Rosicrucians and Swedenborgians. In this group were Court de Gébelin, Chefdebien the alchemist, Clavières, and Pernéty, the Swedenborgian. Although the congress accomplished nothing toward unification, there was extensive exchange of opinion, and correspondence among the delegates continued long after the congress.

The extent to which Illuminism spread throughout the literary and philosophical world of Germany is indicated by the number of well-known writers and philosophers who either were initiates of Freemasonry or had Rosicrucian affiliations. Lessing, Herder, Goethe, Fichte and Pestalozzi were Freemasons, while Hamann, Zacharias Werner, Franz von Baader, Ritter, Schelling, G. H. von Schubert, and Novalis were affiliated with the Rosicrucians. In his biography of Novalis, the critic Spenlé says that there was scarcely any cultivated German who was not a member of some secret society.[21]

Many factors contributed to this general atmosphere of mysticism, the chief one being the initial impact of Eastern thought on Western, both in the discovery of the manuscripts and in the popularizations of the secret societies based upon the Egyptian mysteries. It is not surprising that the country which fostered the Reformation was also the first to perceive the fundamental deficiency of that reform — the lack of mysticism — as the natural consequence of its being severed from the roots of Christian tradition. This essential need for mysticism which inspired German Romanticism and which led Spenlé to call this movement "less a school or a literary doctrine than a true philosophic sect, having alongside its exterior literary activity its mystic belief."[22] It would be an error, however, to consider the visionary aspirations of the lodges, secret societies, and pietistic groups a natural reaction against the excesses of the rationalistic tendencies of the age of enlightenment. At the end of the eighteenth century German and French ideology was characterized by two parallel currents of thought, the rational and the visionary: "This century of 'light' is also one of illuminists" ("Ce siècle des 'lumières' est aussi celui des illuminés"), as the literary historian Jasinski succinctly states it.[23] In the literary and philosophical world, these two currents were exemplified in the persons of Kant and Swedenborg, Schiller and Novalis, Goethe and Lavater. Not until the middle of the nineteenth century did the two parallel currents rush into headlong conflict, when science and faith engaged in a mortal struggle for survival, and not until the twentieth century did man begin to attempt to evaluate the conflict and to salvage for himself what was of value in each.

No individual personified more completely the visionary aspirations of his age than did Emmanuel Swedenborg (1688-1772). He was the prototype of all seers; his influence on contemporary writers can best be compared with that of Kierkegaard on French and German writers of the 1920's and 1930's. Like Pascal, Swedenborg was a scientist and mathematician who, after having made numerous original discoveries, abandoned his scientific studies. Whereas Pascal was a young man of thirty-one, Swedenborg was fifty-five when his visionary experiences began. The son of a theology professor at the University of Uppsala who was also a bishop in the Lutheran Church, Swedenborg made his debut in the natural sciences and engineering. When his studies were finished, he was appointed by Charles XII as assessor on the Swedish Board of Mines, where he first distinguished himself with the invention of a machine for transporting boats overland. Two years later he refused a chair of mathematics at the University of Uppsala believing it a mistake for mathematicians to limit themselves to theoretical work only. His original discoveries became numerous: by 1734 he had written and published a three-volume work, *Opera philosophica et mineralia,* in which he arrived at the nebular hypothesis well before Kant and Laplace. The French chemist, Dumas, credits him with the first attempt to establish a system of crystallology, but most important of all were his discoveries in brain anatomy. In 1901, Max Neuberger of Vienna mentioned that Swedenborg, 150 years before other scientists, had shown that the motion of the brain was synchronous with respiration and not, as previously supposed, with the heartbeat. Although Swedenborg admitted there had been a few earlier intimations of his strange future prior to the year 1743, he nevertheless assigns this date to the time when his spiritual eyes were suddenly opened. Two years later he claimed to have conversations with angels or intermediary beings. His work, *De Cultu et Amore Dei* (1745), marks the change from scientific writing to accounts of his extraordinary visions. In 1749 and 1750 he published the first two volumes of the *Arcana Coelestia;* his later works are too numerous to list here. A detailed discussion of Swedenborgian doctrine would not be relevant, but two of his basic conceptions had a far-reaching effect on the literary world: (1) his idea of correspondence and (2) his theory of a universal language.[24]

Following the *Corpus Hermeticum* and the Kabbala, Swedenborg means by correspondence that every phenomenon in the world of nature has its counterpart, upon which it depends for its existence, in the world of spirit. Since it is by correspondence that the natural world is joined to the spiritual world, a knowledge of correspondence is significant to enable man to communicate with heaven. Among the ancients, an understanding of correspondence was the chief knowledge, Swedenborg maintains, but this knowledge has been almost entirely lost to the modern world.[25] The ancient Egyptians, for example, knew what every kind of animal signified spiritually, and the hieroglyphics on the walls and columns of their temples indicate this knowledge of correspondence.[26] To a lesser degree than this ancient picture writing, modern languages also have both an external form or significance and an internal esoteric meaning. Heaven and earth, the spiritual and the material are, so to speak, joined in the Word:

> Wherefore in the Word there is an internal sense which is spiritual . . . and an external sense which is natural, hence it is that the conjunction of heaven with man is effected by means of the Word.[27]

Similarly, there is an archetypal or universal language to which all earthly languages correspond. In a short chapter, "The Speech of Angels," in *Heaven and Hell* (1757), Swedenborg describes the universal language he claimed to have used when speaking with spirits:

> In the whole of heaven all have one language, and they understand one another, from whatever society they are, whether near or distant. This language does not require to be learnt by them, but is natural to every-one, for it flows from their very affection and thought.[28]

Writing on the same subject in his *Dictionary of Correspondences,* Swedenborg says that men also come into possession of this angelic language at the moment of death. In the case of ordinary human language, "the internal sense of the Word altogether coincides with the universal language."[29] The speech of angels, unlike human language, is instantaneous or, as the modern man would describe it, telepathic: "Because the speech of angels proceeds immediately from their affection . . . angels express in a minute what man cannot express in half an hour."[30] When an angel speaks to a man the words, instead of going through the exterior medium of air into the eardrum, proceed directly into the thought by an interior way and are heard only internally. Angelic language is musical, composed of many vowels, and more exact: "The ideas of their thought and the words of their speech make one as efficient cause and effect; for their words are the effect of which their ideas are the cause; and therefore every word corresponds in itself to a multitude of things." A desire to discover the universal language as a key to the mysteries of nature is expressed by Novalis in *Die Lehrlinge zu Saïs,* by Rimbaud in the *Voyant* letters, and by many others in Germany and France.

The claims of the Swedish mystic were indeed so fantastic that he at length aroused the curiosity of an equally famous contemporary, the philosopher Kant. In reply to a letter from Charlotte Knobloch, asking his opinion about the incredible claims of Swedenborg, Kant decided to weigh the evidence for and against the existence of spiritual beings and the possibility of man's communicating with them. Kant therefore commissioned an English friend, Mr. Green, to visit Swedenborg and to report back on the reliability of the Swedish seer's character and general culture. Green returned from Sweden with very favorable reports and several stories illustrating Swedenborg's extraordinary gift of clairvoyance.[31] These Kant collected in a pamphlet which he wrote on the subject in 1766, *Träume eines Geistersehers* (*Dreams of a Spirit Seer*). Although this work contributed more than anything else to the renown of Swedenborg in Germany, Kant's conclusions about the value and validity of such experiences were altogether negative. Attempts at supernatural knowledge on the part of human beings are in vain, he concluded, and ought to be abandoned in favor of knowledge which is productive of more practical results. In spite of Kant's advice, visionary aspirations continued and produced a tangible effect upon romantic literature.

Swedenborgian thought was naturally favorable to the development of an esthetic based on Illuminist aspirations. The idea of the poet as seer was suggested by Johann Hamann (1730-1788) and again by the Swiss Illuminist, Jean Lavater (1741-1801), who emphasized the religious and prophetic aspects of artistic creation. In its esthetic implications the idea was developed most elaborately by Novalis (1771-1802), but also by a number of his contemporaries: Zacharias Werner (1768-1823), Achim von Arnim (1781-1831), and a group of writers — Franz von Baader (1765-1841), J. W. Ritter (1776-1810), Heinrich Steffens (1773-1845), Johann-Carl Passavant, and G. H. von Schubert (1780-1860) — called "the Romantic physicists" because of their combined training in medicine and their experimentations in "animal magnetism."

Mesmer's theory of animal magnetism, that the bodies of all animals and men are magnetically charged, was considered not a scientific but an occult phenomenon until the end of the nineteenth century.

Mesmerism, which was the subject of as much passionate popular discussion in Germany as it was in France, revived the prestige of occult thought. Many intellectuals, such as Novalis, the Romantic physicists, and finally even the philosopher Schelling, believed that Mesmer's discovery should receive scientific consideration. Swedenborgian societies quickly adopted animal magnetism as a scientific explanation of unusual visionary states. In a novel, *Kreuz- und Querzüge des Ritters von A bis Z* (1778-1781), Theodor von Hippel describes certain initiation rites of the secret societies in which a bold effort was made to free the spirit from the body by using Mesmeric techniques. Upon attainment of the highest degree, the initiates were supposed to be able to communicate with the dead and with spirits who instructed them about their destinies.[32] Similarly, Jean-Paul Richter records in *Die unsichtbare Loge* (*The Invisible Lodge*) that somnambulic states were often provoked in prospective members of secret societies as a part of the initiation rites.[33]

The development of the idea of the poet as seer in German Romanticism can be traced from its first mention in the works of Hamann to its culmination in the works of Novalis and the Romantic physicists, inspired by Mesmerism.

Johann Hamann, a contemporary of Kant and also a native of Königsberg, may be considered the originator and inspirer of German Romanticism in a more profound sense than any other person of his generation. This is true not only because of his intransigent resistance to eighteenth-century rationalism, but also to his personal prestige and influence upon the entire group of *Sturm und Drang* writers, especially upon his protégé Herder, who paid him great tribute for his ideas about the *Ursprache* and *Urpoesie*. Known among his contemporaries as "the Magus of the North," Hamann opposed rationalism with an original adaptation of the Gnostic doctrine of the "Word." Speech or Language preceded Reason in the order of creation, the latter being dependent upon the former, and not vice versa as rationalist philosophers seemed to think. When Reason becomes autonomous it becomes sterile and destructive: "I do not ask so much what is Reason, but what is Language. . . . Without the Word there is no Reason, no world. . . . Language is the mother of Reason and Revelation, its Alpha and Omega," Hamann wrote in a letter to Jacobi.[34] A Swedenborgian influence is seen in Hamann's idea that every phenomenon of Nature is a word in the divine language. Objects do not merely exist, they also signify and are endowed with spiritual meaning. Such was the doctrine of correspondence. All that the first man saw and touched in Nature was a living Word, and Language was thus born from the contact of human sensitivity with the mute symbols of the created world, the signs or characters in the divine language which God had addressed to men. Revelation, therefore, in the sense in which Hamann used the word, means an intuitive receptivity to the images and symbols of the divine language which is Nature. It is an experience which depends upon the senses and the passions. Since the original revelation of God to men was thus made by means of images, poetry is the mother language of the human race. The knowledge which has come to men, Hamann concludes, has not come, as they have imagined, through the tower of Reason which they have constructed in Babel-like fashion, but through the descent of God upon earth, that is, by Revelation.[35]

In his work on esthetics, *Aesthetica in nuce* (1762), Hamann says that the poet must reawaken and reconstruct this lost and primitive language which is true poetry. For this the poet is pre-eminently qualified because of his prophetic and visionary gifts, for genius consists chiefly in a supernatural ability to see. "*True poetry is a natural kind of prophesying*,"[36] he says in the *Biblische Betrachtungen* (*Biblical Meditations*), emphasizing his belief in the religious nature of artistic inspiration.[37] For Hamann there is no conflict between the "spirit of observation" or scientific knowledge, and the "spirit of prophecy" or divine revelation, as he understood it; these two methods of arriving at knowledge seem to complement each other: "What would the spirit of observation be," he asks, "without the spirit of prophecy . . . What would all knowledge of the present be, without a divine remembrance of the past and a premonition of the future?"[38] This power of seeing into the future, which man once had but lost, is inextricably linked with the past and depends upon a true knowledge of the self (or the individual's past) in the Socratic sense. Hamann attached so much importance to this idea, as well as to the Socratic method, that he wrote his first work on this subject, *Sokratische Denkwürdigkeiten* (*Socratic Memorabilia*) (1759). He calls this inner path to the development of visionary powers "the descent into hell," the only hope for man's improvement, as he says in the *Philologist's Crusade,* for "all esthetic thaumaturgy is powerless to replace the least immediate feeling; only knowledge of the self, that descent into hell, can open for us the way to divinization."[39]

Hamann's works contain in essence most of the esthetic theories developed in the nineteenth century. Emphasizing the prophetic and therefore religious character of artistic creation, he laid the groundwork for Novalis' idea of the visionary and priestly role of the poet. In stating that the creative process is related to revelation, Hamann had not said anything particularly new, but the idea that revelation depends upon the Socratic plunge into the depths pointed out not only the unconscious element of artistic creation but also a frequently overlooked idea, namely, that a glimpse into the future can be had only by one in reasonably full possession of his past.

One of the most active popularizers of Illuminist ideas was Jean Lavater (1741-1801) of Zurich, whose extraordinary powers of observation won for him enormous prestige among his contemporaries as a visionary and thaumaturge — few had heard of the inexact theories on physiognomy for which he is today remembered. A member of no lodge or secret society, Lavater nevertheless constantly advocated the formation of a new church based on Illuminist tradition. Of strong pietist as well as eclectic leanings, Lavater hoped that the new church would also revive the faith and miracles of the early Christian apostles. He thought that there was magic power in prayer and that the faith of the Christian disciples conferred upon them supernatural powers, a kind of white magic, which was also capable of producing miracles in the modern world. The discoveries of Mesmer led Lavater to believe that all men possess the powers of a thaumaturge, and he attached a religious significance to the phenomenon of animal magnetism, relating it to the New Testament practice of the laying on of hands. After curing a hysterical servant girl in the town of St. Gallen, Lavater persuaded the doctors that they should also make use of "magnetic cures." So great was Lavater's renown that people came to Zurich from all over Europe to visit him, "as they did the bears in Berne," Viatte says caustically.[40] Particularly sought after by curious French émigrés, whom he often aided materially if not spiritually, Lavater at length made the acquaintance of Saint-Martin (1743-1803), for whose work, *Les Erreurs et la vérité,* he expressed his great admiration. Saint-Martin corresponded with him and also sent him a copy of his *L'Homme de désir.* It was only natural for Lavater and Saint-Martin to admire each other greatly, for in their *Weltanschauung* they had much in common. Both moved primarily toward a mystical and religious outlook and, although deeply influenced by *Illuminism,* they refused to become members of a lodge or secret society. In his works Lavater constantly contrasted what he called the "Inner Church . . . that aggregate of all souls inspired by Christ," with the "Outer Church," or ecclesiastical hierarchy.[41] Saint-Martin also makes a distinction between Christianity and Catholicism. Lavater's *Handbibliothek* (1792) contains one of the early romantic statements of the idea of the poet as seer, emphasizing, as has been pointed out, that artistic creativeness is a religious act: *"Whoever is not a prophet is not a poet. . . . All true poetry is a gift of the Father of Spirits."*[42] Similarly, among the French pre-Romantics, Saint-Martin is the first to have revived the idea of the poet as seer.

A few words should be added in passing about the attitude of Goethe and Schiller toward the Illuminist thought of their time. According to his biographer, G. H. Lewes, Goethe became interested in occult thought in his early youth when he was cured of a stomach disorder by an alchemist. After his cure, Goethe began reading the works of Renaissance alchemists like Paracelsus, Van Helmont, and Basil Valentin, and wrote Fräulein von Klettenberg from Strasbourg during his student days that these studies were his "secret mistresses."[43] However, in 1820, as a much older man, Goethe denied in a letter to von Esenbeck that he was ever deeply interested in the subject:

> Only under the guidance of your trusted hand did I venture a few steps in the direction of the occult. But with the best will in the world I had to turn back very soon for this simply happens to lie outside my province. . . . When I consider the fact that Gassner and Mesmer produced a great stir in my most impressionable years and that I was a friend of Lavater, who attached religious value to this marvelous phenomenon, I sometimes find it strange that I did not respond to the attraction — like a man walking beside a river without feeling any urge to go bathing. My nature must somehow be responsible for this attitude; how else would you account for its having persisted into old age?"[44]

A similar change of opinion may be noted in Schiller who, as a young man of twenty-five, began a novel which he left unfinished entitled *Der Geisterseher* (*The Spirit Seer*) (1786). The hero of this story and his experiences in Venice with an Armenian who could foresee future events and with a group of persons who held seances to communicate with the dead, were modeled by Schiller on the life of Prince Karl Alexander of Württemberg during the years 1733-1737. Later, in 1795, Schiller followed the Kantian line of reasoning about Swedenborg and wrote a poem, *"Das Verschleierte Bild zu Zaïs"* (*"The Veiled Image of Saïs"*), in the periodical *Die Horen* which he published with Goethe. To attempt to lift the veil of Isis, the goddess who symbolizes the ultimate mysteries of Nature and the Beyond, is a sacrilege, Schiller asserts. Furthermore, what such an irreverent person discovers upon lifting the goddess' veil is so hideous that he is forever deprived of all the joy of living.[45] Schiller's attitude of restraint before the ultimate mysteries, so characteristic of the Classical mind, drew from Novalis a refutation in his allegorical story on the same subject, *Die Lehrlinge zu Saïs* (*The Disciples of Saïs*) (1798). In contrast to Schiller's pessimism about the ultimate mysteries of nature, Novalis gives the purely romantic attitude toward them. In *Die Lehrlinge zu Saïs,* all those who out of fear, cowardice, or spiritual imperfection refuse to lift the veil of Isis are not worthy disciples of Truth. What each disciple sees upon lifting the veil is not terrifying at all, it is only himself.[46] By this, Novalis makes the point that ultimate Truth, personal in nature, lies within every person who seeks it. With this denouement Novalis gives artistic expression to Schelling's theory of the identity of Nature and Spirit, when he says "Nature is Spirit made visible and Spirit is Nature invisible."[47] By looking upon ultimate Truth in Nature, man discovers the realm of Spirit and, conversely, when man explores his own spirit he is led back to Nature and its physical laws.

For Novalis, the seer poet was primarily an initiate – one who, like the disciples of Saïs, has been received into a secret society and therefore introduced into the mysteries of Nature as they were taught in ancient Egypt. We have already mentioned the belief among Rosicrucians and Freemasons that all the founders of the great religions were initiated into such a secret tradition. In the second chapter of Novalis' work, *Die Lehrlinge zu Saïs,* some travelers en route to the Egyptian temple of Saïs express their need for a more intimate and complete knowledge of Nature. They believe that revelation can come to them only after such an initiation since man in his present natural state has been cut off from the sources of direct knowledge available to primitive men.[48] Upon their initiation, the disciples of Saïs learn to decipher the sacred and mysterious language in the temple of Nature, which was one of the chief purposes of their journey. This passage on the "language of Nature" from Novalis' work is strongly reminiscent of Swedenborg, Court de Gébelin, and Hamann on this subject: "This great code-writing (*Chiffernschrift*) is to be found everywhere – on eggshells, in clouds, in snow, in crystals, and in the internal structure and the exterior forms of mountains, plants, animals, men, heavenly bodies. . . ." Each is a symbol in the alphabet of a lost and primitive language, says Novalis, which the seer poet, because he has been initiated into the higher mysteries, is particularly capable of deciphering. It is a key to the higher mysteries and the means whereby primitive men communicated with beings of a higher-than-human order. In the contemplation of this language the poet enters into a state in which knowledge and creation are completely interdependent.

Such a striking resemblance exists between Rimbaud's esthetic and Novalis' that a few comparisons are worthy of some notice. In their conception of the nature and function of poetry, both poets achieved a resolution of the esthetic quarrel of the Romantic period – whether pleasure rather than truth is the chief purpose of poetic creation. (Baudelaire was never able to resolve this and one of his contradictions is that while he maintained firmly the theory of art for art's sake he was in fact thinking of art as a means of exploring the unknown.) For Novalis and Rimbaud the magician is the poet's *alter ego*: the magician is a poet (*"Der Zauberer ist Poet"*), and the poet a magician (*"Die Worte des Dichters sind Zauberworte"*).[49] The magician is a poet in the sense that he must bring order out of primitive chaos by means of words, that is, by a spiritualization of the material. He changes outer reality by introducing it into the inner subjective world. On the other hand, the poet is a magician in that he must materialize the spiritual, that is, by means of words he calls objects into being or conjures them up in the Gnostic sense in which to say and to create are one. Thus, the poet in his capacity of magician must give pleasure, and the magician in his role as poet creates something new. In this way, the poet may recover the lost power of his ancestor, Orpheus, who was able to dominate animals and even inanimate nature by his art. In the new world, "the Real Absolute" which the poet creates by the method Novalis appropriately calls "magic idealism," the Fichtean dualities of Nature and Spirit, subject and object, and ego and nonego are synthesized. This new oneness, which is not a mathematical identity, is immanent and organic in nature (as the oak is in the acorn) and it is in this context that Novalis says, *"Ich bin Du"* ("I am thou") to which Rimbaud's famous line, *"Je est un autre,"* makes such a striking parallel. As the following chapters show, both Rimbaud, in the *Saison,* and Novalis, while perceiving that the state of poetic synthesis has something in common with mystical experience, do not make the mistake of equating them. A striking resemblance to lines in Rimbaud's *Voyant* letters are shown in this passage from Novalis:

> The poetic mind has many points in common with the mystical mind. It represents the unrepresentable. It sees the invisible, perceives the imperceptible. . . . The poet is literally subject and object at the same time; soul and universe . . . *The poetic mind is closely related to the prophetic and religious mind, to all forms of seership.* The poet orders, assembles, chooses, invents, but does it in this manner rather than in that.[50]

Novalis describes the state of voyance as being more than a purely visionary experience, as one in which all the senses participate: "It is neither seeing nor hearing nor perceiving, but a composite of these which is more than their sum; a sensation of inner certitude."[51] Here Novalis conceives voyance as a fusion of the senses, which are then able to perceive past, present, and future as one.

The attainment of this state of voyance depends upon the poet's knowledge and mastery of himself, maintains Novalis, elaborating with different details upon the Socratic theme of Hamann.[52] Like Werner, the miner in *Heinrich von Ofterdingen* who studies the geological history of the earth, the poet must also descend into the depths of his own spirit to recapture his lost past and that of the race. "The mysterious road leads into the interior" (*"Nach Innen geht der geheimnisvolle Weg."*) writes Novalis in the *Fragmente*.[53] In this respect Rimbaud has another point in common with Novalis. Both poets were more aware than other Romantics of the unconscious element in artistic creation. Novalis expressed this in the last sentence of the long quotation cited above, and even more explicitly in this passage: "The artist belongs to his work and not the work to the artist."

Paradoxically, the descent into the unconscious is also an ascent to the goal which Novalis calls "the purpose of purposes" in poetry: "Poetry blends everything into its great purpose of purposes—the lifting of man above himself."[54] In this respect particularly poetry may be said to exert magic power, and at this point another parallel may be noted between the esthetic of Novalis and that of Rimbaud, that poetry with its *"alchimie du verbe"* had the power to change life ("changer la vie").[55] Both poets held that the vital element in this alchemy of transforming human nature is love. "Love is the basis of the potentiality for magic. Love alone works magic," Novalis wrote; and Rimbaud, some eighty years later, said: "Divine love alone plays upon the keys of knowledge. I am a musician who has found something like the keyboard of love." They believed that by such means it was possible to transform not only the individual but also humanity itself. In one of the beautiful *Hymns to the Night* (No. IV) Novalis expressed his belief in the redemptive mission of art to humanity, an idea which Rimbaud also expresses in the *Voyant* letters, which is treated in Chapter 6 of this book.

The world of the imagination and the characters which the writer creates enjoy such autonomy in the works of Achim von Arnim (1781-1831) that he constantly asks: Does the work of art really belong to the author at all? Arnim seems to have arrived quite in advance of his times at the modern conception of automatic writing, for he maintains that the writer often does not understand his own works, but must nevertheless have confidence in "what is dictated."[56] Sometimes a writer may have the terrifying experience of meeting in the real world someone he has created, as one finds, for example, in Arnim's work, *Dutch Fantasies* (1826). A young poet writes a tragedy on the myth of Icarus: when the hero falls from the sky his body lands at the feet of a young girl he has seen in a dream. She also recognizes him as a character in her dreams. Later, the author actually meets the girl who appeared in his work. So great is the power of thought and imagination, Arnim believed, that it is possible to excite a series of deplacements in the universe by means of them. A work of art may thus be endowed with dangerous reality. At this point, Arnim, the poet-magician, has led his readers to the threshold of the world of Hoffmann where white magic can become black magic by a mere turn of the screw. Like Hoffmann, Arnim also makes frequent use of prophetic dreams, and his characters in such works as *Countess Dolores* and *Isabelle of Egypt* move easily between the world of dreams and the world of reality.

In his enormous unfinished novel, *Kronenwächter* (*Guardians of the Crown*) (1817), Achim von Arnim, asserting the right of poetry to create history, attempts to recreate medieval Germany in the adventures of two members of the ruling Hohenstaufen family, the knight, Berthold, and his descendant, the painter Anton. Both characters are visited in their dreams by apparitions which make revelations or give warnings of the destiny of the Hohenstaufen family and their own mission in fulfilling it. In "Poetry and History," the preface to *Kronenwächter,* Arnim summarizes many of his esthetic theories. Looking out upon his country estate at Wiepersdorf as he writes,

Arnim compares the life of regularity which must be led by the farmer and by the poet, "that laborer in the field of the Spirit."[57] Comparing the poet to a priest, he says: "The one who calls himself a poet . . . is a true martyr, a hermit who in voluntary celibacy gives himself over to prayer and maceration in order that his fellow men may know joy." To the fear which every writer has that his ideas may only, like himself, "go to sleep in the world of Spirit," Arnim gives the mystical reply that "the Spirit loves even its perishable works." Toward the end of his essay, Arnim distinguishes between historical and poetic truth in a long passage and states his belief that the poet is a seer:

> Poetic works are not true with that truth which we expect of history, and which we demand of our fellow men in our human relations; they would not be that which we are seeking, that which seeks us, if they could truly belong entirely to the earth. For poetic works lead the world, which has been terrestrially alienated, back to the eternal communion. *If we call the sacred poets seers and if the writing of poetry can be called a seeing of a higher kind,* then history can be compared to the lens of the eye, which does not see of itself, but is indispensable to vision in order to gather and bring the light into focus; its nature is clarity, purity, absence of color.[58]

In the opera and the theater two works appeared which reflected the interests of the times in the secret societies, openly presenting Masonic initiation rites on the stage: Mozart's familiar opera, *Die Zauberflöte* (*The Magic Flute*) (1791) and Zacharias Werner's less familiar play, *Die Söhne des Tales* (*The Sons of the Valley*) (1805). After the death of Schiller in 1805 and Goethe's retirement from the theater, Werner had emerged as Germany's foremost dramatist; his play, *Luther,* depicting the chief events of the Reformation, enjoyed a tremendous success in Berlin.

For *The Magic Flute,* Mozart used as the source of his opera a novel, *Sethos, Histoire ou vie tirée des monuments de l'ancienne Egypte* (1731), by an eccentric French scholar, the Abbé Terrasson. This work, translated into English and German in 1732 and considered by French Masonic historians as a standard authority on the Egyptian mysteries, was used by Mozart's librettist, Schikaneder, who borrowed at least two passages word for word.[59] Thomas Love Peacock was the first to point out these borrowings in a review of Thomas Moore's book, *The Epicurean* (1822), a prose romance describing how Aliciphron, a Greek Epicurean, travels to Egypt in the year 247 A.D. to learn the secret of eternal life. Peacock points out that this work, as well as Mozart's opera, was based on the Abbé Terrasson's novel. Although Pope Clement VIII had condemned Freemasonry in 1738, the movement had friends powerful enough to prevent the Papal Bull from being published in Vienna in 1791. Freemasonry was at its height in Austria during the reign of Joseph II when Mozart's opera was presented for, although the ruler was not a Mason himself, his father, Francis I, had been initiated in Holland.

The Sons of the Valley, a play of two volumes in poetry which traced the origin of Masonry to the Templars, produced, says Mme de Staël, a great sensation in Germany.[60] It won for Werner the friendship and patronage of Louis of Hesse, brother of Charles of Hesse. Calling his play "a hymn to pure Masonry," Werner hoped to bring about, through Masonic symbols, "a more enlightened Catholicism."[61] The action of the play involved two opposing forces – the Sons of the Valley and the Templars. The former are Christian knights who have been perpetuating the Masonic tradition in secret, that is, they honor the prophets of all the great religions, an idea especially cherished by the secret societies. The Templars, on the other hand, are avowed initiates of the secret tradition. In the course of the action, the Sons of the Valley make war on the Templars, although both groups are fundamentally striving for the same ideals. The war was caused by the Templars unwisely trying to give the whole truth to all men which, in Werner's opinion, should be reserved for a few more highly developed minds. Moreover such divulgences were incompatible with the fundamental spirit of the secret societies.[62] Thus on the one hand Werner pointed out to Catholicism its error in attacking Masonry and, on the other hand, rebuked Masonry for trying to give to all men what should be reserved for the few (see above). In so doing, Werner hoped to point the way toward a union of Catholicism, Masonry, and the fine arts in a new and truly universal religion. Werner's play calls for the restoration of primitive Catholicism which would contain the essential symbols of all religions. Like other German Romanticists mentioned in this study, Werner saw an intimate relationship between religion and art – he states in a letter of March 30, 1804: *"I believe that the artist is not only a charming man of the world or a philosopher . . . but a priest of the eternal."*[63]

The Romantic physicists – Franz von Baader, J. W. Ritter, Heinrich Steffens, Johann-Carl Passavant, and G. H. von Schubert – so-called because they were either doctors of medicine or physicists, conceived of the possibility of artistic creation by means of magnetic voyance. Around the turn of the century this group, with the exception of Passavant, met frequently in the vicinity of Jena to work experiments in animal magnetism, telepathy, and automatic writing. Taking the discoveries of Mesmer as their point of departure, they arrived at the conclusion that in magnetic sleep (hypnosis) the human spirit makes contact with the "World Soul" ("*Weltseele*") and is thus able to participate in and experience directly cosmic forces.[64] According to their conception, nature is not a vast machine, as the Lockean and Encylopedist philosophers had said, but a living organism, and individuals are only arrested points in the current of vital energy which flows from the whole. Through magnetic contact with this energy it is possible for man's spirit to leave his body and enter into rapport with intermediary beings. Although they considered this relationship of man with nature essentially mystical and magical, they also thought that it could be explained scientifically and used artistically. This is the sense in which Novalis, who also frequented these meetings, used the word "magic"; and "night" in his *Hymns* clearly refers to the night of somnambulistic ecstasy. Original scientific discoveries made in the field of galvanic reflexes by Ritter, whom Novalis had saved from a life of poverty as an apothecary's apprentice, seemed to the Romantic physicists to confirm their interpretations of Mesmerism: the galvanic reflexes, like the somnambulistic states of Mesmer, were related to the autonomic nervous system, the involuntary part of the human organism.

Franz von Baader (1765-1841), a doctor of medicine before beginning his geological studies in Freiberg, was doubtless the most original thinker of this group. He anticipated many of the ideas later appearing in the works of Schelling, Novalis, F. Schlegel, and Steffens. A personal friend of Lavater, Baader had translated and helped him to popularize the works of Saint-Martin in Germany and wrote a book on the teachings of Martinez de Pasqually.[65] When Lammenais and Montalembert visited Baader in Munich, where he finally settled, they were impressed by his striking personality and broad knowledge. Baader's influence upon his contemporaries was undoubtedly greater than his actual productions, consisting of a number of short treatises and obscure fragments on esoteric subjects, which he sent to his friends at various intervals. In these, he discusses the phenomenon of magnetic voyance and elaborates upon its artistic possibilities more than the other Romantic physicists did. Making a distinction between the ordinary use of the senses of sight and hearing, which he calls "exterior" perception, Baader maintains there also exists a corresponding "interior" sight and hearing which take place in man during magnetic sleep.[66] Thus, with the discovery of magnetic voyance, the visions of Christian mystics and other visionaries no longer have to be denied or explained as delusions by skeptics, but may be naturally explained, concludes Baader, identifying the ecstatic state of the mystic and the somnolent condition of a person in hypnotic sleep—agreeing with the French Romantics discussed in Chapter 1. The relationship between magnetic voyance and the arts, explains Baader, is that when he creates a work of art the artist partakes of the same creative energy which God used when he created living beings.[67] In somnambulistic states, the artist is able to make contact with this creative cosmic force, but it is important that he not attempt to work hastily. Ideas and works of art must ripen in time like strawberries in season and it is important, insists Baader, that an author not publish a work until it has matured in his mind. In a treatise written in 1828, Baader says of the poet as seer:

> It is this interior perception, not the one which copies the exterior, which illuminates the progress of genius . . . . *every true artist, every authentic poet is a seer or visionary; every true work of art is the monument of a vision.*[68]

Ritter, whose experiments in galvanic reflexes had led him to reflect upon the implications of Mesmerism, wrote Baader enthusiastically on this subject:

> I think I have made an important discovery: Passive consciousness, the Involuntary . . . many things can only be explained in this way: friendship, love . . . the power of imagination. . . . All our actions are a kind of somnambulism, i.e., answers to questions, and it is we who interrogate. Each one carries in him his somnambulist of whom he is himself the magnetist . . . God in the heart. This phenomenon is absolutely somnambulistic. The waking state has no memory of it.[69]

The discovery of the irrational by those who had been taught rationalism in their youth produced an only-too-human effect upon the conclusions of the Romantic physicists: a tacit assumption that the irrational is superior to the rational. After all, was it not by means of his sleeping consciousness that man was able to contact the cosmic forces of nature? The alternation of sleeping and waking states was compared by Steffens to the rising and setting of the sun: as the sun goes down into its own night, so in sleep consciousness returns into itself or into the Whole. Thus, just as cosmic life consists in an alternation of day and night, so man also participates in the rhythm of the universe.[70] Steffens — who had come to Germany from Norway to study under Schelling at Jena and later with Novalis' teacher, J. J. Werner, at Freiberg remained, and became a professor at Halle and later at Breslau. He wrote numerous works on the natural sciences, philosophical *Märchen* of little literary value, but also a very long autobiography containing valuable information on the Romantic movement in Germany. Unlike the other Romantic physicists in his philosophical thinking, Steffens' attention was turned toward ethics. He was the moralist of the group, always preoccupied with finding a means of perfecting the individual.

Johann-Carl Passavant considered the phenomenon of magnetism as primarily an instrument of communication between man and God. The sacraments and ritual of the Roman church constituted in his opinion a kind of sacred magic whereby Nature became an instrument of Spirit. After having completed his medical studies in Heidelberg, Passavant established his practice in Frankfurt, where he gained a reputation for performing "magnetic cures." A trip to Italy in his youth had inspired his interest in the fine arts and also a great sympathy for Catholicism. Although his interest did not lead to his conversion, it did exert a profound influence on his thinking. In 1832 he became established in Vienna, which had become a center for the study of magnetic clairvoyance. Passavant interested himself in these studies and, like Baader, wrote about the "interior sense," insisting on its great artistic possibilities. He was especially impressed by the fact that the categories of time and space are abolished in magnetic sleep and considered this to be of great importance for the poet: *"The poet is essentially a seer. Poetry is prophecy, ecstatic vision of the past, the future, of the Whole."*[71]

Far more poet than doctor of medicine, G. H. von Schubert (1781-1861) wrote the most important work of all the Romantic physicists insofar as its influence upon literature is concerned. *Die Symbolik des Traumes* (*The Symbolism of the Dream*) (1814) written in Bamberg on command of the wine merchant C. F. Kunz, a drinking companion of E. T. A. Hoffmann, was destined to make an equally original mark on psychology. The son of a Saxon pastor, Schubert, like the other Romantic physicists, had studied theology as well as medicine, natural science, and history — at Weimar and Leipzig. Although he was first attracted by Herder and Jean-Paul Richter, it was Ritter and Schelling who finally inspired him most. Upon establishing himself as a doctor in the village of Altenburg, Schubert wrote and published a novel, *Die Kirche und die Götter* (*The Church and the Gods*), which was an attempt at a mythological novel in the style of Novalis' *Henrich von Ofterdingen.* In fact, the study of Novalis' works which Schubert was making led him to leave Altenburg and go to Freiberg to study geology from Novalis' famous teacher, J. J. Werner. A brilliant series of lectures given by Schubert in 1806 in Dresden on "The Nocturnal Aspects of the Natural Sciences" attracted the attention of such persons as F. Schlegel, Kleist, Mme de Staël, Adam Müller, and others. In these lectures, Schubert outlined an idea which was destined to become a mere banality as Romanticism progressed: primitive man lived in a golden age of perfect harmony with Nature; he was a living Word, expressing the universal Rhythm, and his very language indicated this harmony. The sciences too, which were one and complete rather than fragmentary, included man in their total account.[72] After the fall, provoked by the willfulness of man, the harmony between himself and Nature was broken. The ransom which he must pay for his independence is death, or the loss of immediate consciousness. Only love and death are able to put an end to man's separation from the universe and from other individuals. By means of death the superior forces which sleep in us are restored so that death becomes, in fact, a resurrection. Within life itself man often has supreme moments when he experiences the joy of "dying" to be born to a higher life. Poetry, religion, and the passion for knowledge all tend to prepare man for his final detachment from life.[73]

When Schubert began his teaching career in Nürnberg in 1809, he encountered the full impact of mystical and occult thought of the period. Through his friendship with Matthias Burger, the theosophical baker, he was introduced to the writings of Tauler, Ruysbroeck, and Swedenborg; in his association with Schelling, he came to know the works of Jakob Boehme and, at the instigation of Franz von Baader, Schubert translated in 1811 Saint-Martin's *L'Esprit des choses.* Finally, after a silence of six years while doing research, Schubert published *Die Symbolik des Traumes,* which was praised enthusiastically by Kunz, E. T. A. Hoffmann, Jean-Paul Richter, and the literary world in general. It was far more than a work of mere personal introspection; it was a philosophical study based on the author's medical and physiological knowledge. Schubert states his purpose to be an inquiry into the rapports which exist among the language of dreams, poetry, and nature. Almost a hundred years before Freud, Schubert noted that "in dreams the soul seems to speak a language quite different from the ordinary one" and that ideas in *dreams* are related by a different law of association. There exists in man an innate language, composed not of the abstract signs of his waking language but of images, and it is this which the dream has in common with poetry and prophecy. The Pythia of Delphi always spoke in verses which seemed obscure because she made use of oneiric language. Similarly, the rhythm of *poetry* serves as a magic incantation, appealing to the profound regions of the psyche; for this reason, ritual and the words of religious hymns produce an effect upon the individual far beyond their manifest content. Contrary to what might be expected, the symbolic language of dreams does not differ widely from one individual to another, Schubert maintains. Therefore, by careful observation, the essentials of the language of dreams may be learned. This is, of course, the basic idea Freud supports with numerous case histories in his *Traumdeutung* (1900). More clearly than his predecessors Creutzer and Lichtenberg, Schubert, in still another respect a precursor of Freud and Jung, shows the rapport between dream symbols and myths, which he considered the collective dreams of a people. In order to show the connection between the dream and *Nature,* the third point of his thesis, Schubert makes use of the Swedenborgian and Hamannian idea of nature as the hieroglyphic language in which God reveals himself to men. The original symbols of the oneiric, poetic, and prophetic language may be found in the world of nature which surrounds man "like an incarnated dream."[74] Animals still possess this foreknowledge — which has become dim in man through the process of civilization — as evidenced by the migration of birds and the precautions taken by animals when the winter is to be colder than usual. In spite of Schubert's untenable assumption that the sleeping state is superior to the waking state, one may see how many of the ideas of Freud and Jung existed in a fairly well-developed system almost a hundred years before the appearance of the *Traumdeutung.*

The idea of the artist or the poet as seer in German Romanticism may be said to have reached its artistic culmination in the works of E. T. A. Hoffmann. Most of the ideas of the Romantic physicists find literary expression in his works — correspondence, animal magnetism, second sight, the conception of the "double," the prophetic dream, and others. The heroes of his tales are all seers, and for the most part artists as well, who live on intimate terms with sorcerers and are instructed by them — as is Anselmus, the poet in *Der Goldene Topf* (*The Golden Pot*) by his teacher, the sorcerer Lindhorst, or Johannes Kreisler, the eccentric musician in *Der Kater Murr* (*The Cat Murr*) by his instructor, the magician Abraham. Like the magician, the artist must come to perceive the whole world as enchanted and directed by mysterious forces, as Abraham replies when Kreisler says scornfully that he can explain all his mystifications quite naturally:

> Of course! Of Course! . . . You who are a fairly reasonable man should perceive that nothing is natural in this world, nothing at all. Or do you indeed think, worthy Kapellmeister, that for the simple reason that we are able to produce a determined effect with the same means which we use, we know distinctly the true cause of that effect, the one which has its origin in the great mysterious organism?[75]

The relationship of the musician to Nature is compared with that of the magnetist to the seer by Hoffmann in *The Magnetist*: "The musician has the same rapport with Nature as the magnetist with the seer, his energetic will being the question which Nature never leaves without reply."[76]

The essence of Hoffmann's art consists primarily in his use of the marvelous — not as in the fairy tale where all is enchantment, but in the sudden vivid intrusion of the mysterious into the most commonplace events of everyday life. His procedure is to sketch first a specific place with all the details familiar to his readers, and then to introduce the mysterious. In *The Golden Pot,* for example, it is at a particular place in Dresden, the Schwarzthor (Black Gate), at a specific time, the festival of Ascension Day, that the student, Anselmus, encounters the sinister Liese, and later under an elder bush, beside the Elbe River, sees and hears the enchanted gold-green snakes. In the same way, the dreadful Coppelius in *Der Sandmann* (*The Sandman*) makes his entrance into a happy and otherwise quite normal German household. In Rositten Castle near Königsberg, Theodore, the young man in *Artushof* who had accompanied his uncle to help in the routine affair of drawing up a legal report, suddenly becomes aware of a ghostly intruder. The fantastic must be presented as if seen by an accurate observer, Hoffmann wrote in *Die Serapionsbrüder* (*The Serapion Brothers*). With the painter's eye for concrete details which appeal to the senses, he succeeds in making the mysterious plausible and, therefore, more sinister (or more poetic, as the case may be).[77] In this way, Hoffmann the literary sorcerer succeeds, as Hugo says of Baudelaire, in creating "un frisson nouveau" in literature.

By juxtaposing his dream world, also exactly depicted, with the world of everyday bourgeois reality, Hoffmann succeeds in making the reader take the former as much for granted as the latter. The juxtaposition takes place so adroitly that his heroes move freely and naturally from one world to the other, but not without perceiving acutely the conflicting demands of each existence. The plot, which usually grows naturally from the conflict between these two worlds, is clearest in *The Golden Pot* and *The Sandman.* In the former story, Anselmus' love for the poetic world into which he is introduced by the magician, Lindhorst, must struggle against the designs of Paulmann and his daughter Veronica (bourgeois common sense), who is in league with the forces of evil and black magic in the person of Liese. In the same way, Clara and her brother, Lothar, in *The Sandman* strive in vain to save Nathaniel from his terrible fear of Coppelius. As these two stories indicate, the visionary world of Hoffmann is inhabited by both good and evil influences, by dreams of poetic exaltation as well as by nightmares. In a state of poetic hallucination, Anselmus is transported into the fairy world of Lindhorst; on the other hand, Nathaniel is pursued by an evil fatality in the person of Coppelius. But whether blessed like Anselmus or cursed like Nathaniel, both participate in a force surpassing human nature and both are inhabitants of an extraterrestrial world.

In the denouements of these two stories, the visionary world which at first had only subjective reality for the two heroes finally has also an objective reality. Anselmus and Nathaniel come at last to inhabit completely the world they have constructed out of their dreams. But by dreams, Hoffmann explains in another story, *Prinzessin Brambilla,* he does not necessarily mean those which occur before sleep, but "the dreams which we dream all our lives."[78] "Belief and true love" being the requirements for Anselmus, "once student, now poet," to win Serpentina (Poetry), the two lovers depart for the fabled Atlantis with the golden pot. This contains Serpentina's dowry, appropriately paid in the otherworldly currency of the fire-lily which, explains Hoffmann, holds in its depths the most profound secret of nature, "the harmony of all beings." Serpentina's father, Lindhorst the sorcerer, explains to Anselmus that such knowledge as this, "which, like belief and true love, is eternal," could only be acquired by means of poetry. On the other hand, Nathaniel, who does not dream as well as Anselmus, reaps the consequences of his bad dreams. Olympia, the lady he loves, turns out to be a lifeless automaton which he has mistaken for a creature of flesh and blood. She has been created by Coppelius for the express purpose of destroying Nathaniel, who, ironically, is thus the cause of his own doom of madness. Hoffmann's characters must expiate or be rewarded for their dreams as objectively as if they were deeds.

In the world of Hoffmann the world of poetic vision is an autonomous one, presented with the same objectivity that the realistic writer uses to create the scenes of everyday life. Hoffmann considers the dream a means of artistic creation, of communion with the "World Soul," and thus of the attainment of truth: "To compose is to enter the kingdom of dreams. . . ." he says in *Der Ritter Glück* (*The Knight Gluck*). "Many spend their dreams only in dreaming. . . . they are dissolved there; only a few, having awakened from their dream, arise and pass beyond the kingdom of dreams . . . they attain the truth."[79] The artist must transport the marvelous from his dream world into everyday life; he must know how "to seize what his inspiration reveals to him at the moment of ecstasy." In order to do this he must be something of a magician – "the poet must be endowed with the magic power of poetic truth, for this power alone is able to transport us from ourselves." As one who inspired the French writers in the habit of taking hashish, Hoffmann wrote in the *Kreisleriana* about the phenomenon of synesthesia which Nerval, Baudelaire, and Rimbaud experienced as an effect of the drug and described in their poetry:

> It is not so much in the dream as in that state of delirium which precedes sleep, and particularly when I have heard much music, that I perceive a kind of harmony among colors, sounds and perfumes. It seems to me then that they all become manifest in the sunlight, to be fused into a marvelous concert. The perfume of dark red carnations has an extraordinary magic power over me: involuntarily, I fall into a dream state and then I hear what seems to come from very far, swelling and then disappearing, the sounds of a bass clarinet.[80]

The tales of Hoffmann made the visionary more popular on both sides of the Rhine than did the works of any other German writer. This was especially true in France, where his popularity was even greater than in his native land. The fame of Hoffmann in France began in the late 1820's, when his intimate friend, Dr. Koreff, introduced his works to literary circles in Paris. Dr. Koreff, who was a member of the medical faculty of the University of Berlin and had been mentioned by Mme de Staël in *De l'Allemagne* as "a young doctor of great talent," engaged in revolutionary researches in the field of psychology and attracted attention in the literary world as well as in the scientific with his "mesmeric healings."[81] He frequented the literary circles at the Arsénal, where Nodier and Balzac in particular cultivated his acquaintance, and he was also received in the salons of Mme Sophie Gay, Mme d'Agoult and Mme Récamier. Under the guidance of Dr. Koreff, the journalist Loève-Veimars, born in Paris to a family of German origin, undertook a translation of Hoffmann's works. With the help of Jean-Jacques Ampère and Saint-Marc de Girardin, who were interested in foreign literature, the name of Hoffmann became a legend in France during the 1830's. Using Edouard Hitzig's biography as the source of his information, Ampère introduced Hoffmann to the French public in an article in *Le Globe* (Aug. 2, 1828). Curiously, Ampère compared Hoffmann with Sir Walter Scott, a comparison justified only by the fact that Scott was the most widely read foreign novelist in France at that time. Scott, who either did not think too well of the comparison or who saw Hoffmann as a rival, replied with an article in *La Revue de Paris,* "Du merveilleux dans le roman" ("Concerning the Marvelous in the Novel"). In this article, Scott saw Hoffmann's works as "the imagination abandoning itself to the irregularities of its caprices." Enlarging upon this theme in an introduction to the *Contes fantastiques* (translated by Loève-Veimars and published by Renduel in 1829), Scott contrasted the "unhealthy pessimism" of Hoffmann to the "consoling optimism" of Wordsworth and concluded that it was impossible to submit such stories to criticism.[82] At least part of Hoffmann's sudden rise to fame in France was a result of publicity from the literary battle which Scott's criticism provoked in the French reviews.

Loève-Veimars was the first to protest; in a foreword to the first volume of his translations he included a notice contrasting the easy career of Scott to the difficult life of Hoffmann and his misery resulting from lack of money and chronic illness. Finally, Loève-Veimars pointed out that the first four tales in the volume were simple stories in which the marvelous was entirely absent and, if the latter four contained some scenes of hallucination and magic, these details were quite ordinary and in keeping with scientific discoveries "if one consulted the annals of magnetism." At the instigation of Loève-Veimars, five French reviews published in succession articles defending Hoffmann. The first was Duvergier de Hauranne in *Le Globe* (Dec. 26, 1829), who maintained that the British were incapable of appreciating a literary genre which did not flourish on British soil and that Scott was attempting to fix limits for the imagination, whereas Hugo had already pointed out the tyranny of classical rules. The article of course implied that Scott was the partisan of an outmoded esthetic, and linked Hoffmann with the new school. Within the same month, *Le Mercure* proclaimed that Hoffmann had introduced a new literary genre; *La Revue de Paris,* inspired by Loève-Veimars, published in January 1830, a list of Hoffmann's stories which were to appear in future issues. Saint-Marc de Girardin praised the fantasy of Hoffmann in *Le Journal des Débats,* and Edmond Cavé in *Le Temps* insisted upon the sincerity of Hoffmann, who felt personally the emotions his characters were undergoing — a remark which carried some weight during the height of Romanticism. By the time the third and fourth volumes of Loève-Veimar's translations appeared in May and October 1830, Sainte-Beuve entered into the debate with an article, published in *Le Globe* (Dec. 7, 1830) and later collected in *Les Premiers lundis,* which showed real discernment. According to Sainte-Beuve, Hoffmann had succeeded in changing the marvelous into a psychological phenomenon; his genius consisted in a sixth sense with which he had explored, as a "new Columbus," the unknown spiritual depths of man. Hoffmann, Sainte-Beuve maintained, had succeeded in a veritable transfiguration of the material world, seizing in the most commonplace objects a mysterious hidden significance; in short, he had "extricated and laid bare the magnetism in poetry."[83] Another well-known critic and two prominent writers were also inspired to defend Hoffmann prior to Sainte-Beuve: Philarète Chasle in *Le Journal des Débats* (May 22, 1830), Nodier in "La Fantastique en littérature" (*La Revue de Paris,* Nov., 1830), and the nineteen-year-old Théophile Gautier in an early prose composition not published until much later.

Thus Hoffmann became a legend in France and his name a synonym for the Romantic Bohemian — an artist with hallucinatory vision whose works made "fantastic" a term of high literary praise. Toussenel published an eight-volume work in February 1830, before the translation of Loève-Veimars was completed. Others followed, by Henri Egmont in 1836, Xavier Marmier in 1843, Christian in 1844, and Degorge in 1848.

Although the works of Hoffmann had such an influence on French Romanticism that all whom he inspired are too numerous to be listed here, a few examples follow. Balzac's *L'Elixir de longue vie* (*Revue de Paris,* 1830), which he calls a borrowing from Hoffmann, actually has nothing in common with Hoffmann's story *The Devil's Elixir* except for the magic potion. Much nearer to the German writer are two other stories by Balzac—*La Danse des pierres* (*La Caricature,* Dec. 9, 1830), later revised to form a part of the story *Jésus Christ en Flandre,* and *Le Chef-d'oeuvre inconnu* (*La Silhouette,* 1831). The hallucinatory experience related in the first story, in which the hero has the impression that the stones and columns of the cathedral of Saint Gatien of Tours are vibrating and that the organ and bells are resounding together, might indeed have been done by Hoffmann. Similarly, in the second story, the mad artist Frenhofer, pursued as if by some interior demon, bears a strong resemblance to the characters of Hoffmann. The artistic use which Nodier makes of prophetic dreams in stories such as *Jean-François les Bas Bleus* and *L'Histoire d'Hélène Gillet,* as well as the nightmares of Alfred de Vigny's hero in *Stello,* are reminiscent of Hoffmann's stories, even though there is no direct borrowing of plot. In Alfred de Musset's *Fantasio,* however, a direct borrowing of plot from *The Cat Murr* is apparent: a melancholy but generous artist, like Hoffmann's Johannes Kreisler, frees a young German princess from an Italian prince who has entered her house in disguise. Gautier's first story, *La Cafétière* (1831), tells of a young man who dances all night in his sleep with a ghost; the situation and descriptions at the beginning of the story resemble the first part of Hoffmann's *Artushof.* Gautier's *Albertus* (1831), written in verse, is the story of a young painter who damns himself for the sake of a witch, while *Onuphrius* (1832) tells of a young man pursued by an evil fate, like Nathaniel in Hoffmann's *The Sandman.* For Gérard de Nerval, Hoffmann was the kindred spirit who inspired him to make literary use of the idea of the "double," occurring in particular in *L'Histoire du calife Hakem* from *Le Voyage en orient* and also in most famous work, *Aurélia.* In 1835, while Nerval was helping Henri Egmont with his translation of Hoffmann's works, he wrote and published *Soirée d'automne,* which amounts to a pastiche of Hoffmann. In the course of a long journey by coach, the story's narrator is caught in a heavy storm. In a moment of hallucination, the noise of the tempest is suddenly transformed into the music of an orchestra, and the flashes of lightning, into thousands of small angels who join hands in the sky.[84] These examples indicate to what extent French Romantic writers were influenced and impressed by the genius of Hoffmann.

The works of Hoffmann form a clear and indisputable link between German and French Romanticism. The question of a widespread and general influence from across the Rhine, however, and of the idea of the poet as seer, is by no means a simple one. Several studies on this subject — the best of which is by P. Lévy[85] — have established that the major figures of French Romanticism (Stendhal, Lamartine, Vigny, Balzac, Hugo, Sand, and Musset) were unable to read German. Hugo's long poem on Germany, *Le Rhin,* was not the result of his wide reading of German authors, but of his successful plundering of an obscure predecessor. Stendhal spent three years in Germany but failed to learn the language, while we know from Goethe's accounts that Mme de Staël had to use an interpreter at dinner parties with German men of letters. Furthermore, her work, *De l'Allemagne,* shows that she confined most of her literary discussions to the Classical school at Weimar and was scarcely aware of the leading figures in the new Romantic school. In the preface to his translation of the tales of Hoffmann, Xavier Marmier confirms the fact of a general lack of cultural exchange between Germany and France during this period: "Until then [the time of the Loève-Veimars translations] we scarcely knew the modern literature of Germany except through the slightly too gallicized dramas of Goethe and Schiller."[86] The minor Romantics (Nodier, Nerval, Emile Deschamps, and Gautier), who were the most assiduous translators (along with those already mentioned in connection with Hoffmann), did not really possess a thorough knowledge of German, evidenced by the fact that Emile Deschamps used keys to translate German poetry, while Nerval made many glaring errors in his translation of *Faust.* In spite of this handicap, all these writers knew German well enough to have absorbed a vast amount of information about the Romantics across the Rhine.

Where the question of influence is concerned, an incomplete knowledge of foreign literature can inspire a poet or writer as much as accurate knowledge. One has only to think of the Hellenism of Keats, who never learned Greek. Translations can have considerable influence, as the popularity of Hoffmann in France clearly demonstrates.

Xavier Marmier accounts for the success of Hoffmann by his appeal to the desire of the times for the exotic, for a fresh glimpse at distant horizons:

> Hoffmann was for us one of those new and unexpected apparitions of a foreign land, one of those sudden rays which cause one to catch a glimpse through a mass of clouds, of the heavens and of the contours of a distant horizon.[87]

Two other noted Germanists of this period, Benjamin Constant and Victor Cousin, were preoccupied primarily with metaphysics. Cousin attended the University of Heidelberg in 1817 and later became an eloquent popularizer of German thought at the Sorbonne. The Bibliothèque Universelle of Geneva praised Cousin for having "acclimated to a rebellious land a plant born on German soil," but Hegel's remark about Cousin's metaphysics was: "M. Cousin has taken a few of my fish, but he has indeed dipped them in his own sauce."[88] On the whole, it may be said that Constant's appraisals of Germany are the most accurate and his understanding of German metaphysics the most lucid of any Frenchman of the period before 1850. This is particularly evident in his *Journal intime,* which indicates a wide reading of German authors as well as visits with many of them — Goethe, Schiller, Wieland, F. Schlegel, and Thielmann, Novalis' brother-in-law. *De la religion,* the work of Constant's old age, shows the extent of his real penetration of German philosophy.

Although it is not possible to generalize about widespread influence from across the Rhine during the early decades of French Romanticism, an exchange in both directions may be noted in the case of Illuminist thought and hence of the idea of the poet as seer. The works of Saint-Martin enjoyed great popularity in Germany among the educated classes due largely to the efforts of Lavater; Franz von Baader wrote a work presenting the ideas of Martinez de Pasqually (*Geheimlehre von Martinez de Pasqually,* 1821). On the other hand, Dom Pernéty of Avignon introduced Swedenborgian thought into France after having been librarian to Frederick II. During the last years of his life, Saint-Martin did translations of the works of Jakob Boehme in Strasbourg. There were two other factors in the exchange of ideas: letters and foreign travel on the part of French émigrés during the Revolution which has been thoroughly presented by the critic Baldensperger. Saint-Martin corresponded with Lavater and Kirchberger; Willermoz corresponded with the German Illuminist Turckheim, and Franz von Baader received Lamennais and Montalembert as his guests in Munich. Another of the famous travelers of the mid-nineteenth century was Taillandier (1817-1879), who wrote an article on Charles of Hesse in the *Revue des deux mondes.* An even greater exchange of thought took place at the two international conferences of the secret societies held in Lyons and Wilhelmsbad.

The idea of the poet as seer in French Romanticism may be traced to the posthumous works of Saint-Martin, written in Strasbourg during the period in which he translated Boehme. It seems quite probable that Saint-Martin was inspired in this idea by these translations as well as from his reading of Lavater.

CHAPTER 3

The Seer in French Romanticism

> Today, as in the times of Dr. Sigier [the Middle Ages], the question is to give man wings for penetrating into the sanctuary where God is hidden from our view.
>
> BALZAC, *Les Proscrits,* 1831

In France as in Germany the secret society was the cradle of the occult doctrines which gradually penetrated the literary world. If Court de Gébelin may be considered the intellectual inspirer or St. Thomas Aquinas of French occultism, then Martinez de Pasqually (c. 1715-1779), founder and organizer of numerous secret societies in France, was its St. Paul. Chief among Pasqually's converts was Saint-Martin (1743-1803) who, along with Fabre d'Olivet (1768-1825) and Pierre-Simon Ballanche (1776-1847), has been called a "Gnostic of the Revolution" by André Tanner. Around the writings and teachings of these four Illuminists, the core of French occult thought began to crystallize. But the initiates of the secret societies, or the *Illuminés* as they were called, were more than mere idle dreamers who had revived ancient magical practices unsuited to the modern world. They inspired French socialism with all its revolutionary aims, according to Gérard de Nerval in *Les Illuminés ou les précurseurs du socialisme.* By 1830 their early connections with Illuminism were still everywhere apparent in their writings, and few French Romantics could resist the strong impact of the socialist thinkers. Chief exponents and popularizers of the esthetic doctrines of the poet as seer, the Saint-Simonists and Fourierists had found this idea in the writings of these four Illuminists mentioned above and specifically in the posthumous works of Saint-Martin. Let us examine the different facets of this theme as it appeared in France, with particular emphasis on the aspects which may be found in the cryptic *Voyant* letters of Rimbaud (discussed in Part II of this book).

The Seer as Initiate and Seeker of Spiritual Perfection: Martinez de Pasqually, Saint-Martin, Fabre d'Olivet, and Ballanche

Martinez de Pasqually, founder and organizer of many secret societies in France during the latter part of the eighteenth century, was a man of obscure origin. Contemporaries and near-contemporaries such as Jacques Cazotte, Adolphe Franck, and Franz von Baader described him as a Spanish Jew, but one of his well-known disciples, Willermoz of Lyons, in a letter to Turckheim makes fun of those who called him a Jew. The critic Viatte holds that since a document exists proving the baptism of Pasqually's son and since he did not acknowledge his Jewishness when accused of heresy in Bordeaux, he was in fact a Catholic whose real name, Martin Pasqual, was a common one in Dauphiné. That he had family connections in Spain seems indisputable, however, since he died on the island of Santo Domingo, where he went after having inherited an estate. Whether Jewish or Catholic, Martinez de Pasqually organized Masonic societies at Montpellier around 1754, at Toulouse in 1760, and at Bordeaux. Similar societies were founded in Lyons and Paris by two of his disciples, Willermoz and Bacon de la Chevallerie. It was one of the Paris lodges, "The Nine Sisters," to which Court de Gébelin belonged and into which Benjamin Franklin was initiated during his years as a diplomat in France.[1]

Pasqually's *Traité de la réintégration*, which was still circulating in manuscript form during the life of Gérard de Nerval, constituted one of the chief sources of doctrine of the French secret societies. Dictated by Pasqually to two scribes and disciples, De Grainville and De Champoléon, the *Traité* contains an outline of the occult history of man, presenting the means by which modern man can recover the primordial innocence which he enjoyed before the "fall." Like Prometheus, primordial men were all seers who could communicate freely with beings of a higher order. (Prometheus, as a nineteenth-century hero of Romanticism, represented not only the suffering hero, but also primordial man in all his innocence, and was so godlike that he did not fear to enter heaven.) Modern men also possess these prophetic and visionary powers, Pasqually taught, but only through spiritual perfection can such powers be restored.[2]

His aim was to make all his disciples as learned as he in supernatural matters. The *Traité* contains the usual Kabbalistic doctrines: the theory of the world's creation by a process of emanation, the number mysticism which is related to this cosmogony, the theory of correspondence, and other such themes. Although Pasqually denounced the devices of magic and cartomancy, he did make use of a simple ritual which, says Gérard de Nerval in *Les Illuminés* (1852), revived Kabbalistic rites of the eleventh century. Initiates were called *Elus Coëns*[3], the highest order of which was *Rose-Croix*. One of Pasqually's disciples, Papus, describes the ritual as follows: Pasqually would have all those who "asked for light" enter a room. Circles were traced, sacred words written, and prayers said, "always in the name of Christ." Invisible beings then appeared "in full light" and gave instructions without the use of a medium.[4] In the library of Grenoble there exist today, according to Viatte, some of the manuscripts with the designation "given by the unknown agent" which were not destroyed when the lodges were dispersed in 1790.

The most distinguished of Pasqually's disciples and first among French Romantics to formulate the idea of the poet as seer was Louis-Claude de Saint-Martin. Born to a noble family from Amboise, Saint-Martin possessed a great personal charm which made him popular in the salons. While serving in the army in Bordeaux he was introduced into a secret society presided over by Pasqually.[5] After his discharge and a few years of foreign travel—during which he took lessons from Mesmer and read Puységur, Mesmer's French disciple—Saint-Martin settled in Lyon where he became an active leader in the lodges and tried unsuccessfully for a number of years to persuade his fellow members to resist the increasing popularity of charlatans such as Cagliostro within the lodges.

His first work, *Des Erreurs et de la vérité* (1775), indicated his differences with other disciples of Pasqually which were to increase as Saint-Martin's own doctrine matured. Finally, in 1790, he withdrew completely from the lodges and openly declared himself an enemy of the occult sciences in two works, *Ecce homo* (1792) and *Le Crocodile* (1799). Saint-Martin did not deny the ability of certain thaumaturges to produce marvels, but he attacked their overweening pride and the fact that their performances had eclipsed what he considered the real purpose of the lodges: the spiritual perfection of their members. The fact is that *"le philosophe inconnu,"* as Saint-Martin was called, had gradually become more attached to the type of transcendental mysticism on which saints are nourished. The last three years of his life were spent in Strasbourg, translating the works of Jakob Boehme.

A disciple of Rousseau and Restif de la Bretonne, Saint-Martin approaches in his doctrine the Savoyard vicar's profession of faith in *Emile*. Pointing out, on one hand, the abuse of reason and science by the contemporary philosophers and attacking, on the other hand, the tendency to charlatanry which threatened the lodges, Saint-Martin impresses the present-day reader as one who achieved an inner equilibrium remarkable for his turbulent times.[6] His philosophy centered chiefly on his belief in the enormous capacity of man for perfecting himself: "My entire life," he says, "will be occupied and filled by a single act and that act will be the development of the treasures which are enclosed in the soul of man."[7] The desire for perfection is the essential trait of Saint-Martin's *"homme de désir"* in his work by that title (1790). Men's talents are so varied that everyone can be superior in some respect and can give as well as receive so that "the great commerce of charity and humility can be exercised." Far from being solipsistic, the doctrine of self-development is, in Saint-Martin's opinion, exactly the opposite, for "when man improves himself, he is really working for others." This perfecting process continues even after death: "Men and children who die are plants in a nursery which are transplanted," he says (in a line which is reminiscent of one which Balzac wrote later in *Séraphita*: "Earth is the nursery [*pépinière*] of heaven"[8]). Because of his divine origin, "every man is inspired," thought Saint-Martin, and in another line (corresponding exactly to one of Hugo's) he says that "man is the lyre of God himself."[9] This interior illumination came to man first through language and is most intimately connected with the origin of speech. Following Court de Gébelin, Saint-Martin thought that modern languages "fell" like man from a purer and more perfect state to one less so. Concerning the origin of speech, there must have been a primitive revelation, he reasons, because speech is necessary for the beginning of speech. The theme of the poet as seer is definitely related to the linguistic speculations of pre-Romantic occult thinkers and, in this respect, Saint-Martin's ideas bear an analogy with those of Hamann and Novalis: language was the first revelation of God to man, and when the poet as priest makes use of language he also participates in this original revelation. In his *Oeuvres posthumes,* Saint-Martin makes a connection between poetry and prophecy: *"The right of poets (as in the Bible) marches with a step equal to that of the prophets."*

Among the familiar themes which later achieved their complete expression in French Romanticism, such as the idea that reason alone does not make the whole man, but that the emotions also have their place of importance, may be found this one which has a particular bearing upon the subject of the poet as seer and which gave a powerful impetus to the Romantic belief in the worth of the individual: all men are capable of divine inspiration if they develop their innate capacities — all may become seers, not just priests, since all partake of the divine. Therefore, each man carries within himself his own particular message or revelation to humanity which it is his duty to discover and express. Unfortunately, however, the originality of Saint-Martin's ideas do not seem to compensate for a literary style which lacks the poetic brilliance of Novalis and the strength and power of Rousseau.

Fabre d'Olivet, second of the "Gnostics of the Revolution" and more scholarly in his pursuits than Saint-Martin, was known to the writers of his times chiefly as the translator and commentator of *Les Vers dorés de Pythagore* (1813). A syncretist, linguist, musician, and apostle of the *"culte de l'Orient,"* he was from his youth deeply absorbed in early civilizations and languages. His Huguenot family in the town of Ganges in southern France had suffered persecution, destruction of their home, and almost total extinction during the reign of Louis XIV; thus the background of Fabre d'Olivet was one of heroic nonconformism. During his youth, he studied Arabic with E. Breton, Hebrew with rabbis, and read enormously writers such as Martinez de Pasqually, Court de Gébelin, Saint-Martin, and Swedenborg. During the Terror he went to Germany, where he was initiated into the Pythagorean mysteries. His father's business having been ruined during the Revolution, Fabre d'Olivet became an employee of the minister of war and wrote the text and music of the oratorio for the occasion of the crowning of Napoleon — but his final judgment of the emperor was indeed severe.

In the introductory essay to *Les Vers dorés de Pythagore,* Fabre d'Olivet develops many of the well-known themes of Pythagoreanism: metempsychosis; the triple (body-soul-spirit) rather than the dual nature of man, a conception fundamental to all theosophy; the idea of harmony and the relationship between music and numbers; the concept of a "world soul" or *"le Grand Tout";* and, finally, the purpose of all initiations into the mysteries, which is to "teach the initiate the possibility of that reunion of man with God and to indicate to him the means." Whereas Saint-Martin's ideology developed from occultism to Christian mysticism, Fabre d'Olivet remained all his life primarily a syncretist. Each of the different religions presents a particular way which, if followed, will reunite the follower with *"le Grand Tout,"* he reasons. Like Saint-Martin, however, Fabre d'Olivet places great emphasis upon the perfectibility of man in his introductory chapter. On the whole, many of the most familiar themes of French Romanticism may be found in the pages of these two "Gnostics of the Revolution."

The obvious errors which Fabre d'Olivet made in certain of his linguistic theories should be viewed with indulgence by the modern reader, for they were by no means greater than those of many other linguists of the late eighteenth and nineteenth centuries. The Gnostic doctrine of the Word or *Logos,* which pervades the works of all the Illuminists, is presented in clearest detail by Fabre d'Olivet in *La Langue hébraique restituée* (1815-1816). The following summarizes briefly his basic arguments: It is impossible that language could have developed arbitrarily and by chance, as the philosopher Hobbes suggests, for anyone who studies languages can see logical relationships in their development which could not be the result of mere chance. Man at his origin therefore received a particle or spark of the divine *Logos* and was able to speak the universal language from which all others sprang:

> Particular languages are only dialects of a Universal Language founded on nature and a spark of which from the divine speech animates the elements. One may call this Language, which no people has ever possessed in its entirety, the Primitive Language. This Language, from which all others issue as if from a unique trunk, is composed only of monosyllabic roots, all of which are attached to a small number of signs.[10]

Moreover, there was a primitive alphabet with sixteen characters from which all other alphabets were derived, and a single word without number, gender, or inflexion which Fabre d'Olivet translates into French as *être-étant.* (One is reminded by this of the Masonic legend about the "lost word.") From the primitive language came the two most ancient ones known to the Occidental world, Egyptian and Hebrew, the latter having been derived from the former at the time when Moses was initiated into the the secret wisdom of Egypt. Since

Orpheus the Greek was also initiated into the Egyptian mysteries, both the Hebrew and Greek cultures were fundamentally of Egyptian inspiration.[11] The three great spiritual leaders of the ancient world were Moses, who gave men their laws and institutions; Orpheus, who contributed polytheism and poetry; and Buddha, who introduced philosophy. The Asiatic world had two correspondingly ancient languages – Chinese and Sanskrit.

Finally, Fabre d'Olivet becomes poetic about words in a way which reminds the reader of Rimbaud and Mallarmé. Each word of a particular language may be considered as a living being, he thought, the consonants forming its body and the vowels its soul. Tenses of the verb may be said to have color, for just as there are three primary tenses from which all others are formed, so there are three primary colors. He continues in a passage which may well have inspired Rimbaud's "Voyelles":

> Speech is a means of painting thought. The tenses of the verb are the colored lights of the painting. The more the verbal palette is rich in nuances, the more a people gives flight to its imagination. Every writer makes use of this palette in keeping with his genius. It is in the delicate manner of composing nuances and of mixing them that painters and writers alike distinguish themselves. It is known that ancient painters did not know the art of nuances and of half-tints. They used primitive colors without mixing them. A painting composed of four colors passed for a miracle of art. These colors of speech were not more varied. These nuances of the verbal light, which we call compound tenses, were unknown.[12]

It has been noted that Saint-Martin progressed in his thinking from occultism to Christian mysticism, and that Fabre d'Olivet remained a syncretist who never seemed to emerge from the pre-Christian world. The third "Gnostic of the Revolution," Pierre-Simon Ballanche of Lyon, has aptly been called by Sainte-Beuve "a neo-Christian."[13] This appellation was given him because, like Saint-Martin whose works inspired him, he differed from syncretists of his time such as Fabre d'Olivet. Instead of a new religion composed of elements from all, Ballanche taught that society would improve by a process of palingenesis until all men would be Christian. According to Bédier and Hazard, it was from Ballanche that Chateaubriand took his expression, *"Le Génie du christianisme."*[14] Although Ballanche denied Illuminist affiliations and sympathies, he took the term palingenesis from the Swiss Illuminist, Charles Bonnet, and announced that what Bonnet had done for the individual man, he would do for the collective man, studying the process of palingenesis as it appears in history.[15] This he undertook in his *Palingénésie sociale,* but the neo-Christianity of which Ballanche dreamed — the fusion of all Christendom, Catholic and Protestant, in which exclusivism would be repudiated and the doctrine of eternal punishment abandoned — was certainly not orthodox. Encouraged especially by Claude-Julien Bredin (the prime mover in the cause), Ballanche, with Ampère, Roux-Bordier, and Gasparin (prefect of the Rhône), formed a *Société chrétienne* in which each member was assigned a special task for the purpose of spreading the new Christianity or *Eglise mystique.* Ballanche paid many visits to Fabre d'Olivet, read Lavater, and received as his guests Friederich Schlegel and Zacharias Werner, who had been sent to him by Mme de Staël.[16] After 1830 he thought of himself more and more as the inspired founder of a purified Christianity.

Of particular significance to this study is Ballanche's long epic poem, *Orphée* (1827), which treats the Egyptian initiation of the mythical Greek poet, an Illuminist theme also developed by Court de Gébelin and Fabre d'Olivet. In Ballanche's poem, Orpheus is the poet-priest, the primitive seer, the initiator of the Greeks and thence of all Europe into the mysteries. In these early days when the world is young, poetry is man's speech and his bond with the universal intelligence. There was a universal language which has now been lost but which will be restored by another poet-priest who, like the first Orpheus, will unite men with one language and initiate them into the mysteries. But this age is not yet at hand; in the meantime, it is the poet's duty to discover the particular mystery which the universal mind expects him to, for every age must make its own particular contribution. The poet, more than others, must embody the discoveries of his age, and possess a deep understanding of the nature of things. He must be a prophet who sheds light upon his time and who, like Orpheus, possesses the power of vision and prophecy. Ballanche mentions Saint-Martin and Cazotte in particular as examples of those who possessed second sight; then he asks if this phenomenon is related to animal magnetism:

> In the beginning . . . intuitive faculties had more power and scope than they have at present . . . it was second sight. . . . It is possible that magnetism is destined some day to introduce us into the knowledge of intuitive faculties or at least make us understand them.[17]

Describing briefly the state of second sight, Ballanche says in *Ville des expiations:* "All the senses awaken one another reciprocally. It is as if there were, so to speak, onomatopoeias of colors." Finally, in *Orphée,* Ballanche calls upon poets of the future to liberate their art from obsolete conceptions and to change poetry into something new. At the same time, he maintained that except for the force of tradition many of the ancient masterpieces would no longer be read or cherished.

After the death of Pasqually and Saint-Martin's withdrawal from his lodge, the secret societies became penetrated by many different types of Illuminism, such as the doctrines of Swedenborg, Mesmer, and the socialists, Saint-Simon and Fourier. All these met and mingled, not only in the societies but also in the salons, and found mutual support. The works of Swedenborg were first introduced into France around 1770 by Dom Pernéty, who had served as librarian to Frederick II and had founded a lodge in Avignon. In 1788, Daillant de la Touche wrote a summary of the chief ideas of the Swedish Illuminist, and a complete translation of his works by Moët appeared during the Empire. A revival of interest in Swedenborgianism occurred in the 1820's, when Captain Bernard in the vicinity of Nantes made numerous converts and held discussions in private homes. Le Boys des Guays founded the Church of the New Jerusalem on Rue Thouin in Paris, and also a newspaper, *The New Jerusalem.* As for the magnetists, the official condemnation of Mesmer and his healings in Paris in 1783 had by no means diminished his prestige. On the contrary, his works were widely read during the early nineteenth century, and magnetism became a parlor game. Puységur, Mesmer's French disciple, had discovered the trance state of somnambulism, which was widely practiced in seances, and the answers given by somnambulists were considered to be messages from the Beyond. The leaders of these groups were Deleuze and Du Potet, who also held meetings in the Hôtel-Dieu. Du Potet founded two journals, *Le Propagateur du magnétisme* in 1827, which failed for lack of money, and *Le Journal du magnétisme* in 1845 which enjoyed immense success. The magnetists had become so popular by the 1840's that their cause was advocated from the very chair of Notre Dame by Père Lacordaire.[18]

Prior to 1830 the influence of Illuminist doctrines on French Romantic literature was confined to tales of terror and of the fantastic, written first by Jacques Cazotte (1719-1792) and later by Charles Nodier (1780-1844). These works written before 1830 were concerned entirely with the nocturnal and the nightmarish aspects of occultism rather than the transcendental. About 1830 both Nodier (in such stories as "L'Histoire d'Hélène Gillet," "Jean-François les Bas-bleus," and "Baptiste Montauban") and Balzac (in *Les Proscrits* and *Louis Lambert)* began to see that the literary possibilities of white magic excelled those of black magic. These stories are the first in which Illuminist ideas such as those presented here were used as literary devices; the heroes of these stories are all seers and the plots center around the phenomenon of second sight. At the same time, inspired by Martinist thought, followers of the social reformers Saint-Simon and Fourier began to develop an esthetic based on the social mission of art with the idea of the poet as spiritual leader of humanity. Among the more distinguished partisans of the socialist theory of art were Lamennais, Vigny, Hugo (after 1835), and Sand. Prior to the *Voyant* letters of Rimbaud in 1870, the concept of the seer received its most ingenious and profound treatment in Balzac's prose, *Le Livre mystique* (1831-1835), and especially in the novel, *Séraphita,* while in *Les Contemplations* (1854) Hugo gives the theme its finest poetic expression. Let us trace in more detail this idea as it first appears in early French Romanticism.

Voyance in the Unsophisticated Characters of Charles Nodier

A frequent visitor to the home of Antoine Nodier and his son Charles was Jacques Cazotte, whom the senior Nodier had met through Saint-Martin. Cazotte, a disciple of Martinez de Pasqually and author of *Le Diable amoureux* and other tales of black magic, was something of a visionary in his own right. Gérard de Nerval relates in *Les Illuminés* the well-known story of how Cazotte at a dinner party in 1788 predicted his own death on the guillotine in 1792.[19] The story might be dismissed as legendary except for the fact that in his story, *Ollivier* (1765), Cazotte, in a macabre vision of guillotined heads (including that of his hero) rolling into a ditch, prophesied the atrocities of the Terror and even suggested his own fate. As a boy, Charles Nodier listened to these tales of the marvelous told by Cazotte, and in *Contes de la veillée* he mentions their impression on him. The visits of Cazotte were Nodier's first contact with Illuminist thought. Cazotte was executed when Nodier was twelve years old; at fourteen, he witnessed numerous executions in Besançon which haunted him all his life. Before leaving Besançon, he was initiated into a secret society (Rosicrucian) called the "Philadelphes."[20] Later, when he was approached in Paris by members of the Freemasons, he refused to join them because of his affiliations in Besançon. He did, however, become a member of a group in Paris, the *Méditateurs,* who practiced the smoking of opium in their meetings held at Passy. Under this powerful stimulant, Nodier conceived the possibility of making artistic use of the dreams evoked by the drug. In the Preface to *Smarra, ou les Démons de la nuit* (1821) he describes the dream as the source of poetry, myths, and the marvelous, and says that among primitive peoples and in children there exists between the waking and sleeping state a communication which civilized man has lost: "The world of sleep contains a gate to heaven or to hell, to the sublime dream or to the nightmare."[21] In the prologue of *Smarra,* set in a Lombard village, the lover Lorenzo is delighted to find his mistress, Lysidis, from whom he has been separated for a year. As they celebrate their reunion, Lorenzo tells Lysidis about his terrors during their separation. Abruptly, the scene changes to Thessaly at twilight and the hero, whose name is Lucius, is riding on horseback when, at the point of exhaustion, he has an hallucination: he is surrounded by a group of specters among whom he recognizes his friend, Polémon, who had been killed when the two were on the battlefield. The appearance of Polémon is accompanied by a sort of Walpurgis night scene amid demons and sorceresses. At the sound of a harp all come to order, and Polémon tells Lucius how the sorceress, Méroë, had cast a spell over him and delivered him into the power of Smarra, demon of nightmare. At length, Lucius falls into the clutches of Smarra and sees himself accused of assassination, condemned to death on the guillotine, and his head roll from the scaffold. In spite of this, Lucius' consciousness remains clear enough to be aware of the punishment of Polémon, who was delivered to bacchantes and had his heart torn out by them. With this, the nightmare ends and we are back in Lombardy with Lorenzo, who dreamed he was Lucius, but who awakens to find himself in the arms of Lysidis.

In addition to *Smarra, Jean Sbogar, Le Vampire,* and *Infernaliana,* a collection of stories inspired by a translation of the *Fantasmagoriana,* a similar German work, belong to this same general category of frenetic literature born of the Revolution. About 1830, a marked change may be noted in the writings of Nodier, which Viatte attributes to the fact that he had an experience of illumination in 1828.[22] Whether or not this is true, there was in the life of Nodier a crisis accompanied by acute mental anguish and depression, partly due to the marriage of his daughter, Marie. Although he was still haunted from time to time by nightmares, these became infrequent and less frenzied in his imagination and in his writings after 1830. At this time, he began to turn his creative talents toward more simple, primitive human beings, those who have often been labeled "insane" by society. Nodier said he felt special attraction to them because they remain, even when awake, in the borderland of sleep, being unable to return to a waking state: "How do I know if this alleged infirmity may not be the symptom of a more energetic sensitivity, of a more complete organization, and if nature in exalting all the faculties did not render them fit for perceiving the unknown?"[23] Thus, Nodier peoples his later works with these "innocents" who, because they are pure in heart, possess innate wisdom and visionary powers. The first of such characters is Michel in *La Fée aux miettes* (1832), a simple carpenter, inmate of an asylum in Glasgow, who turns out to have more common sense than the doctors in the institution. The second is Soeur Françoise, the ninety-two-year-old nun in *Hélène Gillet* who refuses to pray for a miracle of some sort to save from the guillotine the innocent Hélène because she "knows" in advance that something extraordinary will take place to save Hélène. Another of these dream-world inhabitants is the hero of *Jean-François les Bas-bleus,* who has become deranged as a result of an unfortunate love affair. On one occasion, after having seen traces of blood in the sky, he predicts the execution of Marie Antoinette; on another, he is seized with horror in the public square of Dijon, where he begins calling the names of members of his family who are at that very moment being guillotined in Paris.[24]

The last two of Nodier's seers are the hero of *Baptiste Montauban* (1833) and Lydia in *Lydie ou la Résurrection* (1840). The first of these, Baptiste, like Jean-François, has become deranged as a result of an unfortunate love affair. In Baptiste's unusual gentleness combined with great strength of character Nodier suggests the idea of the magic power of saintliness, a theme which Balzac develops two years later in the novel *Séraphita.* Baptiste has a supernatural power of communicating with nature, and like Saint Francis of Assisi his particular talent consists in his ability to tame birds.[25] In the second story, Lydia, a young wife, has become deranged since the death of her husband, George, who was killed while saving a family from their burning home. One night, in her sleep, Lydia succeeds in communicating with her dead husband, who conducts her into the Beyond and explains about an intermediary state in which persons remain for a time after death. For a year Lydia lives in continual communication with the spirit world at night and, at the end of this time, when she dies, the narrator is pleased that she has at last joined her husband.

Such is a brief indication of the evolution apparent in Nodier's literary subject matter — from the black magic and the nightmare of *Smarra* to the white magic of his innocent seers, Jean-François, Baptiste Montauban, and Lydia. A forerunner in his introduction of the visionary and the dream into French Romanticism, Nodier not only knew how to create the nebulous atmosphere of the dream but also how to people his world with ethereal creatures. His seers, who are of simple character, instinctive and unlearned, contrast sharply with Balzac's sophisticated and scholarly seers, Louis Lambert and Séraphita. "Revelation," Nodier concludes, "has not been given either to beings of a nature superior to man nor to men obstinate in the sin of knowledge. . . . It has been given to the simple in spirit and in heart, who believe because they feel and not because they know."[26]

THE SEER POET AS HUMANITY'S GUIDE TOWARD SOCIAL PROGRESS: SAINT-SIMON, FOURIER, AND TRISTAN

It has already been noted that after the death of Saint-Martin, the ideas of social reformers Saint-Simon (1760-1825) and Charles Fourier (1772-1837) began to penetrate the secret societies and to stir the imagination of the *Illuminés*. This influence worked in both directions, for the socialists were also moved by Saint-Martin's favorite theme: "love of God and of one's neighbor." In addition, they found it advantageous to adopt his esthetic theory of the poet as seer. With the July 1830 revolution, which gave increased political powers and a wider influence to the bourgeoisie, the followers of these two social reformers came into a position of national prominence. Their two reviews, *Le Globe* (early 1830's) and *La Phalange* (late 1830's, prior to the 1848 revolution), popularized socialist ideas and published articles inspired by Illuminist thought, such as the long article which Gérard de Nerval wrote on the cult of the Egyptian goddess, Isis (*La Phalange,* 1845).

Generally recognized as the father of French socialism and a forerunner of Karl Marx, who is said to have been indebted to him for many of his ideas, Saint-Simon was nourished on the humanitarian teachings of the Encyclopedists. Although he called the social system he wished to inaugurate "The New Christianity" in a work by that title (1825), his orientation toward social problems was far more that of a positivist than that of a religious zealot. In fact, Saint-Simon inspired rationalist ideas in his personal secretary, Auguste Comte, and the idea that an age of science would replace the age of faith. It was therefore the followers of Saint-Simon who changed his philosophy into a cult. After a fabulously colorful career of fighting in the American Revolution and imprisonment during the Terror in France, Saint-Simon amassed a small fortune by speculating on land, but died completely impoverished in Paris in 1825. A prolific writer, he attracted little attention until after his death, when his enthusiastic followers, Armand Bazard and Enfantin, organized a cult, with the latter as the pope of the new religion. Identifying their aims with those of primitive Christianity, the followers of Saint-Simon announced their intention to establish a new Jerusalem on earth. As a means to this end, they advocated complete equality, the emancipation of women, and the abolition of rights of inheritance. Declaring that a despotism founded on science would be difficult to maintain, Saint-Simon urged that a body of scientists called "The Council of Newton," replace the church as God's representative on earth.[27] An interesting reform from the modern point of view was his suggestion that the European states disarm and unite in a single organization which would, nevertheless, preserve the sovereignty of each.[28] In one of his later works, *Lettres d'un habitant de Genève à ses contemporains* (1803), Saint-Simon, relating his dream about the new social order, said that he heard the voice of God telling him: "Women will not only be admitted to the Council of Nations, but they will also vote and be elected."[29] In a similar vein, Olindes Rodrigues, a leader of the religion of Saint-Simon, wrote after the death of his chief: "I await with confidence the revelation of the first woman who will be at the head of the doctrine; she is the woman enfranchized by man, free and ready for the future."

When Pierre Leroux, a friend of George Sand and editor of *Le Globe,* joined the Saint-Simonists in 1830 this magazine became an organ for the dissemination of the new socialist ideas. Upon taking over *Le Globe* in November of that year, the Saint-Simonists deplored the sentimentality, egotism, and despair into which writers of the Romantic school had fallen: art had a serious social purpose, it was maintained in a series of anonymous articles. These articles were written in the same vein as a brochure, "To Artists, Concerning the Past and the Future of the Fine Arts," which appeared in the spring of the same year under the auspices of the Saint-Simonists. Its author, Barrault, a writer of little talent but great enthusiasm, defended Saint-Simon against the attack that he had been indifferent to the role of art and to the artist in society. Barrault called upon artists to become more conscious of their social function in guiding humanity toward a future Golden Age. Art is much more than a mere product of an age of a culture: it is an active social force with power to mold the present and to direct the future. "The artist alone, by his capacity for sympathy . . . is worthy of directing humanity," Barrault said.[30] It is the duty of the artist to awaken the passions of men for social progress, he reasoned, concluding that in the new social order: *"The Beaux-Arts are the cult and the artist is priest."* During the year 1831 *Le Globe* continued in the same vein: *"Poets are seers who open the gates of the future"* (Jan. 26, 1831) and "Poets must sing for the people and fill them with enthusiasm for progress." Much attention to music was in fact given by the socialist leaders during the 1830's and, in the vast garden of Ménilmontant, people's choirs were formed under the direction of Félicien David. Popular songs were encouraged, some adding to the spirit of the movement but most being didactic in nature and lacking in appeal.

Such a flattering conception of the role of art and the artist in the new social order could hardly fail to evoke response from the world of letters. Many writers, including George Sand, Lamennais, Lacordaire, Gerbet, Montalembert, and later even Baudelaire, wrote for or edited socialist magazines. Others, such as Hugo, Vigny, and Leconte de Lisle, campaigned for or aspired to public office and were defeated in the 1848 elections. Even one so aloof as Flaubert had hopes of becoming secretary to the embassy in Rome. However critical one may be today of the aims of the Saint-Simonists, their controversial propaganda awakened the social consciousness of the public and the literary world in general as it rarely had been awakened before.

Filled with the religious fervor which characterized his writings, Lamennais (1782-1854) aspired to rally Catholicism to the cause of social justice for the people, but he obtained instead the condemnation of Rome (Nov. 1831) for his review, *L'Avenir,* which he had founded in October 1830, in collaboration with Lacordaire, Gerbet, and Montalembert. With an eloquence which had profound impact on most of the literary world, Lamennais supported the socialists' belief in an "engaged" art in an article later collected in his *Esquisse d'une philosophie* (1841):

> Useless art, art without spiritual or social action, is without value. . . . The life of art must be sought not in the past which cannot be reborn, but in that which germinates and develops in the womb of the present. Artists of today, the true artists, have only two routes to follow. They can shut themselves up inside themselves, individualize art. . . . But what is man in humanity? To isolate oneself from the common lot is to renounce great inspirations. . . . It is to turn art from its aim. . . . *The old world is dissolving. . . . The religion of the future is projecting its first lights on the human species. . . . The artist must be the prophet of it.*[31]

George Sand, who encountered Saint-Simonism through her friendship with Pierre Leroux, espoused the cause of the people and founded *La Revue indépendente* during the 1840's in collaboration with Viardet and Leroux. In this magazine, two of her socialistic novels, *Horace* (1842) and *Consuélo, la Comtesse de Rudolstadt* (1842-1843) were published. The first of these had been previously rejected by *La Revue des deux mondes* because of several passages on free love; the second had as its theme the occult idea of palingenesis so dear to Pierre Leroux, and contained the Saint-Simonist attitude toward art. Consuélo, the talented young singer who is heroine of this four-volume novel, falls in love with the Count Albert de Rudolstadt on a visit to his château. The young count informs her that he is in reality Jean Ziska, who was born several centuries before and who has been reincarnated. Consuélo then departs for Vienna, where she achieves a brilliantly successful career in music. On one occasion, the young singer, discussing the sacred mission of art with her teacher, Porpora, asks: *"If art is sacred, are we not also its priests and Levites?"*[32] At the moment of her triumph, Consuélo learns that Albert (Jean Ziska) is dying and, in true Romantic fashion, she arrives at his bedside just in time to marry him *in extremis.* Just before he dies, Albert tells her: "I am going to leave you for a time, and then I shall return to earth by the manifestation of a new birth." After numerous adventures, Consuélo is finally put in prison by the King of Prussia and escapes through the agents of a Rosicrucian society. She is initiated into the order of the Grail, and there among the members of this group she finds Albert de Rudolstadt (Jean Ziska) revived and so much like his former self that she is unable to detect any difference!

A rift occurred between George Sand and Leroux when he expounded his doctrines at such length in *La Revue indépendente* that he bored his readers excessively. In 1848, George Sand founded another newspaper, *La Cause du peuple,* in collaboration with Victor Borie, and became editor in chief of *Bulletins de la République,* where she was better able to popularize her ideas. She called the attention of her readers to the desperate living conditions of large numbers of people and counseled them to strike if the elections of 1848 did not bring the amelioration which they expected. When the masses did in fact march on the Hôtel de Ville on April 17, 1848, George Sand, like other literary figures who witnessed the bloody fighting which followed, became disillusioned and abandoned all desire to participate in social reform. After the debacle of 1848, the literary world for the most part did just what Lamennais predicted it would – it began to "individualize art," that is, to detach it from the real world and to cultivate it in the ivory tower of *Parnasse*.

Thus, the followers of Saint-Simon became the *colporteurs* of an artistic and occult as well as socialistic doctrine. From their roots in eighteenth-century rationalism they spread into a nineteenth-century cult, ambitious for social equality. Free from the tyranny of state and church, the New Jerusalem which they conceived would have only artists as priests.

Unlike Saint-Simonism, conceived as the rational application of Encyclopedist belief in social progress and thence changed into a cult by its eager followers, Fourierism, in the tradition of Rousseau and Restif de la Bretonne, was originally inspired by occult thought and ended with followers who favored abandoning this tendency for more practical ones. This system, as conceived by its founder, Charles Fourier, was a curious mixture of Pythagoreanism and primitive Christianity. Taking as his slogan "the love of God and of humanity," Fourier hoped to establish a golden age or a "kingdom of heaven on earth," but by means which differed from those of his predecessor, Saint-Simon. In order for man-the-individual to achieve the state of harmony advocated by Pythagoras as the fundamental principle of the universe, society must also progress toward a more harmonious state, Fourier maintained. This would be eventually accomplished by palingenesis or successive rebirth but, in the meantime, the process could be hastened if man would reorganize society to serve his needs more effectively.

In common with Rousseau and Restif de la Bretonne, Fourier held that the passions, which are essentially good, are the sources of man's creative energies. The new social order was to be based on what Fourier thought would produce the harmonious functioning of the "twelve passions." The happiness of man, and therefore the harmony of society, can come about only when man enjoys the free expansion of his faculties and the satisfaction of his natural desires. Conversely, unhappiness results from inactivity and the suppression of his needs. On its more practical side, Fourier's scheme consisted in dividing society into "phalanges" or working groups of 1,600 persons, who would live together in a large building called a *phalanstère*. Each *phalanstère* would have a portion of soil allotted to it for cultivation, and each worker would be assured a minimum subsistence; the remainder of the earnings were to be distributed among the workers in shares according to a system of merit. Private property was not abolished, nor was the privacy of family life within the *phalanstère*. Of great importance to Fourier was the principle that workers should have the kind of employment best suited to their natural aptitudes. Provisions were made whereby workers could vary their employment from time to time by joining other phalanges and thus prevent monotony.

The five stages through which Fourier believed civilization to have passed should be mentioned here because of a similar reference made by Rimbaud in the *Voyant* letters. Society, Fourier held, has already passed through four stages in its development; the fifth stage lies in the future. From a state of savagery (1. *Sauvagerie*) the patriarchal system developed (2. *Patriarchat*); from the latter came the feudal stage (3. *Féodalisme*), and from it the barbaric modern state based on industrialism and perpetual war (4. *Barbarie*).[33] The fifth stage, that of harmony or true civilization (5. *Harmonie*), can only come about when men radically change the fundamental structure of society.

Having completed two works explaining his system, *Les Quatre Movements* (1808) and *Traité de l'Association domestique agricole* (1822), Fourier went to Paris in 1826 with the hope of finding someone to finance an experiment in a socialistic community. There his ideas attracted little attention until he wrote a polemic against Saint-Simon in 1831. The following year, the first socialistic community was financed by M. Baudet Dulary, deputy for Seine-et-Oise. This community, located in the forest of Rambouillet near Paris, failed from lack of funds. Between the years 1840 and 1850, forty-one such experiments were undertaken, some of them outside France; one of the best known was the Brook Farm experiment of the New England Transcendentalists. After Fourier's death in 1837, Victor Considérant became chief of the group, which remained politically active until the socialist defeat in the revolution of 1848.

The magazine which Fourier founded in 1832 as *La Phalanstère* and which became *La Phalange* in 1836 was the official organ of Fourierist doctrine. It not only published articles about the reorganization of society but also popularized various occult doctrines. Several articles appeared on Swedenborg, who was credited with having inspired Fourier to attempt to establish on earth the harmony which the Swedish mystic thought to exist in heaven. Many articles appeared on Mesmerism and Gnosticism, as well as the aforementioned long treatment by Gérard de Nerval on the cult of Isis.

In a series of articles in *La Phalange,* Hugh Doherty, a frequent contributor, discusses in great detail the social purpose of art. In the Fourierist conception expressed by Doherty, the role of the artist as the inspired guide of humanity is particularly emphasized. The following passage from one of his articles could have been taken from the pages of a modern existentialist writer:

> Art increases therefore to the extent to which the artist sees more into the depth of hearts and farther into the course of existence; to the extent to which it penetrates in some way the destiny of the individual. . . . Art must, by its constant action, re-ally itself to human destiny. The beautiful is more perfect if it reflects better the ideal of the good.[34]

Like Saint-Simon, Fourier was also an ardent champion of women's rights. This aspect of socialist thought appears as one of the themes in Rimbaud's *Voyant* letters and, for that reason, deserves a few remarks. Both reformers insisted with equal intensity upon political as well as social equality for women, and denounced a system in which girls of seventeen were bartered by their fathers to the highest bidders. The emancipation of women, Fourier thought, is a sign of social progress, for in periods of decadence there had been a noticeable decrease in the liberties of women.[35] Conversely, a vigorous and progressive society was characterized by more freedom for women. Men have succeeded in keeping women enslaved, Fourier held, chiefly by denying them an education and making domestic servants of them, "thus, to dispose the slave to brutal treatment, studies which would cause her to evaluate her abject condition are forbidden to her."[36] Insisting upon equal educational opportunities for women, Fourier makes the prediction that when women finally become educated they will enter the fields of literature and the arts.

These inequalities suffered by women have had the effect of a boomerang, Fourier argues, producing an intolerable situation in which women and men constantly deceive each other. If the social destiny of woman remains unfulfilled, so likewise will man's. Reviving the ancient Platonic myth of the androgyne, Fourier prophesies that after a certain number of rebirths men will become morally better until a Messiah comes to reform the church.[37] Similarly, a *Femme-Messie* will appear and bring about the social liberation of women. This woman Messiah together with her male counterpart will reconstruct in their person the Androgyne, *"Le Grand Evadam."*[38]

One woman particularly active in this movement for the emancipation of women was Flora Tristan (1803-1844), grandmother of the famous painter, Paul Gauguin. Under the direction of Fourier, she founded a Union of Women Workers (*Union Ouvrière*), and wrote a pamphlet favoring divorce. In 1838 she published the novel *Méphis,* which is an autobiographical account of her own unhappy life with the young painter who is its hero. Through him, Flora Tristan also expresses the Fourierist doctrine of art:

> The arts are men's communications with God; the arts are religion in its entirety; the prophet, poet, sculptor and musician are the priests of it; the masterpieces its revelation. . . . To create art for art's sake is to isolate oneself from the creator.[39]

Flora Tristan's posthumous work, *L'Emancipation de la femme ou Testament de la Paria,* was edited and published by Eliphas Lévi (L'Abbé Constant), whose occult works will be discussed later in connection with Hugo. This book, written with true Latin vehemence, is filled with such exclamations as: "Their [women's] rights are the same as men's!" and "Now I tell you that the glance of a young girl bought at the price of gold is a prostitution and the one who marries a young girl against her heart makes of her both a prostitute and an adulteress!"[40] Like Fourier, Flora Tristan calls for the education of women: "In order to emancipate serfs, we must educate them!" she maintains. Such an emancipation is essential if the ideal harmony in society is to be achieved, for "woman is queen of harmony and that is why she must be at the head of the regenerative movement of the future." When love at last dominates force, she predicts, "woman will be queen of the world." Finally, she says that it is "intelligence and love which will henceforth make priests as they have made the seers and prophets of all times."

Lamartine, Vigny, and Musset, although not lacking in visionary qualities, will not be listed here as seers in the Romantic sense. While it is true that Lamartine introduced the Eastern theme of animism into his nature poems, his inspiration was nevertheless overwhelmingly Christian rather than occult. Vigny and Musset often express sentiments of revolt against Christianity, but this very revolt is a tacit acknowledgment of their source of inspiration, especially since it is not accompanied by a positive belief in something else. Certainly, there is an absence of the conception of the poet as initiator into the mysteries. These statements do not imply inferiority in the works of these three poets, merely that they are being eliminated here because their works do not relate to the subject at hand. We shall instead turn our attention upon aspects of Gérard de Nerval's voyance not yet discussed.

THE SEER POET AS SYNCRETIST AND INTERPRETER OF MYTH: GÉRARD DE NERVAL

The true seer must be able to decipher myth and legend, especially those of the ancient world, since early peoples concealed their most profound truths under the guise of a simple story. An understanding of the essence of myths was therefore desirable, if not indispensable, in providing the adept with a key to ancient wisdom. Through his assiduous pursuit of occult studies, Nerval possessed and assimilated the symbols of magic more thoroughly than any other seer poet. His natural, spontaneous visionary powers, compared with the more cultivated type possessed by Baudelaire and Rimbaud, has already been mentioned. Nerval's belief in the dream as a means of knowing, of exploring the unconscious and of entering into communication with a spirit world, as related in *Aurélia,* was based upon his personal experiences. Here we shall be concerned with Nerval the syncretist and interpreter of myths who, inspired by his occult research, undertook in 1842 an eleven-month trip to the Middle East. This is the Nerval of *Le Voyage en orient* (1851) and of the twelve cryptic sonnets, *Les Chimères* (1854).

Behind all the picturesque detail of the landscape and the people of the Middle East, as Nerval saw it, lies the mystery of the Orient with its strange and secret doctrines, its initiation into the mysteries which professed to link modern man to the beginnings of his race. In this world charged with mystery the most common events of everyday life are not isolated and without meaning, but possess a secondary or transcendental significance. Second sight in the Nervalian sense means the ability to see and to decipher the spiritual significance of events. Extending further than the Swedenborg-Baudelaire correspondence, in which only objects signify, Nerval's second sight is much more uncanny, but it never produces a shock because the supernatural is treated as if nothing in the world could be more natural. Two legends from *Le Voyage en orient* clearly reveal Nerval's application of occult knowledge to the process of deciphering events and to the creation of atmosphere which gives his works their distinctive character: the first of these is the legend of the Kalif Hakem, and the second, the legend of Adoniram, master builder of Solomon's temple. Through a series of events, the heroes of both stories discover the secondary or spiritual meaning of their lives.

The Legend of the Kalif Hakem

Escaping by night from his palace in Cairo, the Kalif Hakem wanders in disguise through the city streets. He finds this experience of becoming another person so pleasant that he decides to repeat it. On one of these occasions, the Kalif meets a simple boatsman, Yousouf, with whom he takes hashish. In accordance with the effects said to accompany the taking of this drug, the Kalif perceives himself to be divine. While still partially under the influence of this perception, he is approached the next day in the streets by a blind beggar who throws at the crowd money which the Kalif had given him out of charity. The beggar asks instead for bread for his starving people. When the Kalif reproaches the beggar for addressing in such a peremptory manner someone whom he has not seen, the latter replies: "All men are blind before God."[41] Astonished at the man's reply, the Kalif asks him if it is God whom he is addressing, to which the beggar answers: "It is you, Lord." From this moment on, Hakem begins the realization of his divine nature. One evening, when he is again walking through the streets in disguise, he is seized by the police and sent to Moristan, a prison and insane asylum.

His arrest had resulted from a plot of his vizir, Argevan, to seize power for himself and marry Hakem's sister, Sétalmulc, whom Hakem also loved and hoped to marry in accordance with Egyptian custom. After struggling all night to free himself, Hakem again realizes the next morning his divine nature and perceives the spiritual significance of this event as the Gnostic symbol of the imprisonment of the spirit by matter. No one in the prison recognizes Hakem as the Kalif. When Argevan and Sétalmulc, on a charity visit to Moristan, also do not recognize him, Hakem begins to doubt his own identity. Only the blind beggar is able to identify him as the Kalif and a god. After a series of events, the Kalif's divine nature becomes apparent to all the prisoners, who revolt and deliver him. Hakem returns to his palace to find another man occupying his chair beside Sétalmulc. Suddenly recognizing this man as his "double" or *ferouer,* considered by Orientals to be an omen of approaching death, Hakem flees from his palace into the night. On the Nile he meets Yousouf, the boatsman, who tells Hakem of his love for the beautiful lady in the palace. Hakem then recognizes Yousouf as the man who had been seated beside his sister in the palace. On the following night, Hakem is assassinated. Yousouf had defended him, but their bodies were never found. The inhabitants of Cairo said that they were both seen thirty years after their official death. The Drusians maintained that they withdrew into a mountain where they founded their religion.[42]

The Legend of Adoniram

At the time of the construction of the temple, when Solomon is beginning to grow old, the Queen of Sheba visits his court. There she meets and falls in love with a young man, Adoniram, master-builder of the temple, and a mysterious character. No one knows whence he came nor who his ancestors were. He lives a solitary life. It is known, however, that this master artist dreams constantly of marvelous works of construction resembling those of a race which disappeared during the flood in the city of Henochia. This was the city of the lineage of Tubal-Cain upon whom Solomon had pronounced his curse. Their art, Solomon maintained, belonged to darkness, whereas his own partook of light since it had been blessed by Adonai, god of brightness. Adoniram possesses, therefore, the Promethean spirit – clever, full of dreams and ambitions, and rebellious against the established god.

One night, as Adoniram is working on the dangerous project of constructing a coulee on the Dead Sea, traitors among his workers cause him to throw water on the hot metals and thus interrupt him and threaten the ruin of his work. As the steam and hot metals fly in every direction, all his workers flee and Adoniram himself, stunned by the impact and lying upon the ground half senseless, suddenly becomes aware of a presence near him and is carried away in a vision.

In a true Orphic descent into hell, the mysterious person leads Adoniram underground. As they begin their descent, Adoniram asks the presence who he is; the latter replies: "Your ancestor, man . . . an artist, your master and your superior: I was Tubal-Cain." Greatly surprised by this reply, Adoniram begins to doubt both himself and the reality of his impressions as the two penetrate further underground. By the time they reach the fire lying at the center of the earth, Adoniram has learned that Tubal-Cain, the master blacksmith, was the father of a secret race, the descendants of Cain, who escaped the Flood by going underground. There they preserved their esoteric traditions, the knowledge which man possessed before the Flood. Adoniram sees men at work everywhere on metals and various precious stones. Ingenious, industrious, but accursed and oppressed by the world to whose conformism they have refused to submit, these people are aided by the Elohim, divine forces which in Jewish Kabbalistic tradition are said to help men secretly. To these spirits Tubal-Cain opposes Adonai, the god of brightness and of officialdom (the Apollo of the Greeks) who has always repressed inventive genius and allowed more vulgar mentalities to oppress it. Here, in their secret traditions, Tubal-Cain explains, men may partake of the Tree of Knowledge without perishing from it. Adoniram immediately identifies himself as belonging to this race of the Elohim and learns that they were the real builders of the Pyramids. At length, Adoniram meets Cain, whom he recognizes as that part of man which revolts in sincerity against what he believes to be the injustice of the Creator. Cain accepts full responsibility for being the original revolter against Adonai and the cause of all the sufferings of his race. Cain then explains the nature of the curse which was pronounced upon his descendants: their bodies will be weak, their lives short, and solitude will be their lot. Although superior to their fellow men in intellect, and for that reason their benefactors, they are nevertheless doomed ever to be hated and misunderstood because of this superiority. Only their tombs will be honored. Cain exhorts them to have courage in spite of all this, for from their numbers will come a royal family which will restore upon earth the worship of the sacred element—fire—which has been lost.

Upon his return to earth, Adoniram begins to repair the destruction of his coulee on the Dead Sea. Upon its completion, he finds again the Queen of Sheba, who renounces Solomon for him, and as the two are making plans for their wedding, Adoniram, like the unfortunate Hakem, is assassinated by three of his jealous companions.[43]

Using the framework and details of an Oriental story, similar to those found in the *Arabian Nights,* Nerval effects a complete change in this literary genre. The events of an Oriental tale, for the most part, are viewed by the raconteur from an exterior point of view, that is, the narrator remains outside the tale and detached from it. In these two legends, however, the narrator has woven his own personality into the stories to such an extent that the events are seen from the interior in the personal manner characteristic of Romantic writers. Nerval is both Hakem and Adoniram, and it is quite possible that he chose these two legends because of his feeling of identification with the two oppressed but superior heroes. Nerval is Hakem the prince who discovers his duality and his mysterious divinity, who is frustrated, misunderstood, and finally committed to an asylum. In spite of this, his divine nature triumphs and the liberated hero leaves the asylum to become the founder of a new syncretic religion — exactly what Nerval hoped his occult studies would accomplish. Hakem is therefore Nerval the poet-priest. The Drusian religion interested Nerval immensely because it provided him with a living example of syncretism actually in practice in modern society. The Drusians, he discovered, found no conflict between their religion and those of their Christian and Moslem neighbors; on the contrary, these neighbors were constantly persecuting the Drusians in the name of their religion. As modern descendants of the Gnostics, Pythagoreans, and Essenes, the Drusians, according to Nerval, held the cardinal principle of all syncretists, namely, that there have been many incarnations of God in the course of history, of which the founder of their own religion is only one. Dating their religion from the year 1000 A.D., the Drusians believed Hakem to be the latest of these incarnations of God.[44] Nerval maintains finally that this was the source of Masonic mysticism brought into the Western world by the Templars during the Middle Ages.

Adoniram is Nerval the artist and initiate into the mysteries, the creative genius to whom an unusual vision has been given and who, because of his superiority, is doomed to be hated and accursed by men. Initiation into the mysteries is reserved for these superior ones; it is their way of salvation and spiritual progress since they are unable to fit into the established religions because they see too clearly the fallacies which these contain.

It is probable that the twelve sonnets composing *Les Chimères* received this title because each possesses a multiple meaning, as the body of the mythical Chimera was said to have triple form. Not only do the events of Nerval's personal life signify, but they also form a pattern parallel to the various steps of the alchemical process and also to the religious past of man. The sonnets are twelve in number, suggesting the twelve steps considered essential in the alchemical process of changing the baser metals into gold. Although the cryptic allusions of a personal and alchemical nature have been worked out with much care and precision by Jeanine Moulin and Le Breton, the relationship of the poems to each other and the over-all pattern of their progression has not yet been shown by other critics. It is this which will be pointed out here.

The first three poems, "El Desdichado," "Myrtho," and "Horus," correspond to the Kabbalistic tradition, to the alchemical process, and to the poet's own life. El Desdichado, the black and melancholy prince, is the primordial chaos, the masculine principle with relation to Myrtho, "the divine enchantress," the feminine principle of the second poem. Their union produces "Horus," the divine child, or the third emanation, which in Kabbalistic symbolism is called the "Word."[45] In alchemical symbols, the black prince is the disintegrated matter as it descends into the crucible; in terms of the poet's own life, it is Nerval bereft of his two loves, Adrienne and Jenny Colon, who died prior to the composition of these poems. It is for this reason that Nerval says, comparing himself with Orpheus, that he has twice crossed the Acheron. But as the black metal of the alchemical process begins to whiten in the heat, the poet begins to find consolation in "the pale hortensia" of the second poem, who is Octavie in his personal life. As the white metal begins to turn red in the crucible, so the pale hortensia becomes entwined with the myrtle, the red flower sacred to Venus. In the poet's own life his love for the pale and pure Octavie becomes mingled with the more carnal love for the Neapolitan girl whom he encountered on his travels.

Horus, the divine son of Isis and Osiris, was considered by syncretists to have been a prefiguration of Christ and one of the incarnations of God. His birth in the primitive world, marking the end of that epoch, was said to be comparable to the coming of Christ in the Greco-Roman world. As his birth marked the beginning of a new religion so, in alchemical terms, the "philosophic child" or "the treasure of the philosophers" meant the first suggestion of the appearance of gold, which was preceded by a rainbow of colors. This is suggested by Nerval in the last line of the poem with his allusion to the "scarf of Iris." In terms of the poet's personal life, the philosophic child was born when, after a series of disappointments in love, he dedicated himself seriously to the discovery of a synthesis of occult symbols to serve as a basis for solving the mystery of existence. From this point on the sonnets indicate the religious evolution of man:

HORUS – *The Egyptian Religion.* It marks the end of the more primitive gods.

ANTEROS – *Greek Polytheism.* Anteros was the son of Aphrodite and Ares, born of the union of opposites which was said to have created the harmony of Grecian culture. Anteros is the champion of ancient polytheism in its struggle against monotheism. Compared in the poem with Cain, Anteros is considered by Nerval to be another revolter who has "sown the dragon's teeth" which will produce a race of intellectual giants. The last tercet of this poem contains a reference to the alchemical process of the triple absolution of the philosophic mercury, necessary for its purification. This would seem to correspond with the three stages of religious development – Egyptian, Grecian, and Roman – through which religious thought had to pass in the process of its purification.

DELFICA – *The Roman Religion.* As the name Delphica implies, this religion developed from the Greek. As Daphne was changed into a laurel, so the Grecian religion changed into the Roman which finally "sleeps under the arch of Constantine." The poet prophesies that the ancient gods will return, just as he and Octavie have found again, in Pompeii, the temple of the Egyptian goddess, Isis. In his references to the laurel (Apollo), the myrtle (Venus), the olive (Minerva), and the sycamore (Christianity), Nerval suggests that it will be through the syncretism of ancient thought with Christianity that this return will occur.

ARTEMIS – *The Virgin.* Between the ancient world and the Christian world about to be born comes another manifestation of

Isis, the queen of heaven, who is also the queen of the night and its mysteries. In the person of the Virgin, past and future are contained, since the pagan goddess prefigures the mother of Christ. Thus Nerval asks: "The first or the last?" The number thirteen is associated with Artemis because there are thirteen lunations annually. Thirteen is considered an unlucky number because, in the tarot cards, it is the symbol of death. For the poet, it means the death of Aurélia. We know he associated Aurélia with Artemis because he first gave the title *Artemis ou le rêve et la vie* to his work *Aurélia*. Aurélia-Artemis is the actress Jenny Colon who, the poet says, belonged to him more in her death than in her life (Cf. "*C'est la mort – ou la morte*"). In her hand, Artemis carries the *rose trémière* (hollyhock), the rose of the Orient, which suggests again the poet's idea of syncretism. In the last stanza, the poet orders the white roses to fall – that is, the two early Christian women saints mentioned in the preceding stanza – since he considers the pagan Artemis, "saint of the abyss" and goddess of the night, to be preferable to them. In alchemical terms, the white roses refer to the matter which has become volatilized. As the alchemist urges the volatilized matter to fall back to the bottom of the crucible lest it escape upon the world, so the poet is somewhat reluctant to see the birth of Christianity.

LE CHRIST AUX OLIVIERS (5 SONNETS) – *Christianity*. Nerval's Christ in Gethsemane is unmistakably the Christ of the syncretists – the eternal victim who has had other incarnations (Cf. Sonnet 5). The real agony of Nerval's Christ is that he is torn between two worlds, one dying and the other in the process of being born. In the third sonnet, his is the only breath of life in this intermediary stage of civilization. All in the universe is dead except Christ. Only he is aware that if he dies everything is dead. Like Vigny's Christ, Nerval's is also an anguished being who doubts the existence of God, but who, unlike the former, does not become an embittered revolter before the abyss surrounding him. Particularly dramatic are the last two stanzas of the fifth sonnet, in which the oracle invoked by Caesar is forever silenced. Now only Christ can explain the mysteries.

VERS DORÉS – *Syncretism*. One would have expected the sonnets to end with the five mentioned above. What, then, is the significance of this one added on at the end? Since a progression has been noted in the other sonnets, it would seem logical for this one not to lack connection with the others, but to represent what Nerval believes will follow Christianity — a rediscovery of the spiritual essence of the ancient mysteries. The true gold of the alchemist or "the mystery of the metal" mentioned in this sonnet, is spiritual in nature. It consists in man's realization that everything in the universe is alive — mineral and metal, plant and animal — that in the most obscure human being "a hidden God dwells," and finally in man's perception of his identity with this totality of life through love (Adonis).

As Nerval sought a common denominator to reconcile all religions, he also attempted to fit the events of his personal life into this meaningful whole. *Les Chimères* are the bright and many-faceted jewels formed from the slowly deposited sum of his research and experience — the jewels of the alchemist in search of perfection. In these sonnets, he has interwoven the events of his life and the transcendental fabric of his mystical research so skilfully that philosophy, art, and the personal events of his life form a closely knit whole. For this reason, a slight flaw anywhere in the warp or woof of his existence could result the more easily in a break of this unity. No conflict existed for him between his vocation as artist and as seer. Perhaps a truly visionary spirit such as Nerval does not perceive the possibility of such a conflict as easily as does a mind like Balzac's, which possessed a more earthy side along with the visionary.

The Conflict between Artist and Seer: Balzac

To enter the *Comédie humaine* is to take a trip into the nineteenth century with a guide who was more thoroughly acquainted with the territory and its inhabitants than any other French writer of the time. It was therefore only natural for the comprehensive mind of Balzac (1799-1850) to carry the theme of the seer to its peak in early Romanticism (in his trilogy *Le Livre mystique,* 1831-1835). These appeared in the years of his early maturity when, at the height of his creative powers, he turned his serious artistic attention to the Illuminist ideas of his time. Balzac's originality consists in the fact that he saw the literary possibilities in the more transcendental aspects of occult thought. Novels dealing with black magic were commonplace, but a series in white magic based upon Swedenborg and Mesmer made him something of an innovator and later earned for him the title "voyant." That there was more to Balzac's interest in Illuminism than mere curiosity was not apparent to the critics of his time, who considered him a realist until after his death, when Philarète Chasles and Baudelaire pointed out that this "realist" had actually been the most Romantic of them all. But Philarète Chasles' remark, "He was a seer, not an observer," intended to bring out the neglected side of Balzac's genius, was again only partly true.[46] Balzac was an observer who looked at the world with the precision of a scientist and as a seer who gazed with inspired clarity into the depths of the human spirit and beyond. This rare mentality, combining the scientific with the visionary, manifested itself clearly in his attitude toward two of the great philosophical controversies of his time.

The first was a dispute in 1830 between the biologist Cuvier and Geoffroy Saint-Hilaire on the subject of "transformism," the pre-Darwinian idea that the animal kingdom developed from the plant kingdom. Cuvier, with a rigorously scientific approach and method, maintained that the evidence to support such a conclusion was insufficient. On the other hand, Saint-Hilaire, more philosopher than scientist, began with the inspired idea of the unity of all matter and maintained to the French Academy that the biological connection between the plant and animal kingdoms could no longer be denied. It was indeed an early version of the Darrow-Bryan "monkey trial," and Balzac reacted to it in a typical way: in *Le Cousin Pons,* he admired and praised the exact methods used by Cuvier, but in *La Peau de chagrin,* he said that the truth lay with Saint-Hilaire. If biological links exist between the plant and animal kingdoms then, by analogy, as Balzac reasons in *Louis Lambert,* links also exist between the plant and animal kingdom and man and, even more important, between man and God: "My idea," Louis writes to his uncle, "is to determine the real rapports which may exist between man and God. . . . You will ask what comparative anatomy has in common with a question so serious for the future of society. Is it not necessary to convince oneself that man is the end of all terrestrial means in order to ask oneself whether he might not be the means of some end?"[47]

The second controversy, which lasted the entire century and which culminated in Bergson's *Mind and Matter* (1896), was between the materialists (heirs of Locke, Hume, and Condillac) and the spiritualists (descendants of Berkeley, led by Royer-Collard). The materialists maintained that matter is the ultimate reality and that which we call mind is merely highly refined matter; the spiritualists insisted that the very existence of matter depends upon and is a manifestation of mind. Although Balzac wrote much on this subject, which enraged many people, he considered the argument a specious one and said so frankly in *Louis Lambert*.[48] He refused to take sides, because he considered thought to be both material and spiritual in nature—thus being a true psychosomaticist (before the coining of that term). Although a relentless seeker of the Absolute, Balzac was nevertheless unwilling to deny the reality of the material world. On the other hand, he did not allow the scientific materialism of his time to blind him to the profound mystery surrounding his mundane human comedy. The author of the *Contes drolatiques* was also the author of *Séraphita.*

However, it is the visionary side of Balzac's genius, culminating in *Le Livre mystique,* which is the focus of this discussion. Before proceeding to the trilogy, a few brief remarks should be made about the theme of the seer in Balzac's novels of the 1820's. Not only do these *Oeuvres de jeunesse* reveal his early interest in Illuminism, but the chief characters of *Le Livre mystique* exist here in germ. Three of Balzac's early heroes—Jacob Del Ryès in his first novel, *Sténie ou les erreurs philosophiques* (1821), Tullius in *Le Centenaire ou Les Deux Béringheld* (1822), and Victor Morillon in the Preface to *Gars* (1827), a first version of *Les Chouans*—suggest the character of Louis Lambert even in minute details. Jacob and Tullius are mystical scientists of extraordinary perception and intelligence who suffer deeply in love and in their contact with worldly affairs in general. Victor Morillon is a child prodigy like Louis Lambert, and also comes from Vendôme, is the son of a tanner, and is an orphan from early childhood. A fourth character from the novels prior to *Le Livre mystique,* Etienne Hérouville in *L'Enfant maudit,* is a Louis Lambert without the education; he is the instinctive seer, like Godefroid in *Les Proscrits,* whose life consists in the perpetual contemplation of nature. In addition to these early sketches of Louis Lambert and Godefroid, Séraphita and Minna are also prefigured in two works, both entitled *Falthurne.* The first *Falthurne,* an unfinished novel of 1821-1822, presents a supernatural being, Falthurne, whose name, Balzac says, means "tyranny of light."[49] A beautiful young "initiate of the mysteries of Moses, Isis, Hermes, and the Brahmins of India," Falthurne possesses such uncanny wisdom that people believe her to be a sorceress in league with the devil, although there is nothing diabolic about her in reality. Falthurne aspires only to use her knowledge to control nature for the good of mankind, an ideal greatly emphasized by the secret societies. Balzac conceives of his Falthurne as a priestess of a new syncretic religion of the kind which was advocated by Victor Cousin when Balzac was a student at the Sorbonne during 1818-1819.

The second Falthurne is a prose poem in two parts, the chief character of which is Minna, whose name is used for one of the principal characters in *Séraphita.* In the poem, Minna, the young girl who lives in a peaceful Italian village, is taking care of an old crusader who has leprosy. A mysterious being, Falthurne, a kind of archangel, whose presence emanates goodness upon the inhabitants of the valley, appears to Minna. In the second part of the poem, Falthurne, Balzac the syncretist informs us, who is the partisan of no religious sect, orders the assumption of Minna into heaven because of her unselfish devotion. The first Falthurne of the novel achieved her supernatural knowledge or voyance through her own efforts to develop spiritually, whereas Minna has a divine gift bestowed upon her as the result of her charitable vocation. In this contrast of the two Falthurnes, Balzac has seized the essential difference between the Illuminist seer and the Christian mystic. For the latter, visions are an act of grace, a special gift of heaven, and not a power attained by the individual himself, as is true of the Illuminist seer. Balzac has also wisely transformed the Séraphita of *Le Livre mystique* into a much more human character than Falthurne.

The Count of Béringheld in *Le Centenaire,* like Falthurne of the novel, is also an initiate of the secrets of Magism. Without making a pact with the devil, but merely as a result of his own researches, Béringheld discovers the elixir which makes him immortal. For this reason, Balzac first gave the title *Le Savant* to this novel, parts of which suggest the more mature later work, *La Recherche de l'absolu.* Although *Le Centenaire* belongs to the category of the *roman noir,* the Count of Béringheld does not kill out of a frenzied desire for murder, but with great regret and only out of the necessity of prolonging his own existence. In expiation for his crimes, he performs acts of charity, using his magnetic powers to heal the sick by the imposition of his hands, after the fashion taught by Mesmer. To his descendant, Tullius, he gives the *liqueur* which cures him. Tullius' fiancée, Marianne, has visions similar to those of Louis Lambert, which Balzac describes, taken almost textually from Swedenborg and used later in *Le Livre mystique*:

> The extraordinary thing about this magic vision is that it was capable of being seen not by virtue of the exterior eye but by an interior vision, in such a way that it is still a problem to be resolved to know whether places were drawing near and were appearing in it, or whether it was carried away to those places.[50]

The final paragraphs of *Le Centenaire* contain a discussion by the frequenters of the Café de Foy on the subject of Mesmerism and the doctrines of the Rosicrucians (*Rose-Croix*), whom the author designates by name. There Balzac advocates the rehabilitation of the occult sciences with a view toward utilizing all the knowledge at man's disposal to prolong life.

Two Illuminists who aroused the youthful Balzac's interest and curiosity — Swedenborg and Mesmer — have already been mentioned; the third was Saint-Martin from his native Touraine. The Swedish and French mystics held at least one idea in common with the Austrian doctor, and it was this which attracted Balzac to them: each saw within man immense, undiscovered, and undeveloped psychic powers — telepathy and second sight, or voyance, and a third called Mesmerism after its founder, but now known as hypnosis. The works of Mesmer in popularized editions were widely read during the first four decades of the nineteenth century and "animal magnetism" (hypnosis) became a dangerous parlor game. It was in these discoveries of Mesmer that Balzac felt he had found the true link between science and mysticism. The Preface to the 1842 edition of the *Comédie humaine* contains a long tribute to Mesmer and "to all those who for fifty years have worked on thought as opticians have worked on light — two things almost similar."[51] In *La Peau de chagrin,* Balzac predicted that the discoveries of Mesmer would "open a new route to a human science," a science of man which would include more than his biological functions.[52]

Having thus laid his foundations upon what seemed to him the best scientific thought of his time, Balzac proceeded to build on it his own mystical theory about the phenomenon of voyance. He even coined a term to designate it — "the gift of Speciality" (*le don de Spécialité*) or "Specialism" (*le Spécialisme*) — from the Latin word *species,* "vision." In *Louis Lambert,* specialism is defined as an interior vision whereby the seer (*voyant*) is able to perceive, as if in a mirror, a given situation in its entirety, that is, in its past, present, and future aspects.[53] Although Balzac uses as his example the most ancient symbol of magical wisdom, the mirror, he insists that specialism is a completely natural phenomenon. It occurs quite automatically, he explains in *Louis Lambert,* when the inner being (*être intérieur*) has reached a certain stage of spiritual development or perfection. At this time, the human spirit emerges from its chrysalis and is released into a new existence. The seer is then able to communicate with "intermediary beings invisible to ordinary sight, a phenomenon which has long been known to the Hindus as *Le Tokeiade.*[54] During this extraordinary experience, the five senses, ordinarily differentiated in man for practical purposes, function as a single sense (Cf. Louis Lambert's aphorisms). This is doubtless the basis of the experience of synesthesia which captured the imagination of Nerval, Baudelaire, and Rimbaud and which inspired the famous lines: "Oh mystical metamorphosis/Of all my senses dissolved into one!"[55]

Balzac connects the phenomenon of voyance with the discoveries of Mesmer in the following way: All bodies of men and animals, Mesmer had said, are magnetically charged (hence the term "animal magnetism"). This force Mesmer called the "universal fluid," and he believed it was purely physical in nature and could be concentrated at will to influence another body or bodies, even when these were at a distance. But Balzac considered this dynamic force to be psychic as well as physical in nature. In Louis Lambert's aphorisms, he calls it "the ethereal substance" and says it is by means of this that men sometimes receive presentiments of future events. In other words, Balzac held that man has within himself a magnetic connection with a universal mind or psychic force outside himself. On this subject Mesmer has written:

> It is probable that we are endowed with an internal sense which is related to the totality of the universe; exact observations may be able to assure us of it; from this one could comprehend the possibility of presentiments.[56]

To further satisfy the rational side of his nature, Balzac explains mental telepathy, another manifestation of voyance, by comparing it in *Le Cousin Pons* with the recently invented daguerreotype:

> Just as bodies are being projected today into the atmosphere, allowing a specter to remain there which is seized by the daguerreotypist, who stops it in passage; so ideas, real and acting creations, express themselves in what must be called the atmosphere of the spiritual world . . . and from there certain creatures endowed with rare faculties can perceive these forms or these traces of ideas.[57]

In *Le Réquisitionnaire* (1831), a mother, upon receiving a telepathic vision of the death of her son in a distant village, dies instantly from shock. At the end of the narrative, Balzac predicts that such telepathy will some day form the basis of a new science.

"In order to understand specialism," Séraphita tells Minna, "one has to possess it," and there is ample evidence in the *Comédie humaine* to indicate that it was not in the scientific world but in his personal experience that Balzac found the most adequate confirmation of the existence of this extraordinary vision.[58] The following passage from *Le Lys dans la vallée* (1835) reveals that at some time during his adolescence (later, biographer Curtius thinks, than this passage indicates) Balzac had a mystical experience which was intimately related to his art:

> At the time of my first communion I threw myself into the mysterious depths of prayer. . . . Quickened by an ardent faith, I prayed to God to renew in my favor the fascinating miracles which I was reading in the *Martyrology*. . . . My ecstasy caused untold dreams to come forth within me, which furnished my imagination, enriched my tenderness and fortified my thinking faculties. I often attributed these sublime visions to angels who had the task of fashioning my soul for divine destinies. They endowed my eyes with the faculty of seeing the intimate spirit of things; they prepared my heart for the magic things which make the unhappy poet, when he has the fatal power, compare what he feels with what he is, the great things desired with the little which he obtains. They wrote in my head a book in which I could read what I was supposed to express; they put on my lips the burning coal of the improvisor.[59]

The great seer who most inspired Balzac's inclination to mystical vision was Swedenborg. It is probable that, like the adolescent Louis Lambert, he also read the work of the Swedish mystic, *Heaven and Hell,* since an abridged translation of Swedenborg's works by Daillant de la Touche had appeared in France as early as 1788 and another definitive translation by Moët during the Empire. Or Balzac may have heard of Swedenborg first as a student at the Sorbonne in 1819 when his professor, Victor Cousin, had just returned from Germany. At any rate Balzac himself mentions in a letter of October 8, 1832, to Charles Nodier that he possessed the works of Swedenborg as well as those of other mystical writers — Madame Guyon, St. Theresa, Mademoiselle Bourignon, and Jakob Boehme. Direct references to the works and ideas of Swedenborg in *Le Livre mystique* are too numerous to be discussed fully here; some of them will be noted as we analyze the trilogy. What Balzac actually saw in the works of the Swedish mystic may, however, be stated quite briefly. Besides a confirmation of his own experience of second sight, he perceived in the works of Swedenborg the possibility that a liberal and universal religion could be established, based on the ideal of syncretism. In *Séraphita,* Balzac foresees the possibility of man's development of his psychic powers to achieve a nobler, more charitable existence. Just as the "Word was made flesh" in the ancient world, the flesh must be made Word in the modern one. This is the essential meaning of the controversial novel, *Séraphita.* Finally, we cannot pass lightly over Balzac's unequivocal statement of personal faith in Swedenborgianism, as Catholic critics have sometimes been inclined to do. In a letter to Madame Hanska, the Polish noblewoman whom he finally married, he wrote: "I am not orthodox at all and I do not believe in the Roman Church. . . . Swedenborgianism, which is only a repetition in the Christian sense of ancient ideas, is my religion, with the addition which I make to it of the incomprehensibility of God."[60]

Another impetus to Balzac's interest in Illuminism came from his friendship with Henri de Latouche, who was interested in the Swedenborgian church and was an initiated member of a Martinist secret society. Balzac met Latouche in 1825 in the office of his publisher, Urbain Canel, at the time of the publication of his novel, *Wann-Chlore.* The friendship ripened, and it was Latouche who assumed the financial responsibility for Balzac's first successful novel, *Le Dernier Chouan* (1829). Considerable evidence exists, summarized by the biographer André Billy, that under Latouche's influence Balzac was initiated into a Martinist society. There is, for example, the statement of critic Emile Ferder insisting that the Martinist archives have very interesting documents on Balzac, and also the study of Van Rijnberg of the University of Amsterdam, on Martinez Pasqually, maintaining that a member of the supreme council of the Martinist order, M. Chaboseau, revealed Balzac's initiation to him.[61] Was it perhaps of his membership in one of these secret societies that Balzac was thinking when he wrote to Madame Hanska: "I am inexplicable for all, for no one has the secret of my life and I am not willing to divulge it to anyone."[62] Whether he was initiated or not, Balzac at any rate wrote about the Martinists in *Le Lys dans la vallée* in highly commendatory terms:

> The disciples of this philosopher [Saint-Martin] practiced the virtues advised by the highest speculations of mystical illuminism. This doctrine gives the key to the divine worlds, explains existence by transformations in which man sets out for sublime destinies, liberates duty from its legal

> degradation, applies to the sufferings of life the unchangeable gentleness of the Quaker, and commands scorn for suffering by inspiring something inexplicably maternal for the angel which we bear to heaven. It is Stoicism which has a future. Active prayer and pure love are the elements of this faith, which comes out of the Catholicism of the Roman Church to return into the Christianity of the primitive Church.[63]

Let us now turn to an analysis of *Le Livre mystique* in order to see exactly how Balzac meant such a work to be construed. In *Les Proscrits* he suggests that there are three different paths to mystical knowledge; in *Louis Lambert* he depicts the precarious relationship between artist and seer, the danger which he himself feels that mysticism may destroy his art; finally, in *Séraphita,* he notes the possibility of the regeneration of man by means of mystical illumination.

Les Proscrits, first and shortest of the trilogy, serves as a fitting prelude, presenting three distinct kinds of seers, each having arrived at spiritual illumination by a different path. Dr. Sigier, professor of mystical theology at the University of Paris in the year 1308, represents the philosopher-seer, one who has discovered mystical experience by means of his esoteric studies. A gifted orator who expounds a most unorthodox doctrine, Dr. Sigier (like Balzac) announces that he will discuss the subject of divine revelations. The lecture contains, for the most part, an exposition of the basic tenet of theosophy — the linked existence of all life — which was mentioned in connection with the Cuvier-Saint-Hilaire debate. One additional aspect of this subject is of particular significance to *Le Livre mystique,* namely, the Swedenborgian idea that beings have the power to ascend or descend the ladder of creation according to their deeds. Sometimes angels fall and become men; conversely, human beings sometimes achieve angelic status. The second seer, the young boy Godefroid, Balzac indicates as a kind of fallen angel, an instinctive rather than intellectual seer, constantly haunted by memories of a previous life, completely bewildered by his new earth life, and obsessed by the desire to return "home." (This is the exact reverse of the situation in *Séraphita,* in which a human being has evolved out of the human condition and attained the status of a higher being.) The third seer in *Les Proscrits* is the poet Dante, whose sojourn in Paris has been brought about by his political exile from Florence. Like Godefroid, he too is an exile, a *proscrit.* In the narrative, Dante saves the young Godefroid from suicide by reminding him that such an act would only cast him into a lower sphere of heaven. The passages in which the great poet describes the heirarchies of heaven with much pictorial detail is intended to make a contrast with the abstract presentation of the same idea in Dr. Sigier's lecture. What Balzac implies in *Les Proscrits,* then, is that there are three different paths to mystical illumination — the intellectual way of the philosopher, the poetic way (or the way of the imagination), and the instinctive way of one who is born a seer. The knowledge which each of the seers in *Les Proscrits* possesses is essentially the same, but their means of achieving and of stating it are quite different.

In *Louis Lambert,* Balzac, whether consciously or unconsciously, has symbolized a conflict which he had begun to feel between his roles as artist and as seer. In this story Louis, called a seer by Madame de Staël, has as his companion and alter ego in the Collège de Vendôme the *je* of the narrative, who is a poet: "The Poet-and-Pythagoras," as they are called jocularly by the other students. Among critics there is general agreement that Louis Lambert and his friend represent a *dédoublement* of the author — that he is presenting two different aspects of his personality. Louis is Balzac the seer or the "spiritualist," while the *je* of the story is Balzac the artist and man of the world, the "materialist." When Louis' companion leaves the school, that is, when the poet takes leave of the seer, each one experiences the deep sense of personal loss natural to two minds which have come to feel their mutual dependence. Like his counterpart in *Louis Lambert,* Balzac the artist also departed from the seer-self of his adolescence. Later, as a young man, he met his seer-self again, probably between the years 1825 and 1829 when, inspired by Latouche, he was either initiated into a secret society or at least rediscovered his former visionary self in Swedenborg and Saint-Martin. It is significant that when the poet finds Louis again no communication is possible since the seer has gone beyond the domain of Art and the artist. Louis has been living in a trance-like state comparable to that described by Swedenborg, and the poet is able to salvage only a few scattered aphorisms from the ultimate silence of the mystic. Thus in *Louis Lambert* it is the artist who survives or triumphs over the seer, just as the latter predicted he would at the time of their separation at the Collège de Vendôme. "You will live," said Louis, "but I will die."[64] In *Le Chef-d'Oeuvre inconnu* and *Gambara,* two other novels of the *Etudes philosophiques,* the situation is the reverse of that in *Louis Lambert,* that is, it is the seer who triumphs over the artist, with the result that both the painter Frenhofer and the musician Gambara destroy their own art. Behind the plots of these three novels lies the spiritual dilemma of the author: Balzac the artist fears that his visionary self might ultimately triumph over his artistic self, that if he should become too absorbed in mysticism he might either produce the unintelligible, like Frenhofer and Gambara, or be reduced to the trance-like silence of Louis Lambert. Since Balzac is not willing to destroy his art, it is therefore Louis Lambert who must die, while the artistic alter ego survives. But why, one may naturally ask, did Balzac feel the existence of such a dilemma? After all, it is possible to be both artist and seer, like Plato, Dante, Blake, and many others? Balzac was undoubtedly correct in feeling that for him a conflict existed, particularly in view of the sheer quantity of literary production which he had undertaken. Let us turn now to the last novel of the trilogy, *Séraphita,* where Balzac gives free rein to the opposite of the denouement of *Louis Lambert* — the full development of the seer mind.

Out of the Platonic myth of the androgyne, Balzac has recast a modern one personifying what he believed to be the spiritual potentialities of man. *Séraphita* is therefore a myth which gives the reader a glimpse into the future of man, as seen through the eyes of Balzac. Because critics have been too literal in their approach, the novel has been a highly controversial one ever since the time of Balzac, thus supporting his statement in *La Vieille Fille;* "Modern myths are even less understood than ancient ones."[65] But since Balzac is not an obscure writer, *Séraphita* may be clearly understood if one takes into account its allegorical or mythical as well as its literal meaning. The myth of the androgyne had been recreated by Romanticists before Balzac: in Germany, Ritter, a friend of Novalis and Franz von Baader, had revived it; in France, it had appealed in particular to the social reformers Saint-Simon and Fourier. However, certain differences between the Platonic myth and its Romantic version are readily apparent. In the ancient myth, the human being is represented as having lived during his remote past in a Golden Age or state of perfection and sexual undifferentiation whereas, in the modern version, the implication is that another such Golden Age lies in the future, when the human being will reattain his lost unity and perfection. For all these Romanticists the myth of the androgyne meant more than a mere nostalgic dream of Eden: it was rather a personification of their unshaken belief in man's capacity for spiritual progress. Balzac, who believed that society would never improve until the individual first improved, differed from the social reformers who were thinking in terms of collective progress to be brought about by drastic changes in the social structure. "I do not share the belief in indefinite progress where societies are concerned," he said in the preface to the *Comédie humaine,* "but only in the progress of man over himself."[66]

In addition to its more abstract meaning, Balzac's myth of the androgyne has a much more personal and poignant meaning for him. Séraphita is also the incarnation of Balzac's dream of the perfect woman — the wife whom he sought pathetically all his life but never found. She is Madame Hanska as he wished she were and as he often indeed dreamed she was.

Let us examine briefly the mythical or allegorical aspects of *Séraphita,* which Balzac calls *"une histoire vraiment céleste."*[67] Against a background of snow and altitude, suggesting the solitude, purity, and height of the supernatural, Wilfrid and Minna (Humanity) fall deeply in love with Séraphita (Perfection), who dwells among them in the obscure Norwegian village of Jarvis. Both want to marry this mysterious creature who appears to each in an altogether different light. The young girl, Minna, is convinced that the androgyne whom she calls Séraphitus is masculine, while for Wilfrid "she" is Séraphita and a very beautiful young girl. For both of her friends, Séraphitus-Séraphita is able to complete what is lacking in their personalities. To Minna (the feminine or love-principle in humanity), Séraphitus gives a deeper understanding and wisdom (Chap. I); to Wilfrid (the masculine or force-principle in humanity) Séraphita imparts a more unselfish conception of love. Séraphita, born of parents who had already attained a high level of perfection, was thus especially endowed by birth with the talents of a seer and is able to practice telepathy, to foretell future events, and to detach spirit from body at will. The suggestion here that biology may take a hand in the development of unusual psychic powers in man again reveals the psychosomatic reasoning of Balzac. The climax of the novel comes when the androgyne is engaged in her last struggle to break the bonds of the human condition. This consists in the total triumph within Séraphita of *agape* over *eros,* of the impartial love of all creatures over the partial possession of one. Angels and demons struggle with each other in a titanic combat in which the former triumphs over the latter. At the end of the novel, in some of the most poetic passages ever penned by Balzac, the eyes of Wilfrid and Minna are opened (i.e., they become seers) and they are permitted to witness Séraphita's entry into heaven after her death. Like Balzac in his life, Wilfrid and Minna, being human, are unable to follow the seer "into the kingdom of light." Nevertheless they return to their village completely transformed by their vision.

This denouement does not imply that "only angels have wings" while ordinary mortals must content themselves with more mediocre attainments; Séraphita tells her friends clearly before her departure: "The divining rod belongs to us all."[68] Again, in *Les Proscrits,* Balzac suggests the meaning of the denouement of *Séraphita*: "Today, as in the time of Dr. Sigier [the Middle Ages], the question is to give man wings for penetrating into the sanctuary where God is hidden from our view."[69] To Séraphita, Balzac has obviously given "wings," which is a figurative way of saying that she has become illuminated or possesses a mystical second sight. This cannot be sought or achieved in itself, as Balzac indicated in *Louis Lambert,* but results from fulfilling certain conditions which mystics of various faiths have known for centuries.

THE SEER POET AS PRIEST: HUGO

The difference between the attitudes of Hugo and Balzac toward the Illuminists of their times deserves a few brief comments. Unlike Balzac, Hugo was not attracted during his early youth by either temperament or interest to mystical or occult currents of thought. Whereas the youthful Balzac aspired, like Louis Lambert and other heroes of his early novels, to the comprehensive knowledge of a philosopher, Hugo was absorbed chiefly in writing lyric poetry. It was through the socialists during the late 1830's, in particular Pierre Leroux, that Hugo made his first contact with Illuminism. On the other hand, while Balzac assumed as a fundamental premise that the social structure was inherently evil, he nevertheless vigorously resisted the Saint-Simonists and the Fourierists, believing that society could improve only as the individual improved. Finally, it is significant that Hugo's acquaintance with the transcendental aspects of Illuminism was accidental and that his active pursuit of the subject came only after he had suffered a number of personal losses. This does not deny the sincerity of his interest, but indicates that he did not pursue it altogether spontaneously and for its own sake as did Balzac, but partially because it served to alleviate his grief.

A glance at the evolution of Hugo's esthetic theories between the years 1820 and 1840, as stated in certain of his prefaces, will serve as a background for the final emergence of his theory of the poet as priest and Magus. In the prefaces of two early poetic volumes, *Odes et Ballades* (1822-1828) and *Les Orientales* (1829), he announced his belief in the independence of the poet, who serves only the cause of his own imagination and fancy. Hugo denied in these prefaces that the best art has any connection with the events of the period in which it is written. The works of Chateaubriand and of Mme de Staël, for example, were not products of the French Revolution, he argued. A remarkable reversal of this opinion began to appear in the prefaces written during the 1830's; significantly, the first sign of it came two years after the banning of his play, *Le Roi s'amuse* (1832), in the Preface to *Lucrèce Borgia* (1834). Here Hugo maintained that although the writer must not go outside the impartial limits of his art, he must be aware that the drama has a national mission, "a social mission, a human mission."[70] In that same year he also wrote, in *Littérature et philosophie mêlées,* that "present-day art must not be subservient to an ephemeral political cause,"[71] and that the writer must of necessity present "the sum of the ideas of his time." In his private correspondence at this time, Hugo showed less restraint, echoing in a letter to Victor Pavie the ideas of the Saint-Simonists: "The theater is a sort of church; humanity is a sort of religion."[72] By the time of Gautier's famous Preface to *Mlle de Maupin* (1834), Hugo was no longer a partisan of art for art's sake; the following year he even turned to political satire in *Les Chants du crépuscule* and, two years later, gave definitive poetic expression to the Saint-Simonist conception of art in *Les Voix intérieures* (1837):

> Like a priest at church
> I dream of art which charms, of art which civilizes
> Which changes man a little,
> And which, like a sower who throws his seed afar
> By sowing nature through the soul
> Will cause God to germinate there.[73]

But the changes in Hugo's esthetic theories merely reflected the evolution which had taken place in his entire political and religious thinking during the 1830's. These changes are described categorically in *Littérature et philosophie mêlées*:

> My former royalist-Catholic conviction of 1820 has been collapsing piece by piece for ten years in the face of age and experience. There still remains something of it in my mind, but it is only a religious and poetic ruin. I sometimes turn away from it to consider it with respect, but I no longer go there to pray.[74]

The 1840's brought a great increase in the intensity of Hugo's interest in the cause of the people, although he moved with great caution, refusing to identify himself with any particular group. He had indeed come under Socialist influence. This was the time of the composition of *Les Misérables,* a period when fortune smiled upon him and misfortune dealt him a most cruel blow: he was elected to the Academy in 1841 and made a peer in 1845; the failure of *Les Burgraves* was eclipsed by the death of his eldest daughter, Léopoldine, and her husband, Charles Vacquerie, who were drowned in the Seine on their honeymoon in 1843. At length, the socialist defeat of 1848 followed by the *coup d'état* of 1851 dealt the final blow to all Hugo's political aspirations. Like thousands of others, he had supported Louis-Napoleon believing that sorely needed social reforms would be effected, but was completely deceived. Though they were grandiloquent and bombastic in part, Hugo's discourses to the National Assembly during the years 1845 to 1851 show remarkable prophetic vision. He spoke courageously and eloquently in favor of universal suffrage, freedom of the press, education of the masses, and the democratic union of all Europe. When the *coup d'état* came, little was left for him except exile – first in Belgium and then on the islands of Jersey and Guernsey. In exile, he continued to execrate the tyrant and, although there was a personal element in his hatred of Napoleon III, most of his bitterness was based on love of liberty. Was there not some consolation in the fact that deploring social injustice and becoming the champion of liberty in exile was not without a certain dramatic appeal?

One of his companions in exile was Pierre Leroux, who had bluntly criticized Hugo's novel, *Notre-Dame de Paris,* for its lack of social consciousness, and who now prevailed upon Hugo to use his art to serve humanity. Hugo, in *Le Journal de l'exil,* and Pierre Leroux, in *La Grève de Samarez,* record their long discussions on the Jersey beach, each attributing to himself the more persuasive arguments and the intellectual victory. Nevertheless, Leroux's words were to Hugo the voice of the people, and they appealed to his conscience. He had found other Illuminists (during the 1840's) more attractive to his imagination. There was Alexander Weill, the Jew who translated the Kabbala and later wrote a work explaining Kabbalistic cosmogony entitled *Les Mystères de la création* (1855). It was to Weill that Hugo showed the first pages of *Les Misérables* in 1847. Another was the magnetist, Henri-Marie Delaage, editor of *Le Journal du magnétisme,* the official organ of a group founded in 1845 by Du Potet. Delaage, a prolific writer, dedicated one of his numerous occult works to Hugo, who in turn mentioned Delaage and his theories in *Choses vues,* written during the 1840's but published posthumously.[75] Delaage's *Le Monde occulte* (1850) contains an account of what actually took place in magnetist *cénacles,* particularly those frequented by men of letters. One incident related by Delaage in this work caused a great stir in the newspapers in 1847. Alexandre Dumas, in order to get material for his play, *Urbain Grandier,* attended one of these séances and was so impressed by the performance of a certain medium, Alexis, that he gave a detailed account of his experiences to the newspaper *La Presse* (Sept. 7, 1847).[76] Dumas' story aroused the interest of the literary and artistic worlds. Two days later, Théophile Gautier, the sculptor Pradier, Jules Sandeau, the musician Adam, the painter Chassériau and Madame de Girardin, wife of the journalist who was one of Hugo's early colleagues, attended another performance. Shortly after that a séance was arranged at the home of Hugo at Rue de la Tour d'Auvergne. There, all marveled again at the performance of Alexis and her magnetizer, Madame de la Fontaine. Many similar séances followed in the salons frequented by the artistic and literary people.

The Illuminist whose works enjoyed the greatest prestige during the 1850's and 1860's was Abbé Alphonse-Louis Constant (1810-1875), better known by the pseudonym, Eliphas Lévi. Leaving the priesthood before having taken his final vows, the Abbé turned his pen to the cause of socialism. In the prison of Sainte-Pélagie, where he was sent for his work *La Bible de la liberté* (1841), he met the Abbé Lamennais, also imprisoned for writing a pamphlet, *Le Pays et le Gouvernement.* There, Flora Tristan visited Lévi and brought him food until his release in April 1842. Mention has already been made of the fact that Lévi completed Tristan's work, *L'Emancipation de la femme,* upon her death two years after his imprisonment. Out of prison but no longer able to live by his pen, Lévi turned to art, which he had always pursued as a hobby, and painted a number of murals in the church of Choisy-le-Roi (Seine). Just prior to his imprisonment, he and his friend, Esquiros, had founded a publication, *Les Belles Femmes de Paris* (1839-1840), in which he drew flattering portraits of society women. Among these portraits was one of Mme de Girardin; while Lévi was doing it, he made the acquaintance of Balzac, then at the height of his fame. At the home of Saint-Simonist

Charles Fauvéty, Lévi had met two more friends of Hugo: Alexander Weill and Pierre Leroux; other frequenters of this group were Victor Considérant, Charles Renouvier, Emile Littré and Louis Ménard. Although Lévi had been interested in the theoretical aspects of occultism since his early youth, it was not until his meeting with the Polish mathematician Hoëne Wronski in 1850 that he actually became an initiate.[77] By 1856 he had completed his two-volume work, *Dogme et rituel de la haute magie,* which was followed by numerous other works, the most important being *Histoire de la magie* (1860) and *La Clef des grandes mystères* (1861). In these various works, Lévi attempts a synthesis of the different kinds of occult thought in an effort to show that behind them all was the doctrine of the Kabbala, the key to all the ancient mysteries and the best foundation for a new, universal religion.[78] In 1860 and 1861, Lévi was a member of a Masonic lodge, "The Rose of Perfect Silence," and received the grade of Master, but he retired, saying that the Freemasons who preached tolerance themselves displayed intolerance of Catholicism which they tried to justify by the fact that the church had excommunicated them.[79]

In 1862 Lévi, who greatly admired Hugo, dedicated a poem to him, calling him "this new Prometheus"; this poem was later printed in *Le Grand Arcane.* In a prose passage in the same book, Lévi calls Hugo "a great magician without knowing it." When Lévi was at length introduced to Hugo by Catulle Mendès in 1873, Hugo complimented him on his "talent for rhapsody" and even borrowed an idea from one of Lévi's more poetic passages in *Dogme et rituel de la haute magie.*[80] Here Lévi, by no means an untalented writer, presents Lucifer in a long passage of poetic prose as the "angel Liberty," exactly as Hugo characterized him later in *La Fin de Satan.*[81]

About 1850, the popularity of the magnetists began to be supplanted by another group, the Spiritualists (*Spiritistes*), who finally attracted Hugo's attention. The movement began in Hydesville, New York, in 1848, where phenomena such as wall tappings and table-turnings were allegedly observed in the home of the Fox brothers. The rapidity with which these ideas spread, and with them a literature complete with specialized vocabulary, was surprising. By 1852 there were three hundred spiritualist circles in Philadelphia and more than 30,000 professional mediums in the United States.[82] Spreading quickly to France, Spiritualist ideas were popularized by

Allan Kardec, who used them to attack the magnetists as "materialists." At length, Kardec published his definitive work on the subject, *Le Livre des Esprits* (1857). In the meantime, "the turning tables," (*les tables tournantes*) which spelled out answers at the touch of a medium, became a favorite pastime in the salons in France during the 1850's and 1860's – a game which many took seriously.

Among its serious adherents was Madame de Girardin, who introduced it to the Hugo family in September 1853, while they were in exile on the island of Jersey. In the parlor of Marine-Terrace, Hugo's son, Charles, served as medium, while the poet discovered to his great pleasure that he himself was not altogether lacking in mediumistic abilities. On Sunday evening, September 11, 1853, the Hugo family was convinced that they had made contact with the deceased daughter, Léopoldine.[83] "They wept and they believed," Auguste Vacquerie, brother of the drowned son-in-law, remarked acidly.[84] Skeptical at first, Vacquerie later became the most enthusiastic believer of all. This was the beginning of a large number of sessions in which members of the family took copious notes on what they thought was being communicated to them from the Beyond. The original account of these communications may be found in the *Procès Verbaux* of Vacquerie, published by Gustave Simon, and in the *Journal de l'exil,* kept by Adèle Hugo, the daughter. One fact becomes absolutely clear to one perusing these curious accounts: the absolute sincerity of Hugo and his family in the belief that they had contacted not only Léopoldine but many great men of the past – Moses, Mohammed, Chénier, Shakespeare, Luther, Molière, and many others. The contents of a few of these alleged communications should be noted for illustration.

Moses, for example, in his discourse compares the turning tables to the oracles of Delphi and Epidaurus: "You are touching the ancient tripod," he says. He continues thus in a passage which resembles the style of Victor Hugo more than that of Moses:

> God speaks eternally to man through the voice of revelations. The first revelation was nature; the second, conscience; the third, the miracle. When conscience and nature are no longer listened to, the miracle speaks. . . . When man chases God from his home a trembling of the conscience takes place, and matter, indignant against the rebellious soul, rises up, takes command, and the soul obeys.[85]

Perhaps the most curious session was the one in which André Chénier gave an account of his impressions at the time of his execution under the Terror, and proceeded to dictate lines completing some of his unfinished works. To the explanation that the verses were Hugo's pastiche of Chénier, critic Souchon contends that Hugo was not present at this particular session and the verses were taken down by others.[86] When Hugo did join the session with Chénier, a discussion ensued between the two poets on the subject of the corrections which Chénier suggested. Shakespeare, in his discourse, is supposed to have reported that he encountered in the Beyond many great writers of the past — Homer, Aeschylus, Sophocles, Dante, Rabelais, and Cervantes — and that none of them, himself included, cared to engage any further in literary production, but were all pensive and attentive in the presence of immensity.[87]

Among these communications was one which had especial influence on Hugo's literary production. On September 19, 1854, a spirit announced itself as the *Ombre du Sépulchre* and ordered Hugo to terminate the work which he was then writing. When the poet asked for further particulars, the dark spirit answered at great length. The substance of its remarks may be paraphrased thus: Every person during his life constructs two works — his work as a living being and his work as a phantom; the former is constructed during the day in his mundane contacts; the latter he builds silently at night during his sleep. Finally, the Shadow counseled mysteriously: "Be the Oedipus of your life and the Sphinx of your tomb."[88] The next evening the Shadow cautioned him against the dangers of continuing his efforts at communication with the Beyond, and at length revealed to the poet this important message:

> Arrange your posthumous works at ten year or at five year intervals. . . . You though dead will aid the living. . . . Therefore do for the twentieth century an affirmative work rather than a doubtful work for the nineteenth century.[89]

A connection may be seen between this message and the number of Hugo's works which were in fact published posthumously. Between the years 1886 and 1902, eighteen volumes of Hugo's works appeared, arranged by his friend Paul Meurice. Among these were *La Fin de Satan* (1886), *Toute la Lyre* (1889, 1893), *Dieu* (1891), *Les Années funestes* (1898), *Post-Scriptum de ma vie* (1901), and *Dernière Gerbe* (1902). The publication of *Quatre-vingt-treize,* which Meurice began in 1904-1906, was completed by Gustave Simon after Meurice's death. As late as 1942, another volume of prose and verse was collected, *Océan, Tas de Pierres,* and finally, in 1951, H. Guillemin published another volume, *Pierres.*

The *Procès-Verbaux* of Gustave Simon ended on July 2, 1855, three months before Hugo left Jersey for Guernsey. There, the séances were not resumed, as far as is known, and Hugo settled down to vigorous literary production. In view of the fact that Hugo believed the messages communicated to him would form the basis of a new religion (Cf. Balzac's similar beliefs about the Swedenborgian messages), why do we find such an abrupt silence and an end of the séances? Two explanations for this may be offered. First, that Hugo's doctor, fearing that the poet would go mad, forbade him to continue this dangerous pursuit. Second, as Auguste Viatte points out, there had been the terrifying example of Victor Hennequin, magnetist and mutual friend of Hugo and Emile de Girardin, who did in fact go mad and had to be confined.[90]

As Hugo looked back upon these experiences after ten years and the sensationalism of the moment had gone, what was his final estimate of the strange phenomena? Did his faith in them continue? In one of the less well known of Hugo's prose works, *William Shakespeare,* he indicates his conclusions clearly. Although the book was written on the occasion of the three-hundredth anniversary of the English poet's birth, most of it is not actually concerned with him, but with Hugo's own reflections on art and the relationship of the artist to society. It is clear that Hugo still held to the Saint-Simonian belief in the social function of art and continued to maintain that the role of the poet in society is that of prophet and magus: "The poet is priest," he reiterates.[91] In many passages, so lyrical that translation distorts them, Hugo writes in favor of art, which is the "servant of Truth" cooperating with Progress:

> Art is the azure, but the azure from the height of which falls the ray of sun which swells the wheat, turns the corn yellow, rounds the apple, turns the orange golden, sweetens the grape. . . . The amphora which refuses to go to the fountain deserves the jeers of pitchers. . . . To dream dreams is fine, but to dream Utopia is better.[92]

Not only is the poet a priest, but so also are all other men of genius — scientists, philosophers, explorers, musicians, etc. — since it is through them that society moves forward. This was the same idea developed in the poem, "Les Mages," in *Les Contemplations,* written ten years earlier. Comparing the poet to Prometheus in a line recalling the famous one of Rimbaud, Hugo asks: "What is this gift of man to set fire to the Unknown?"[93] Again discussing the function of the poet Hugo alludes to the myth of Orpheus and the legend of Amphion:

> The poet arrives in the midst of those who go and come, who are called the living, to tame, like Orpheus of antiquity, evil instincts, the tigers which are in man, and like the legendary Amphion to move all stones, the prejudices and superstitions, to put in movement new blocks, to remake the foundations and the bases and to rebuild the city, that is society.[94]

On the subject of the turning tables Hugo is indignant that the so-called scientific attitude is that of mockery rather than examination. He says bitterly:

> the turning table . . . has been greatly mocked. To speak briefly, this mockery is meaningless. To replace examination with mockery is convenient but unscientific . . . the unexpected must always be expected by science. . . . Science has only the right of visa on facts. It must verify and distinguish. All human knowledge is only selection. The fact that the false complicates the true by no means excuses a total rejection.[95]

On the other hand, Hugo believes that the poet has no real need of a mechanical or human medium such as a tripod or a turning table since "the poet himself is the tripod of God."[96] At the same time, he has not forgotten the example of Victor Hennequin and in *Post-Scriptum de ma vie* he urges that caution be exercised by all who approach the "promontory of dream": "Don't forget this . . . the dreamer must be stronger than the dream." And again in the same work: "These encroachments upon the darkness are not without danger. Dreaming has its dead, the insane."[97] Finally, Hugo began to think as Balzac did of voyance, that it is a natural phenomenon provided one does not hold too narrow a view of what is natural. Hugo had learned from the Jersey séances that voyance, which is a very vital part of a larger religious experience, is not reserved for a few especially elected or gifted persons, but exists as a possibility for all who choose to pursue it. This is summed up in what is doubtless the finest and most poetic passage in the entire work, *William Shakespeare*:

> Every man has in him his Patmos. He is free to go or not to go onto that terrifying promontory of thought from which darkness is perceived. If he does not go there, he remains in . . . ordinary consciousness, in ordinary virtue, in ordinary faith or ordinary doubt; and it is just as well. For interior peace it is obviously better. If he goes on that peak

he is caught. The profound waves of the marvelous have appeared to him. No one sees that ocean with impunity. Henceforth he will be the broad thinker . . . that is, the dreamer. *He will touch at one point the poet and at the other the prophet.* A certain quantity of him now belongs to darkness. The boundless enters into his life, into his consciousness, into his virtue, into his philosophy. . . . He distinguishes in this twilight enough of his former life and enough of his ultimate life in order to seize these two ends of dark thread and tie his soul again.[98]

Before examining the texts in order to pinpoint the exact relationship between Hugo's poetry and his preoccupation with the occult, a few factual matters about the works with which this study is concerned should be mentioned. *Les Contemplations* (1856) and the long poem, *Dieu,* both written during this period, reflect more than any of the other poetic works the influence of the Jersey séances. An enthusiastic public eagerly bought 60,000 copies of *Les Contemplations* during the first year, and although many readers were somewhat shocked by the poet's audacity in the prophetic poems, such as "Ce que dit la Bouche d'ombre," and critics made fun of his occultism, most were forced to admit that Hugo at fifty-two was a greater poet than he had been at thirty. Although this is not unique in literary history, it is nevertheless relatively uncommon and, among romantic poets, exceedingly rare. Of the 139 poems in the two volumes, only 28 were composed before the death of Léopoldine in 1843, as the critic Vianey has pointed out.[99] It should be added that of the 111 written after her death, 92 date from the years 1854-1855, so that *Les Contemplations* may not be considered, as Hugo claimed, the work of twenty-five years, but primarily the work of nineteen months — to be precise, those nineteen months after the visit of Madame de Girardin to the island of Jersey, when Hugo was so actively engaged in the affair of the turning tables.

Many factors entered into the general deepening of Hugo's poetry. His grief over the death of his daughter had wrought a profound change in him. Having known the ultimate in human suffering and having struggled personally with the problem of evil, he was undoubtedly able to give these emotions a more authentic and richer lyrical expression. The emotional content of these poems of exile convey an impression of greater sincerity than the earlier poems. They are also less rhetorical. But the most important factor in the poetic excellence of *Les Contemplations* consists in their extraordinary imagery. Whatever secondary sources Hugo may have used, this imagery is Kabbalistic in origin, as examination of the texts show.

A comparison here might be made with the poet Yeats who, before his occult studies, was only a light and superficial poet, but who found in his esoteric pursuits an integration of his ideas and, what is of greater importance for poets, a rich body of symbols from which he could draw. Let us examine Hugo's exotic symbolism in order to have a fuller understanding of his poetry and to participate somewhat in his seer experience.

The Kabbalistic symbolism of *Les Contemplations* and the long poem, *Dieu,* is particularly apparent in three of the major themes of both works: (1) the conception of God which Hugo presents, (2) the explanation of the problem of evil which he offers, and (3) the idea of the chain of being, which is related to the Kabbalistic theory of emanations. Although in all probability Hugo utilized commentaries on the Kabbala or other secondary sources for his information, and his knowledge was not that of a scholar, he nevertheless absorbed some of the basic ideas. In addition to these fundamental concepts, four images in their context reveal a Kabbalistic inspiration: the mirror, the ladder, the giant, and the tree.

The problem of a dual universe had preoccupied Greek philosophers, both during Plato's time and later. This was – to repeat one of the most familiar of ancient philosophical problems – if God created the world out of nothing, then man inhabits a dual universe, that is, there must be both God and the *Néant.* Plato resolved the problem by reducing all sense phenomena to the unity of the idea, and he and his school were constantly discussing the concept of "the one and the many." Zeno offered as his solution to the problem the multiplicity of the universe as only an illusion of the senses. The cosmogony of the *Zohar* resolves the problem of the Greek philosophers in the following manner: The infinite transcends the finite but does not exclude it, for Creator and created are in reality one. This being maintained, the problem of evil imposes itself of necessity, for if man and all material phenomena are one with the Creator, then an explanation must be given for the suffering which man inflicts and endures in the world. This the *Zohar* explains in the idea upon which its entire cosmogony depends, namely, the dual aspect of God, who is represented as having one side which is positive, tangible, and measurable and another, like the opposite face of a coin, which is negative, intangible, indefinable, and nameless. In the figurative language so characteristic of the *Zohar,* God in his first aspect is called *En-Sof* (the Boundless) and is represented as the luminous point of a circle, the circumference of which is infinity.[100] The luminous point possesses a dark side, which is the shadow cast by its own brilliance. This is called *Ayin,* by which is meant the *Néant* or the mysterious unknowable aspect of deity.[101] The relationship between the two aspects of God is that of the positive to the negative. According to the account of creation in the *Zohar,* God did not call the world into being out of nothing, rather the universe emanated from God by a process of cosmic parturition. It should be noted that this idea is not the same as the pantheistic conception which makes God and the universe identical, for while the child who issues from his parents bears many of their characteristics, he is nevertheless independent of them and possesses a personality uniquely his own. Similarly, the universe, which came from perfection, if different in any way, could only be less perfect. Such was the origin of evil according to the *Zohar.*

Furthermore, the creation of the universe began with a burst of light which was in reality a thought of God. It consisted of ten emanations, called *Sephiroth* (from the Hebrew word meaning to number) since each of the emanations had not only symbolic and metaphysical significance but also a numerical value.[102] It is not possible to discuss all the emanations in detail here, but a few will suffice. The first emanation was called the Crown (*Keter*) because it represented symbolically the plenitude or the unity of the Creator with all created phenomena. It corresponded to the number One and also to the first letter of the Hebrew alphabet, Aleph. The second emanation, corresponding to the number Two and to the letter Beth, was called Wisdom (*Hocma*). This was an active, masculine principle – the Creator in search of an object of his thought. The third emanation, corresponding to the number Three and to the letter Gimel, was called Intelligence (*Binah*). In relation to the second emanation this was a passive or feminine principle. According to French Kabbalistic commentator Karppe, the first three emanations formed a kind of sacred trinity:

> The first three Sephiroth, namely, the Crown, Wisdom and Intelligence, must be considered as one and the same thing. The first represents knowledge or Wisdom; the second that which knows and the third that which is known.[103]

Karppe also identifies the third emanation with the speech of God or the "Word."

Hugo, in the fourth poem of the sixth book of *Les Contemplations,* makes an allusion to the connection between numbers and the process of creation:

> Listen. I am John. I have seen somber things,
> I have seen the infinite shadow where the numbers disappear.[104]

Again, in "Ce que dit la Bouche d'ombre," he says:

> Did you, therefore, imagine the universe otherwise?
> Do you believe that God, by whom form issues from number,
> Would have made the forest forever somber?[105]

Two other emanations should be mentioned: the fifth, which is the microcosm or man, and the tenth, which is the macrocosm. The digit one in the number ten corresponds to unity or *En-Sof* from which the world or multiplicity, represented by the zero, emanated. Conversely, the circle, since it is that to which nothing can be added, also symbolizes the primordial unity. Thus the Kabbala teaches this paradox about creation; just as the beginning included the end, so the end is itself a beginning. In the last few lines of his long poem, "Ce que dit la Bouche d'ombre," Hugo expresses the same idea:

> The brightness will mount into everything like sap;
> . . . .
> In all the darkness griefs will end; an angel
> Will cry out: Beginning![106]

As man and the universe emanated from God, so in the end both will return to their Creator. This is perhaps also what Saint John meant by the cryptic lines: "I am Alpha and Omega, the beginning and the end." At any rate, Hugo, in three volumes—*Les Contemplations, Dieu,* and *La Fin de Satan*—insists, contrary to Christian theology, not only upon the final salvation of all humanity, but also upon the salvation of evil itself in the person of Lucifer.

We have said that Hugo uses Kabbalistic symbolism to present his conception of the deity in *Les Contemplations* and in the long poem, *Dieu.* Let us examine the latter first, since the Kabbalistic concept is more obvious in it. In an apocalyptic Introduction, the human spirit is confronted by a dark point overhead. He interrogates it, demanding to know God. In answer to the poet's question, voices from the past offer the various historical replies which have been given to the question. The Introduction and each of the nine chapters which follow begin with the sentence: "And I saw above my head a dark point."[107] In each of the chapters through the Christian era, the dark point takes the form of an apocalyptic animal, which presents its particular point of view. After the Introduction, which the poet calls "Ascension into the darkness," and the replies given by the various animals, the dark point becomes transformed into a luminous point in the last two parts of the poem, "La Lumière" and "Le Jour." It surrounds the poet and announces that God exists and that what appears to man as a dark shadow is in fact a consuming light. The poet is overcome by the awareness that "All is light."[108] Thus, in the very climax of the poem, not only is the imagery of the point Kabbalistic in origin, but also the dual nature of God which is represented by the dark and luminous aspects of the point. As the Shadow had spoken about God in the first part of the poem, the light now also speaks on the same subject:

> He is X, element of radiance, number
> Of the infinite, formidable brightness of the shadow,
> Light on the Koran as on the Missal.
> . . . .
> God is the living flame in the depth of all things.
> . . . .
> The brightness stops, as if completely dazzled,
> I was fainting, and sight and hearing,
> And even the beatings of my heart interrupting each other,
> Would go out of me like water which spills over.[109]

In the final chapter, paradoxically bearing the title "Le Jour," the dark and luminous point changes into a death shroud and advises the poet to give up his quest, saying that he has seen all a human being can endure:

> Do you wish, trembling arrow, to attain the target finally?
> Do you wish to reach the goal, look at the invisible,
> The unnamed, the ideal, the real, the unheard;
> To understand, to decipher, to read? to be one dazzled?
> Do you wish it? Reply.[110]

When the poet answers this question in the affirmative, the finger of the Eternal touches him on the forehead and he dies.

In *Les Contemplations,* the *Néant* symbolizes the problem of evil which is uppermost in the poet's mind. He chooses this as his symbol because of what he describes as "the lugubrious intimacy of evil and the abyss."[111] The *Néant* is represented poetically with varied imagery – sometimes it is "the universal chasm" ("*le gouffre universel*"), "the shadowy Mouth" ("*la Bouche d'ombre*"), or "the sewer of universal Evil" ("*l'égout du mal universel*").[112] An important difference exists, however, between the *Néant* of Hugo and that of the modern existentialist writer, Sartre. Hugo's *Néant,* like that of the Kabbala, is a plenitude, the opposite of being, whereas Sartre says explicitly that his *Néant* is not the opposite of being, but its contradiction. It is a breach of consciousness, of that which separates what a man is from what he will become. "Nothingness is not, it nullifies itself" ("*Le Néant n'est pas, il se néantise*") he says in *L'Etre et le Néant.*[113] An imperfect universe was necessary, Hugo maintains in the first part of "Ce que dit la Bouche d'ombre." If being were not imperfect or heavier than the primordial spirit, then it would return immediately to that brightness from which it descended and there would exist as in the beginning no differentiation between Creator and creature. "Evil is matter," he says.[114] "Ce que dit la Bouche d'ombre" ends with a prediction that the entire universe, including all that is evil, will be finally drawn back into the primordial light, as if by a magnet.

As a poet who could capture and communicate a feeling for spatial vastness and the cosmic solitude surrounding man, Hugo is unsurpassed in the French language. This atmosphere pervades the entire sixth book of *Les Contemplations,* entitled "Au Bord de l'infini." To communicate this feeling of the insignificance of man in the face of this vastness, Hugo describes society as "a whirlpool of beings in the *Néant*" ("*un tourbillon d'êtres dans le Néant*").[115] Entire civilizations of men are swallowed up by the insatiable *Bouche d'ombre*:

> Into Eternity, chasm where the tomb empties itself
> Man flows endlessly, somber river which flows
> Into a somber sea.[116]

Although it is true that man inhabits the *Néant* "like a tiger in his lair," it is also true that the *Néant* inhabits man:

> We are the *Néant;* all our virtues could be contained
> In the hollow of the rock where the bird comes to drink.
> The good that we do is, like us, a specter.[117]

Again, in the poem "Horror," Hugo devotes some of his finest lines to this sentiment of cosmic vastness which lies both within man and without:

> We are the agitated abyss
> . . . .
> We are the flakes of eternal snow
> In eternal obscurity.[118]

Although the concept of the *Néant* is not necessarily a Kabbalistic idea, the belief that it is one of the aspects of the dual nature of God does serve to identify Hugo's frame of reference. Many passages can be found in *Les Contemplations* where Hugo expresses poetically the idea of the dual nature of God:

> God, for the saddened thinker,
> Always opens in the darkness
> Brusque chasms of brightness
> The great hidden one of Nature
> Comes out of his lair at their appeal,
> At their call the symbolic shadow
> Speaks; the mystery is explained.[119]

In a second verse, Hugo expresses the same idea of the duality of God:

> Being shows eternally its dual face
> Good and Evil, fire and ice;
> Man feels both his pure soul and his somber flesh
> And the kiss of God.[120]

Finally, in "Ce que dit la Bouche d'ombre," Hugo expresses the idea of the oneness of the Creator with all created phenomena:

> God, the sun in the blue sky, the spark in the ash,
> Is outside of nothing, being the universal end,
> The lightning flash as well as the sunbeam is his glance.[121]

We will now examine the four other Kabbalistic symbols mentioned – the ladder, the mirror, the tree, and the giant. In a long passage which is among the finest in "Ce que dit la Bouche d'ombre," Hugo uses the image of the ladder and the mirror. The mirror, it will be remembered from the discussion of Balzac, is a symbol of correspondence; the ladder symbolizes the idea that creation does not stop with man but continues into the higher forms of life. The words "rebinds" and "joins" near the end of the passage suggest the linked nature of all created beings:

> Do you believe that this enormous life, filling
> With breath the foliage and the head with light,
> Which goes from rock to tree and from tree to beast,
> And mounts from the rock to you insensitively,
> Stops on the abyss at man, an escarpment?
> No, it continues invincibly, admirably,
> Enters into the invisible and into the imponderable,
> Disappears there for you, vile flesh, and fills the azure
> Of a resplendent world, the mirror of an obscure world,
> Of pure beings, of seers whose splendors bear witness
> To angels made of light as man is made of instincts;
> It plunges through heavens never reached,

Sublime ascension of starry ladders,
From enchained demons mounts to winged souls,
It makes the somber forehead touch the radiant toe,
Rebinds the star spirit to the archangel sun,
Joins, while crossing millions of leagues,
Star-studded groups and blue legions,
Peoples the heights, the depths, the borders and the middle,
And in the depths vanishes into God.[122]

Since the phenomenal world is one of infinite multiplicity, the number of correspondences is also countless. Man therefore exists in a "forest of symbols" (Cf. Baudelaire's poem, "Correspondances"). Swedenborg, in his *Dictionary of Correspondences,* says that trees represent the complexity of sensory impressions: "On this account the ancients, who were skilled in the knowledge of correspondences, held their sacred worship in groves."[123] In the *Zohar* the "tree of life," also mentioned in the book of Genesis, is the symbol of primordial sources of nourishment and of the powers of creation. The trunk and branches of this tree correspond to the ten emanations, while the tree itself is called by Kabbalistic commentators, "the Sephirotic tree." Hugo describes this mysterious tree in his poem, "Pleurs dans la nuit":

The tree Eternity lives without summit and without roots;
Its branches are everywhere, near to the worm, neighbor
To the great golden star;
Space sees the endless growing of the branch Number
And the branch Destiny, somber vegetation,
Fills up frightened man.[124]

In the symbol of the giant, the *Zohar* represented the idea that the entire universe formed an enormous man, a celestial being of whom terrestrial man was only an image. This primordial man, the prototype of creation, was androgynous (like the Biblical Adam from whom Eve came) and was called Adam Kadmon. Serouya, a modern French critic of the Kabbala, gives this explanation of Adam Kadmon:

> For Kabbalists the celestial world is divided into as many parts as the body of man. The head of man corresponds to the world . . . of angels; the part included between the neck and the navel corresponds to the region of the stars and other celestial bodies; the lower part of the human body beneath the navel, to the sensual world, to this world below.[125]

In *Les Contemplations,* Hugo makes two allusions to Adam Kadmon without calling him by name. In the poem, "Spes," he says: "The entire universe is a sinister giant"; and in the long passage about the ladder of being cited above from "Ce que dit la Bouche d'ombre," Hugo says that the ladder "makes the somber forehead touch the radiant toe."[126] The "toe" referred to is the toe of Adam Kadmon, and Hugo is making an allusion to the Kabbalistic idea that being in its entirety forms this symbolic man. Swedenborg expressed the same idea in these words: "It has been shown that the whole heaven is in the human form and likeness and is therefore called the Grand Man."[127]

Such was the imagery chosen by Hugo in his role as poet-magus and initiator into the mysteries. The poet's resolve to penetrate this unknown world reaches its culmination in the poem, "Ibo," of *Les Contemplations.* The rituals of fire and water and the entrance into the "tabernacle of the unknown" referred to in these stanzas of the poem were a part of the ceremonies of the secret societies:

Why hide these profound laws?
    Nothing is screened.
Into your flames and into your waves
    I shall pass;
I shall go and read the great Bible;
    I shall enter naked
Up to the terrible tabernacle
    Of the unknown.[128]

In this poem, Hugo calls himself a *magus* and identifies the *magus* with Prometheus, whose task it is to possess the mysteries of heaven. With these stanzas we have reaced the Rimbaldian conception of the poet as a stealer of fire:

Man in this troubled epoch,
    A somber ocean,
Must act like Prometheus
    And like Adam
He must steal from the austere heavens
    The eternal fire
Conquer his own mystery,
    And rob God.[129]

PART II

Culmination of the Doctrine: The *Voyant* Letters

CHAPTER 4

The Four Seasons in the Development of Arthur Rimbaud

> With Rimbaud . . . it is not French which one needs to know but the forgotten tongue of the poet. . . . Out of all the glittering constellation of French writers I am forced to choose him, a nova. . . . I choose Rimbaud because through him I understand France best. With his own youthful hands he created a monument as lasting as the great cathedrals.
>
> HENRY MILLER, *Remember to Remember*

Although Balzac and Hugo often elaborated on the subject of seers, it was Rimbaud who perceived most clearly the artistic possibility of the phenomenon of voyance and formulated an esthetic based on it. For this reason, his *Voyant* letters, analyzed in detail in Chapter 5, represent a culmination of this theme, so familiar in the literature of Romanticism. Yet, since an original mind so often revitalizes everything which passes through it, so in these letters the theme of the poet as seer is recreated and re-emerges as the poet's original discovery.

Contrary to the literary manifestoes which poets so often make, only to abandon later (and often with profit), or which they formulate after the fact of what they have written, Rimbaud's esthetic was no idle theory, but one which he actually used in poetic creation. To him, the connection between creed and creation was so close that when he at last rejected his esthetic creed he also abandoned his poetry. It was quite natural for so young a poet to hold tenaciously to his doctrine, since he could not draw on the wider experience of a more mature person. Therefore, he exclaims in "Matinée d'ivresse": "Je t'affirme, méthode!"

Because of the extent to which Rimbaud put faith in this esthetic theory, it seemed possible to use an exact textual analysis of the *Voyant* letters as a key to a clearer understanding of *Les Illumina-*

tions. With this in mind, the inquiry into the theme of the poet as seer was originally undertaken. It is by no means implied here that Rimbaud read or had any direct knowledge of the German writers mentioned in Chapter 2. While it is not impossible that he did, this cannot be proven from any known facts. The first three chapters of this study serve as an illuminated screen or background against which the texts of the cryptic *Voyant* letters might be projected in order for their meaning to be clarified.

The great need for a completely different approach and a more tangible solution to the problem of understanding the poetry and personality of Arthur Rimbaud becomes apparent from even a brief survey of what his critics have written about him. Among these critics, chaos reigns, and although this study does not contend that unanimity of opinion should exist among critics, nevertheless such a mass of contradictory opinion indicates certain fundamental errors. Depending upon the mood of the critic concerned, Rimbaud is angel or devil, voyant or *voyou,* atheist or mystic, child or scholar, genius or impostor, invert or convert, existentialist or surrealist – in short, more than any other poet, Rimbaud is the product of his critics' self-projection. In a recent study of Rimbaud, American critic Wallace Fowlie (*Rimbaud's Illuminations,* 1953) considers it a mark of the poet's genius that each one sees in Rimbaud what he himself is looking for. While this may suffice for the general reader, the function of the critic is to recreate as nearly as possible the thoughts and emotions which the poet intended to communicate.

It would be difficult to name any other modern poet who has provoked more contradictory reactions among his critics than Rimbaud. Denounced and even cursed by some, Rimbaud, that "furious angel" – or demon – of French letters has nevertheless escaped his critics every time, but he has not been neglected nor outmoded. The triumph is his, and so this "alchemist of the Word" remains uncaptured. The freshness and intensity of his poetry continues to enchant and to possess men deeply. In the literary world, this prodigious boy was indeed a nova, for what other country could name a poet who at sixteen wrote poems comparable to the "Bateau ivre" or at seventeen and eighteen wrote the first free verse in his language?

Until 1947, Rimbaud's critics turned most often to biography, or to critical works which were largely biographical; and although this was valuable in itself, it was seldom that a critic actually came to close grips with the poetry. Among the earlier biographer-critics, the divergence of opinion about Rimbaud's personality was as wide and contradictory as the different interpretations of his poetry. While it is not possible to discuss here at great length all the numerous critical works, a general indication can be given of the main points of view held by the leading exponents.

There was, first of all, the group who either wanted to annex Rimbaud to the church or to emphasize the drama of his conversion. The first of these were the Berrichons, Rimbaud's sister, Isabelle, and her husband, Paterne, who between the years 1897 and 1921 wrote several works depicting the poet as a convert to mysticism and saintliness. Isabelle Rimbaud in particular left no stone unturned to prove that Rimbaud died a good Catholic; she even refused to allow Aragon and Breton to publish in 1924 a poem which she thought might be prejudicial to this impression.[1] The Berrichons received strong support for their viewpoint from two well-known contemporaries, Paul Claudel and Jacques Rivière. Claudel wrote in a letter to Berrichon: "It is to Rimbaud that I owe, humanly speaking, my return to the faith."[2] Coining a phrase which became famous, Claudel called Rimbaud "un mystique à l'état sauvage," in the Preface to the poet's works which he published in 1912.[3] In an earlier letter to Jacques Rivière, Claudel explained at some length why the discovery of Rimbaud had meant so much in his life:

> Rimbaud was the chief influence which I experienced. Others, and chiefly Shakespeare, Aeschylus, Dante and Dostoievsky, were my masters and showed me the secrets of my art. But Rimbaud alone had an action which I shall call seminal and paternal and which really made me believe that there is a generative power in the order of minds as there is in bodies. I shall always recall that morning in June of 1886 when I bought that small issue of the "Vogue" which contained the beginning of *Les Illuminations*. . . . I finally came out of that hideous world of Taine, Renan and the other Molochs of the 19th century, of that penal servitude, of that frightful mechanism entirely governed by perfectly inflexible laws and as a culmination of horror, knowable and teachable (automatons have always inspired me with a kind of hysterical horror). I had a revelation of the supernatural. Genius reveals itself there in its purest, most sublime form, as an inspiration come one knows not from where.[4]

Jacques Rivière, also profoundly inspired by the young poet, maintained in his posthumous work, *Rimbaud* (1930), that although it was not accurate to call Rimbaud a Christian, he was nevertheless a "wonderful introducer to Christianity." Defining an angel as a being who possesses a greater quantity of existence than a man,

Rivière says: "In this respect Rimbaud is an angel. A furious angel. He has not been touched; he carries intact the resemblance of God." A being of complete innocence who dwelt outside the moral sphere, Rimbaud in Rivière's opinion was not immoral but amoral, "a fallen angel."[5] Also following the Claudelian line of criticism were Daniel-Rops in *Rimbaud, le Drame spirituel* (1936), emphasizing the poet's conversion and spiritual dilemma, and René Silvain, who points out the role of Rimbaud as the originator of the religious awakening of the 1920's in his work, *Rimbaud le précurseur* (1945).

But the Rimbaud of this group of critics was not destined to go unchallenged. Opponents existed even among Rimbaud's contemporaries in the person of Verlaine, who was the originator in *Les Poètes maudits* (1884) of the body of criticism which considers Rimbaud as the evil genie of French letters and a Bohemian rascal. Among the critics of the 1920's, Marcel Coulon was the first to attack the idea of Rimbaud as saint and mystic and to point out that there were falsehoods in Isabelle Rimbaud's testimony. But Coulon, in the harshness of his judgment, wanders farther from the truth than Claudel and Rivière in the generosity of theirs. Although Jean-Marie Carré in *La Vie aventureuse de Jean-Arthur Rimbaud* (1926) also judged Rimbaud to be "amoral and atheistic," his criticism is not harsh; the Rimbaud he presents is essentially a great adventurer, in his younger years as a literary figure as well as in his later life in Africa.[6] Benjamin Fondane, taking up the theme of the *poète maudit* and carrying it to the most extreme conclusion of all, insists that the *voyant* was in fact a *voyou* (*Rimbaud, le voyou,* 1933). Harsh also in their criticisms of other critics as well as of Rimbaud, Etiemble and Gauclère (*Rimbaud,* 1936) tried to explain the poet by analyzing the psychological reasons for his renunciation of literature: he was discontented, they believe, with the partial success which he had actually achieved and would have nothing less than absolute achievement. Two psychological studies, emphasizing Rimbaud's lack of mental stability, were written during the 1920's by psychiatrists, Lacambre and Delattre (1928). Lacambre judged Rimbaud to be a constitutional psychopath suffering from hallucinations. Although he was not a psychologist, C. A. Hackett, in *Le Lyrisme de Rimbaud* (1938), discussed at length the mother complex of Rimbaud and presented the poet as a *Petit Poucet* to whom the writing of poetry was an "infantile game."[7]

In a class apart is critic Rolland de Renéville who, although he saw in Rimbaud no Christian at all, curiously presented Rimbaud as a devotee of Hindu mysticism (*Rimbaud le voyant,* 1929). Rolland de Renéville's thesis is of interest in this study because it represents the first attempt to explain what Rimbaud meant by his theory of the voyant. His error stems from his assumption that the concept of the seer and also Rimbaud's idea of the universal intelligence must of necessity have come from the sacred books of Hinduism. To support his arguments, Renéville cites several passages from the *Upanishads* about seers and some from the *Bhagavad-Gita.* But the reader of Rimbaud looks in vain for other possible allusions to Hinduism, for such words as *yoga, brahman,* or *atman.* Instead, one finds throughout *Les Illuminations* and the *Saison* such words as *mage, alchimie, magie,* and *sorcellerie.*

The only other attempt among the earlier critics to explain what Rimbaud meant by his voyant theory was Godchot in *La Voyance de Rimbaud* (1934). Instead of analyzing the text of the *Voyant* letters in detail, Godchot discusses only one or two points in them. His conclusion, no longer supported by any critic at the present time, is that the theory of the poet as seer was taken by Rimbaud from the Bible. To support his argument, Godchot quotes[8] the following obscure passage from the Old Testament:

> Now in the time past, in Israel when a man went to consult God, he spoke thus: Come let us go to the seer. For he that is now called prophet, in time past was called seer.
>
> [I Samuel 9:9]

It is true that Old Testament prophets were supposed to have possessed visionary powers, but all ancient cultures, especially those of the East and Middle East, had seers. They also existed among the Greeks and Romans. One fact alone refutes the theories of both Rolland de Renéville and Godchot: a seer in the Hindu or Biblical sense was an individual who lived a life of great austerity and asceticism and such is not the tone or the import of Rimbaud's letters, as this analysis will show.

Even Rimbaud's merits as a poet have met fierce disputation: F. Ruchon in *Jean-Arthur Rimbaud, sa vie, son oeuvre, son influence* (1929) maintained that the poet's works are altogether lacking in logic and that he was not a man of letters in any serious sense. On the other hand, André Dhôtel in *L'Oeuvre logique de Rimbaud* (1933) considers that the poetry constitutes a logically constructed whole and proceeds to attempt a demonstration of this. Most severe of those holding the point of view of Ruchon is a recent critic, Roger Caillois, who insists that the poet was an impostor in *Les Impostures de la poésie,* (1945). The majority of critics take the opposite point of view about the literary merits of Rimbaud. On this point, Claudel and Rivière join in agreement with Gide, Breton, and others. Among Rimbaud's contemporaries, the first to praise his genius and to describe it accurately as well as poetically was Mallarmé. Although he never met Rimbaud personally, he saw him once in a café with Verlaine and other members of a group of bohemians of the artistic and literary world, the *Vilains bonhommes.* In reply to a letter (April, 1896) of a Harrison Rhodes in the United States, who wrote him inquiring about Rimbaud, Mallarmé says that he had "the perfectly oval face of an angel in exile, with light brown hair in disorder and disturbing, pale blue eyes."[9] Describing Rimbaud's genius, Mallarmé writes this poetic passage in *Divagations*:

> The flash of a meteor, he, lighted with no motive except his presence, sole issue, extinguishing itself. Everything certainly would have existed since without this luminary of consequence [ce passant considérable], since no literary circumstance really prepared it: the personal case remains, with force.[10]

Gide and Breton gave their highest tribute to the genius of Rimbaud, while André Fontaine devotes an entire work to the analysis of this genius. Gide wrote in his *Journals*: "The reading of Rimbaud . . . has made me ashamed of my works and disgusted with everything that is merely the result of culture. It seems to me that I was born for something different."[11] Breton, claiming Rimbaud as the precursor of Surrealism, gave Rimbaud credit for having revolutionized French poetry with free verse. He explains in *Les Pas perdus* his interest in Rimbaud:

> It would not be less of an error to consider art as an end. The doctrine of art for art's sake is as reasonable as the doctrine of life for art's sake seems to me to be foolish. We know now that poetry ought to lead somewhere. It is on this certitude that the passionate interest which we have for example in Rimbaud is based.[12]

Also emphasizing the genius of Rimbaud is the work of André Fontaine, who says in *Le Génie de Rimbaud* (1934) that the boy was motivated primarily by the desire to have his work published, and that had he attained the success for which he hoped, he would never have abandoned literature. Also in accord regarding the literary genius of Rimbaud are: English critic and biographer Enid Starkie in *Arthur Rimbaud* (1938; rev. ed., 1947); the American critics Edmund Wilson in *Axel's Castle* (1931) and Henry Miller in *When Do Angels Cease to Resemble Themselves? A Study of Rimbaud* (1946); and Wallace Fowlie in *Rimbaud* (1946).

Such were the general trends in Rimbaud criticism prior to 1947. The years 1947-1950 brought a great increase in critical activity during which many of the critics of the 1920's and 1930's rewrote their works with zeal and enthusiasm but little appeared which could be called definitive. Serving as the stimulus to further research were the appearance in 1946 of the Pléiade edition of Rimbaud's works together with the correspondence, compiled by Rolland de Renéville and Jules Mouquet, the critic who discovered the Latin poems of Rimbaud's school days, and of Irish biographer Enid Starkie's revised edition of her biography in 1947. Using a suggestion made by Starkie about the possible influence of the occult system of Eliphas Lévi on Rimbaud, Jacques Gengoux in *La Symbolique de Rimbaud* (1947) attempted to explain all the poetry, even the Latin verse of the poet's school days, in terms of Lévi's occult system. His work is far-fetched and unconvincing, but he made a bolder attempt at close textual analysis than anyone had attempted on such a scale. It was doubtless the work of Gengoux which inspired Rolland de Renéville to rewrite his *Rimbaud le voyant* (1947), enlarging his original idea of the Hindu inspiration of Rimbaud's poetry to include a general Oriental influence.

Attacking the theories of Rolland de Renéville and Gengoux, a new critic, Debray, wrote *Rimbaud le magicien désabusé* (1947). Debray denied an Oriental influence in the poetry of Rimbaud, but rejected also, in spite of the postscript by Daniel-Rops, the theory of the poet's conversion. Debray states that his is an existentialist approach to Rimbaud, attempting to show the poet in his social situation. Debray's conclusions are somewhat disappointing in that the idea upon which he dwells, the theme of Rimbaud the great revolter, has been discussed at such great length by other critics. Debray holds that the poet attempted to break all the conditions of existence, both human and cosmic, and in the end he came to revolt against his own revolt. This final rejection of his revolt does not necessarily imply, in Debray's opinion, that Rimbaud returned to Christianity.

To add variety to the numerous and contradictory theories, Rimbaud was hailed by P. H. Paillou as the "father of existentialism" (*Arthur Rimbaud, père de l'existentialisme,* 1947). C. A. Hackett, rewriting an earlier work, elaborated again in *Rimbaud l'enfant* (1947) with greater detail upon the theme of the poet's mother complex, but added at the end of his volume a very useful bibliography. The critic of 1947 who seems to show the greatest discernment (with the exception of Starkie's work, which is more biographical than critical) is Guy Michaud in the section on Rimbaud in his *Message poétique du symbolisme.* In Michaud's criticism, which displays admirably the French virtue of *mesure,* Rimbaud is neither angel nor devil, but the "poet of the pure image," an intuitive rather than a rationalist, whose genius Michaud acknowledges and appreciates.[13]

The year 1949 proved to be the stormiest of all in the Rimbaldian field. It brought both a literary scandal and a real discovery involving actual works of the poet, also a critical work by Henry de Bouillane de Lacoste which caused the largest stir of all the recent criticism. In the same year, Jean-Marie Carré rewrote his biography, *La Vie aventureuse de Jean-Arthur Rimbaud,* stating in the Preface that he had no thesis to defend, his only purpose being to resuscitate Rimbaud as he was from the documents which exist. The literary scandal which came in the summer of 1949 involved the false "discovery" of Rimbaud's lost work, *La Chasse spirituelle,* which was quickly detected and denounced as a hoax by André Breton.[14] A *bona fide* discovery of the *Lettre du baron de Petdechèvre,* a pro-Communist pamphlet sent by Rimbaud to the review *Nord-Est* in September 1871, was made by Jules Mouquet, who in a similar manner had found Rimbaud's Latin poetry.[15]

In *Rimbaud et le problème des Illuminations* (1949), Bouillane de Lacoste attempts to prove, chiefly by graphology and then by internal evidence, that *Les Illuminations* was written in 1875 — two years after *Une Saison en enfer* — and not in 1872, as all critics had previously believed. The importance of the change in date is that if the prose poems of *Les Illuminations* were written after the *Saison,* the latter is no longer the poet's *adieu* to literature as it would seem to be from its content, but merely his *au revoir.* To have proceeded in a truly scientific manner, Bouillane de Lacoste should have given short excerpts of a few lines from at least ten of the prose poems from *Les Illuminations* so that the similarity of the handwriting in them, and the difference between them and the poems in verse, would have been immediately apparent. Instead, he printed four poems in their entirety: "Scènes," "Promontoire," "H," and "Bottom" and one short excerpt from "Conte." Two of these four – "H" and "Bottom" – were on the same page of a manuscript and therefore should count as only one example. Four examples are certainly not sufficient to prove his point. The question also arises immediately as to whether it is impossible for the poems selected by Bouillane de Lacoste to have been composed in 1872 but copied by Rimbaud at a later date. Graphology being an extremely dubious "science," Bouillane de Lacoste has increased its uncertainties by his constant allusions to what Rimbaud's handwriting reveals about his character. The handwriting of 1870, for example, is supposed to show "childish pride" ("*orgueil puéril*"), whereas that of *Les Illuminations* is supposed to show that he was in a calm and happy state of mind.[16] Perhaps what the handwriting really shows is whether or not Rimbaud wanted to make a good impression on the recipient: the smoothest and most beautifully penned of the reproductions are the "Devoir de Classe" of 1870 (opp. p. 24) and the letter to Théodore de Banville (opp. p. 15), whom he wanted to publish his "Soleil et chair." We are finally reduced to a choice between the statements of two of Rimbaud's contemporaries regarding the date of these two works: Verlaine's that the *Saison* was written first, and Delahaye's that *Les Illuminations* preceded the *Saison*. In his memoirs of 1871, Delahaye, describing the musical and literary "soirées" at the home of Bretagne, said: "Pour finir, on lisait les vers ou quelques-uns des premiers poèmes en prose de Rimbaud."[17] According to biographer Enid Starkie, Verlaine's testimony is unreliable because he was a chronic alcoholic at the time of the publication of *Les Illuminations* (1886) and contradicted himself several times as to their date of composition.[18]

After many hesitations about the work of Bouillaine de Lacoste, Jean-Marie Carré, who directed the thesis, said that he was convinced of its accuracy. Bouillane de Lacoste published a critical edition of Rimbaud's works rearranged according to his new dating, but critics André Breton and Etiemble protested vigorously. Breton said in *Flagrant délit* that Bouillane de Lacoste's theories "show that its author has never been in profound communication with Rimbaud."[19] In 1950, Etiemble and Gauclère published a reedition of their critical work of 1936 (*Rimbaud*) in which they agreed with André Breton's criticism of Bouillane de Lacoste's thesis. They added that Bouillane de Lacoste's theory can be proven only when he can demonstrate that the poems he cites were not copied by Rimbaud at a later date. In this recent study, Etiemble and Gauclère present Rimbaud as essentially one who was torn between his own dream world and the world of reality. Still harsh in their judgment of Rimbaud, they maintain that without all the scandal connected with the Verlaine affair, Rimbaud would not be any better known than Nerval or Raymond Roussel.

Using his *Symbolique de Rimbaud* (1947) as the basis of a more detailed study, Jacques Gengoux published in 1950 a 700-page tome, *La Pensée poétique de Rimbaud.* Prior to Gengoux's work, little had been done to show the extent to which Rimbaud's thought is rooted in that of his century — the emphasis having always been placed upon his great originality. To show that Rimbaud drew constantly upon the ideas of his time in no way nullifies his originality. Gengoux, however, errs greatly in his work in constructing from the poetry of Rimbaud a system so filled with numerous references to the poet's alleged sources that it would have taken the boy poet, however brilliant, at least ten years longer to have acquired such erudition. One would say that the erudition belongs instead to Gengoux, especially the excellent knowledge of Hegelian metaphysics which Gengoux attributes to Rimbaud.

Such is also the case insofar as many of the other critics are concerned. Even a cursory glance at the point of view taken by many reflects far more strongly the personality of the particular critic himself and his own personal ideology than Rimbaud's. In many cases, the self-projection is quite apparent: for example, what is more natural than the opinions of Claudel and Rivière, themselves devout Catholics, or of Rolland de Renéville, interested in Oriental thought and editor of the occult magazine "Cahier d'Hermès," of Benjamin Fondane's outraged sense of bourgeois propriety; or of Paillou's considering Rimbaud the father of Existentialism in a post-war work which coincides with that movement and reveals chiefly Paillou's interest in it? By what means, then, can the same error be avoided in this study? By awareness of the pitfall, and by a detailed textual analysis of the *Voyant* letters in an effort to show whatever relationship may exist between them and certain trends in nineteenth-century thought.

But the general confusion and the number of contradictory opinions among Rimbaud's critics have not arisen entirely from self-projections. Some are due to the fact that the *Saison en enfer* contains passages which are self-contradictory if taken out of context. To arrive at a true understanding of the poet one must first face this fact. There is, however, an explanation for these contradictions, so obvious that it is surprising that none of the critics — particularly Debray, for example, who said that he would present Rimbaud from an existentialist point of view — has called attention to it. All have considered the personality of the poet to be a static essence instead of a living, growing adolescent existence. They have tried to seize this essence, which they believe to be Rimbaud lurking somewhere behind the poetry. Small wonder that he has eluded them; Rimbaud as a static essence does not exist. The school year 1870-1871, for example, was a year of extraordinary growth for the poet, both physically and intellectually. According to a footnote in Delahaye's memoirs, Rimbaud grew seven inches during that year.[20] Even if this is an exaggeration, the poet's growth was so rapid and so sudden that it caused a comment from his friend. It is not without significance that this was also a year of great spiritual crisis and of the composition of the *Voyant* letters, which describe this change in considerable detail. Adolescence, especially that of a genius, may not be considered a block of marble to be seized by the critic, rather it is a flowing stream only to be described in its various seasons.

Four distinct phases or seasons through which the poet passed from the time of his entry into the Collège de Charleville in 1866 at the age of twelve until his final abandonment of literature in 1874, may be designated by a close examination of the poetry and biographical data. This does not mean that each of the phases may be cut off from the others with mathematical precision, like blocks of wood, or that strains of an earlier phase may not appear again much later, but if Rimbaud's life and poetry are regarded in this manner much that is contradictory becomes clarified. Especially significant is that corresponding changes may be noted in the poetry produced in each of the four seasons.

(1) *The Season of the Docile Schoolboy*

The first of these periods — extending from the time of his entrance into the Collège de Charleville in 1866 at the age of twelve to the departure of his teacher, Georges Izambard, in June 1870 — may be clearly designated as that of Rimbaud the docile and ambitious schoolboy, the brilliant prize-winning pupil. During these years there is no real evidence, either in the poetry or in the biographical data, of the troublesome and rebellious boy which he would become during the summer of 1870. On the contrary, the evidence shows him to have been a hard-working as well as gifted child who wrote Latin verses with great facility and supplied less talented classmates with poems to submit. Rimbaud won a large number of scholastic prizes as well as two regional prizes in a Latin verse contest held by the schools in the neighborhood of Douai. "Il suait d'obéissance," he wrote when he was sixteen, describing himself in these earlier years.[21] From this period prior to his sixteenth birthday, six Latin poems were published; a seventh, of which only the title remains, was lost; two French essays (one of which was written when the poet was only eight years old) remain but were not published during these years; and finally, seven French poems were written, only one of which was published at the time of its composition.

(2) *The Season of Rebellion*

From July-August 1870 to March-April 1871 is a second clearly defined period, characterized chiefly by Rimbaud's efforts to gain his independence, economic and moral, from a mother who allowed him no freedom. The reasons why the docile schoolboy developed so suddenly into the *révolté* and rascal which the critic Fondane saw him as will be discussed later in this chapter. During these months, Rimbaud ran away from home three times and refused to complete the one year he lacked on his *baccalauréat* — and he had so recently been the best student. In contrast to the more sentimental and bookish poetry of the first period, the poems written during these months were inspired by his newly acquired experiences and hence reveal much more originality. The poetry of this period also shows that his revolt expressed itself in three directions common among adolescents — sex, religion, and politics. A number of scatological works indicate clearly Rimbaud's sexual dilemma; a second group of poems reveal not only his anticlericalism but his total rejection of Christianity; while a third group shows him to have been radically republican in his political views and, if not an actual participant in the battle of the Commune, at least deeply sympathetic with it.

(3) *The Creative Season*

The formulation of the esthetic doctrine expressed in the *Voyant* letters of May 1871, marks a third period which was one of such intense literary creation that it may be said Rimbaud truly lived for his art. The spiritual crisis which led him to announce that he would become a seer is reflected in an even greater change in his poetry:

the poems of *Les Illuminations,* both prose and verse, are vastly different in form and content from the poems written during the second period.

(4) *The Season in Hell and the Vision of Eternity*

In the autumn of 1873, Rimbaud had a second spiritual crisis. This was partly the result of the Brussels affair, in which he was shot by Verlaine, and partly due to his loss of faith in his esthetic doctrine and therefore to his feeling of failure as a poet. Finally, just before his nineteenth birthday, this most precocious of all poets bids farewell to literature in *Une Saison en enfer.* From the depths of the mental and spiritual anguish through which he had passed, Rimbaud experienced a mystical vision. But the *Saison* contains no hint of compromise with the church. On the contrary, the poet's refusal of organized Christianity is adamant. In this chapter, the first two periods of the life and poetry of Rimbaud will be examined; the last two phases will be treated in Chapters 5 and 6.

The Poet of the First Season

The circumstances of the Rimbaud family during the poet's formative years are quite well known but may be stated briefly. Rimbaud had a brother, Frederick, who was a year older than he and two sisters, Vitalie and Isabelle, who were younger by several years. The father, Frederick Rimbaud, a captain in the French army, had deserted the mother, Vitalie, when Arthur was only six years old. Lest Madame Rimbaud be too harshly condemned for lacking understanding of her gifted son, the difficult task of rearing four children without help should not be overlooked. Her greatest weakness consisted in her determination that her children should turn out well, as she doubtless considered their father had not. With unrelenting vigilance, she guarded her two boys in particular, meeting them every day after school and walking home with them lest they get into mischief. The only refuge the young poet found from the ubiquitous eye of his mother was the latrine — "Il pensait là tranquille," he wrote of himself in "Les Poètes de sept ans."[22]

In order to prepare Frederick and Arthur for the *lycée,* Madame Rimbaud sent them to the Pension Rossat and supplemented what they learned there by making them memorize quantities of Latin poetry, slapping them when they did not know what she had assigned. The year of Arthur's entrance into the Collège de Charleville was also the year of his first communion, and he devoted to his religion all the ardent love which found no outlet in the home. He longed to be a martyr, and on one occasion almost had his wish when he attacked a group of older boys who were playing with holy water in the church font. When it became clear at the school that Arthur possessed extraordinary scholastic talents which his brother did not share, Vitalie Rimbaud engaged the schoolmaster, M. Lhéritier, to give Arthur private lessons. It was Lhéritier who first encouraged Arthur to write original verse in both Latin and French, and under whose guidance Rimbaud won almost all the first prizes in his class as well as the first prize in Latin verse in 1869 at the *Concours Académique,* in which all the *collèges* and *lycées* in the vicinity of Douai participated. Of the six Latin poems published in the *Moniteur de l'enseignement secondaire* and the *Bulletin officiel de l'Académie de Douai,* one was the prize-winning poem of 1869, "Jugurtha." Unfortunately, a seventh poem which won the prize for the year 1870, "Sancho Pança à son âne," supposed to have been published in June of that year, was lost when the review had to suspend publication on account of the war. Five of the extant poems are original and one is a translation of the invocation to Venus from the *De Rerum Natura* of Lucretius. The critic Mouquet, who discovered these Latin poems in 1932, pointed out an amusing fact about the translation from Lucretius: Rimbaud had the audacity to take a previous translation by the well-known poet, Sully-Prudhomme, which had been published by Lemerre in the *Bibliographie de la France,* make corrections in it which actually made a noticeable improvement in the poem, and submit it undetected to the *Bulletin officiel de l'Académie de Douai.*[23]

When Georges Izambard came to the Collège de Charleville in January 1870, he was something of a scholastic prodigy himself. He obtained his *baccalauréat* at the age of fifteen, his *licence* from the University of Paris at eighteen, and was then appointed teacher of the highest class at the Collège de Charleville at the age of twenty-one. At the time of Izambard's arrival, Rimbaud had just published his first French poem, "Les Etrennes des orphelins," in *La Revue pour tous* (Dec. 1869), in addition to three of the Latin poems already mentioned. Izambard soon became an important influence in Rimbaud's life, and perhaps the only person who ever really understood him and liked him. Izambard shared Rimbaud's literary ambitions, possessed a large library of Parnassian poetry which he freely lent to Arthur, treated the boy as an equal, and talked to him about literature. All the evidence indicates that Izambard's influence on Rimbaud was good, in spite of the fact that Vitalie Rimbaud complained to him for having lent her boy a work so immoral as Hugo's *Les Misérables* and blamed him for her son's final break with all discipline.[24] Under the influence of Izambard, Rimbaud wrote six more poems in French and four in Latin between January and June 1870, even while receiving intensive preparation for the July examinations.

Then quite suddenly in June 1870, the young poet's world came crashing in on him. News of his prize-winning Latin poem in the *Concours Académique* arrived simultaneously with that of the outbreak of the Franco-Prussian War. The schools closed immediately, and Rimbaud, threatening in every breath to run away, accompanied his two friends Izambard and Deverrière to the railroad station on July 24. Izambard pleaded with Rimbaud to remain and pass his *baccalauréat,* reminding him that his mother would be softened by the prizes soon to be awarded him. Two weeks later, in the midst of his admiring family and friends, Rimbaud was decorated with honors – a medal from the Academy of Douai for his Latin poem, "Sancho Pança à son âne," many red-bound volumes for class honors, and varnished laurel wreaths for his composition in French. But this meant little to him since the one person who had meant anything to him or understood him had gone. The letter Rimbaud wrote to Izambard after his departure contains a pathetic picture of adolescence in time of war: the summer vacation which the family had planned in the country had to be abandoned; confinement in a small town with nothing to do left Rimbaud bored and restless beyond endurance and this, in turn, increasingly strained relations with his mother. His only escape was the access which he had to Izambard's library, the key to which his teacher had left with the landlord with instructions that Rimbaud be allowed to go there and read. After he had read all of Izambard's books, Rimbaud, undoubtedly inspired by his brother Frederick's escape from home into the army, suddenly took the train for Paris on August 28. He had obviously acted on an impulse, since what he did was poorly planned. He left without money to pay his fare and was promptly taken to jail on his arrival in the capital. In his distress he wrote to Izambard, who promptly secured his release, but as it was no longer possible to return to Charleville because of the state of siege, Izambard sent Rimbaud money to come to his home in Douai.

There the young poet remained for about three weeks, enjoying the affectionate treatment accorded him by Izambard's elderly aunts, the Gindre sisters. When news arrived of the defeat at Sedan, Izambard enlisted, but was not sent to the front immediately because he was untrained and because of a weapon shortage. He served temporarily in the National Guard and gained permission for Rimbaud to be enrolled in his company. They drilled with broomsticks until Rimbaud drew up a protest against the lack of weapons directed at the mayor of Douai. An ardent supporter of the Emperor, the mayor had deliberately withheld the arms, blaming the lack on the new government of the National Defense. Rimbaud was in the process of gaining signatures for his protest when his mother interrupted his activities. Having received from Izambard the news of her son's whereabouts, Vitalie Rimbaud responded so violently that Arthur absolutely refused to return home and quarreled with Izambard about it. At length, however, the quarrel was settled amicably by Izambard's elderly aunts and it was agreed that Izambard would take the culprit home lest he escape a second time. When the two arrived in Charleville, Madame Rimbaud did not express her appreciation to Izambard for his kindness, but instead deluged him with more of the abusive language with which she had addressed him in her letter. For Arthur, there was only a cuff on the ear. It is therefore not surprising that Rimbaud ran away again only a week after his return home, this time to Belgium; while the distressed Madame Rimbaud now pleaded with Izambard to try to find her son.

At this point we reach the end of the first phase in the poet's life: here a definite and radical change may be noted in him as well as in his poetry. Before moving on to the second period in Rimbaud's development, it will be worthwhile to examine the themes of the five original Latin poems, the two essays, and seven poems in French which belong to the first period, so that the difference between the poetry of this season and that of the one which follows may be made clear.

The Poetry of the First Season

Since Mouquet's discovery and translation of Rimbaud's Latin poems, the only critic who has seen fit to analyze their content is Gengoux. Unfortunately, he sought only to show what he considered to be their occult sources. Other critics have preferred to ignore this body of Rimbaud's work, possibly because they considered them only school exercises. While this is true, these classroom assignments contain documentary evidence about their greatly disputed author and it is worthwhile to give them brief attention.

All five of the original Latin poems have a common theme which is most suggestive: they treat the subject of an unusually gifted child or youth at the moment when he has just become aware of his exceptional talents. In the first of these poems which begins "Ver erat . . ." a truant schoolboy enjoying a pleasant spring day in the country falls asleep beside a brook. In his dream, a flock of doves bring him a laurel wreath and as they put it on his head the heavens open and the god, Apollo, gives him his lyre and writes on his forehead: "Tu vates eris."[25] Then a choir of muses sings a religious annunciation of his high calling. This indeed suggests the fantasy of a gifted child who has just awakened to an awareness of his own genius. In another passage, the fourteen-year-old poet indicates that he has perceived directly the divine element of his own being. This is not stated presumptuously, but rather as a natural quality in all human beings.

This awareness of his divinity occurs again in the poem Mouquet has titled, "L'Ange et l'enfant," in the idea of world strangeness and nostalgia for a world beyond—which later became an important theme of *Les Illuminations.* "L'Ange et l'enfant" relates the incident of a small child who, having enjoyed his New Year's *étrennes* and about to fall asleep, sees an angel bending over him. Too close to heaven to be frightened by his celestial visitor, the child merely contemplates the wonderful being with pleasure. The angel asks the child to return to heaven, assuring him that he will be more at home there. As he dies, the child's face is covered with celestial light, like the boy-poet in the first poem when he was visited by Apollo.

Three more "enfants merveilleux"—Jesus, Hercules, and Jugurtha—appear in the Latin poems. The boy Jesus is a child artist whose carpentry is so beautiful that the villagers are astonished by its excellence. They compare him with Hiram, the architect of Solomon's temple, and ask, "Quis est puer ille?"[26] It is not difficult to see in this poem the schoolboy of Charleville who had astonished people with his art and who was pleased with recognition at so early an age. Hercules, the mythological child of extraordinary physical strength, is presented in a fourth poem as a young man who uses his superhuman powers unselfishly. When the river Achelous overflows its banks, Hercules steps into the rushing torrent and stops it. That

Rimbaud identified himself with Hercules is evident later when he signs the poem "Ce qu'on dit au poète à propos de fleurs," addressed to Théodore de Banville, "Alcide Bava," signifying that he himself intended to be the Hercules who would clean the Augean stables of *Parnasse*.[27]

In the poem "Jugurtha," the longest and most original of the Latin poems, the idea of the "enfant merveilleux" appears as a refrain, which Monquet translates thus: "Il naît dans les montagnes de l'Arabie un enfant qui est grand."[28] Ingeniously, Rimbaud uses the idea of palingenesis as a means of linking his hero, Abd-El-Kadir, with the great Jugurtha of antiquity. But the idea of palingenesis is clearly used only as a literary device in this poem, for nowhere does Rimbaud attempt to elaborate on the theory itself. Abd-El-Kadir, the Arab chieftain who united his people to fight against French domination of Algeria (1832-1847), was taken prisoner by the French and kept in the Château of Amboise until his liberation in 1852 by Napoleon III. At the end of the poem, Jugurtha appears to Abd-El-Kadir, telling him not to grieve about his defeat since prosperity and a better age would come for his people under French domination. Such were the patriotic and conservative political views of the schoolboy who one year later wrote a plan for a Communist constitution. As a very young child he must have heard stories about Abd-El-Kadir, since his father had participated brilliantly in these very campaigns in North Africa and had been decorated with the Crimean medal and the military medal of Sardinia; in the year of Arthur's birth, Frederick Rimbaud had been made a member of the Legion of Honor.

Among the earlier works, three themes become important in the poetry of the second and third periods of Rimbaud's literary development: the young poet's instinctive love of vagabondage, his nostalgia for Eden, and an indication of the mother image in reverse.

The wanderlust of Rimbaud finds its equal among French men of letters only in the character of François Villon, with whom he appropriately identifies himself in a long essay, *Charles d'Orléans à Louis XI* (1870). The defense which it contains of Villon and his vagabond colleagues on the occasion of their being condemned to death was written by Rimbaud in fifteenth-century French style and put into the mouth of medieval poet Charles d'Orléans. In this impassioned plea, Rimbaud identifies himself with Villon — an association he carried out in fact during the next year and which found expression in the lovely poem, "Ma Bohème." The sensuous love of nature which so characterizes some of Rimbaud's finest poetry is related to his propensity for wandering. This is indicated in the first Latin poem, "Ver erat," in this version of the French translation by Mouquet:

> I delighted in looking at the distant fields
> And in observing the happy miracles of the earth in springtime.
> A child, I sought only vain wandering in the country:
> My small heart held higher aspirations.
> I know not what more divine spirit added wings
> To my exalted senses; mute with admiration my eyes contemplated
> These sights; into my breast there crept
> A love of the warm countryside; such a ring
> Of iron as the magnesium magnet draws by a secret
> Force and attaches itself noiselessly by invisible hooks.
> However, I had broken all the parts of my body by my
> long vagabondages.[29]

"What a walker he was!" exclaimed Verlaine about Rimbaud in *Les Poètes maudits,* and Rimbaud himself in later life comments upon this subject in two letters to his mother from Aden:

> Don't count on the fact that my humor might become less vagabond. On the contrary, if I had the means of traveling without being forced to stop and work in order to earn a living, I would not be seen two months in the same place. The world is very large and full of magnificent countries. . . . But on the other hand, I should not like to be a vagabond in misery . . . to live always in the same place, I always find that very unpleasant.[30]
>
> [Jan. 15, 1885]

Five years later, discussing the possibilities of a job in France and of marriage, he wrote: "Speaking of marriage, I have always meant that I intended to remain free to travel, to live in foreign countries and even to continue to live in Africa."[31]

The quest for Eden, or the longing for a completely pure state of being, is indicated in the poems, "Ver erat" and "L'Ange et l'enfant." The poet who is crowned by the gods in the first and the child who is carried away by the angel in the second are both surrounded by the beauty of a world superior to this one and to which they are aware of belonging. The imagery of light, water, and crystal used by Rimbaud in "Ver erat" to indicate the purity of the other world suggests vaguely his later masterpiece, "Mémoire":

A light of brilliant whiteness
Spread around my shoulders, clothed all my body with its pure rays:
And this light was not at all similar to the somber light
Which, mixed with shadows, obscured our glances.
Its celestial origin has nothing of terrestrial light.
. . . .
Into my body there slipped then
An extraordinary warmth: thus, splendid in its pure crystal
A limpid fountain becomes inflamed with rays of the sun.[32]

In "L'Ange et l'enfant" Rimbaud expresses his regrets for the sincerity and purity of spirit which he finds so seldom in people:

Mortals do not ever
Caress with sincere happiness; even from the perfume of the flower
Something bitter surges, and agitated hearts know nothing
Except sad joys; never does pleasure delight in anything
Without clouds, and a tear lights up ambiguous laughter.[33]

It is for this reason that the boy is not unhappy to be taken out of the world and to become a "fils du ciel."

The mother image, which appears in two of the Latin poems and a French essay written when the poet was eight years old, constitutes psychologically the most significant aspect of the early works of Rimbaud. As the poet represents her here, the mother is everything that his own was not – gentle, girlish, deeply sensitive, and very affectionate toward the child. In his first essay, "Le Rêve de l'enfant," written when Rimbaud was only eight years old, he describes his mother as very different from his father – "a sweet, calm woman who feared little, and yet who kept her house in perfect order. She was so calm that my father would amuse her like a young girl. I was the most loved."[34] The poem "L'Ange et l'enfant" and the one about Jesus as a boy present two more brief images of the sensitive and affectionate mother: in the first, that of the mother weeping over the body of her dead child and, in the second, that of the Virgin kneeling and kissing the fingers of her son who had been wounded by a saw on his carpenter's bench and had attempted to hide his injury in order not to grieve his mother.

The fantasies of children are noted for their wishful thinking. Obviously, however, in the examples cited, Rimbaud does not wish himself dead or injured; what he really wants is a situation in which he would receive the attention and affection he lacks and needs. Fantasies of death or injury are extremely common, even among children less emotionally deprived than Rimbaud. In all three cases cited here, the young poet has presented his mother as she obviously was not, but as he wished she had been, as the biographies affirm. In a letter written a year later than the Latin poems, Rimbaud admits that his mother was "as inflexible as seventy-three administrations of iron helmets"; in still another letter to Paul Demeny he calls her "la bouche d'ombre" after Hugo's long poem by that title.

It is unnecessary to analyze in detail the first seven French poems belonging to this first literary period in the life of Rimbaud. In contrast with the Latin poems which have been grossly neglected by critics, the early French ones have been thoroughly discussed. Moreover, their meaning is clear to anyone who reads them attentively, and their inspiration, for the most part, is bookish and imitative. "Les Etrennes des orphelins" and "Le Forgeron" are imitative of Hugo; "Bal des Pendus" is pure Banville; the long poem, "Soleil et chair," which Rimbaud sent to Banville in the hope that he would publish it in *Le Parnasse contemporain,* treats the Rolla theme of De Musset in a Parnassian style. It should be said to Rimbaud's credit that his "Soleil et chair," which contains many fine passages, is better than most of the poems which were in fact published in this issue of the *Le Parnasse contemporain.* "Ophélie" and "Première soirée" possess the light and graceful charm of some of the best Parnassian poetry, but are undoubtedly derivative in their inspiration. Only one of the group, "Sensation," seems to have been taken directly from the young poet's personal experience. Inspired probably during one of Rimbaud's long walks in the country, the poem is particularly original in the sensuous love of nature which one encounters frequently in the more mature poetry:

SENSATION

During blue summer evenings I shall walk along paths
Pricked by wheat and crush the slender grass:
A dreamer, I shall feel its freshness in my feet.
I shall let the wind bathe my bare head.

I shall not speak, I shall not think of anything,
But infinite love will mount into my soul,
And I shall go far, very far like a gypsy,
As happy with Nature as with a woman.[35]

Derivative and bookish though the other poems may be in their inspiration, it is no exaggeration to say that they are unparalleled in literary history for a boy of fifteen years.

THE POET OF THE SECOND SEASON

Neither the French poems nor the Latin verse give the slightest indication of the revolt which was to take place in Rimbaud during the late summer of 1870. The poetry which he wrote prior to this date is as conventional as his own life; he is even conventional in his choice of literary models — Hugo, Banville, and Musset. Nor do the biographical data add anything of real significance to explain the change which was about to come. From it, we know there was friction between mother and son, but this in itself is hardly unusual with adolescents eager for more freedom from parental restraints. How then can Rimbaud's revolt be accounted for? The picture is not too difficult to reconstruct with the clear psychological evidence furnished by the Latin poems. The fantasies of death and injury indicate the young poet's great emotional need for affection and understanding from his mother. When Izambard came, he at least partially filled that need and thus made the harshness of the poet's mother somewhat more endurable. Having once enjoyed the kindness and understanding of his teacher, Rimbaud was unable and unwilling to return to the sterility of life without Izambard. The departure of Izambard served therefore as a spark in the powder keg of resentments against his mother. Biographical facts seem to confirm such an explanation, for prior to Izambard's departure there is no indication of revolt in Rimbaud. Thus it was with shrewd peasant insight that Madame Rimbaud blamed Izambard for her son's revolt against discipline. However, the only fault which may be truly attributed to Izambard (unpardonable from Madame Rimbaud's point of view) is that he had unwittingly usurped and filled the role of beloved adviser and counselor which was rightfully that of the poet's mother, but which she, perhaps because of the difficulties of her own life, had become incapable of fulfilling. This she could never forgive, and it accounts for her hostility toward Izambard.

An equally important but purely impersonal factor in Rimbaud's revolt which should not be underestimated was the war. It was this which precipitated Izambard's departure, caused the closing of the schools and, therefore, brought Rimbaud's bright prospects to an abrupt end. In all probability, if the schools had reopened in September 1870 the prize-winning student would have returned to finish his last year; but events were destined to take another and different turn.

The conflict with his mother proved to be merely the starting point in Rimbaud's revolt, which spread in all directions at once and was aimed at all the restraints of society. He had reached an age when most adolescents demand some independence, especially a highly gifted one. Swiftly and unannounced his repressed genius burst its confinements and sought freedom in the air and sun of the open road. Rebellion in the young can have healthful or unhealthful results; more often, as in the case of Rimbaud, the effects are mixed. On the positive side, he undoubtedly wrote better poetry as a result of his experiences; on the negative side, from August-September 1870 until the time of the writing of the *Voyant* letters, Rimbaud was engaged too much in rebellion for its own sake. There were the months during which he developed into the rascal which critic Benjamin Fondane saw in him. To attempt to ignore or excuse this period would be merely to by-pass the facts. During these months, Rimbaud ran away from home twice, had an unpleasant initiation into sexual experience, refused to return to school when it reopened in February 1871, wrote such obscenities as "Merde à Dieu" on the park benches in front of the railroad station at Charleville, and went about the streets of that town just prior to the Prussian invasion shouting in front of the small shops, "Beware, your hour has come!"[36] He believed that by upsetting the status quo the invasion would make way for a new socialistic regime, and he therefore wrote a project for a Communist constitution. Since this has been lost, we know of its existence only through Delahaye's memoirs.

Clearly, the poet's personality underwent a complete but natural metamorphosis. The departure of Izambard served as the spark which set off Rimbaud's rebellion, but this had its deeper cause in the lack of understanding on the part of his mother.

The Poetry of the Second Season

The second phase in Rimbaud's life was accompanied by a comparable change in his poetry; he became as independent in his art and thinking as he was in his actions. Whereas the poems of the first period are largely bookish in their inspiration, those of the second period are based almost entirely on Rimbaud's personal observation and experience during his wanderings. This new poetry possesses the extraordinary freshness and originality of one seeing the world outside his small town for the first time. Therefore, each poem is a small fragment of that life as he captured it whole, with all its color and sound, its sensations of touch and smell. One who reads Rimbaud for the first time receives an immediate impression of a highly colored poetry wrought by one who possessed a painter's feeling for color. Perhaps the only other poet who used color to this extent was Edmund Spenser.

The poems of this period are so closely related to the events of the poet's life at this time that it is worthwhile to observe them in juxtaposition. Two scatological poems, "Le Châtiment de Tartuffe" and "Venus Anadyomène," which coincide with the departure of Izambard, mark the beginning of the second literary period, while several others of varying degrees of salaciousness were written during these months. Before examining these scatological works, three of which were incorporated into the *Voyant* letters, this study will summarize briefly the events of the second period, relating the poetry to them as we proceed.

If the poems written between August-September 1870 and May 1871 are arranged chronologically and according to subject matter, they give a coherent picture of Rimbaud's experiences on his second flight from home into Belgium. Consider them in this order: "Ma Bohème," "Tête de Faune," "Rêve pour l'hiver," "Le Dormeur du val," "Les Douaniers," and "Le Buffet." "La Bohème" has been placed first in this group because the month of September is mentioned in the poem itself as the time of Rimbaud's wanderings. The exultant mood of "La Bohème," celebrating the joys of the open road and the poet's pure delight in his freedom, also indicates that it was probably written at the outset of his journey, before he had become fatigued and disillusioned or suffered the great hardships of his trip. From biographical data we know that Rimbaud spent his first night at Fumay with his friend and classmate, Leon Billuart, and from there he set out for Charleroi to visit another school friend, Des Essarts, whose father was editor of a local newspaper.[37] Rimbaud had hopes of finding a journalistic job in Charleroi with Des Essarts' father, but he used such abusive language as he described certain political figures of the times, calling them scoundrels and traitors, that he shocked the bourgeois sensitivity of M. Des Essarts, who finally asked him to leave. "La Bohème" was probably written on the road between Charleville and Charleroi, for Rimbaud says in the poem that he wrote en route at intervals when he stopped to rest. The poet's pure delight in his new freedom makes this and "Le Dormeur du val," quite different in its subject but also written en route, the best poems of this period:

MY GYPSY DAYS

Off I would go with fists in my torn pockets;
My overcoat transformed into an ideal wrap;
Under the sky, Muse, I was your wandering knight
Oh what splendid loves I dreamed of there!

My only trousers had a large hole.
———Tom Thumb the dreamer, plucking rhymes like grapes
Along the way. The Big Dipper was my only inn.
———My stars in the heavens gave a soft rustle.

Seated beside the road, I would listen to them
Those fine September evenings, when I felt
Drops of dew like heavy wine upon my brow;

When rhyming amid fantastic shadows,
As if I played a lyre, I'd pluck the elastic laces
Of my wounded shoes, one foot pressed against my heart![38] (Gallimard)

Another poem of the open road which probably celebrates the beauty of the forests of the Ardennes through which he was passing is the fantasy, "Tête de Faune." Here the poet fancies that he sees the eyes of a faun staring at him from the foliage and hears its muffled laughter from among the branches:

FAUN'S HEAD

In the foliage, a green jewel-box, golden spotted,
In the foliage, uncertain and in bloom
With fine flowers where a kiss sleeps,
Alive and bursting the exquisite embroidery,

A frightened faun shows his two eyes
And bites the red flowers with his white teeth;
Burnished and bloody like old wine
His lips burst into laughter under the branches.

And when he was fled — like a squirrel —
His laughter trembles still on every leaf,
He may be seen frightened by a bullfinch,
The golden Kiss of the Wood rapt in meditation. (Gallimard)

As the young poet continued his journey he passed through a region where there had been fighting; there he encountered the body of a dead soldier — "Le Dormeur du val." The great restraint of emotion characterizing this poem gives it a power which, combined with its musical quality, reminds the reader of English literature somewhat of Christina Rossetti:

THE SLEEPER OF THE VALE

It was a verdant dell where sings a stream –
Silver tatters clinging madly to the grass
Where the sun illuminates the proud mountain.
It was a little vale all frothy with sunbeams.

A young soldier, mouth open, head bare,
His neck bathing in fresh blue watercress,
Sleeps; he is stretched out on the grass under the sky,
Pale on his green bed where the light weeps.

His feet in the gladiolas, he sleeps. Smiling
Like a sick child, he is taking a nap.
Nature, cradle him warmly: he is cold.

Perfumes no more cause his nose to tremble;
He sleeps in the sun, his hand on his chest,
Quietly. He has two red holes in his right side. (Gallimard)

Somewhere along the road between Fumay and Charleroi, Rimbaud caught a ride in a little wagon which he describes as rose-colored with blue cushions. In "Rêve pour l'hiver" he relates that during the ride he exchanged a kiss "which ran down her neck like a foolish spider" with the young girl to whom he dedicated his poem. It is inscribed anonymously, "To . . . Her" and is signed "en wagon, le 7 octobre 70."[38] The next day Rimbaud reached Charleroi, as his letter of October 8 from that city to his friend Billuart in Fumay indicates.

Three poems, "Au Cabaret vert," "La Maline," and "L'Eclatante victoire de Sarrebrück," relate his experiences in Charleroi. The first two contain references to the city and present two restaurant scenes filled with all the odors, sights and sounds of the Belgian cuisine. In the first line of "Au Cabaret vert" we are informed that the poet had been walking for a week when he arrived in the city. Consequently, few if any poets ever wrote more eloquently about a slice of ham – the reader can almost smell it cooking. In "La Maline" Rimbaud describes the interior of another restaurant, making the same direct appeal to all the senses and, as in the former one, relates an episode of his flirtations with the waitress. In the streets of Charleroi, a Belgian print, "brilliantly colored" and selling for thirty-five centimes, caught his eye. It was a representation of the Emperor Napoleon III (whom Rimbaud accurately describes as "fierce like Zeus and gentle like a papa") standing in a "blue and yellow apotheosis" among his soldiers, who were having a siesta. In the poet's imagination, one of the soldiers gets up shouting, "Long live the emperor!"[39] But in the center, a shako rises "like a black sun" and asks ironically, "On what?" With the same irony, the poem "L'Eclatante victoire de Sarrebrück" refers to the first battle of the Franco-Prussian War, which was anything but a victory for Napoleon III.

Unfortunately, no poems have survived which refer to Rimbaud's experiences in Brussels. From biographical data, it is known that he called at the home of one of Izambard's friends, who gave him money and a change of clothing.[40] It is probable, however, that he did not remain long in the Belgian capitol, but set out rather promptly for Douai. The poem "Les Douaniers" suggests that the poet may have had some difficulties at the border, due undoubtedly to the necessary securities which accompany war. But the customs officers were only one group of petty officials who annoyed the poet greatly — these "retired soldiers and sailors" whom he describes as the "débris of the empire," who "slash the azure frontier with large hatchet blows and lead their hounds on a leash."[41]

Upon his arrival in Douai, Rimbaud went to Izambard's home, where his teacher finally found him after having traced him all through Belgium. In the living room of Izambard's own home sat Rimbaud, peacefully copying the poems inspired by his journey, to which three more, probably written in Douai, may be added: "Le Mal" and "Rages des Cesars," which will be discussed presently, and "Le Buffet," probably inspired by a piece of antique furniture owned by the elderly Gindre sisters. When Izambard dutifully and promptly informed Madame Rimbaud of her son's whereabouts, she refused to pay his fare home, insisting that he be returned to her by the police.[42] Izambard made all the arrangements for this, exacting from Rimbaud the promise that he would henceforth remain at home. The physical hardships endured by the young poet during his wanderings had made him more resigned to remaining at home, and if the schools had reopened this might have been Rimbaud's salvation; but the war continued.

Grim months followed of bombardment, siege, privation, and occupation by foreign troops. Mézières, the neighboring city of Charleville, was bombarded and Delahaye's house was burned. Both towns were occupied by Prussian troops in December 1870, but the occupation did not last long since the armistice was signed on January 27,

1871. Rimbaud spent these three valuable months reading avidly in the library of Charleville, especially the works of the French socialists Saint-Simon, Fourier, Prudhon, and Louis Blanc.[43] Annoyed again by petty officialdom, he wrote the satirical poem "Les Assis" about the complaining librarians who were so reluctant to bring him the books he requested. Considerable evidence exists to prove that Rimbaud was a voracious reader. In a letter to Izambard dated August 25, 1870, Rimbaud mentions that he has permission to use his teacher's library but that he is bored because he has read all the books and can find nothing new. He then gives a long list of works which he has read and ends the letter with a plea for Izambard to buy him a copy of Verlaine's *La Bonne Chanson.* In another letter (April 1871) Rimbaud mentions a long list of Parnassians whose works he had read while he was in Paris on his third flight from home.[44] Delahaye devotes over forty pages to a discussion of certain works which he and Rimbaud discussed, and he also says that Rimbaud read avidly. In addition to the socialist writers, Delahaye mentions in particular such names as Helvétius, Rousseau, Michelet, Lamartine, and Quinet.[45] Finally, Verlaine devotes a paragraph in *Les Poètes maudits* not only to the quantity of Rimbaud's reading but also to its strange character:

> when he [Rimbaud] felt himself — finally! fatigued from striding along for nights and days over mountains, woods and plains, for what a walker he was! he would come to the library of a city and ask there for works which were evil sounding to the ears of the librarian-in-chief . . . but what difference did a name make to a fellow in this accursed work? The excellent bureaucrat, whose very duties forced him to hand over to Rimbaud on his request, many Oriental stories and libretti of Favart, all mixed with some vague scientific books, very ancient and very rare, would curse at having to get up for this child and willingly sent him back by the ear to his studies, which were not very dear — to Cicero, to Horace and to we don't know which Greek authors.[46]

It is possible that the very ancient and rare scientific works mentioned in this passage refer to alchemical or occult works which Rimbaud read. If so, this vague hint along with the clear indications of the *Voyant* letters constitute the only external evidence which can be cited to support the theory of the occult inspiration of Rimbaud's works.

It was also during these months darkened by war that Rimbaud and a group of his friends met, according to Delahaye's memoirs, at the home of Charles Bretagne where the poet read some of his prose poems.[47] In all probability Delahaye's date on this is correct, because the next winter Rimbaud was in Paris with Verlaine. This being the case, it would seem likely either that Rimbaud formulated his esthetic doctrine some months before he actually wrote it down or that he wrote some of his *Illuminations* before he had formulated his doctrine. Delahaye attributes Rimbaud's first efforts at writing prose poems to Baudelaire's inspiration; this too would seem to fit the date, since we know that Rimbaud must have become acquainted with Baudelaire's poetry at some time before the spring of 1871 because of the great praise given him in the longer *Voyant* letter.

Another group of poems written between August 1870 and February 1871 (which like the Latin poems have remained virtually untouched by critics) are the scatological poems. Documentary evidence may also be found in them of the nature of the changes taking place in the young poet's development during these months. One has only to think of the difference between the hymn in praise of the goddess Venus in "Soleil et chair" (May 1870) and the cynical, bitter disgust recorded in the scatological poem, "Vénus Anadyomène" (August 1870) to see that a drastic change took place during the late summer of 1870 in Rimbaud's attitude toward sex. The innocent prelude of a romance is indicated in the poem, "Roman," which gives an account of a summer date with a young girl with whom the poet had walked under the lindens, drunk lemonade in a café, and who laughed when he read her his poems. The last stanzas of the poem, "A la musique" (August 1870) record the strong, awakened sexual drives of a normal adolescent as he attends a musical concert in the town park on a hot summer afternoon. Finally, the poem, "Vénus Anadyomène," indicates a knowledge of female anatomy which seems more than merely bookish. Any further specific details about this romantic affair are unknown, but the bitterness and cynicism of "Vénus Anadyomène," contrasting as it does with the joyous but bookish Venus in "Soleil et chair," indicate that the poet may have had an unpleasant and unsuccessful initiation into sex. It is quite probable that this took place during July-August 1870, rather than at the later date Enid Starkie suggests.

Although "Les Réparties de Nina" cannot be classified as scatological, it is another in the series of poems which indicate Rimbaud's attitude toward the opposite sex. Here, the poet attempts to persuade a young girl to accompany him on his travels, and gives her a lengthy poetic description of their life together on the open road. But at the end of his long speech the girl reveals that she is only interested in his business prospects and replies tersely: "And the office?" From November 1870, until February 1871, Rimbaud faithfully kept his promise to Izambard not to run away from home, but on February 15 he sold his watch and left for Paris. Delahaye refers to the fact that Rimbaud had a mistress, a young girl about his own age, who accompanied him to Paris on his third flight, but he says that Rimbaud refused to talk about her, and indicated extreme unhappiness in connection with the episode. Whatever the details of this affair may have been, two facts emerge clearly from the poetry, namely, that Rimbaud expresses the normal passions of an adolescent toward members of the opposite sex, but that these met with complete frustration. The longer prose poems, "Un Coeur sous une soutane" and "Les Déserts de l'amour," give similar accounts of frustrated love and the physical distress of puberty. The frustration soon turned into bitterness toward all women, expressed particularly in "Mes petites Amoureuses," one of the poems included in the *Voyant* letters, and in a later poem written after the time of the *Voyant* letters, "Les Soeurs de charité."

Of the four poems Rimbaud included in the *Voyant* letters – "Le Coeur supplicié," "Chant de Guerre Parisien," "Mes petites Amoureuses," and "Les Accroupissements" – "Mes petites Amoureuses" indicates the ambivalence which he feels toward the opposite sex as a result of his frustration; "Le Coeur supplicié" expresses a definite homosexual attraction. Let us examine these two poems in greater detail in order to make these points more precise. In the first three stanzas of "Mes petites Amoureuses" the poet recalls an idyllic picture of young love on a spring day in the country: "We loved each other at that time," he says.[48] The two young people (the girl wearing rubbers) had stopped during a shower under a tree which was dripping upon them and ate their lunch of boiled eggs together, while the leaves of the tree overhead made a "cabbage-green sky" – a suggestion of the light greenness of early spring. The youth recalls that the girl had recently anointed him a poet and then quite suddenly, without suggesting the reason why, in the midst of a pleasant recollection, he intersperses terms of contempt "my ugly ones" ("*mes laiderons*"). The number of minute descriptive details which the poet gives would suggest that the situation was taken from his personal experience. Not only does the youth begin to think sadistically, "Come down here so that I may whip you" ("*Descends ici que je te fouette*") but also obscenely, and this obscenity is clearly derived from frustrated love.[49] Being unable to avenge himself physically, he takes out his outraged feelings in violent and abusive language. This is very clear in the following stanza:

> And yet it is for the sake of these embraces
> That I have rhymed!
> I should like to break your haunches
> For having loved![50]

One has the impression from this poem that Rimbaud hoped by piling up loathsome epithets as he described the female body to get revenge on women in general: "Blond laideron . . . Noir laideron . . . Roux laideron."[51] Moreover, his repeated references to female anatomy make it quite clear that his loathing is one of fascination, that he is obsessed with desire for its object, and that it is this ambivalence which accounts for his outbursts of anger in the poem.

"Le Coeur supplicié" also records the fascinated loathing which the young poet felt as a result of a first homosexual experience. The events of the poem take place around a camp of soldiers, probably in Paris while Rimbaud was on his third flight from home during February-March 1871. In the first stanzas of the poem a scene of revelry is suggested, of soldiers drinking and singing, in the phrase, "les refrains bacchiques."[52] The young poet has been smoking shag along with the men, no doubt to make himself feel more mature. Then the soldiers begin telling obscene jokes, doubtless indulging in sexual exhibitionism ("*ithyphalliques et pioupiesques*"), and finally either Rimbaud himself actually participated in a homosexual act or he witnesses others doing it. This is not stated precisely in the poem, but it is implied as he describes his revolted sensibilities ("*J'aurai des sursauts stomachiques*") and his feelings of guilt. Ordinarily, one does not feel guilty for the misdeeds of others. "Depraved" is the word which he uses to describe his feelings, and in the same stanza he expresses his wish to be purified by the magic power of healing in the waves, probably of the Seine ("*flots abracadabrantesques*"). But his disgust exists only on a conscious level; unconsciously, he is attracted and fascinated to the extent that he feels a conflict which makes him powerless to act or to extricate himself: "*Comment agir, ô coeur volé?*," he asks. Obviously, if he really felt repelled by the events described in the poem, he would have left the scene quickly and there would have been no question or conflict about it. It is his unconscious fascination which causes him to hesitate about his course of action:

THE TORMENTED HEART

My sad heart drivels at the stern,
My heart concealed with shag:
They are throwing sprays of soup at it,
My sad heart drivels at the stern:
Under the jokes of the troops,
Uttering general laughter,
My sad heart drivels at the stern,
My heart concealed with shag.

Ithyphallic and pioupiesque,
Their jokes have depraved it!
At the helm frescoes appear
Ithyphallic and pioupiesque.
O abracadabrantesque waves,
Take my heart so that it may be cleansed!
Ithyphallic and pioupiesque,
Their jokes have depraved it!

When they have finished their quids,
What will you do, O ravished heart?
There will be bacchic hiccups
When they have finished their quids:
I shall have a sick stomach,
If my heart is debased again:
When they have exhausted their quids
What will you do, O ravished heart? (Gallimard)

To say that this poem proves that Rimbaud was by nature a homosexual would be grossly incorrect. Psychologists know that at some time or other during adolescence many people experience interest in members of the same sex and that this is not serious unless it becomes fixed. In Rimbaud's case, however, it did become fixed when he met Verlaine, who was ten years older and who already possessed homosexual habits. If he had not met Verlaine when he did, it is probable that Rimbaud's strong natural passion for the opposite sex, evident in the poems discussed, might never have turned toward homosexuality. Two further indications that Rimbaud was not basically a homosexual are that (1) toward the end of his life, when he was in Abyssinia, he had a mistress, and (2) the correspondence of these years shows him making plans to return to France for the express purpose of getting married.[53]

Rimbaud included "Le Coeur supplicié" in the first and shorter *Voyant* letter of May 13, 1871, with the suggestion that his teacher destroy it as a silly work with no meaning. Izambard, however, who did not understand the poem, replied by writing a manifestly nonsensical poem and sending it with remarks to the effect that anyone could write nonsense. Wounded by Izambard's jibe, Rimbaud wrote only one more letter to his beloved teacher, and addressed himself henceforth to Paul Demeny. The conclusion to be drawn from this is that the poem meant more to its author than he pretended it did in the first *Voyant* letter.

"Accroupissements," included in the longer *Voyant* letter, belongs to a group of anticlerical and atheistic poems, no doubt inspired by Rimbaud's reading of Helvétius and other eighteenth-century philosophers. In this group, the development of his religious revolt may be traced step by step from "Le Châtiment de Tartuffe" (late summer 1870), "Le Mal" (written during the poet's flight into Belgium in the early autumn of 1870), and the very obscene poem, "Oraison du soir" (probably dating from the winter of 1870-1871) to the height of poetic intensity in two of the best poems of this category, "Les Pauvres à l'église" and "Les Premières communions" (written shortly after the time of the *Voyant* letters, on the occasion of the first communion of the poet's younger sister, Isabelle). On the whole, Rimbaud's revolt in religion was more than a Voltairean rebellion directed against ecclesiastical hierarchy; it went further and struck at the very roots of Christianity in "Les Premières communions" with its famous line: *"Christ! O Christ, éternel voleur des énergies."*[54]

What Rimbaud attacks specifically in the "Le Châtiment de Tartuffe" and "Accroupissements" is the sensuality and hypocrisy of priests. In both poems the attack is so strong that the question arises as to whether the poet is projecting his own excited passions upon others and condemning them vigorously. One's own faults often appear more detestable when seen in another. "Le Châtiment de Tartuffe," relating the incident of a malicious individual who purposely tears the robe of a priest to reveal that the latter is wearing nothing underneath, would seem a case in point. Further evidence of the poet's preoccupation with sensuality may be found in the most blasphemous of all his poems. "Oraison du soir," where he compares his creation of poetic dreams with the "warm excrements of an old dove-cote" and describes his urination after having drunk beer as his evening orison.[55] One can hardly go farther than this, but readers who are inclined to be harsh with Rimbaud should bear in mind that some of the greatest of poets – Shakespeare, for example – have indulged in poetic obscenities and blasphemies.

"Accroupissements" would have been a humorous poem, a verbal caricature of the priest Milotus, were it not for the fact that the poet, instead of smiling at his creation, dipped his pen in vitriol. Many of the poem's descriptive details are humorous, but the over-all tone or mood which prevails and reflects the poet's attitude is one of angry sarcasm. The reason for such a mood is clear: Milotus' sensuality is meant to exemplify that of the entire priesthood which Rimbaud attacks perhaps in order to justify the same fault in himself – or at least to make it appear less reprehensible by comparison. Briefly, the details of the poem are as follows. The priest Milotus, who rises late in the morning, long after the sun is up, is awakened only by his cravings for food. He breathes in the sunshine "like a sensual polyp." As he cooks his breakfast, the heat from the fire makes Milotus, who is so fat that his "lip rests on his stomach," become extremely aware of his body: Quelque chose comme un oiseau remue un peu / A son ventre serein comme un morceau de tripe![56] The priest's room is in utter confusion, stuffed with rough furniture and filthy rags. "His brain is stuffed with rags too," Rimbaud adds angrily. A sickening heat gluts the narrow room and "gravely clownish hiccoughs" can be heard occasionally. In this context, the last stanza of the poem, which might perhaps present some problem of interpretation, should be construed as follows. In the evening, as Milotus crouches on the ground in the shadows, he pursues in the heavens with his nose – the most animal-like of the sense organs – not the Virgin, but Venus.

Behind Rimbaud's revolt against religion lies the physical stress of adolescence, but this also takes an intellectual and philosophical form: his *Poète de sept ans,* in the poem by that title, is an eighteenth-century rationalist "who loved not God but men."[57] The poem "Le Mal" reflects the poet's disgust at the devastating spectacle of war, which he must have witnessed on the occasion of his flight into Belgium, and at what seems to him the indifference of God to human suffering. In these lines the ancient problem of evil is made so specific that it loses all triteness:

EVIL

While the red spittle of grape-shot
Whistles all day through an infinite sky;
While scarlet or green near the King who rallies them,
Battalions crumble en masse in the fire;

While frightful folly grinds to powder
And turns into a smoking heap a hundred thousand men;
— The poor dead who in summer lie in your joyous grass —
O Nature, thou who made these men in holiness!

There is a God who laughs at the damasked cloths
Of altars, at incense and at the large golden chalices
Who during the lull of the hosannahs falls asleep

And awakens when mothers rise up
In anguish, weeping under their dark old bonnets
And give him the large penny tied in their kerchiefs. (Gallimard)

In politics as well as in sex and religion, Rimbaud was a *révolté,* as the "Chant de Guerre Parisien" indicates. In two other poems, "Rages des Césars" and "L'Eclatante Victoire de Sarrebrück," the young poet protested against and satirized Napoleon III; and in the fourth poem included in the *Voyant* letters, "Chant de Guerre Parisien," he leaves no doubt about his sympathies for the Commune. Whether he actually participated in the fighting is relatively unimportant, but his identification with those who were resisting the government and his sudden trip to Paris in February-March 1871, reveal that his sympathy for the Commune was strong enough to be expressed in action. Thiers, Picard, and Favre, mentioned in the poem, were the chief figures in the capitulation at Versailles. Thiers in particular succeeded in convincing the deputies that they must, in the interests of their country, make peace with Bismarck. In this poem, as in "Paris se repeuple ou l'Orgie Parisienne," Paris is personified as a woman who has been robbed and raped (*"le vol de Thiers et de Picard"*).[58] Extending the metaphor further, the poet describes the suburbs of Paris, "stripped by Thiers and Picard" as "délirants cul-nus." This is a reference to Thiers' order of March 1871 for the disarming of the National Guard, which was the immediate cause for the outbreak of the affair of the Commune. Other details in the poem recreate the atmosphere of the times: the shakos, sabers, and the tom-toms of the soldiers, their general state of debauchery (*"nous bambochons plus que jamais"*) and the descriptions of fire which refer to the particular incendiary techniques used by the national troops against the Commune, namely, pouring gasoline on the houses and setting fire to them.[59] Rimbaud makes two references to this in the poem:

> With petrol they are making Corots
> . . . .
> The Great City has its pavements hot
> In spite of your showers of petrol.

Finally, in the last stanza, the young poet expresses his disgust over the historical fact that the provinces did not participate in the revolt of the Commune.

As abruptly and unannounced as in the summer of 1870 when the docile schoolboy took the train for Paris, another change took place in Rimbaud during March-April 1871. In the case of this second change, the immediate cause was the emotional shock which the young poet received from the experience recounted in "Le Coeur volé." His return to Charleville just at the moment when the affair of the Commune was beginning to look promising represents a definite recoil from action. Having abandoned political action, he turned his psychological need for revolt in a direction where the chances for success were greater. The energy which he had been putting into fruitless political, religious, and sexual rebellion now became concentrated into an artistic and esthetic revolt. It was a most fortunate turn of events, for in this direction his iconoclasm had some chance of producing positive results.

Prior to the *Voyant* letters of May 1871 there is absolutely no mention of the poet as seer or of the phenomenon of voyance, and no allusions in the poetry written before this date to indicate that Rimbaud had any knowledge of Illuminism. Furthermore, in the long list of books of current interest which the poet found in Paris during February-March 1871, mentioned in the letter of April 17 to Paul Demeny, not one had any connection with the doctrine of the poet as seer. This letter does, however, indicate a certain contempt on the part of Rimbaud for the poor state into which he feels contemporary literature has degenerated, and this becomes one of the chief ideas motivating the formulation of his own esthetic. His trip to the capital and his discovery of the inferiority of many of the Parnassian poets gave him greater confidence in his own ability to write something better. To use his own figure of speech, he now thought of himself as the literary Hercules who would clean the Augean stables not only of *Parnasse* but of French poetry in general. Perhaps on his long solitary walk back to Charleville from Paris, he formulated some of the ideas appearing in the *Voyant* letters. Such inspirations are never really sudden, but are nourished by much thought and reading, the more so in the case of Rimbaud who, because of his extreme youth, could not draw as freely upon experience. With the formulation of his esthetic doctrine in the *Voyant* letters, the young poet entered upon a new period of intense literary creation. He now became a more conscious and self-confident artist, and in the months following the formulation of his doctrine he produced such masterpieces as "Bateau ivre," "Mémoire," and most of the *Illuminations.*

The question raised by the presence of the four poems — "Le Coeur volé," "Chant de guerre Parisien," "Mes petites Amoureuses," and "Accroupissements" — within the text of the *Voyant* letters is whether Rimbaud intended them to illustrate his new esthetic doctrine, and if so, to what extent he actually carried out his theory in these poems and in later ones. While Enid Starkie states flatly that these poems could not possibly illustrate Rimbaud's doctrine of the poet as seer, the poet himself indicates otherwise within the longer *Voyant* letter.[60] Here he even labels his "Chant de guerre Parisien" an example of the new literature which he hopes to produce: "I am beginning with a psalm of present-day interest." It seems possible that Starkie based her opinion on the belief that voyance is a mystical concept, and these poems are manifestly incompatible with mystical thought as she understands it. In this she is quite correct if she is thinking of Christian mysticism, but the doctrine which is being set forth in the *Voyant* letters is not this, but the mysticism of the unconscious and of occult thought. Assuming, then, that the poems included in the *Voyant* letters do in fact illustrate Rimbaud's conception of the poet as seer, the question of the connection between them and the doctrine can best be dealt with by examining the letters in greater detail.

CHAPTER 5

The Esthetic Doctrine of Rimbaud

Reality invents me,
I am its legend!
JORGE GUILLÉN

The two *Voyant* letters – the shorter one of May 13, 1871, from Rimbaud to his friend and former professor, Georges Izambard, and the longer one of May 15 addressed to Paul Demeny, the poet and friend of Izambard – constitute the most tangible evidence which can be produced for connecting Rimbaud with the current of Illuminism covered in the first three chapters of this book. In fact, these letters are the only external evidence for such an interpretation, since the poet himself makes no mention of this interest in his other letters, nor do any of the persons with whom he corresponded – Izambard, Demeny, Delahaye, Verlaine, or any relative. The memoirs of Delahaye add nothing to the subject except the small bit of information that Charles Bretagne, the violinist and the friend of Rimbaud who urged him to write to Verlaine in an effort to make himself known in Parisian literary circles, was an occult enthusiast. But Verlaine does not mention it in *Les Poètes maudits*. The case for the occult inspiration of Rimbaud's poetry rests then upon the evidence contained in these letters and upon the internal evidence, largely to be found in *Une Saison en enfer*. The significance of these letters, in relation to the works of Rimbaud as a whole, consists in the fact that they serve as a key to the understanding of both *Les Illuminations* and *Une Saison en enfer*. Insofar as the idea of the poet as seer is concerned, these letters contain the most elaborate treatment in Romanticism of a theme which has touched many different writers. Although Balzac and Hugo discussed the phenomenon of voyance at great length, it is Rimbaud who relates it most elaborately and intimately with the process of poetic creation and advances it as an esthetic theory.

The two letters were not published until long after Rimbaud's death – the first and longer one to Demeny in October 1912 in *La*

Nouvelle Revue Française by Rimbaud's brother-in-law, Paterne Berrichon, and the shorter one to Izambard in October 1926 in *La Revue Européenne,* by Izambard himself. A tone of insolence and sarcasm characterizes the letter to Izambard – a surprising change in tone and attitude toward his once beloved professor. Instead of the teacher scolding the wayward pupil, it is the pupil who now scolds his professor for having shown such a lack of originality in his poetry. It was pointed out in Chapter 4 that Izambard also had literary ambition and wrote poetry. The fact that Rimbaud writes to Izambard so briefly and so insolently, and then only two days later at such greater length to Demeny, indicates that a rift has taken place in their friendship, at least as far as Rimbaud is concerned. The longer Demeny letter develops the ideas of the first letter much more fully without a tone of discourtesy and contempt. It is characterized by such great earnestness and enthusiasm on the part of the poet for his new ideas that some of it gives the effect of notes hastily taken, reflecting Rimbaud's impatience to begin putting his newly discovered theory into effect. Sometimes the sentences are incomplete; a lack of transitional phrases often obscures the connection between ideas, or the omission of elaborating details gives an elliptical effect. Yet the letters also contain some of the poet's most brilliant lines, such as the famous one: "The poet therefore is really a stealer of fire."[1] In the translation of the letters appearing in Appendix A, an attempt has been made to preserve in English the peculiarities which exist in the French. The letters will not be analyzed separately here, but simultaneously according to the various topics presented. To make a close textual analysis is essential for exactness and to avoid the pitfalls of other critics. Indeed, in Rimbaldian research in general, the more precise the textual analyses, the fewer generalities needed.

The topics discussed in the two letters fall into these general categories:

The four ages of poetry
A proposal for a new, objective poetry
The role of the poet as seer
The future of poetry and the poet
An estimation of certain contemporaries

The Four Ages of Poetry

The Demeny letter opens with the announcement that the poet intends to present the world with a new kind of poetry, and that he would like to discuss the future of poetry as he conceives it. But before proceeding to the future of poetry, he must outline briefly the several stages through which poetry has already passed. The following outline, based exactly on the text, summarizes the stages of poetry as Rimbaud conceived them:

1. Ancient Poetry Culminating in the Age of Greece

The poetry of the ancient world, culminating in the age of Greece, was characterized by "harmony." This was the result or the product of harmonious living in a world where ordinary, everyday actions were made rhythmical by the poets. For the Greeks, poetry was not a game; it was taken seriously in a way it has not been since. What Rimbaud implies here is that among the Greeks, poetry was life and life was poetry, so intimate was the connection between them. Because this attitude toward poetry and life was lost, everything from the end of the Age of Greece to Romanticism is decadence — "moyen âge," he says vehemently. Further on in the letter, Rimbaud maintains that the poetry of the future will in some respects resemble the poetry of Greece.

2. From the Middle Ages to the Age of Romanticism

FROM ENNIUS TO THEROLDUS: The first period of poetic decadence began with Latin poetry and ended with that of the Middle Ages, Theroldus being a reference to the alleged author of *La Chanson de Roland* mentioned in the last line of that poem. This period and the next were, according to Rimbaud, the ages of the "versifiers," its poetry being "rhymed prose," "a game," and "the impotence of innumerable generations of idiots."

FROM THEROLDUS TO CASIMIR DELAVIGNE: This period extends from the Middle Ages to the very early part of the nineteenth century, Delavigne (1790-1868) being generally credited as the first dramatist to attempt, though feebly, to free French drama from the Classical rules. The only great poet of this entire period is Racine, Rimbaud asserts; after him "the game became stale." Unfortunately, however, the game lasted two thousand years, he adds sarcastically. Assuring his readers that his observations are not to be taken jokingly, Rimbaud maintains that "such is the state of affairs in poetry." Nor are these statements to be interpreted as the natural desire on the part of youth to execrate its elders, he claims, saying: "Let the newcomers execrate us, if they will!"

3. From Romanticism to the Voyant Period

FIRST GENERATION ROMANTICS: This age has never been accurately judged, Rimbaud asserts, for who would have been qualified to do so? Certainly not the critics who, he implies, would surely have been prejudiced against it; or the Romantics who, he suggests, could not be expected to find fault with it. The young poet accurately perceives here the difficulty of judging one's contemporaries or near contemporaries. Rimbaud's own criticism of the first generation Romantics shows remarkable perception: their emotional outpourings, he says, are too often insincere — "the song sung is so seldom the work, that is, the singer's thought sung and understood." The reason for this insincerity is that their art is based upon a false conception of the ego: "If only these old imbeciles hadn't discovered only the false meaning of the ego, we wouldn't have to sweep away these millions of skeletons."

Yet the first Romantics were seers although they were not aware of it themselves, the cultivation of their souls having begun by accident. They were "abandoned locomotives which the rails take for a time."

Three such individuals are mentioned by name and commented upon. Lamartine: "sometimes *voyant,* but stifled by the old form." Hugo: "too pigheaded . . . he has SIGHT in his last volumes. *Les Misérables* is a real poem. . . . I have *Les Châtiments* close at hand: 'Stella' gives almost the extent of Hugo's *sight.* . . . Too much Belmontet and Lamennais, Jehovahs and columns, old broken-down monstrosities." Musset: "the fourteen times execrable. . . . Every schoolboy who has the means acts Rolla, writes a Rolla!" It should be pointed out here that Rimbaud himself was one of the schoolboys who wrote his "Rolla" — "Soleil et chair." His dislike of Musset is now so great that he writes a whole paragraph of tirade against him.

SECOND GENERATION ROMANTICS: The second generation of Romantics are very "seeing" (*voyants*), Rimbaud maintains, mentioning in particular Gautier, Leconte de Lisle and Banville. But the first real *voyant* is Baudelaire who lived, however, in a milieu which was too artistic, and the form which is so praised in him is poor ("*mesquine*"). "The discoveries of the Unknown demand new forms!," Rimbaud exclaims. Finally he mentions two poets of the Parnassian school whom he believes to be *voyants*: Albert Mérat and Paul Verlaine.

4. *The Poetry of the Future: Voyant Poetry*

This is the new poetry which Rimbaud believes will be produced in the future and which he discusses in the three other topics included in the *Voyant* letters.

Such a summary of the ages of poetry furnish concrete evidence of certain bookish sources on which the young poet drew and provides us with objective data in the attempt to reconstruct other more original parts of Rimbaud's works. In this outline of the ages of poetry may be seen the tendency of the nineteenth century to acquire a more intelligent understanding of the various periods of history. Voltaire, in *Le Siècle de Louis Quatorze* (1751) had been the initiator of such speculation: he had said that there were four great eras – the age of Pericles, Augustus, Michelangelo, and Louis XIV. Similarly, Condorcet outlined the various periods of history as he conceived them in *Esquisse d'un tableau des progrès de l'esprit humain* (published posthumously in 1801). These eighteenth-century speculations assumed much greater proportions in the nineteenth, when Herder and Hegel in Germany and Michelet in France each wrote universal histories which attempted to trace the development of the various civilizations and to formulate an intelligent philosophy of history. Inspired by the spirit of the times, socialist philosophers Saint-Simon and Fourier made their own curious outlines of man's social development as they conceived it. Fourier held that society had passed through four stages: (1) *Sauvagerie,* (2) *Patriarchat,* (3) *Féodalisme,* and (4) *Barbarie* (the modern state based on industrialism and perpetual war);[2] the fifth era, *Harmonie,* can come about only when the fundamental structure of society is changed.

Theories of a similar kind began to be developed regarding the history of poetry, for example, Thomas Love Peacock's *Four Ages of Poetry* (1820), to which Shelley replied with his *Defence of Poetry*. Peacock outlines the ages of poetry as follows: (1) The Age of Iron – the poetry of primitive man. (2) The Age of Gold – the Age of Greece, which Peacock describes thus:

> Poetry has now attained its perfection: it has attained the point which it cannot pass; genius therefore seeks new forms for the treatment of

the same subjects: hence the lyric poetry of Pindar and Alcaeus, the tragic poetry of Aeschylus and Sophocles. Even Herodotus' history is half a poem and was written when the whole field of literature belonged to the muses.[3]

(3) The Age of Silver – the poetry of Rome, about which Peacock says: "The poet of the Age of Silver recasts the poems of the Age of Gold. . . . Poetry had taken a step toward its extinction." (4) The Age of Brass – the age of Peacock's contemporaries, of whom he says: "This age professes to return to nature and revive the age of gold. This is the second childhood of poetry. . . . This is the poetry of the Lake poets."[3]

Although it is most unlikely that Rimbaud ever read or heard of Peacock's work, he would not have had to look far to have found the same ideas. That after Homer poetry declined is an idea as old as the Pléiade. Diderot also developed this theme in his article on Homer in the *Encyclopédie.* It was Herder, however, who in the late eighteenth century gave an almost lyrical expression to the belief that the Age of Greece corresponded to the adolescence or springtime of humanity and that for this reason there was more vigor in the art of that period. He says in *Zur schönen Literatur und Kunst*:

In spring and in youth man sings; in winter and in old age the music becomes mute. The origin of the poetry of Greece coincides with the springtime of their culture and disposition. . . . Of the poetry of the oldest singer and of the formation of speech through hymns, of Alcaeus and Sappho, of Pindar and the chorus . . . we have spoken and everywhere noticed a youthful, aspiring spirit. . . . Everything in the world has its hour. There was a time when Poetry contained in itself all of human wisdom. . . . It sang of the gods and related the deeds of its Fathers and Heroes; it taught men the wisdom of living.[4]

In a chapter entitled "The Decline of Poetry among the Greeks and Romans," Herder maintains that there was some decline even in the Age of Greece after Homer, but that by the time of the Roman domination, poetry had definitely become decadent:

For them [the Romans] poetry, in particular the lyric hymns, always remained, so to speak, a foreign art; the odes of Catullus and Horace are only an echo of the Greek lyre. Already in Virgil and in Ovid, in Propertius and Horace, one notices that the traditions of the past linger with little impulse. . . . One feels that the old lessons of the Gods have been used up. Doubtless this was the source of why most Roman poets – Ennius, Lucan . . . preferred to write stories rather than heroic poems, and some even chose unpoetic subject matter. The old flower garden had faded.[5]

To Herder may also be traced the nineteenth-century idea of "The Greek Unity," the belief that the Greeks had achieved a harmony of mind and body not to be found in other cultures. This idea inspired the esthetics of both Schiller and Hölderlin.

In France, the same boundless admiration for Greek literature, together with a belief in the decadence of Latin poetry, may be found in the writings of Edgar Quinet (1803-1875), a disciple and translator of Herder. From Delahaye's memoirs we know that Rimbaud did read Quinet and, this being the case, it is probable that he read Quinet's *Histoire de la poésie* (1857). Certain passages from Quinet's work should be compared with Rimbaud's briefer remarks on the subject of Greek and Roman poetry. Greek poetry was great, Quinet insists, because it was lived and sung by the people as well as by the poets. It was an integral part of life: "Among the ancients poetry was a necessary condition of life; everything was an occasion for verses: morning, evening, meals, festivals, work, weddings, arrival, departure."[6] Such poetic heights were never achieved in the history of poetry because the same harmony of living has never been again achieved:

> Each song, to the extent to which it was understood, fell into the domain of public tradition. It was there also that the poet went to look for it when he had need. All lived around him by means of his work; all sent it back to him. . . . The people really worked as much as the poet. The poet invented, the people remembered. The former was the voice; the latter the echo.[7]

Whereas poetry for the Greeks was a religion, among the Romans, Quinet continues, it was merely an "arbitrary invention" created for the amusement of patricians (Cf. Rimbaud's statement that after the Grecian period poetry became a "game"): "Among the Romans . . . poetry is fiction, falsehood; in their eyes it is of great merit to be able to defy it."[8] The chief law of this poetry was imitation: "it is equally evident that Roman art should necessarily adopt as the supreme law the law of imitation. This was the rule to which it had submitted at birth."

Roman poets had long ceased to be the guides of the people and became merely actors; Quinet continues: "cet histrion était le grand Ennius" while Virgil was "that melancholy initiator of the Middle Ages."[9] (Cf. Rimbaud's idea that the Middle Ages really began with the Roman period insofar as the history of poetry is concerned.) The Roman poets were furthermore conspicuously lacking in the power of prophecy; there were no Jeremiahs, no Isaiahs – not even a René or a Childe Harold; Quinet complains: "Among so many official prophets, augurs and soothsayers . . . not one had any presentiment of what was menacing the ancient world." The decline of Roman poetry was due, as in the case of Greek poetry, to the fact that the equilibrium which existed between the world of action and the world of ideas was broken:

> The real world dominated too strongly . . . the ideal world in order for there to be established between them the just proportion from which harmony is born; action surpassed thought, history oppressed the poem.[10]

The poetry of the Middle Ages as well as that of Rome and the sixteenth century were decadent and imitative, Quinet held in *Histoire de la poésie,* making still another point in common between this work and Rimbaud's *Voyant* letters. Quinet compares the writing of the epics of the Middle Ages with architectural construction – "epic mechanism," he calls it, and adds: "Under their helmets all the knights are alike; poetry is without nuances, without individual expression."[11] The church and feudalism Quinet considers two embodiments of the period; these were followed by woman in the seventeenth century, who replaced the religious ardor of the Middle Ages:

> The heavenly ardor which consumed hearts had ended by being concentrated upon an earthly object. . . . The vase of Christ's passion filled the philtres of enchantresses and the tears of lovers. . . . Woman replaced the church.[12]

Finally, Quinet concludes, the period of political violence and Revolution produced the chaotic and lawless art of the Romantics.[13]

Mention should be made of another critical work which treats the subject of the decadence of poetry after the Age of Greece: Leconte de Lisle's *Préface des Poèmes Antiques.* Written five years earlier than Quinet's *Histoire de la poésie,* this Preface along with Quinet's work would seem to be likely sources of Rimbaud's ideas. Not only does Leconte de Lisle's preface contain remarkable similarities of content with the *Voyant* letters, it also possesses the same trenchant tone and peremptory assertions regarding the poetry of past ages:

> Since Homer, Aeschylus and Sophocles, who represent Poetry in its vitality, in its fullness and in its harmonious unity, decadence and barbarity invaded the human spirit. As for original art, the Roman world is on the level of the Dacians and Samaritans; the entire Christian cycle is barbarous. Dante, Shakespeare and Milton only prove the strength

> and the height of their individual genius; their language and their conceptions are barbarous. Sculpture ceased with Phidias and Lysippus; Michelangelo did not produce anything. . . . What remains then of the centuries since Greece? A few powerful individuals, a few great works without connection and without unity.[14]

Leconte de Lisle also attacks Romanticism in much the same vocabulary as Rimbaud does:

> A second-hand art, hybrid and incoherent; archaic products of insomnia, nothing more. . . . Never had thought, overstimulated beyond measure, come to such a paroxysm of rambling. Poetic language here is analagous to nothing except the barbarous Latin of Gallo-Roman versifiers of the fifth century.[15]

Further analogies will be made later between the *Préface des Poèmes Antiques* and other parts of the *Voyant* letters; it will suffice now to say that Rimbaud, like Leconte de Lisle, was always dreaming of wild forests and rivers, of a lost Eden and of a primitive freshness.

In his cursorily given appraisal of the first- and second-generation Romantics, Rimbaud not only reveals considerable literary insight, but he also gives several clues connecting his idea of the seer with Illuminist thought. If this can be definitely established in this analysis, then it is probable that the poems of *Les Illuminations* are not merely a succession of pure images as Guy Michaud and Etiemble believe, but that they have a definite ideological content. In his general criticism of the first-generation Romantics, Rimbaud perceived at once that as innovators they lacked artistic consciousness, and he is accurate in saying that there was, for this reason, something accidental and haphazard in their success. Nevertheless, they were sometimes seers, and Rimbaud mentions in particular the later works of Hugo. This obviously refers to those works which Hugo wrote when he was in exile on the islands of Jersey and Guernsey, notably *Les Châtiments* and *Les Misérables,* which Rimbaud mentions by name, and *Les Contemplations,* which he must have known since he called his mother "la Bouche d'ombre." Rimbaud's remark that *Les Misérables* is a poem may also be found in Gautier's *Souvenirs romantiques* (1857): "It is a novel constructed in the manner of a poem, in which each character is an exception only in the hyperbolic manner with which he represents a generality."[16]

The poem "Stella" from *Les Châtiments* which, according to Rimbaud, shows the extent of Hugo's "VUE," gives some suggestion as to what Rimbaud meant by the term voyant. In this poem, Hugo describes an experience he had on the beach at Guernsey. He was awakened suddenly by a great radiance:

> It was a brilliance which was thinking, which was living.
> It would calm the reefs where the waves break;
> One would think one saw a soul within a pearl,
> It was still night, darkness reigned on high,
> The sky was lighting up with a divine smile.[17]

The rest of the poem is a description of the poet's mystic intuition of the oneness of all consciousness and of universal animism: an awakening flower tells the poet that she is sister of the morning star; the ocean "watches" the poet's vision. He hears birds speak to each other in their nests, and finally the voice of the star says: "I am ardent Poetry — the ocean is in love with me and the angel of Liberty and the giant Light send me ahead first."[18] Now the poem records an experience of supranormal vision, an intuition of the oneness of all being and of the aliveness of the so-called inanimate world. This is indeed one of the distinguishing features of Hugo's later works, and what Rimbaud wants to point out is that this first manifestation of voyance among the early Romantics must become a conscious artistic method. In his chapter on Victor Hugo in *Souvenirs romantiques,* Gautier calls attention to this perception of universal animism as characteristic of Hugo's type of visionary experience:

> The poet possesses that visionary eye of which he speaks regarding Albrecht Dürer; he sees things from their bizarre angle, and life hidden underneath the forms reveals itself to him in its marvelous activity. The forest teems strangely; roots dig the soil with their claws, like serpents re-entering their lairs; branches with gnarled elbows, with deformed fingers extend themselves like spectre's arms; the knots of the old trunks seem to be eyes which stare at one, and under stirred-up leaves one believes he sees the flight of dresses or shrouds.[19]

Although it was Lamartine who first introduced the Eastern theme of universal animism into French Romanticism, his inspiration on the whole was Christian rather than Illuminist, whereas the reverse of this was true of Hugo in his later works. Nor does a mere fascination with the idea of pantheism seem sufficient reason for classifying Lamartine as a seer. Among Parnassians it was customary to attack Lamartine and Musset in particular, and Rimbaud makes the usual attack on both — Lamartine for his form and Musset for his immaturity. Gautier expresses their attitude toward Lamartine in *Souvenirs romantiques* in the following passage: "He ignores or disdains all these questions of form, and with the negligence of a gentleman who rhymes at his leisure, without submitting himself more than is necessary to question of craft . . ."[20] Even harsher in his judgment of Lamartine, Leconte de Lisle writes in his *Préface des Poèmes Antiques*: "He possesses neither creative gifts nor the objective sense. . . . Lamartine lacks a religious respect for Art."[21]

The remainder of Rimbaud's remarks about the first generation Romantics is confined to a tirade against Alfred de Musset. Here it would seem that he is definitely making use of Gautier's judgment found in "Les Progrès de la poésie française," for the following passage is too similar for mere coincidence:

> Alfred de Musset is the poet of the twentieth year. *His muse has known only the spring. Namouna* has given birth to a numerous family. . . . Every young man has made a volume of verse, printed from the imitation of the preferred master.[22]

Like Gautier, Rimbaud uses the word "*printanier*" to describe Musset's works; instead of *Namouna* he substitutes *Rolla* as the inspiration of every schoolboy. Another objection which Rimbaud raises in regard to Musset is curious but piquant: his work is so essentially French that it is therefore despicable. "The same loathsome genius which inspired Rabelais, Voltaire and Jean de la Fontaine, commented upon by M. Taine," Rimbaud says in disgust. One might think that Rimbaud had placed Musset in good literary company, but his reference to Taine's work clarifies what he had in mind. In his work, *La Fontaine et ses Fables* (1853), Taine says, but not in a spirit of scorn, that La Fontaine is one of those writers who is most typically French: "He is a Gaul speaking to Gauls. Along with Rabelais, Voltaire and Molière, he is our most faithful mirror."[23] In this case, therefore, Rimbaud gives his own source. Taine, in the passage to which Rimbaud refers, proceeds from these remarks to one of his sweeping conclusions about French writers: he makes the statement that the *légereté* and the *esprit gaulois* to be found in such writers as Rabelais, Voltaire, and La Fontaine are typical of the French as a race. Taking Taine's conclusions literally Rimbaud hastened to apply them to Musset and attacked them, doubtless because the essential rationalism and wit of the *esprit gaulois* seemed to him incompatible with the doctrine of the poet as seer.

Among the second generation Romantics, Rimbaud mentions as seers the same three poets to whom Baudelaire also gives the most importance in his *Art romantique* – Théophile Gautier, Leconte de

Lisle, and Théodore de Banville. Exactly as Rimbaud implies in his classification, Baudelaire also curiously ranks Gautier and Leconte de Lisle as better poets than Lamartine and Hugo:

> but men of the world, those who have been elated or have pretended to be elated with *Les Méditations* and *Les Harmonies,* are overlooking this new treasure of enjoyment and beauty. It is true that Lamartine and Hugo have too long enjoyed a public more curious about the games of the Muse than the one which was going along sluggishly at the time when Théophile Gautier became definitely a famous man.[24]

Baudelaire couples Leconte de Lisle with Gautier as a poet who was similar in spirit:

> The only poet with whom one could without absurdity compare Leconte de Lisle is Théophile Gautier. These two spirits take equal pleasure in travel; these two imaginations are naturally cosmopolitan. Both like to change the atmosphere and dress their thought in the variable modes which time scatters in eternity. But Théophile Gautier gives to detail a more vivid relief and a brighter color, while Leconte de Lisle is especially attached to the philosophic armature. Both love the Orient and the desert; both admire repose as a principle of beauty . . .[25]

The modern reader who approaches Gautier's poetry is more apt to regard the poet as one who had primarily a painter's or a sculptor's vision for external objects and describes an almost purely external world. However, this is not altogether correct and is not what his contemporaries saw in him, nor does it agree with the conclusions of a more recent Dutch critic, Velthuis, who made a study of Gautier's mysticism. Like Lamartine and Hugo, Gautier expresses his belief in the animism of all natural phenomena, for example, in the poem "Affinités secrètes." Here Gautier states that every object as well as every being is animated by a universal soul and that at the time of death or disintegration all goes

> . . . into the profound melting pot
> To enlarge the universal paste
> Made of the forms which God melts.[26]

In "La Nature chez elle" Gautier attributes a mysterious life to trees and plants; in "Thébiade" he expresses his desire to be absorbed by the *Néant*. On the subject of Gautier's belief in metempsychosis, Velthuis remarks: "it is astonishing how Gautier, an enlightened artist of the XIXth century, could have such a resolute belief in occult powers."[27] But it was precisely this quality his contemporaries admired in him. Baudelaire praises in *L'Art romantique* Gautier's astounding capacity to perceive "correspondences":

> If one reflects that to this marvelous faculty Gautier unites an immense innate intelligence of *correspondence* and of universal symbolism, this collection of every metaphor, one will understand that he can, without ceasing, without fatigue as well as without error, define the mysterious attitude which the objects of creation hold before the view of man.[28]

This inclusion of Leconte de Lisle's name among the seers, although it would scarcely have pleased that master of the Parnassians, is highly significant. Rimbaud was not so uninitiated in literary matters as to have been unaware that Leconte de Lisle held more tenaciously than any of the other Parnassians to the doctrine of art for art's sake; he was the arch enemy of Romanticists like Hugo who expounded their philosophic ideas openly in their poetry, not to mention the contempt which he felt for the socialists who had popularized the idea of the poet as seer. If this was not an error or oversight on the part of Rimbaud, why does he list as a seer poet one who so openly attacked others who held the idea of the poet as seer and who would so obviously have disagreed with such an esthetic? He does this because the process of voyance as he conceives it, and as the analysis of the second and third topics of the *Voyant* letters will reveal, is only partially intuitive; it includes a rational and "objective" evaluation of the discoveries of the unconscious. Aware that his method would be a synthesis of certain aspects of Romanticism with the Parnassian ideal of objectivity, Rimbaud did not hesitate to include Leconte de Lisle in his list of seers. Although it is true — as many modern critics such as Maurice Souriau and Joseph Vianey have pointed out — that Leconte de Lisle's poetry was not as completely "pure" of all ideas as his contemporaries considered it, on the whole it is not primarily his own philosophy or even that of his age which he attempts to convey, but rather the ideologies of past civilizations. These he hoped to recreate poetically by means of numerous pictorial details and with the precision of an archaeologist. Rimbaud, young though he was, shared with Leconte de Lisle the savant's passion for facts. One of the latter's works which very probably came to Rimbaud's attention was the long poem, "Quain" ("Cain"), which appeared in the 1869 *Parnasse contemporain,* the issue in which Rimbaud had hoped to publish his "Soleil et chair." Leconte de Lisle's poem, which depicts the life of a Biblical man at the time of the Flood, records the prophecy of Thogorma the Seer, who predicts that a day will come when Yahveh the hunter will tell man to adore him; but man will refuse, having found the knowledge and mastery of the universe which makes him free.[29]

Théodore de Banville was perhaps the most overrated poet of his day: Gautier praises him in *Souvenirs romantiques;* Baudelaire in *L'Art romantique;* Mallarmé compares him with Orpheus and Heine in *Divagations;* and Rimbaud lists him as a seer. Baudelaire describes eloquently his own personal reactions to the genial writer of *funambulesque* poetry, and for those who are acquainted with Sartre's essay on Baudelaire the passage will have additional significance:

> But Théodore de Banville refuses to stoop to the morass of blood, to these abysses of mud. His art, like that of the ancients . . . expresses only what is beautiful, joyous, noble, great, rhythmic. Thus in his works you do not hear the dissonances, the discords of the music of the witches Sabbath. . . . His poetry is not only a regret, a nostalgia, it is itself a voluntary return to the state of Paradise.[30]

In praise of Banville's lyricism Baudelaire writes:

> There is truly a lyric manner of perceiving. The most deformed men, those to whom fortune gives the least leisure, have sometimes known this sort of impression, so rich that the soul is almost illuminated by it, so vivid that it is almost exalted by it. The whole interior being, in these marvelous instants, soars into the air from too much lightness and dilation, as if to attain a higher region.[31]

In regard to what might seem to a modern reader to be an artificial use of mythology in Banville, Baudelaire and his generation considered that

> Mythology is a dictionary of living hieroglyphics, hieroglyphics known by the whole world. Here the landscape is reclothed, like the faces with a hyperbolic magic; it becomes scenery. Woman is not only a being of supreme beauty comparable to that of Eve or Venus . . . but it becomes necessary to endow Woman with that kind of beauty such as the mind can only conceive as existing in a superior world.[32]

The first letter (May 1870) which we possess of Rimbaud's correspondence was addressed to Banville, whom Rimbaud asked to publish his "Soleil et chair." The poem was never published by *Parnasse contemporain* which Banville edited, but poems of much less excellence appeared, whose authors were better known. Two months after he had praised Banville in his letter to Demeny, Rimbaud, undoubtedly annoyed by the rejection of his poem, wrote a pastiche of Théodore de Banville and of Parnassian poetry in general, in the poem "Ce qu'on dit au poète à propos de fleurs." But more was involved in Rimbaud's attack on *Parnasse* than a mere personal grudge: the esthetic doctrine he had formulated gave him the self-confidence which he had previously lacked and an awareness that he was now a poet in his own right and therefore justified in attacking others with whose methods he disagreed.

"But since to inspect the invisible and to hear the unheard is something other than to recapture the spirit of dead things, Baudelaire is the first *seer,* the king of poets, a real God." This sentence from the Demeny letter indicates that the process of voyance as Rimbaud conceived it goes beyond what Leconte de Lisle and the Parnassians were able to do, namely, "recapture the spirit of dead things." Voyance was even more than supranormal vision, it also included supranormal hearing, or clairaudience. How precisely and succinctly Rimbaud seized the essential of Leconte de Lisle's poetic aim and at the same time accurately gave first place to Baudelaire! His only reproach for the first seer was his failure to seek new forms to express his new discoveries; the freeing of poetry from its conventional forms and the invention of free verse became the signal contribution of Rimbaud to modern French poetry.

Although Baudelaire shared many of the esthetic ideas of Leconte de Lisle and Gautier — the doctrine of art for art's sake, a belief in the aristocracy of poetry and the poet, a scorn for what he considered the sentimentality and shoddy craftsmanship of the Romantics — his esthetic differed from theirs in at least two fundamental respects. First, he did not adhere to the Parnassian ideal that poetry should be impersonal or "*impassible.*" Instead of the ideal of Platonic beauty in the abstract, beauty as Baudelaire conceives it has two aspects, the absolute and the relative or temporal; it is personal as well as impersonal. Second, in contrast to Gautier and Leconte de Lisle, Baudelaire does not engage in poetic description for its own sake — as the reader often has the impression that the former two poets do — for he holds that it is not the function of the artist to copy nature, whether the world around him or that of past civilizations, but to interpret and decipher his world in luminous metaphors. In a world of hieroglyphics, the poet deciphers and interprets the mysteries; his role is that of priest in the temple of Nature. In *Souvenirs romantiques,* Gautier points out this quality in Baudelaire's art and calls him a *voyant* in the following passage:

> He possesses also the gift of *correspondence,* to employ the same mystic expression, that is to say he knows how to discover, by a secret intuition, rapports invisible to others and how to unite thus through unexpected analogies what only the *voyant* can seize, objects which are the most far-removed and the most opposite in appearance. *Every true poet is endowed with this quality, more or less developed, which is the very essence of art.* [The words "correspondence" and "voyant" are italicized by Gautier.][33]

When the symbols have at last been penetrated and deciphered, the poet then achieves an understanding of correspondence and of universal analogy, or the ability to grasp the spiritual meaning and to perceive the subtle rapports between this world and the next. Such was the true function of the seer poet as Baudelaire conceived it. In *L'Art romantique* he expresses his expectation to be able by means of this vision to penetrate the mystery of death itself:

> It is this admirable, this immortal instinct of the Beautiful which makes us consider the earth and its spectacles as a glimpse, as a *correspondence* with Heaven. The insatiable thirst for all which is beyond and which veils life, is the most living proof of our immortality. *It is both by means of poetry and through poetry that the soul foresees the splendors beyond the tomb.* [The word "correspondence" is italicized by Baudelaire.][34]

The last lines of this passage clearly reveal the esthetic contradiction which was pointed out in Chapter 1: Baudelaire states repeatedly his belief in art as an end in itself, yet in this passage and in many others he indicates that poetry for him is a *means* of penetrating the unknown. He thought he had discovered in hashish the key to unlock the world of spirit, whereas in fact he had found the doorway into another world, important in its own right — that of the unconscious.

A Proposal for a New Objective Poetry Based upon a Different Conception of the Ego

While the discussion of the four ages of poetry shows Rimbaud to have had one foot in Romanticism, this topic of the *Voyant* letters will show him also to have had the other foot deeply in *Parnasse.* Although he admired the Romantics for having sometimes been seers, he execrated them in true Parnassian fashion for their "subjective" poetry, egotism, and excessive sentimentality. In the letter to Izambard, also interested in writing poetry, Rimbaud says:

> Your subjective poetry will always be horribly insipid. Some day, I hope — many others hope the same thing — to see in your principles objective poetry. I shall see it more sincerely than you would!

In another passage from this letter he writes: "At bottom you see in your principle only subjective poetry"; and in the Demeny letter, referring to the Romantics, he writes: "So many egotists proclaim themselves to be authors."

The ideal of "objective" as opposed to "subjective" poetry was one of the fundamental tenets of two leading Parnassians — Leconte de Lisle, who expounded this view at length in his *Préface des Poèmes Antiques,* and Sully-Prudhomme, in his Preface to the translation of the *De Rerum Natura* (1869), the invocation to which Jules Mouquet has shown to have been plagiarized by Rimbaud. Due partly to a natural reaction against the excesses of Romanticism, but in a more positive sense to the dawn of a new scientific era, many Parnassians held that the best poetry would be produced if the poet viewed his work with the same detached objectivity as a scientist his experiment. Like the scientist, the poet should also be a savant, subordinating all personal sentiment to the objective truth which he seeks.

On the whole, the *Voyant* letters contain too many of the ideas expressed in the *Préface des Poèmes Antiques* for mere coincidence. In addition to his announcement of the ideal of "objective" poetry which will remain "far from the world of action" and in which "personal emotions have left only a small trace," Leconte de Lisle's Preface contains many other points which appear in the *Voyant* letters: the idea that the poet is the guide of humanity, that poetry fell into a state of decadence and barbarity after the Age of Greece, that the poetry of the future will again achieve the lost harmony of the Grecian Age. Furthermore, Leconte de Lisle also attacks the Romantics for their sentimentality.

In his attack on the Romantics, Leconte de Lisle states that, as in all ages of literary decadence, the language has been reduced to petty personal impressions, such as was the case in the early part of his century: "The personal theme and its too often repeated variations have exhausted the attention; indifference has followed deservedly . . . it is indispensable to abandon as quickly as possible this narrow and banal way."[35] Addressing the poets of his age, he tells them that they are no longer the instructors of human souls, that they have in fact ceased to be heard because their pupils know instinctively more than they who express only "sterile complaints" and their own inanity. Such poetry can no longer inspire either heroic actions or social virtues because the sacred language, as in all ages of literary decadence, has become the slave of individual tastes and caprice. Such an excess of personal emotion is not possible in so sophisticated an age, he reasons, and a new generation of poets has begun to renew art at its source and rediscover its lost Harmony (Cf. Rimbaud's idea that the new poetry would achieve a harmony similar to that of the Age of Greece). This, Leconte de Lisle indicates, can come about through a union of art with science in an effort to produce a more erudite poetry: "art and science, separated for a long time as a result of the divergent efforts of intelligence, must therefore tend towards uniting closely with each other, if not towards becoming confused with each other." The great literature of the past – the Mahabharata, the Bible and Greek tragedy – did not indulge in personal sentimentality, but was philosophic and impersonal: "for every true and high poetry actually contains a philosophy – whatever it may be – aspiration, hope, faith, certitude or renunciation, deliberate and ultimate to the sentiment of our identity, which survives terrestrial existence."[36] Finally, Leconte de Lisle predicts that perhaps in a century or two "poetry will become the inspired and immediate word of the human soul" (Cf. the Demeny letter).

A lengthy philosophical discussion of what is meant by the subjective (as opposed to the objective) manner of thinking may be found in Sully-Prudhomme's Preface to his translation of the *De Rerum Natura.* It is probable that Rimbaud read this Preface, since he saw fit to plagiarize the translation. But a closer examination of its contents will also reveal that it contains the germ of Rimbaud's famous line, "Je est un autre," over which so much explanatory ink has been made to flow. Sully-Prudhomme states the distinction between the subjective and the objective in these words: "But today reflection has caused us to analyze our sensations in their very essence, and teaches us to separate what in the sensation is ourselves, the *subjective,* from what the exterior phenomena expresses by which we are impressed, the *objective.*"[37] Using arguments unmistakably taken from Schelling's philosophy of identity in his *System of Transcendental Idealism* (1800), Sully-Prudhomme attempts to resolve the quarrel which lasted a century between the Materialists and the Spiritualists (to which reference was made in Chapter 3 in the section on Balzac). The reason for this quarrel, Sully-Prudhomme explains, is that there are two kinds of thought and therefore two kinds of knowledge. First, there is perceptual or spontaneous knowledge which we receive from direct contact with the material world. Second, there is reflective knowledge (Kant's conceptual knowledge) which weighs and discriminates between the perception and matter as such. However, just as the apprehension of the external by the individual is never entirely objective but always a construct of consciousness (as Kant points out), so the ego is never entirely subject but is created by the "otherness" of the universe. The latter part of this statement forms the basis of Schelling's point of divergence from Kant and Fichte and the central idea of his philosophy, which he defines as "the constant objectivation of the subjective." Schelling, objecting to the Kant-Fichte thesis that the phenomenal world is the product of the subjective consciousness, maintains that it is not correct to say that the ego produces the nonego without also agreeing to its converse: that the nonego also produces the ego. Just as there is no object without a subject, so there can be no subject without an object; it was therefore an error on the part of Fichte to neglect the material aspect of reality. Since the ego originates through its knowledge of itself, it is therefore a knowledge which creates itself. Such intellectual intuition is the whole aim of transcendental philosophy, Schelling held: to transform into its own object that which would otherwise be no object; to produce and to perceive at the same time what is being produced in such a way that the producing and perceiving are in fact absolutely one.[38]

The ego as thinking subject must be capable of regarding itself as object, and this part of the identity philosophy Sully-Prudhomme states quite clearly in his Preface: "The being of the ego is for the mind which studies it an unknown object with the same claim as exterior things." A longer passage bears a close resemblance to the *Voyant* letters:

> Every man pronounces "I" spontaneously, as soon as he feels some interest in distinguishing himself from other beings, but few men are capable of descending into themselves to consider this ego and to seek to make of it an idea. Reflexive consciousness does not limit itself to feeling the ego; it thinks it (*elle le pense*).[39]

This last sentence is quite probably what Rimbaud had in mind when he said to Izambard: "It is false to say 'I think.' One should say 'I am thought' (*on me pense*)." Or, as the modern Latin American poet Jorge Guillén says: "Reality invents me, I am its legend!"

The world of phenomena is not so external to us as we imagine it to be; Sully-Prudhomme continues: "If the very being of exterior things is not absolutely strange and unknown to us, it is precisely because it communicates with ours." The reverse of this is also true: "in order to know, man must communicate with the object, that is to say . . . he must participate in its nature; he knows it only to the extent to which he participates in its nature."[40] Thus in the process of self-reflexiveness, when the ego becomes aware of itself as an object, subject and object become identical, and then in the true Rimbaldian sense, "*Je est un autre.*" This elusive sentence which has baffled critics for so long becomes clear only when the young poet's ideas are viewed in the light of the thought of his times; detached from this, it is obscure.

Rimbaud uses four metaphors to illustrate the means by which the new creative process will replace the subjective poetry of the Romantics with a new "objective" poetry. Two of these metaphors — the comparison of the poet with the violin and the clarion — emphasize the new passive role which the ego must take in the creative process. The other two — the blossoming of a flower and the musician's stroke of his bow — indicate only a slightly more active role for the ego in the creative process. Let us examine the first two metaphors as they are stated in both letters:

> So much the worse for the wood which finds itself a violin and insolently defies the unconscious ones who split hairs over matters of which they are entirely ignorant. (Izambard letter)
> If the brass wakens as a clarion, that is not its fault. (Demeny letter).

Just as the materials out of which the instruments were made (the wood and the brass) did not choose to become musical instruments but were chosen by an outside agency, so a man cannot choose to make himself a poet; this depends upon something more than the material out of which he is made. In both passages the important idea, however, is that the wood "discovers" or "finds" itself to be a violin, and the brass likewise "wakens" to the fact that it is a clarion. In other words, the poet must first realize himself as an *instrument* through which music may be produced by the otherness which he calls the "Universal Intelligence."

The other two metaphors are more original and poetic in their expression. In the first, the role of the ego-as-subject is not altogether passive as in the case of the first two metaphors. It consists in the passive activity of watching and listening and proceeds to the growth and burgeoning, or the really vital creative process which takes place in the depths of consciousness and not on the surface: "I am present at the blossoming (*éclosion*) of my thought: I look at it, listen to it . . ." In terms of the identity philosophy, the poet is regarding his thought as if it were a concrete object. In the last metaphor, the ego-as-subject takes a still more active part: "I give a stroke of the bow: the symphony makes a stir in the depths and comes with a bound on the scene." The most active role which the artist or musician can take in this part of the creative process is at best only a mechanical gesture on the surface; again Rimbaud repeats the idea that the real music must come spontaneously from beneath. These metaphors describe the creative process in its passive aspect, that is, when the ego looks upon itself as an object. But the role of the ego also has an active aspect – which will be discussed under the next topic. Such, then, is the new attitude toward the ego advocated by Rimbaud in opposition to that of the Romantics. It is an idea which comes through Sully-Prudhomme from Schelling, but it nonetheless becomes original when Rimbaud gives it concrete poetic form.

Following Sully-Prudhomme's Preface still further in comparison with the Demeny letter, the former states that the ego conceived as object will be studied like any other unknown phenomenon: "The being of the ego is for the mind which studies it an unknown object with the same claim as exterior things." Similarly, Rimbaud advocated self-study in the following passage from the Demeny letter:

> The first study for the man who wants to be a poet is knowledge of himself, completely. He searches his soul, he inspects it, he tries it, he learns it. That seems simple: in every brain a natural development is accomplished; so many egotists proclaim themselves to be authors; there are many others who attribute to themselves their intellectual progress.

This implies more than one understands by the ancient Delphic oracle: "Know thyself!" The kind of cultivation Rimbaud advocates here means more than the ordinary self-development experienced in the process of reaching maturity. This cultivation will depend upon something which is outside as well as inside the poet – in this "otherness" in which his ego participates.

A further indication that Sully-Prudhomme was drawing upon Schelling's identity philosophy consists in the fact that he resolves the dualism of the ego-as-subject with the ego-as-object in the same manner as his German predecessor: by saying that both become identical in "le Grand Tout," Schelling's *Weltseele,* a Universal Intelligence including them both. There can therefore be no absolute dichotomy between mind and matter or Nature and Spirit, Schelling reasons and Sully-Prudhomme also maintains in his Preface, since these are only two aspects of the same thing. It is in this conception of the World-Soul that Schelling's philosophy is at once most original and at the same time reflects the influence of the theosophical thinkers of his time such as Baader and other Romantic physicists mentioned in Chapter 2: Nature is not a pure mechanism, but an animated organism, the unconscious part of the Absolute Mind. Like the Kabbalists, Schelling posits a dualism within the nature of God and presents philosophical thought with its first dynamic conception of the deity in the modern era: Nature is that part of God which is not yet Spirit, but which is in the process of becoming Spirit; God is not therefore infinite, but subject to finite limitations in the process of achieving perfection.

For Hegel, the substance of history itself consists in the gradual unfolding of this universal mind (*Weltgeist*), or "the development of Spirit in Time."[41] While notable historical characters such as Alexander the Great or Caesar have ostensibly pursued their own egoistic desires for personal power and fame, they have at the same time been the unsuspecting instruments of the *Weltgeist.* Hegel says in *The Philosophy of History*:

> It was not, then his [Caesar's] private gain merely, but an unconscious impulse, that occasioned the accomplishment of that for which the time was ripe . . . such individuals had no consciousness of the general Idea they were unfolding, while prosecuting those aims of theirs; on the contrary, they were practical, political men. But at the same time they were thinking men, who had an insight into the requirements of the time—*what was ripe for development.* This was the very truth for their age, for their world. . . . It was theirs to know this nascent principle; the necessary, directly sequent step in progress, which their world was to take.[42]

Put into poetic terms by Rimbaud in the *Voyant* letters is a similar conception:

> The Universal Intelligence has always scattered its ideas naturally; men picked up a part of these fruits of the brain: they acted by, they wrote books from them: in such a way went the advance, without men straining, not being yet awakened, or yet in the fullness of the great dream! [Demeny letter.]

If Rimbaud acquired his knowledge of Schelling's identity philosophy through Sully-Prudhomme's Preface, which seems highly probable, it is also possible that he may have discovered from some other secondary source the Hegelian idea of the Universal Intelligence unfolding itself in history. The most likely possibility is one from his native Ardennes – Hippolyte Taine, who knew Hegel from German texts. In his detailed study of the influence of Hegel on Taine, D. D. Rosca concludes that all the important esthetic ideas held by Taine came to him from Hegel, from the early theories expressed in *La Fontaine et ses fables* (1853) and *Histoire de la littérature anglaise* (1863) to the several volumes on the history of art written between 1865 and 1869 and later included in *La Philosophie de l'art* (1882).[43] Among the Hegelian ideas to be found in Taine's work is the one in question here, namely, that the artist or the writer is the representative and interpreter of the century and the nation in which he lives: "the artist discerns and expresses better than anyone the salient and durable traits of the world which surrounds him,"[44] he says in *Histoire de la littérature anglaise.* Because this is true, Taine held that

> A great poem, a fine novel, the confessions of a superior man are more instructive than a pile of historians and histories; I would give fifty volumes of charters and a hundred volumes of diplomatic documents in exchange for the memoirs of Cellini, the letters of Saint Paul, the debates of Luther or the comedies of Aristophanes. . . . It is therefore chiefly through the study of the literary figures that one can construct the spiritual history and arrive at the knowledge of psychological laws upon which events depend.[45]

Like Hegel, Taine believed in Intelligence or the Idea as a generative principle in the universe and, in this respect as well as in many others which Rosca points out, Taine was far more Hegelian than positivist. In the first chapter of *Les Philosophes classiques,* Taine attributes all particular ideas to this universal Idea or Intelligence and says: "Every form, every change, every movement is one of its acts."[46]

THE ROLE OF THE POET AS SEER

We have now arrived at the heart of Rimbaud's esthetic doctrine, and also to that part of his thought which is most intimately linked with the ancient mysteries and with the occult current of Romanticism. Two well-known myths are invoked by the poet which relate this part of the Demeny letter with the ideas presented at the beginning of Chapter 1: they are the myths of Prometheus and Orpheus, the two great seekers after the unknown, who embodied more than any others the aspirations of the nineteenth century — as Sisyphus (the man condemned to endless and meaningless toil) and Orestes (the hero driven to madness by conflicting loyalties) seem to represent the spirit of the twentieth century. Although Rimbaud does not refer to Prometheus and Orpheus by name, his allusions to them are unmistakable in the lines: "The poet is therefore really a stealer of fire" and "He [the poet] is in charge of humanity, even of the animals." Then, as if to strengthen his own resolve as well as to emphasize the importance of his purpose, he says: "I say that one must be a seer, make oneself a seer"; in the second allusion to the Promethean myth he calls the seer "the great criminal, the great accursed one — and the supreme Savant." In examining more closely the finer points of these familiar myths, the meaning of this last statement becomes clear.

Prometheus and Orpheus represented more to Rimbaud than two suffering heroes of Romanticism; both were prototypes of the seer chosen by the poet as his ideal. Prometheus, by his ascent into heaven, and Orpheus, by his descent into hell, attempted to wrest for mankind the secrets of existence; the one braved the blinding light of heaven, the other the impenetrable darkness and uncanny terrors of the underworld. Prometheus, whose name means "foreknowledge," and who, according to legend escaped destruction by Zeus (for his crime of stealing fire and giving it to mortals) only because he knew by his power of prophetic vision the one who was destined to overthrow Zeus. As a seer, therefore, Prometheus possessed the most profound secrets of heaven, and not even Zeus could force the Titan to disclose his information. Orpheus, on the other hand, also possessed supranormal knowledge, but in a different realm. Since Orpheus, according to one legend, was the son of Apollo and the muse Calliope, it would seem likely that it is he with whom Rimbaud identifies himself a second time when he refers to himself and Verlaine as "fils du soleil" in the poem "Vagabonds." Court de Gébelin, Fabre d'Olivet and in particular Ballanche in his long poem *Orphée,* present Orpheus as the poet-priest, initiated into the mysteries of antiquity. Court de Gébelin even worked out the strange etymology that *Orphée* meant *"fils d'Hor"* (son of Horus) or *"fils du soleil."*[47] In any event, Orpheus was believed to be the incarnation of the god Dionysus and the founder of the Dionysian mysteries to which Christian doctrine bears such a striking resemblance in its ideas of original sin, incarnation, virgin birth, redemption, and immortality. Aristophanes in *The Frogs* describes Orpheus as a missionary of civilization; Cicero praises the humanizing effects of the Dionysian mysteries upon the ancient world. Indeed, what could be a more fitting origin of Greek culture than that their finest artist became a priest and introduced this greatest of all ancient peoples into the mysteries?

The allusions to these two myths in connection with the phenomenon of voyance suggests that the role of the poet as seer, as Rimbaud conceived it, has two aspects — an active and a passive. In his passive role, the seer-poet listens to the dictates of the unconscious and descends like Orpheus into its depths, passing through the gates of ivory and of horn, of sleep and of death; in his active role, the poet like Prometheus penetrates the secrets of heaven and possesses the power of foreknowledge or prophetic vision. The latter represents symbolically the path of the mystic, while the former suggests the way of the *mage* used in the broadest sense, as Hugo does in his poem "Les Mages," to refer to all those scientists and artists who have increased human knowledge.

A definite connection existed between the Promethean myth and the secret societies of the eighteenth and nineteenth centuries. Eliphas Lévi divides the occult thought of the societies of his times into two main branches — the Eastern, extending from Zoroaster to Manes, the founder of the powerful Manichean sect of the third century A.D., and the Western, extending from Orpheus to Apollonius of Tyana, the leader of the Gnostics.[48] Not only was fire the material symbol of the universal light and the principle of goodness among the Persian Magi and the Manicheans, it was also important in the Egyptian initiation rites in which Osiris was the personification of the sun. Expounding upon the Promethean myth, Eliphas Lévi writes: "The great magic secret is therefore . . . the sacred fire stolen by Prometheus." Lévi calls this fire "astral light" and "the world's soul" in two other passages, explaining that as the world is lighted by the sun so man is animated by spiritual astral light. Second sight, Lévi holds, is related to astral light in the following way:

> Second sight is the faculty of seeing in astral light. This sight is natural like first sight or the ordinary sight of the senses. Somnambulists and ecstatics enjoy naturally second sight; but this sight is more lucid when abstraction is complete. Abstraction is produced . . . by a superabundance of light . . . which renders the nervous instrument more inert.[49]

For Lévi, there is no such thing as an "invisible world," strictly speaking, but only different degrees of perfection in the organ of sight.

What we call imagination is also the capacity to apprehend in astral light:

> Thus for the sage to imagine is to see . . . the imagination of the adept is diaphanous while that of the vulgar is opaque . . . Men of genius differ from simple seers [voyants] by the faculty which they possess of causing other men to feel what they themselves see, and to cause them to believe by enthusiasm and sympathy.[50]

This is the great force which the *mage* must control, for it is the source of his power as well as the "universal mirror of visions":

> there exists a mixed agent, a natural and divine, corporeal and spiritual agent, a plastic universal mediator, a common receptacle of vibrations. . . . By means of this force all nervous systems secretly communicate together; from this are born sympathy and antipathy; from it come dreams; by means of it the phenomena of second sight and extranatural vision are produced . . .[51]

In possession of the Promethean fire or "astral light," the seer is able to fulfill his Orphic role which Lévi describes as "sovereign pontiff of nature" and "thaumaturge of earth."[52] In this capacity the seer-poet, like his famous predecessor, may also exert a magic power and domination over animals:

> Man becomes king of animals only by controlling them or by taming them; otherwise he would be the victim or the slave. Animals are the symbols of our passions; they are the instinctive forces of nature.[53]

A feeling of mystery toward the animal world which pervades the poetry of Hugo and Baudelaire in particular and also that of the anti-Romantic Leconte de Lisle may be traced directly to the occult current of Romanticism. Gautier, for example, remarking upon Baudelaire's fondness for cats, says that these animals have "a nocturnal side, mysterious and Kabbalistic," reminding one of witches, alchemy, and necromancy.[54]

But what exactly, according to Lévi, does the seer perceive in the mirror of astral light? A reflection of the so-called invisible world which he is able to interpret and communicate to others only to the extent to which he understands the analogy between it and the visible world: "Analogy is the key to all the secrets of nature."[55] Quoting Court de Gébelin, Lévi maintains in another passage that the tarot cards contain the secret of universal analogy or correspondence, and that the Rosicrucians and Martinists knew these secret symbols, which among the ancients also were revealed only to the initiated. Now the twenty-two tarot cards corresponded to the twenty-two letters of the

Hebrew alphabet, each of which had a numerical and symbolic equivalent.[56] In addition to this, each represented a stage in the alchemical process, a correspondence with the signs of the Zodiac and with the symbolism of magic, all of which were considered related branches of knowledge which it was the duty of the *mage* to understand and to master. A chart compiled from several writers — Lévi, Karppe, Serouya, and various encyclopedias — indicates some of these correspondences.[57] The symbolic meaning of the numbers and letters is particularly interesting in the light of recent works of Simone Weil on the subject of the intuitions which the pre-Christian world had of Christianity.

It is often typical of occult writers to describe in vivid detail the marvels of their experiences and then leave the reader questioning the most essential point, namely, how such powers may be acquired. In this respect, Eliphas Lévi is no exception, since he also is silent on this subject. But for Rimbaud, the method or technique to be used by the seer was all-important, and it was in the pages of Baudelaire's *Paradis artificiels* that he found it. Rimbaud's description of his method as "a long calculated disordering of all the senses" accurately summarizes the experience which Baudelaire relates. In the *Paradis artificiels,* the effects of hashish are also described as a distortion of the senses: "in your whole being you feel a stupor and a perplexing stupefaction. Your eyes become enlarged; they are so to speak pulled in all directions by an implacable ecstasy."[58] And in another passage:

> But what is more important, I believe, for the spiritual man, is to know the action of the poison on the spiritual part of man, that is to say, the enlargement, the deformation and the exaggeration of his habitual feelings and of his moral perceptions, which present in such a case, in an exceptional atmosphere, a true phenomenon of refraction.[59]

Rimbaud then compares his method of self-distortion with the fiendish work of the *comprachicos* (a Spanish word meaning "child buyers"): "But what is required to make the soul monstrous on the order of the *comprachicos.* What! Imagine a man planting warts on his face and cultivating them" (Demeny letter).

This is a reference to an association of seventeenth-century outlaws in Spain and England, who were discussed at length by Victor Hugo in *L'Homme qui rit* (1869). They bought and sold children, whom they distorted physically for the purpose of amusing audiences in the streets. Such a one was Gwynplaine, the hero of *L'Homme qui rit.*

This comparison and the remarks which follow indicate that for Rimbaud the taking of hashish was a form of inverted asceticism. The poison-imbibing poet is described as a kind of martyr in the cause of developing the new poetry, while the poet himself, far from enjoying his plunge into evil, refers to it as "ineffable torture" and calls the suffering "enormous." Describing his first experience with the drug in the poem "Matinée d'ivresse," he calls it "Little drunken vigil, holy [sainte]" and adds that he has "faith in the poison."[60] It makes no difference if the poison kills the poet or drives him mad, he reasons in the Demeny letter, for if he perishes, others will come after him. To break down the domination of the conscious ego in order to discover a new domain is the obvious purpose of the drug. It will be the fertilizer for new flowers of poetry which will spring from a new type of consciousness.

Although the indebtedness of Rimbaud to Baudelaire is generally acknowledged by critics, many of the specific details of this debt need to be pointed out, such as, for example, the striking parallels between Rimbaud's "Matinée d'ivresse," and Baudelaire's *Paradis artificiels.* A textual analysis of this poem furnishes excellent clues to the meaning of other more obscure poems in *Les Illuminations.*

MORNING OF DRUNKENNESS

O my Good! O my Beautiful! Atrocious boasting [*fanfare*] in which I never falter. Rack of enchantments! Hurrah for the unbelievable work and for the marvelous body, for the first time! It began with the laughter of children; with their laughter it will end. This poison will remain in all our veins even when, the boasts shifting, we shall be returned to the old inharmony. O now let us who are so worthy of these tortures fervently claim that superhuman promise made to our body and soul created: that promise, that madness! Elegance, science, violence! They have promised us to bury in darkness the tree of good and evil, to take away tyrannic honesty so that we may bring forth our very pure love. It began with a certain disgust – and it ends – unable to seize this eternity on the spot – it ends with a riot of perfumes.

Laughter of children, discretion of slaves, austerity of virgins, horror of faces and objects here, holy be all of you in the memory of this vigil. It began with every sort of boorishness; lo, it ends with angels of flame and ice!

Little drunken vigil, holy, if only because of the mask which you have bestowed upon us. We swear by you, method! We do not forget that yesterday you glorified each one of our ages. We have faith in the poison. We know how to give our entire life every day. Behold the time of the Assassins.[61]

As Baudelaire, in the first pages of the second part of *Les Paradis artificiels* addresses opium: "O just, subtile and powerful opium!"[62] so Rimbaud begins "Matinée d'ivresse" with an apostrophe to the drug. A detailed analysis of the text follows.

Atrocious boasting in which I never falter! According to Baudelaire, novices waiting for the first effects of the drug to begin often indulge in boasting and buffoonery. Rimbaud uses the word "*fanfares*"; Baudelaire, "*fanfaronnades*":

> Most of the time novices, at their first initiation, complain of the slowness of the effects. They are awaiting them with anxiety, and since that does not pass quickly enough for their taste, they make boasts [*fanfaronnades*] of their incredulity which delight very much those who know . . . the manner in which hashish behaves.[63]

Rack of enchantments is a poetic paradox meaning the "torture of the marvelous" ("chevalet" being an ancient instrument of torture). This is a direct reference to Baudelaire's chapter, "Tortures de l'Opium," while the word "*féerique*" is the exact word used in *Les Paradis artificiels* to describe the visions produced by hashish. In this connection, it should be added that Baudelaire also calls the visions a "*fantasmagorie*," while Rimbaud, recalling these experiences later in the *Saison*, says: "I am master of fantasmagories."[64]

Hurrah for the unbelievable work and for the marvelous body, for the first time! This line expresses the poet's delight that his body was able to withstand the effects of the drug on the occasion of his first attempt.

It began in the midst of the laughter of children, with their laughter it will end, refers to the initial effects of hashish as Baudelaire described them in the following passages:

> At first a certain hilarity, ridiculous and irresistible takes possession of you. . . . This gaiety is unbearable to you; but it is useless to resist. . . . You laugh at your stupidity and at your folly; your comrades laugh in your face, and you bear them no grudge because good will is beginning to be manifest.
> This foolishness and these bursts of laughter which resemble explosions, appear like real madness, or at least like the silliness of a maniac, to every man who is not in the same state as you.[65]

This poison will remain in all our veins even when, the boasts shifting, we shall be returned to the old inharmony. The debilitating and enslaving effects of hashish, which last long after the immediate effects have passed, are objectively presented by Baudelaire: "The man who has recourse to a poison in order to think, will soon be unable to think without poison."[66] Rimbaud's words, "the old inharmony," refer to the state of everyday living, which is inharmonious by contrast with the state of ultimate beatitude achieved under the drug and described by Baudelaire in these lines:

> The third phase . . . is something indescribable. It is what Orientals call *Kief*; it is absolute happiness. It is no longer something turbulent and tumultuous. It is a calm and immobile beatitude. All philosophic problems are solved. All arduous questions against which theologians battle, and which cause the despair of reasoning humanity, are limpid and clear. Every contradiction has become unity. Man has exceeded God![67]

It is this experience of complete happiness and beatitude which Baudelaire calls *"cet état d'ivresse,"* and from which Rimbaud takes the title of his poem, "Matinée d'ivresse." This climax of happiness achieved under hashish doubtless throws some light upon one of Rimbaud's later statements in *Une Saison en enfer*: "happiness was my fatality."[68] (The modern reader who may have read Aldous Huxley's book, *The Doors of Perception,* might conclude that the effects of hashish, though somewhat similar to those of mescalin, are doubtless more dramatic.)

O now let us who are so worthy of these tortures fervently claim that superhuman promise made to our body and soul created: that promise, that madness! Believing that his body has now proven itself worthy, the poet would like to redeem the "superhuman promise" which is, according to Baudelaire, the realization of himself as God. "I have become God,"[69] says Baudelaire. For this reason, he calls the promise a madness in the last few words of this passage.

Elegance, science, violence! They have promised to bury in darkness the tree of good and evil . . . so that we may bring forth our very pure love. In the first three words here, Rimbaud has summarized the first phases of the effects of the drug as Baudelaire described it. The word "elegance" refers to Baudelaire's recommendation that hashish be taken in a leisurely fashion and, if possible, in favorable surroundings – "an apartment poetically decorated," Rimbaud suggests.[70] "Science" pertains to the exact details for the preparation of the drug, which Baudelaire gives in the chapter, "Qu'est-ce que le haschisch?" The word "violence" refers to the state directly preceding the climax described above, of which Baudelaire says: "The definitive crisis, determined by the digestion of the food, is in fact very *violent* . . . such a state would be unendurable if it lasted too long and if it did not give way to another state of drunkenness."[71] Finally, the burying of the tree of good and evil refers to the state of beatitude or *Kief* which Baudelaire described in the passage cited above. One reaches a state "beyond good and evil" or what Rimbaud calls a state of "pure love" and what Baudelaire describes as a state of "natural goodness":

> But the expansion of the benevolent sentiments caused by the opium is not an attack of fever; it is rather man primitively good and just restored and reintegrated into his natural state, detached from all the bitterness which had occasionally corrupted his noble temperament.[72]

It began with a certain disgust — and it ends . . . with a riot of perfumes. This line clearly refers to the experience of synesthesia, well known to readers of Baudelaire. It consists in a kind of hallucination or acuity of the senses in which sound, color, and perfumes may be perceived as one and is described at length by Baudelaire[73] in more than one passage. What may be seen in this is the origin of Rimbaud's famous sonnet, "Voyelles," in which he claims to have discovered the color of vowels and also an explanation of that baffling line in the *Saison*: "I was damned by the rainbow."

Laughter of children, discretion of slaves, austerity of virgins, horror of faces and objects here . . . it ends with angels of flame and ice! Here again Rimbaud summarizes in different words the stages of the drug, the "laughter of children" making a parallel with Baudelaire's description of the first stage as one of "childish gaiety." The "discretion of slaves" refers to Baudelaire's statement of the enslaving effects of the drug, while the "austerity of virgins" may be found in his statement that, in the state of *Kief,* the hashish taker believes himself to be "the most virtuous of all men."[74] The "horror of faces and objects" is felt by the poet as the drug begins to reach its climax, that is, objects in his physical environment become distorted: "Hallucinations begin. Exterior objects assume monstrous appearances. . . . Then they become deformed."[75] Physical sensations of extreme heat and cold as well as dryness of the throat were reported by Baudelaire:

> The throat closes up. . . . The palate becomes dried up by a thirst which it would be infinitely sweet to satisfy. A light coolness had already become manifest at the tips of my fingers; soon it was changed into a very keen coldness. . . . The coldness was still increasing . . . I considered myself like a statue carved from a single block of ice.[76]

Hunger and thirst accompanies these corporeal sensations, but thirst is the most persistent. The sensations of extreme coldness serve to explain Rimbaud's "angels of flame and ice." Since the physical sensations produced by the drug are similar for all persons, Rimbaud's descriptions resemble Baudelaire's to a certain extent, but the psychological effects and the ideas evoked differ widely from one individual to another: "Hashish reveals nothing to the individual except the individual himself," Baudelaire concludes.

The last paragraph of "Matinée d'ivresse," in which Rimbaud refers to this experience as "holy," indicates that his intention in taking hashish is an inverted form of asceticism. In the *Voyant* letters, as well as in this poem, he expresses his willingness to sacrifice himself, if need be, in order to make new poetic discoveries: "Ineffable torture in which he has need of all faith, of all superhuman strength, in which he becomes the great sick man, the great criminal . . . For he arrives at the Unknown!"[77] The meaning of the last line of "Matinée d'ivresse" is quite clear, since the word "assassin" refers etymologically to a Mohammedan secret society, the "Hashishin," whose members during the Crusades practiced secret murder under the influence of the drug. Rimbaud indicates that the time has come for him to avail himself of this ancient practice of drug taking and although it is not murder which he expects to practice, he nevertheless takes a vow to do violence to himself. Such was Rimbaud's drastic method of "arriving at the Unknown" – which explains why he tells Izambard in the shorter *Voyant* letter: "Now I am debauching myself as much as possible."

The Future of Poetry and the Poet

The first problem which the poet of the future must face is one of communication. For the *mage* as for the mystic, the chief difficulty is how to communicate his unfamiliar findings. He must "find a language" ("*trouver une langue*") to communicate accurately the impressions received from this new terrain of the psyche which he has entered by means of the drug. In short, the poet of the future will have the linguistic obligation of aiding in the discovery of a universal language: "The time of a universal language will come," Rimbaud predicts. His brief description of this mysterious language in the following passage suggests that it will be both extra-verbal and telepathic: "This language will be soul for the soul, summarizing everything: perfumes, sounds, colors, thought hooking thought and pulling" (Demeny letter). In the two sentences which precede this one, Rimbaud emphasizes the irrational nature of this language by saying that all attempts to think, (the word "think" is underscored by the poet) about the first letter of the alphabet of such a language would merely lead to folly. Thus the poet insists upon the instinctive nature of the language and its direct relation to the unconscious. His famous sonnet on the vowels doubtless represents his own first effort in the direction of the new poetic language. He elaborates upon this later in the *Saison* in this passage:

> I have discovered the color of vowels! . . . I have regulated the form and movement of each consonant, and with instinctive rhythms, I flattered myself for having invented a poetic word accessible . . . to all the senses. I reserved the translation. At first it was a study. I wrote silences, I wrote nights. I recorded the inexpressible. I fixed frenzies in their flight.[78]

This reference to a universal language which will be both instinctive and telepathic recalls the mystical Swedenborgian theory of language discussed in Chapter 2 and serves as a further indication that the *Voyant* letters were inspired by the current of Illuminist thought. It would be useful here to recapitulate a few of the salient ideas about this language as Swedenborg, and later Romantic writers, conceived it. The Swedish mystic believed in the existence of an archetypal language, innate in all men, but which most people could come into the possession of only after death. He described it as a soft harmonious language full of vowels, possessing a perfect correspondence between idea and word and telepathic in nature. In its written form, this language consisted in a series of numbers all of which possessed symbolic significance. This seems to be what Rimbaud meant when he said that the poetry of the future, written in the universal language, would be "full of Number and Harmony." This does not imply that Rimbaud read Swedenborg, although it is not impossible that he did. It is more likely that he read articles popularizing the ideas of the Swedish mystic, such as those that may be found by Hugh Doherty in *La Phalange* or the abridgment and commentary on Swedenborg by Daillant de Latouche which Balzac read.

The universal language was related to the idea of correspondence in this way: man before the fall made use of the universal language and enjoyed by means of it immediate revelation and communication with higher beings. After the fall, revelation took place by means of correspondence, and when, still later, men forgot the knowledge of correspondence, the Word was written. This written Word, which possessed an external meaning apparent to men and an internal or spiritual sense for purposes of communication with heaven, constituted man's chief bond with heaven. Swedenborg identifies the "internal sense of the word" and the universal language in his *Dictionary of Correspondences*.[79]

Inspired by Swedenborg, the idea of the universal language permeated German Romanticism, and although Herder refuted the theory of the divine origin of language, he still maintained that all modern languages "fell" from one perfect universal language or *Ursprache*. Fichte maintained that the *Ursprache* was hieroglyphic in nature, while Hamann and Novalis in the literary world were the most inspired by Swedenborgian linguistic mysticism. Hamann held that language had preceded both Reason and Revelation and that these had only come about through the medium of the Word; Novalis rhapsodized upon the mysterious and hieroglyphic "language of nature" and also upon the "internal meaning" of the Word. Novalis' disciples of Saïs, who had traveled so far to learn the language of nature

> felt themselves especially attracted by this sacred language which had been the bright link of these kinglike men of the past with supraterrestrial regions and their inhabitants. . . . The pronunciation of it was a marvelous chant, the irrestible accents of which penetrated to the heart of natural beings and analyzed them. Each one of these substantives seemed a proverb which expressed the soul of each one of these beings. These vibrations, by their creative virtue, awakened all the images of universal phenomena and one could indeed say that for them the life of the universe was an eternal dialogue with innumerable voices, for all power, all sorts of activity seemed to be miraculously united in their language.[80]

Novalis hoped to find the lost word which would be the key to all the mysteries of Nature and which would reunite Nature and Spirit as they had been in primitive times. This lost word, Novalis said, resumed all others, united body and soul, and the mere pronunciation of it gave one creative powers such as God had used in the beginning, when to say and to create were one.

This original and primitive language, according to Court de Gébelin, was composed of a small number of hieroglyphic characters, monosyllabic in form and copied directly from Nature. This rapport of words with Nature he considered to be the very basis of poetry and harmony.[81] Although no living language could be identified with this primitive language, its key has been preserved and handed down in the tarot cards.[82] Eliphas Lévi hailed this discovery of the tarot cards as the key to the wisdom of the ancient world and described this key which was lost for centuries and then recently discovered:

> Now this key which was believed lost for centuries has been re-found, and we have been able to open all the tombs of the ancient world, make the dead speak, see again in all their splendor the monuments of the past, understand the riddles of all the sphinxes and penetrate into all the sanctuaries. The use of this key among the ancients was permitted only to the high priests, and the secret of it was not even entrusted to the elite of the initiates. Now here is what this key was: It was a hieroglyphic and numerical alphabet expressing by characters and by numbers a series of universal and abstract ideas.[83]

Only Martinists and Rosicrucians possess and have kept intact the true tarot, Lévi insists. Lévi considered that his own unique contribution to the knowledge of numerical and letter symbolism was the meaning of the quartenary. The number four, corresponding to the Hebrew letter *Daleth,* represented the four seasons, the four points of the compass, and so the material universe with its pairs of opposites. The sacred Tetragrammaton, or the four consonants, JHVH, forming the incommunicable name of the deity and represented in the form of a cross, was a well-known symbol in the pre-Christian world. Identifying JHVH with the sacred words of the Dionysian bacchantes, IO EVOHE, Lévi says that both meant the same: *J*ed, *H*e, *V*au, *H*e.[84] The Kabbalistic tetragrammaton which these letters represented expresses the idea of God in humanity and humanity in God.

According to Kabbalistic legend, King Solomon possessed a signet ring on which the name of God, JHVH, was engraved, and by which Solomon was able to perform miracles. Arabic writers declare that Solomon received four jewels from four angels and set them in this ring so that he could control the four elements. On one occasion, Asmodeus obtained possession of the ring and threw it into the sea, thus depriving Solomon of his power until he discovered it again inside a fish. Eliphas Lévi says this about the ring: "Solomon's ring is all the knowledge and all the faith of the Magi resumed into one sign. It is the symbol of all the forces of heaven and earth. . . . It is the talisman of talismans. . . . Solomon's ring is all-powerful."[85]

Now Rimbaud makes a cryptic allusion to this ring in the *Saison* in a passage giving enough details to support this interpretation: "Do you want me to vanish, to dive after the *ring?* ["Ring" is underscored by Rimbaud, signifying that he meant a very particular ring]. Is that what is wanted? I will make gold, remedies."[86] The last sentence is obviously an allusion to a magic ring possessing the powers usually attributed to the philosopher's stone.

Gerard de Nerval similarly mentions his discovery of this hieroglyphic language and its alphabet while he was studying the Kabbala. He said that only by learning it could the poet acquire power in the world of spirits. Like Novalis, he too sought the lost word: "The magic hieroglyphic and mysterious alphabet reaches us only incomplete and falsified by time. . . . Let us find again the lost letter and the effaced sign; let us recompose the dissonant scale and we shall have power in the world of spirits."[87] In the alchemical as well as Kabbalistic legend there were accounts of a magic word which had been lost, and the rediscovery of which would bring about the final chemical marriage and the production of gold. Was this perhaps the word to which Rimbaud referred in "Alchimie du verbe" in the line quoted previously: "I flattered myself to have invented a poetic word accessible . . . to all the senses" (see note 78).

The last of Rimbaud's prophecies are concerned with the poet as a citizen and with his function in society. At this point the young poet clearly breaks with the Parnassian ideal of the poet in the ivory tower. "Poets will be citizens," he predicts, and more than this, they will participate actively in the march of humanity toward progress. They will accomplish this by defining the amount of the unknown "within the universal soul" which is allotted for their time. Rimbaud adds this bit of mysticism, in the midst of all the down-to-earth predictions about progress, meaning that the poet will serve the society of the future as a sort of divining rod, and that his role will be essentially the priestly one it was in ancient times. The new poetry will be more than the poetry of the past, that is, songs in praise of the noble deeds of heroes, "rhymed action." It will hold a place of importance in society: "*elle sera en avant,*" Rimbaud predicts. This prophecy cannot fail to cause the modern reader to reflect that, since Hugo's *Hernani,* the theater rather than poetry has traditionally held a position of avant-gardism in France. Exactly when Rimbaud expects this veritable Renaissance to take place involves the last of his prophecies about the future of poetry and shows definitely the influence of the socialist thinkers upon his creative imagination. The poets of the future will come, he says, "when the infinite servitude of woman will be broken, when she will live for herself and by herself; man . . . having given her her discharge, she will also be a poet! Woman will find the unknown! Will her world of ideas differ from ours?"

The poet as a leader of humanity, art which will have a social function, and the freedom of women were all familiar aims of the socialists, especially the Fourierists, who were discussed at some length in Chapter 3. It was noted there that these themes were developed in *Le Globe* in such statements as "Poets are seers who open the gates of the future" (Jan. 26, 1831) and "Art has a mission other than to amuse the imagination of the idle."

> Artists have for their tasks at every epoch in civilization to cultivate the sentiments necessary for the development of humanity. They are priests, the directors of souls, even more necessary than the government and the Church . . . They exercise a veritable sacerdotalism.[88]

Saint-Simonists used the theory of the poet as seer to combat the idea of an independent art or "art for art's sake," a phrase first coined by Victor Cousin, in *Du Vrai du beau et du bien* (1818). Ideas about the social mission of art were also repeated in *La Phalange* by the Fourierists during the 1840's in such articles as "De la mission de l'art":

> Art . . . expresses in its most elevated flight the most advanced social tendencies; it is a precursor and a revealer. Now, in order to know whether art is fulfilling its role as initiator, whether the artist is truly at the vanguard, it is necessary to know where Humanity is going, what the destiny of the Species is. . . . Art must by its constant action re-ally itself to human destiny. The beautiful is the more perfect in the extent to which it reflects better the ideal of the good.[89]

The development of Hugo's esthetic thought in his prefaces was traced from the ideal of independent art which he held during the 1820's to his complete reversal of this opinion and final enunciation of his belief in the poet as priest and *mage* in *Les Contemplations*. This was the esthetic view which finally crystallized in his thinking and which he still held in later years, elaborating upon it at length in *William Shakespeare* in the chapter "Le Beau Serviteur du vrai," where he summarizes his opinions on this subject in such lines as:

> Art for art's sake may be fine, but art for the sake of progress is finer still. To dream is fine, but to dream Utopia is better. Ah, do you need a dream? Very well, dream of a better man. Do you want a dream? Here's one: the ideal. The prophet seeks solitude, but not isolation.[90]

The last of Rimbaud's prophecies, regarding the emancipation of women, comes as a surprise in view of the enclosure within the Demeny letter of an anti-feminist poem "Mes petites Amoureuses." We may conclude that Rimbaud disliked women as he found them, but was not lacking in hope for their improvement. Love could only be "re-invented," as he advocates in the *Saison,* when woman has changed, that is, when she can be educated and can vote. Although Rimbaud speaks only of woman's liberation, these two other points were advocated by the socialist writers who inspired this passage. Saint-Simon, Ganneau, Rodrigues, Enfantin, Bazard, Considérant, and Prudhon had all advocated the emancipation of women in many ardent paragraphs, but none more violently than a woman herself, Flora Tristan, grandmother of Paul Gaugin, whose posthumous work, *L'Emancipation de la femme,* was edited and prefaced by Eliphas Lévi.

Saint-Simon proposed that women be admitted to the future society of nations and that they be allowed to vote and hold office. This new emancipated woman would regenerate society, Saint-Simon believed, by using her mitigating influence against male aggression. Society should be directed by both men and women, insisted the followers of Saint-Simon in many pamphlets. Fourier held that the extent to which women have been emancipated serves as the truest indicator of social progress, for in societies which are vital and in the process of social development, women enjoy more liberties, whereas in decadent cultures their enslavement is almost total. Fourier held that in modern society the social inequalities which man has imposed upon women had only served to react against him. Having deprived woman of an education, man has consequently found himself without companionship. Finally, Fourier predicts — as does Rimbaud in the Demeny letter — that the educated woman of the future, when she is liberated at last from household toil, will invade literature and the arts: when women have become educated "we will witness the downfall of those prejudices about the incapacity of women."[91] Agitation for social reforms for women continued on all sides, and in this connection the myth of the androgyne was revived by the Fourierists. The aim of marriage, they held, was to re-establish the harmony of the original marriage of Adam and Eve. As Adam was regenerated by Christ, Eve must be regenerated by the Virgin, so that they can form a harmonious couple in the society of the future. Concerning the myth of the androgyne, Eliphas Lévi writes: "The two sexes will then make one . . . the great Androgyne will be created, humanity will be woman and man, love and thought, tenderness and strength, grace and energy."[92]

AN ESTIMATION OF CERTAIN CONTEMPORARIES

These were the ideas of Rimbaud's times which entered into his esthetic judgments and inspired his prophecies about the future of poetry. Although the *Voyant* letters contain many familiar Romantic and Parnassian themes, Rimbaud added his own personality to them to such an extent that they attained freshness and originality. Furthermore, his estimate of his contemporaries is remarkably accurate. Certain of their works may be named specifically as having had a large part in the formulation of Rimbaud's doctrine: Edgar Quinet's *Histoire de la poésie* (1857) for Rimbaud's ideas about the four ages of poetry; Leconte de Lisle's *Préface des Poèmes Antiques* (1852) for his ideas about Grecian poetry; Gautier's *Progrès de la poésie française* and *Souvenirs romantiques* (1857) and Baudelaire's *L'Art romantique* for Rimbaud's judgments upon the first and second generation Romantics; Sully-Prudhomme's *Préface* to his translation of the *De Rerum Natura* for Rimbaud's ideas about the ego-as-object; Baudelaire's *Paradis artificiels* for the method which he would use for the *"dérèglement de tous les sens."*

In addition to these specific works is the definite influence of the socialist and occult thinkers whose writers are legion and who repeat each other; but it is impossible to say definitely which socialist or occultist inspired the passages about the process of voyance, the universal language, or the emancipation of women. It is only important that we be able to recognize these two currents of thought in order to understand more clearly Rimbaud's frame of reference and therefore the meaning of his more cryptic allusions. The fundamental error of Gengoux's criticism is that he attempts to pour all of Rimbaud, even the Latin poems, into the mold of one occult writer, Eliphas Lévi. Why Lévi any more than any other occultist? Lévi, for example, does not expound upon the subject of the universal language. In all probability Rimbaud encountered this idea either in Fourierist popularizations of Court de Gébelin found in *La Phalange* or in some popularization of Swedenborg. Gengoux's argument is weakened by the fact that a poet like Rimbaud, who relied so much upon spontaneity and insisted upon the role of the unconscious, would not likely have taken a couple of Lévi's volumes and followed them as rigidly as Gengoux claims.

Two final aspects of the *Voyant* letters remain to be discussed. One is the list of Parnassians given by Rimbaud at the end of the Demeny letter; the other is the question raised at the end of Chapter 4 as to whether the poems included in the two *Voyant* letters may be considered illustrations of the esthetic doctrine.

With regard to the list of Parnassians cited by Rimbaud, it is not difficult to see that he took their names from the index of the *Parnasse contemporain* of 1869, the issue in which he had hoped that Banville would publish his "Soleil et chair." (These names appear in Appendix C with a short paragraph of identification.)

As for the relationship between the four poems included in the two *Voyant* letters and the esthetic doctrine, Rimbaud indicates in connection with the first poem, "Chant de guerre Parisien" in the Demeny letter, that he considers it to be an example of the new poetry as he conceived it: "I am beginning with a psalm of present-day interest," he says. Enid Starkie finds these semiscatological works incompatible with the theory of the poet as seer, probably because to her the concept of the seer suggests a mystical experience with which the poems would obviously be incompatible. But since the visions of the unconscious produced under drugs or hypnosis do not resemble in nature those of mystic vision, and are described by mystics in altogether different terms and metaphors, there is no essential contradiction between these poems and the esthetic doctrine as Rimbaud conceives it. The four poems were intended, however, to illustrate in particular the ideal of "objectivity" as opposed to the subjectivity of the Romantics. This, it will be remembered, was an integral part of the doctrine, but the question arises immediately as to whether Rimbaud in fact achieved the poetic objectivity which he advocated. Pure objectivity in any realm, least of all in poetry, is doubtless nonexistent. When we call a poet or poetry objective, we can only speak relatively, that is, one poem may be said to be more or less objective than another, but not objective in any absolute sense.

On the whole, a large proportion of the poems written by Rimbaud between the time of the *Voyant* letters and the composition of the *Saison* — notably most of *Les Illuminations* and a few other poems — possess both objective and visionary qualities. *Les Illuminations* is objective in the sense that it is recordings made by the poet of what he saw under the influence of hashish; but the terrain described is the poet himself and thus is inevitably subjective as well as objective. Some readers have found these poems too cold and impersonal, while others object to their obscurity. But *Les Illuminations* are dreams written in that symbolic language which is doubtless the lost one sought by the Romantics from Hamann and Novalis to Rimbaud and the Symbolists. To read these poems is to make a translation, the accuracy of which depends upon the translator's understanding of the symbols.

CHAPTER 6

The Orphic Vision

> A God can do it. But can a man expect
> to penetrate the narrow lyre and follow?
> His sense is discord . . .
> For song, as taught by you, is not desire,
> not wooing of something finally attained;
> song is existence . . .
>
> RILKE, *Sonnets to Orpheus,* J. B. Leishman

Although Rimbaud had identified the poet with the Promethean as well as the Orphic legends, he realized that the latter was the more accurate comparison when, two years later, in 1873, he looked back upon this period of his life and called it his "season in hell." He made no further allusions to the Promethean myth after the time of the composition of the *Voyant* letters, but thenceforth thought of himself as Orpheus, the initiator of men into the mysteries; nevertheless, for the brief space of two years, Rimbaud had made the error of identifying the vision of the unconscious, *the Orphic vision,* with that of the mystic. It was the same error made by other Romantics, which have been noted in detail in Chapter 1, except that Rimbaud finally discovered the nature of his mistake. Describing later his aspirations during this voyant period, which was the peak of his brief poetic career, he said: "I am going to unveil all the mysteries, religious mysteries or natural mysteries: death, birth, future, past, cosmogony, nothingness."[1] Although Romantic irony is apparent in such an overstatement, Rimbaud's descent into the unconscious was not without positive results and definite artistic revelation. One of his first discoveries was that of his "double" or his genie (*"Génie"*) as he called his spirit-self.

THE VISION OF THE DOUBLE ("CONTE," "BEING BEAUTEOUS," AND GÉNIE")

The prose poem "Conte" relates in the form of a simple fairy tale or fable the inner drama of the transition which took place within the young poet during the spring of 1871, at the time he composed the *Voyant* letters. The destructive prince of this symbolic fable is, of course, the poet himself during his rebellious phase. Dissatisfied not only with his personal life but also with the world at large, the prince in the poem has, like the poet, dreams of changing society. The first change which he hopes to make is in the relation of the sexes: "he foresaw astonishing revolutions of love" and considered women capable of more than mere "compliance graced by heaven and luxury." In other words, the poet believes that the sexes have something more positive to offer one another than mere submissiveness blessed by the church and motivated by financial interests. The prince of the poem "wanted to see the truth, the time of desire and essential satisfaction," that is, he dreams of an honest relationship between the sexes based upon desire and its satisfaction. In order to bring about these changes, however, he launches upon a program of unlimited violence and destruction, doubtless in the belief that the old order of things must first be destroyed before the new one can be established. Omnipotent as the princes of dreams and fairy tales always are, this one takes a frenzied delight in unleashing his sadistic impulses upon society at large: killing women indiscriminately, setting fire to the palace like some Erostratus, and rushing upon men in the street in order to cut them to pieces. The rage and sadism of the adolescent Rimbaud are apparent in this fantasy, but fantasies such as this are probably not uncommon among adolescents.

But the prince's orgy of destruction really changed nothing: other women merely replaced those whom he had killed and, what was even more exasperating, no one took even the slightest notice of the evil he had done. Then one evening he has an extraordinary experience: he meets a Genie of "ineffable, even inadmissible beauty." In Illuminist terminology, the poet encountered his "double" or his spirit-self. This first encounter with the double is described by all Illuminists as one of the great moments of their lives (cf. Gérard de Nerval's account of this in *Aurélia* and also those of a modern Illuminist Rudolph Steiner in *Erkenntnisse der höheren Welten,* Chapter 6). Rimbaud remarks here that the prince experienced "a promise of unspeakable, even unbearable happiness" from the meeting. The identification of the Genie in the poem with the double is emphasized by the poet himself near the end of his narrative: "The prince was the Génie. The Génie was the Prince." When Rimbaud says that the two of them "annihilate each other in essential health" he means that when his destructive self or *voyou,* met his seer self or voyant personality, the latter brought a healthy end to the former, while the former doubtless kept the latter from soaring too far above the world of commonplace reality.

Abruptly, the Genie of the poem disappears, as Genies in fairy tales are accustomed to do, for the vision of the double is not one which lingers. The connection between this fable and the last line of the poem, "Learned music is lacking to our desire," is not immediately apparent; what Rimbaud probably means by it is that to express such an inner spiritual event as the one related here, he preferred the simple form of a fable such as this rather than a more complex poetic genre.

"Being Beauteous" also gives an account of the phantom self which Rimbaud encountered on his descent into the unconscious. The title of this poem was suggested in the poem "Conte," in which the Genie is described as a "being of ineffable beauty." In this poem, Rimbaud calls his "Being Beauteous" a "Vision" (capitalization in original) and mentions in particular its height (*"un Etre de Beauté de haute taille"*). This is an allusion to the fact that the double or spirit-body in Illuminist parlance is always described as much larger than the physical body of the given individual. The effects of phantasmagory, which were doubtless produced by hashish and of which the poet said he was master (*"je suis maître en fantasmagorie"*) can be noted in this poem when the poet says that the noises of the world and its "hoarse music" cause the adored body of the being to grow larger, to rise, and to tremble like a specter. So resplendent does the vision become that by comparison with it "life's own colors darken, dance and stand out around the vision," he says, suggesting that colors were visible to him which were not "life's own" but which belonged only to the vision. This part of the poem recalls Baudelaire's account of his extraordinary perception of color under the influence of hashish, which Rimbaud had also undoubtedly experienced himself. Not only is Rimbaud filled with wonder at the discovery of his spirit-double but also with delight that his Genie is fundamentally a being whose true essence is love: "Oh, our bones are clothed again with a new, loving body," he exclaims, as if he were relieved to be rid of his *voyou* self. The sadistic prince has encountered once more his spirit-self, who is filled with love instead of hate. But at this point the ideas of "Being Beauteous" approach those of a third poem, "Génie," in which the double is again discussed.

Although the subject of "Génie" is the same as that of "Conte" and "Being Beauteous," the atmosphere is altogether different. "Conte" was in form a symbolic fable or fairy tale; "Being Beauteous," a visionary experience of an hallucinatory kind. In "Génie" the poet speaks of his double with more familiarity, as if he has by this time become accustomed to him and has indeed come to love him. Here, as in "Being Beauteous," the Genie's chief characteristic is love — the re-invented love mentioned in "Conte" and expressed in these terms: "He is love, perfect measure re-invented, marvelous and unlooked-for reason, and eternity: loved instrument of fatal qualities." The paradox contained in the last part of this statement may be explained by the fact that the Genie is the instrument or the means whereby the poet has acquired qualities which were fatal to his destructive self. Such was the situation in "Conte" when the prince met the Genie; his destructive self perished. This interpretation receives further support in "Génie" where Rimbaud mentions specifically having acquired a healthier attitude: "O relish of health, the soaring of our faculties . . . and passion for him who loves us for his infinite life." He has been released from the rage and sadism which possessed him in the first part of "Conte" and his spirit is at last able to soar. In that he is a spirit, the Genie belongs to eternity ("He is love . . . and eternity") and since he is also attached to a physical body, he belongs to time ("He is affection and the present. . . . He is affection and the future").

Other opposites are mentioned in the poem as existing together in a kind of synthesis within the Genie nature — "love and force," "love and reason" as well as time and eternity. These pairs of opposites existing in equilibrium suggest the spiritual perfection of the Genie. In fact, the poet considers that his contact with the Genie has been altogether beneficial and inspiring: he has become more sensitive to nature, the change of seasons, "foamy winter," and the "murmur of spring"; all that he eats and drinks has been purified since the spirit purifies everything with which it comes into contact. At the time of the composition of this poem the Génie is not present, but his words are still ringing in the poet's ears: "Away with those superstitions, away with those ancient bodies. . . . It is this present age which has foundered!" Thus, the modern world is at fault, the poet is saying, if it cannot free itself from the tyranny of the past.

A negative comparison between the Genie and Christ follows in the next paragraph which begins: "He [the Genie] will not go away, he will not come down again from a heaven . . ." What the poet means here is that unlike Christ, the Genie will not go away and return from heaven nor will he engage in a redemption from sin. This is unnecessary because he can accomplish his redemptive process merely by his presence and by the fact of his being loved. In other words the poet feels that his encounter with the Genie has wrought a profound change within him which is more effective than the usual methods of conversion. A more recent description of the Illuminist belief that an encounter with the double effects a complete conversion of the personality may be found in the writings of Rudolph Steiner previously mentioned. In the last part of the poem, Rimbaud breaks out in an unrestrained panegyric of the Genie. One line of the panegyric, "O he and us! Pride more benevolent than lost charities!" contains the paradox that the pride which he now feels in his experience with the double (a sin from the Catholic viewpoint) is more benevolent than charity, normally considered a Christian virtue. The poem "Génie" ends with the poet's insistence that all recognize this wonderful being and follow his direction.

THE VISION OF EXISTENCE ("APRES LE DÉLUGE," "ENFANCE," "AUBE," "JEUNESSE," "VIES")

One enters a luminous and enchanted world in the first two prose poems of *Les Illuminations*, "Après le déluge" and "Enfance." These should be read and analyzed simultaneously, because their atmosphere is similar and because the second poem also refers to the Flood. The reader receives the immediate impression of having just stepped through the looking-glass into a fresh new world, still glistening with primordial rains which have not yet stopped, and bright with a rainbow, magic flowers and precious stones, which are alive, as all things are in the world of childhood. The poet suggests that we are in a dream state by saying that at the edge of the forest "dream-flowers tinkle, flash and flare." It is a country inhabited by all the fabulous persons encountered in children's fairy tales: giantesses, sultanas, princesses, "superb black women," Bluebeard, "the girl with the lips like oranges," and the "witch who lights her embers in an earthen pot and will not tell her secrets." As one would expect of a child's paradise, it is filled with many animals: beavers, a rabbit, a spider, a bird, "beasts of fabulous elegance" – all these the poet mentions. In short, Rimbaud's Eden is magically alive with vivid color and movement, marvelous animals, and extraordinary human beings, and the child-poet is the spectator and discoverer of all this wonder. The shedding of blood which led to the disaster of the Flood is also present in this new Eden: the slaughter of animals and murder of the sort which may be found in fairy tales: "The blood flows from Bluebeard's house." Death also appears in the midst of all these wonders when a little girl is found dead behind the rose bushes ("Enfance"), and the fact that her mother, who has already died ("*trépassée*"), is seen coming down the steps, is stated as a mere commonplace.

Abruptly, the scene shifts in "Après le déluge" from the wonders of the outdoor world to an indoor setting. Children in mourning are sitting inside a house looking at marvelous picture books while outside the last rains of the Flood beat against the window. One of the children gets up, goes out, and swings his arms about as a signal to the weathervanes and steeplecocks, who understand him immediately, since communication among man, other creatures, and even objects was immediate in these early days. This is clearly a dream representation of the birth of an individual as well as the arrival of a new people upon the earth after the Flood. The symbols of blood and milk mentioned by the poet lend even further support to this interpretation. It should be noted that the children who are about to arrive are in mourning over the occasion: birth, in other words, is an occasion of mourning for the unborn. The child who goes out of the house surveys the world and sees all institutions in their formation: in the Alps, Mass and first communions are celebrated at 100,000 altars. Commerce begins when the caravans depart, and man builds himself a luxurious protection against the elements and the chaos from which the newly made earth has come. At length, Eucharis the nymph tells the child, who is standing in a bed of violets, that spring has come; and at the sight of the new rains, swollen streams and the sound of thunder, the child wishes that the flood would return ["*relevez les Déluges*"]. As the child longs to return to the womb, so mankind too desires to return to a time when the world was still unspoiled and fresh. Since that time, much that was precious has been lost, people have become bored; and above all, the Witch, the Queen (Nature) "who lights her coal in the earthen pot," refuses to tell the child what she knows, i.e. she refuses to explain the meaning of existence, and he is left in a world — as Albert Camus has described it — where everything is given and nothing explained.[2]

Another brief reference to the Flood was made by Rimbaud in a third poem, "Movement," indicating that this event had a further significance for him:

> They are the conquerors of the world,
> Those who personally seek a chemical fortune;
> . . . .
> They take along the education
> Of races, classes and beasts on this ship.
> Repose and vertigo
> In the diluvian [diluvienne] light
> Through the dreadful nights of study.[3]

The vessel with the beasts, races, and classes, coupled as they are with the word "diluvian," seems to be a reference to Noah's ark, while a "chemical fortune" and the "dreadful nights of study" may be interpreted as an allusion to the origins of alchemy. (According to one of the legends, alchemy was supposed to have originated with Noah's son, Shem or Chem; from his name, together with the Arabic article, *al,* the word alchemy was derived.[4] The ark was considered by medieval alchemists to have been the original laboratory; Eliphas Lévi likewise traces the origin of magic to the time of the Flood in his *Histoire de la magie.*)[5]

When read together, these references to the Flood form a total picture: the child upon his arrival in the world is comparable to man as he appeared on the earth after the Flood; both are surrounded with wonder and mystery, both seek explanations which Nature of herself cannot give since she herself is a part of the mystery. The only knowledge which exists in this primitive age of innocence is that of legends and fairy tales or of magic and alchemy, the heavenly wisdom which Enoch obtained from the angels before the Flood, the last few remnants of which survived on the ark. Believing that "It is this present age which has foundered!" Rimbaud resolved to return to this ancient wisdom, as he later confessed in *Une Saison en enfer*: "I returned to the Orient and to the first and eternal wisdom" and "I believed in all the enchantments."[6]

The means whereby the poet was able to enter this wonderland are indicated in the first paragraph of "Enfance," and then expanded on in the last part of this poem. Certain of these allusions were explained in Chapter 1 and will be recapitulated here. The first line of "Enfance" which begins cryptically: "Cette idole, yeux noirs et crin jaune . . ." recalls to the reader of *Les Paradis artificiels* that Baudelaire, quoting De Quincey, calls opium "the dark idol" or the "Mater Tenebrarum" in at least three passages. The word "crin" as used here by Rimbaud also suggests the drug, for it denotes not only a horse's mane but also the fibrous stem of a plant such as hemp, from which the drug hashish is derived. The extraordinary use which Rimbaud makes of color, not only in these two poems but also in *Les Illuminations* as a whole, may be partly explained as the effect of drugs. The last paragraph of "Enfance" makes it evident that this interpretation of the first sentence is correct. Here, the wonderland evoked in the first part of the poem has abruptly vanished and the poet describes the basement room ("*mon salon souterrain*"), perhaps in Paris ("*Ville monstrueuse*"), where he had been reading as he awaited the more potent effects of the drug. Three phases in this last paragraph bear a rather striking similarity with *Les Paradis artificiels*:

Rimbaud: "Peut-être des gouffres d'azur?"
Baudelaire: "un gouffre limpide . . . l'immensité bleue de la mer."[7]

Rimbaud: "des boules de saphir, de métal."[8]
Baudelaire: ". . . je vis un soleil couchant semblable à du metal en fusion qui se refroidit."[9]

Rimbaud: "nuit sans fin."
Baudelaire: "la durée d'une nuit représentait pour lui la valeur d'un siècle."[10]

If such interpretations are to be made of the first three and the last sections of "Enfance," how may the meaning of Part IV – which begins: "I am the saint in prayer on the terrace. . . I am the scholar of the dark arm chair . . ." – be related to the poem as a whole? One recalls Baudelaire's account of the sensation of "multiplication of the personality" and the feeling of identity with others experienced during the state of beatitude: "One lives several men's lives in the space of an hour," he says.[11]

"Aube," which is perhaps the loveliest of all *Les Illuminations,* is another poem of beginnings, and possibly for this reason it has an atmosphere similar to that of "Après le déluge" and "Enfance." Here the poet evokes the stillness of a summer's dawn, doubtless that of his own small town, Charleville. To one who has visited there the lines, "Nothing was stirring yet on the fronts of the palaces; the water was dead," suggest that the poet walked from his home across the Place

Ducale with its seventeenth-century architecture resembling that of the Place des Vosges in Paris, down to the waterfront beside the Meuse. Here the trees along the river make "camps of shadows" and all is quiet in the early morning when even the birds fly away noiselessly. Little stones "stare" at him and a flower tells him its name. On the other side of the Meuse, he sees through the pines a blond waterfall letting down its hair and, at the top of the falls, he recognizes "the goddess" (Dawn). In love with the Dawn, the child begins lifting her veils, but the goddess escapes him and flees among the bell towers and the domes as the child pursues. Near a laurel grove, he overtakes her with the veils piled up beside her and he feels "her immense body a little." The poem ends with the two statements: "Dawn and the child fall in the depth of the wood. On awaking it was noon."

Like "Conte," "Aube" is also a symbolic fable which contains beyond its simple literal meaning another of deeper significance. There are two persons in this little drama — the child and the goddess of the Dawn. These two bear a special relationship to each other in that both represent beginnings; the Dawn in that she is a personification of all beginnings and the child in that he is a specific and individual beginning. This is doubtless why the child feels so strongly attracted to the goddess of the Dawn; it is the attraction of like for like. The goddess is represented as wearing veils for the reason that the one who personifies beginnings is naturally clothed in mystery: the future is a mystery. When the child attempts to lift the veils, he is making an effort to see the future, and the goddess appropriately eludes him, but only for a time. The child pursues her unceasingly until he overtakes her, this time finding her without her veils which are piled up beside her. He discovers her mystery and makes a physical contact with her, but this is only partial because he is a small child in comparison with the immensity of the goddess ("*son corps immense*"). The choice of words is erotic from the very beginning of the poem; "I embraced a summer's dawn" to ". . . I felt her immense body a little." Upon touching her, however, the child falls asleep. Childhood is indeed a sleep and a forgetting — if not in the Wordsworthian sense, at least in the psychological — for the man remembers very little of what he experienced as a child. When he awakens from the sleep of childhood, "it is noon," that is, it is youth or young manhood.

In contrast to those poems which record the experiences of childhood, "Jeunesse" indicates the increasing self-reflexiveness of the young poet. Having fully awakened from the sleep of childhood, he is now meditating upon his own as well as on the whole human condition. In its form, this poem resembles "Enfance," and like that poem the first and the last parts should be read together. An atmosphere of contemplation, absent in the poems previously discussed, is created by the poet in the very first sentence of Part I, called "Dimanche." The situation described is a most familiar one: it is one of those quiet Sunday afternoons in a small town, when the poet, deep in concentration, relaxes from his study for a few moments. Sounds, even distant ones to which he had been impervious because of his concentration, now invade him. (For many people, such moments of pause after intense concentration can be times of illumination even without the use of hashish.) The last paragraph of this poem records another hallucinatory account, such as may be found in "Being Beauteous." Here the poet says that "perfect and unpredictable beings" offered themselves to him for "experiments." In the face of these visions, the poet is acutely aware that he is still only in the stage of the "temptation of St. Anthony," that is, of acute suffering from the temptations of the flesh (cf. Baudelaire's mention of the thirst, hunger, and sexual excitement which accompany the taking of hashish). Then, as if to make his own resolution the more firm, he says to himself, "But you will begin this work." As was pointed out in Chapter 5, Rimbaud's taking of hashish was always an inverted form of asceticism, and here he mentions the struggle which he had with himself—his diminished zeal and his "childish insolence, weakness and fright"—as if these were all things of the past. Now that he has reached young manhood, he must show more resolution. After thus strengthening his will to pursue his course with more firmness of purpose, he calls attention to some of the more attractive features of his experiments, among them the "perfect and unpredictable beings" mentioned above, and also the state of harmony (cf. Baudelaire's statement that Orientals call this kief) and "architecture," doubtless of the dream type which may be found in such poems as "Ville I"—"even the peoples of ancient times will move in dreamily," he says, confirming again that he has been speaking of the visionary effects of the drug. On the subject of the architecture of his dreams, Baudelaire writes: "Astonishing and monstrous architectures would rise up in the brain, similar to those moving constructions which the eye of the poet sees in clouds colored by the sunset."[12] The cryptic last lines of Rimbaud's poem may therefore be interpreted in this way: the poet knows that his memory and senses will serve to feed his creative impulse and that it can survive without the visionary world, but what, he asks himself, will happen to his illuminated world when he departs from it? (*Quant au monde, quand tu sortiras, que sera-t-il devenu*?") His answer to this in the last sentence is: "Nothing in any case will remain of present appearances." All will vanish, as he knows very well, for his world is of such stuff as dreams are made.

The two middle parts of the poem "Jeunesse" fit together quite logically. In the one, entitled "Sonnet," the poet evokes his childhood memories; in the other, "Twenty Years Old," he reflects upon the fact of his approaching manhood. In both parts, the problem which he attempts to analyze is that of the body and its physical desires. In childhood all was simple, "O childhood days! Wasn't the body a treasure to spend?" he exclaims, summarizing with brisk exactness the inexhaustible energy of childhood. In still another metaphor he asks, "Wasn't the flesh a fruit hanging in the orchard?" The physical pleasure which the child takes in his games may be enjoyed, like the fruit in the orchard, as a natural pleasure without social censure. The child's idea of adult love is the one which he finds in legend and fairy tales, such as the myth of Psyche, for example: "O to love, the peril or the strength of Psyche." Here, love is represented as merely incidental to adventures involving great danger to the heroes and heroines and is a source of strength to them in their trials. The youth, however, awakens to discover that love is quite different, and the attitude of the adult world toward it is quite the reverse of that of childhood. But this is merely implied here, and not stated explicitly until the last section of the poem.

At this point, Rimbaud makes a digression which may be interpreted in the following way: As it is with man the individual, so it is with the race. The earth too was once "fertile in princes and artists," but the descendents of the ordinary man drove them to crime and mourning, and the world became both man's fortune and his peril. As the common man acquired political power, his responsibilities increased along with his fortune. But all this is done, Rimbaud continues, and all the calculations of the ordinary man, his plans and his impatience, are only "his dance and his voice, not fixed and not forced." By this, the poet means that the recently acquired power which the ordinary man possesses has not yet become firmly established (at the time this poem was written the Republic was only about a year old) nor does it yet have force behind it; nevertheless, the "dance and the voice" are responsible for scientific invention and for creating a more brotherly and discreet humanity "throughout the imageless universe." This phrase, if interpreted as meaning "religious images," implies that this newly acquired power of the common man has to some degree spread the ideal of the brotherhood of man in a world which has lost its religious faith. In the new socialism, religious images could certainly be dispensed with as unnecessary. The last sentence of this part of the poem seems to confirm such an interpretation: "Force and right reflect the dance and the voice which are only now ["*à présent*"] appreciated," he says. This means that the forces of law and order under the new regime have only begun to reflect this formerly unstable voice of the common man which had then only recently come to be appreciated.

After this digression the poet returns, in Part III of "Jeunesse" entitled "Vingt ans," to the topic which he originally introduced. As a youth he discovers with much bitterness that the body can no longer be a source of pleasure, but must instead be regarded as something to be subdued ("*L'ingenuité physique amèrement rassise* . . ."). He does not linger on this subject, however, but passes quickly on to other aspects of youth, recognizing objectively "the infinite egoism of adolescence" and its "studious optimism." Then he recalls a particularly happy summer (perhaps the summer of 1870 before the war began) and says wistfully: "How full of flowers the world was that summer!" But the music died, or rather was replaced by another kind, that of a choir "to calm impotence and absence!" This seems to be a rather clear allusion to the fact that he was powerless to join his friends Izambard and Deverrière in their departure and had to remain behind and endure their absences. The thought of it still makes him bitter and he says: "A choir of glasses, of nocturnal melodies . . . indeed the nerves go quickly on the hunt." It was then that his delinquency began, as it was shown in Chapter 4 – drinking, vagabondage, and sexual experimentation. At this point it becomes clear how this section moves logically into the last, which has already been discussed, for the poet realizes that he has not yet fully outgrown the temptations of the flesh, and that he is "still at the stage of the temptation of St. Anthony."

The poem "Vies," which is similar in form to "Enfance" and "Jeunesse," is also related in meaning to Part IV of "Enfance." As in the latter poem, Rimbaud conveys his sensation of what Baudelaire describes as the multiplication of the personality under hashish, or the feeling of having lived more than one life ("One lives several men's lives in the space of an hour"). Here the poet finds himself in the exotic surroundings of the Holy Land, in a pepper field near the terraces of a temple. The flight of the famous "red pigeons" which the poet says "thunders around my thoughts" and which has caused so much consternation among critics, would be too extraordinary even for the exotic setting mentioned, except that the lines which follow indicate clearly that he has seen red pigeons because he is under the influence of a drug (either hashish or opium). A companion is with him (Verlaine, perhaps?) who has also taken the drug, for the poet asks in the last sentence of this part: "What is my void in comparison with the stupefaction awaiting you?" Doubtless he had some reason to believe that the drug would have a more potent effect on his friend than it had on him. Just before the last sentence the poet suggests that he has been reading, and we recall the same fact in the last part of "Enfance," where he was reading while awaiting the effects of the drug. In "Vies" Rimbaud mentions that he had a stage on which to "perform the dramatic masterpieces of all literatures." This stage, doubtless an interior one, he feels to be the source of "unheard-of wealth," but he is also so interested in the "treasures" which his friend has discovered that he has neglected his own.

The second part of "Vies" is in reality a defense by the poet of his activities, for here he summarizes what he considers to be his accomplishments. He believes, for example, that he is a "more deserving inventor" than all his predecessors. The noun "inventor" is used here in its Latin sense of "discoverer," just as Rimbaud used the verb "*inventer*" in the first line of his sonnet, "Voyelles," and again in "Alchimie du verbe": *"J'ai inventé la couleur des voyelles."* The poet feels that he is a more deserving discoverer than others who have used drugs before him, in that he has dared and suffered more for art than they did. As a second achievement, he mentions that he is a "musician who has found something resembling the key of love." This key of love which the poet discovered by means of hashish came from the profound sense of identity with others which Baudelaire discusses in the *Paradis artificiels* and which is the subject of Part III of the poem. In spite of his discoveries, the poet says that at present he is only a gentleman from "a harsh country with a dark sky," but he does not feel sorry for himself because of the hardships which he endured during his childhood. Nor does he miss the religious happiness ("*la gaité divine*") which he once enjoyed: "the calm air of this harsh country nourishes my terrible scepticism quite actively," he says, but since he has discovered that his scepticism was ineffectual (after his return to Charleville from his third flight and at the time of the composition of the *Voyant* letters), he has devoted himself to "a new worry" — doubtless the injurious effects of hashish, for he adds that he expects to "become a very wicked fool."

In Part III of the poem "Vies" Rimbaud returns to the theme of the first paragraph — his perception of the multiplication of personality, of having lived many different lives in various parts of the world. The first five sentences of this part of the poem each mention a different place and a varied activity in which the poet feels he has been engaged: in an attic he was a painter who "illustrated the human comedy"; in a wine cellar he learned history; in a Northern city he frequented artistic circles where he met the wives of former painters; in an old back street in Paris he was taught the classical sciences; as his final pursuit, he finished a "long work" in a magnificent dwelling "surrounded by the entire Orient," where, he says, "I spent my illustrious retirement." This part of the poem should be compared with a passage from the *Paradis artificiels* in which Baudelaire, describing the effects of opium on De Quincey, says that for a long time the English writer "no longer evoked images," but they came to him "spontaneously, despotically."[13] De Quincey was particularly annoyed at this time by numerous visits from a certain Malayan who became multiplied until it seemed that the Malayan "became Asia itself — China, India, and in short the whole immense and fabulous Orient." Every night in his dreams De Quincey was transported by the Malayan to an Asiatic milieu: "I rescued myself in pagodas, and I was the priest, I was adored, I was sacrificed. I fled the wrath of Brahma through the forests of Asia; Vishnu hated me, Shiva set an ambush for me. I suddenly fell into the hands of Isis and Osiris." It is this kind of hallucinatory experience which Rimbaud describes in Part III of his poem.

In the final passage of "Vies," Rimbaud says that he has been released from duty and that he must not even think of it any longer. This is a reference to the sensation Baudelaire mentions of having arrived at a high stage of morality without effort, so that one seems to be beyond good and evil. Rimbaud later attacks himself in the *Saison* for having thought this: "I who considered myself Magus or angel [*mage ou ange*] free from all morals!" he says scornfully. At the time of the composition of "Vies," however, he declares: "I am really from beyond the tomb and without errands."[14] As pointed out in

Chapter 2, the belief was widespread among the Romantics that persons who were either in a trance state as a result of Mesmeric practices or under the influence of drugs were automatically in contact with the Beyond, and they were consulted as if they were oracles. In this last sentence, Rimbaud also believes that he is "from beyond the tomb" and therefore no longer has petty duties to perform — he is dispensed from them, in order to be free for his mission as seer poet.

THE VISION OF ETERNITY ("ANTIQUE," "ETERNITÉ," "AGE D'OR," "CHANSON DE LA PLUS HAUTE TOUR," "FÊTES DE LA FAIM," "COMÉDIE DE LA SOIF")

For a brief time the young poet believed that he was actually having a glimpse of the mysteries of Eternity, and the poems which we have listed here record this experience. Before approaching them, however, attention should be directed to a statement which Rimbaud made in the rough draft or "Brouillon" of *Une Saison en enfer*. There he says: "I was damned by the rainbow and religious magic (*les magies religieuses*)."[15] When Rimbaud made his final draft of the *Saison* he retained the first part of this sentence but omitted the last part, "and religious magic." This reference to his Illuminist studies was probably omitted as he preferred to keep them secret. The reason why Rimbaud felt that he was damned by the rainbow, in that this was connected with the poisonous drug and the colors which he saw while under its influence, has already been explained, but why did he also consider that his magical studies had damned him? Certainly not because these were forbidden by the Catholic church, for we find no other indications that he would have strained himself to be orthodox. The reason is that he discovered his error of mistaking the Orphic or Illuminist vision for that of the mystic. He thought that these studies were the "key to the great mysteries" (to use the title of one of Eliphas Lévi's chief works) but concludes in the *Saison* that "Charity is that key."[16] Like the other seer poets, he was unaware of the real value of his explorations of the unconscious.

On the same page of the Graux manuscript with "Being Beauteous" is the poem "Antique," in which the poet presents himself in relation to his Génie. Whereas in his first encounter with this Being in "Conte" he recognized him as his alter ego, in "Antique" he becomes aware of an opposing truth, namely, of his own earthiness and animal-like nature in comparison with the spiritual nature of the Genie. While one part of him is a "lithe son of Pan" or Nature, the Genie, his double, is a creature above the human order. It was a natural reaction for him to have after the awesome vision of his double. In common with primitive man, described by Illuminist writers as androgynous, the poet perceives within himself his own androgynous nature ("in this belly where sleeps the double sex"). This is a quality which primitive man had in common with the spiritual man who is yet to come for, according to Eliphas Lévi, the Golden Age belongs to the future as well as to the past. As primitive man was androgynous, modern men must also move toward an equalization of the sexes in order to restore the Androgyne, as the Fourierists advocated.

Equilibrium of opposites was one of the most important magical concepts. The Magus must possess this knowledge and master the opposites within himself before he can control the forces of Nature. A brief digression here will illustrate this point and at the same time shed some light upon another of Rimbaud's poems. Although the poem "Ce qu'on dit au poète à propos de fleurs" is chiefly a long pastiche of Théodore de Banville's poetic style, it contains these two lines which are related to the subject at hand: "But neither Renan nor the Murr Cat / Have seen the immense blue thyrsus."[17] In connection with this line a second passage should be read from the prose poem "Thyrse" in Baudelaire's *Les petits Poèmes en prose*:

> What is a thyrsus? According to the intellectual and poetic meaning, it is a sacerdotal emblem in the hands of priests and priestesses honoring the divinity of whom they are the interpreters and servants. But physically it is only a staff. . . . Around this staff, in capricious windings, stems and flowers sport and frolic, the latter sinuous and fugitive, the former inclined like bells or cups turned upside down. And an astonishing glory bursts forth from this complexity of lines and colors, soft or striking. Would one not say that the curved line and the spiral woo the straight line and dance around it in mute adoration? . . . The thyrsus is the representation of your astonishing duality, powerful and reverent master, dear Bacchante of mysterious and passionate Beauty. . . . the staff is your will — straight, firm and inflexible; the flowers are the winding of your fantasy around your will; *it is the feminine element performing around the male its bewitching pirouettes.*[18] [Italics not in original.]

The thyrsus was a magic staff used by the Dionysian Bacchantes in their rites and so was a symbol of the initiation into the mysteries of antiquity. The connection among Renan, Hoffmann's Cat Murr, and the blue thyrsus of Rimbaud's poem may therefore be construed to mean that neither by means of the purely rational side of man (the masculine principle), personified in the poet's mind by Renan, nor by pure fantasy embodied in the Cat Murr (the feminine principle), can the poet become a true initiate of the mysteries symbolized by the thyrsus, but only when the masculine and feminine principles exist in equilibrium.

The poem "Eternité," which possesses all the profound simplicity of one of Blake's *Songs of Innocence,* records the climax of the poet's spiritual quest. Here Eternity is represented as a synthesis of opposites, and this explains why the poet attached so much importance to the idea of equilibrium. Such a concept of Eternity as a state of harmony in which all opposites have been reconciled is not particularly strange or far-fetched. The ideal of saintliness constantly upheld in the *Bhagavad-Gita,* for example, is to free oneself from the "pairs of opposites." Also it has been noted in the poem "Vies" that Rimbaud believed he had reached a state which was beyond good and evil. In this poem, he expresses the joy which he feels in his discovery:

ETERNITÉ	ETERNITY
Elle est retrouvée. Quoi? – L'Eternité. C'est la mer allée Avec le soleil.	It has been found again. What? – Eternity. It is the sea gone With the sun.
Ame sentinelle, Murmurons l'aveu De la nuit si nulle Et du jour en feu.	Sentinel soul, Let us murmur the vow Of the night so void And of the day on fire.
Des humains suffrages, Des communs élans Là tu te dégages Et voles selon.	Human franchise, Common urges There you free yourself And fly accordingly.
Puisque de vous seules, Braises de satin, Le Devoir s'exhale Sans qu'on dise enfin.	Since from you alone, Satin embers, Duty is exhaled Without one saying finally.
Là pas d'espérance, Nul *orietur.* Science avec patience, Le supplice est sûr.	There no hope, No *orietur.* Science with patience, The punishment is sure.
Elle est retrouvée. Quoi? – L'Eternité. C'est la mer allée Avec le soleil.[19]	It has been found again. What? – Eternity. It is the sea gone With the sun.

It will be noted that most of the stanzas in this poem contain two words in sharp contrast: (1) la mer, le soleil, (2) la nuit, le jour, (3, 4) élans, Devoir, (5) Science, patience, (6) la mer, le soleil (or fire and water). In a second version of the same poem, later cited by Rimbaud in the *Saison,* one notes the substitution of the word *mêlée* for *allée* in the first and last stanza. Now the idea of eternity as a union of sun and sea or fire and water — the masculine and feminine principles in occult thought — is a well-known alchemical symbol, according to John Read in a recent study of alchemy, *Prelude to Chemistry.*[20] The *prima materia* of the philosopher's stone, which was supposed to cure all diseases and turn the baser metals into gold, was symbolized by "fiery water," Read holds, citing the following Latin verse under an alchemical drawing of 1625: "Fire and flowing water are contrary to one another; happy thou if thou canst unite them: let it suffice thee to know this!" Read concludes that the philosopher's stone represented a union of the masculine and feminine principles: "Thus both the preparation of the stone and its application as a transmuting agent could be regarded . . . as essentially the union of masculine and feminine principles." Likewise, in Kabbalistic terminology, *En Soph* (the infinite), sometimes referred to as "astral light," was also a harmony of opposites, and is called "a symbol of eternity" in the dictionary of occult terms compiled by Manly P. Hall.[21] Astral light, according to Eliphas Lévi, is the medium of the seer's visions and the means whereby the magus is able to work miracles: "The science of miracles is therefore the knowledge of this marvelous force, and the art of working miracles is simply the art of magnetizing or illuminating beings according to the invariable laws of magnetism or of astral light."[22] Lévi maintains that it is from this "great magic agent" that the term *illuminés* was taken: *"Illuminés* means simply the knowers and possessors of the light, whether by means of the knowledge of the great magic agent or by means of rational and ontological conceptions of the absolute."

In the *Saison,* Rimbaud prefaced his second version of the poem "Eternité" with this statement, indicating further that he attached a particular significance to the conception of light: "Finally, O happiness, O reason, I brushed from the heavens the azure which is dark [*noir*], and I lived, a golden spark of the light *nature*" (the underscoring is Rimbaud's).[23] The opposites mentioned in the phrase "the azure which is dark" suggests the Kabbalistic conception of the dual nature of God as light and darkness; this makes the passage as a whole the expression of joy which the poet feels in being a small particle of this spiritual light which is God. It is possible that this passage from the *Saison* is related in meaning to the following one, from Henri Delaage's *Doctrines des sociétés secrètes* (1852):

> this light [lumière] is the igneous force which in the name of *nature* [*nature*] has developed seeds, has given them the power to pierce the ground, to lift themselves with leaves, flowers and fruits.[24]

Here Delaage indicates that he is using the concept of light in an unusual and mystical sense as the life force or the power which produces growth in nature. Not only was this mysterious light the medium of visions and the "substance" of the double or astral body, but it also possessed particular symbolic significance in the initiation rites of the secret societies. Delaage's work contains a lengthy account of the various stages of an initiation rite symbolizing the regeneration of the neophyte who, if successful, was no longer a "child of darkness" but a "child of light."[25] He was then led into the sanctuary of Isis and Osiris where he was given an eye made of diamond to indicate that he was a priest of Osiris, meaning *"oeil de Dieu."* Delaage expresses the idea of Illuminists that the Egyptian mysteries were the origin of the Western religions:

> Thus the light communicated in the sanctuaries of Isis molded the revealers and the teachers of religion who spoke the language of the eternal wisdom; this same light communicated in the sanctuaries of Mithra trained the Magi, prophets whose eye saw the future, whose hands performed miracles.[26]

"Eternité" and three other poems express the poet's pure delight upon reaching the summit of his experience: "Age d'or," "Chanson de la plus haute tour" and an untitled one beginning, *"O Saisons, ô châteaux."* In these verses, we can at least partially reconstruct and so share somewhat in his experiences. Although similar to "Eternité" in their brief lines, these poems possess the more haunting rhythms of an incantation. A reference to the seasons and the castles appears as a refrain in the last of the poems mentioned — the French is cited here because the rhythm is difficult to maintain in English without changing the words:

> O Saisons, ô châteaux,
> Quelle âme est sans défauts?
>
> O Saisons, ô châteaux,
> J'ai fait la magique étude
> Du bonheur que nul n'élude.[27]

In "Age d'or" another allusion is made to the castle:

> O! joli château!
> Que ta vie est claire!
> De quel âge es-tu,
> Nature princière
> De notre grand frère?[28]

The connection here between the seasons and the castles, not at all an apparent one to a reader unfamiliar with Illuminist thought, contains a reference to one of the most beautiful legends of the *Zohar,* where it is related that the soul of the seer on its way to spiritual perfection and union with the divine *En Soph* must travel through seven palaces (often called castles, tabernacles, houses, or halls) representing different levels of spiritual attainment.[29] The soul of the seer supposedly left the body and traveled on a celestial journey, under the guidance of Enoch, through the seven castles until it reached the final stage of prophetic vision and illumination. The recitation of verses or hymns having short lines served as a sort of magic incantation to induce the gates of the castle to admit the seer. Knowledge of the stars and the seasons was entrusted to Enoch, who walked with God, and was delivered by him to men. But knowledge about the mystic ascension in the castles was reserved for the chosen few, the seers. Therefore, in the line *"O Saisons, o châteaux!"* the poet is doubtless thinking of the celestial trip of the seer, past the mundane knowledge of the seasons to the mystical knowledge of the castles. In the second line, *"Quelle âme est sans défauts*?" the poet is thinking of his imperfections as he approaches the castle, since it is supposed to represent a new level of perfection achieved.

In "Age d'or" the poet, rejoicing in his newly discovered state of harmony, hears angelic voices. He has many questions to ask the celestial beings but, realizing the futility, refrains from doing so. Then one of the angelic voices begins to sing and becomes visible to the naked eye (*"visible à l'oeil nu"*). The poet joins in the singing. It is a song about the wickedness of the world, which the angelic voice advises him to leave to the fire, and about the beauty of the castle by contrast (*"O joli château!"*). In the last stanza, other angelic voices have joined in the singing: "Multiples soeurs! Voix / Pas du tout publiques!"[30]

Also in agreement with these interpretations is the "Chanson de la plus haute tour," in which the poet celebrates his ascetic withdrawal from the world into the tower of his mystic castle. Aware that his life has been wasteful, lazy, and "a slave to every pleasure," he decides that the highest good is to depart from men. This he does, casting aside all fears and sufferings except for the morbid thirst ("*La soif malsaine*") which is constantly with him as a result of the hashish he has taken. He even succeeds in forgetting the prairie, which was probably the most tempting pleasure to the vagabond side of his nature. He carried this inverted asceticism to such lengths that he "ended by finding the disorder of my mind sacred," as he says in the *Saison* immediately preceding the re-quotation of this poem. Instead of saying prayers to the Virgin — the soul is poor who has only her image ("*la si pauvre âme, Qui n'a que l'image de Notre Dame!*") — he says farewell to the world with ballads (*Saison*). The second version of this poem, quoted in the *Saison,* should be noted because it differs greatly from the first and shows improvement in poetic technique. Here the well-known refrain produces the effect of an incantation: "Qu'il vienne, qu'il vienne, / Le temps dont on s'éprenne."[31]

The physical pangs of hunger and thirst which the poet suffered in his practice of an inverted asceticism are recorded in the two poems "Comédie de la soif" and "Fêtes de la faim." The titles of both these poems are ironic, for the feast mentioned in the latter is nonexistent and the "comedy" of the first would be more accurately called a tragedy. "Fêtes de la faim" is another poem re-quoted with changes in the *Saison.* Both versions are brief and consist chiefly of the poet's expression of the great anguish which he suffers from hunger: "I always dine on air, rock, coal, iron," he laments. But not all Rimbaud's hunger can be traced to the effects of hashish; he was often hungry on his flights from home, lacking money with which to buy food. The poet's thirst was more intimately related to hashish and to absinth, which he mentions specifically in the "Comédie de la soif." In the first stanza, the poet's most remote ancestors offer him fine wines mellow from aging underground, but he declines them. His ancestors, buried in the nearby fields, ask him to descend into their cellars and have cider and milk, but these he also refuses, in the second stanza. Next, his immediate grandparents, who tell him that they will return from the cemetery, offer him fine liqueurs and the rare drinks, coffee, and tea; these he also rejects. Then a spirit appears and bids the water sprites ("Ondines") to give the poet water, and the wandering Jews, exiled in Norway, to give him snow, but says that pure drinks do not quench his thirst, which he compares with that of the Hydra, the nine-headed monster slain by Hercules. At length, his friends urge him to taste of the wines along the shore and then offer to lead him, like a wise pilgrim, to the "green-columned Absinth." To this the poet replies that he would rather rot in a swamp than have anything further to do with such "landscapes," which we interpret to mean the landscapes of his absinth dreams, in view of the line, *"Jamais l'auberge verte ne peut bien m'être ouverte"* ("Never could the green inn be open to me"). The poet then dreams that death will perhaps come to him one evening when he has been quietly drinking in some old city and he will die content since he has finally learned patience. But if, on the other hand, he becomes resigned to his trouble (*"mon mal,"* i.e. his terrible thirst) he wonders whether he will choose to live "in the North or in the Country of the Vines." Such speculations are idle, he concludes, resolving that if he should ever become the wanderer which he once was, he will have nothing further to do with the "green inn," or absinth. In the last stanza, the poet, suffering from his great thirst, reflects upon the fact that the animal world also knows thirst like this—"the pigeons which tremble on the prairie, wild game and the last butterflies." Finally, he expresses the wish that he could dissolve where the cloud before him has and "expire in these humid violets."

The state of equilibrium which the poet discovered at the height of his experience was of brief duration. Numerous obscure allusions to the "chaos" and "tumult" of the "poles" appear in *Les Illuminations*, indicating that the poet was not always able to maintain the high point of his experience recorded in the poem "Eternité." Four of these are:

> the chaos and ice of the poles ["Après le déluge"]
>
> from the tumultuous pole to the castle ["Génie"]
>
> this ice . . . these blue rays and these purple perfumes of the sun of the poles ["Métropolitain"]
>
> This evening at Circéto of the icy heights . . . colored like ten months of the red night. . . . For my prayer alone, mute as those nocturnal regions and preceding *feats more violent than the chaos of the poles* ["Dévotion"]

In these passages it should be noted that the ice of the poles is contrasted with the sun or the rays of the pole, and that there is a connection in the poet's mind between the pole and the castle. The reference to the poles is an allusion to the Illuminist idea that the astral light in which the seer was said to have his visions was polarized: there was a positive pole which was red, and a negative one which was white. The ice of the poles then would refer to the negative or white end, while the rays or light of the pole would refer to the positive or red end. The center of this polarized light was the point of equilibrium, the place of the union of all opposites, from whose luminous center came forth harmony of sound, the colors and the resplendent paths to the castles. By contrast with the equilibrium of the center, the poles are described as being chaotic. The first passage from "Après le déluge" contains an allusion to the chaos from which the new world has emerged after the disaster of the flood; while the second, from the poem "Génie," refers to the emergence of man, the individual from his own interior chaos to the celestial palace of spiritual illumination. The poet urges all men to follow the Génie from the polar chaos or the domination of the opposites to the point of equilibrium and harmony. The purple perfumes mentioned in the third passage refer to the experience of synesthesia, which accompanies the extraordinary vision of the seer. Further discussion of the red and white or the positive and negative forces will be discussed in the following section on the subject of the colors (cf. the poem "Barbare").

THE VISION OF THE RAINBOW ("VOYELLES," "LES SOEURS DE LA CHARITÉ," "LES POETES DE SEPT ANS," "BARBARE," "VILLES II" AND "BATEAU IVRE")

It is in the vision of the rainbow that the two chief sources of Rimbaud's inspiration — or damnation, as he preferred to call it later — became united. The extraordinary presence of color, which is everywhere apparent in Rimbaud's poetry and which perhaps impresses most the reader who approaches these works for the first time, is due not only to the effects of hashish, but also to what he called his *"magies religieuses."* This is true because the colors of *Les Illuminations,* like the objects which he evokes, are charged with symbolic and Kabbalistic significance. Rimbaud's visions are therefore not grey and misty apparitions, but alive with color, meaning, and mobility. Describing as synesthesia the heightened perception of colors which he saw under hashish, Baudelaire also writes:

> Hallucinations begin. . . . Sounds have a color, colors have a music. Musical notes are numbers and you work prodigious arithmetical calculations with terrifying rapidity, as the music swells in your ear.[32]

Also commenting upon the extraordinary perception of colors which he saw under the drug mescalin, Aldous Huxley writes in *The Doors of Perception*:

> how significant is the enormous heightening, under mescalin, of the perception of color! . . . Mescalin raises all colors to a higher power and makes the percipient aware of innumerable fine shades of difference, to which, at ordinary times, he is completely blind.[33]

Why Rimbaud's poetry is so charged with color is easily understood, but whether or not the colors are used symbolically and, if so, to what extent and with what significance, will require more detailed analyses.

Since the concept of light held a position of central importance in Illuminist thought, it is natural to find Kabbalistic commentators Karppe and Serouya concluding that "the rainbow occupies a particular place in the *Zohar*."[34] Light was a synthesis of the colors, and each of the emanations which came from the primordial light possessed a corresponding color as well as a number, both having symbolic significance. Not only was the rainbow itself a symbol of rebirth, but its very existence was a result of the union of the two opposites — light (or fire) and water. As in the cosmos emanation was a process by which the dark, invisible, and unknown aspects of the deity moved in the direction of becoming visible and manifest, so in the rainbow black is linked to white by seven intermediary colors. Similarly, in Illuminist initiation rites, as Delaage points out, the "child of darkness passes through seven degrees before arriving at the white and pure light which binds him again to God."[35] His initiation symbolizes his rebirth just as the rainbow represents the rebirth of the world. Now the whole system of emanation is based upon what Serouya describes as a kind of pansexualism which existed from the very beginning within the deity where light, the male element, is thought of as having united with darkness, the female element.[36] The emanations and the colors were similarly considered to have been wedded to each other, beginning with the second and third emanations. The first one, the Crown, was considered to be colorless, differentiation not yet having taken place until the appearance of the next two, Wisdom and Intelligence, which were black and white, masculine and feminine, respectively. The next pair of colors were red (Justice, masculine) and white (Grace or Mercy, feminine) which gave birth to green, and so on until the last emanation, which is blue or sapphire, the heavenly or spiritual color. In the progression red, green, and blue, the order of the prism is followed, while the complete progression black, white, red, green, and blue is the order of the colors in the alchemical process and also the same succession mentioned by Rimbaud in his famous sonnet, "Voyelles."

Of all the disputed parts of Rimbaud's poetry "Voyelles," published October 1883 in the review *Lutèce,* provoked the most diversified criticism by its very nature. With a fine sense of humor, artist M. Luque drew a caricature of Rimbaud which appeared in *Hommes d'aujourdhui* (1888), showing a picture of the poet dressed in child's clothing and seated on an enormous green "U." On the floor beside him were several freshly colored vowels and a can of paint. Among the early critics of the famous sonnet was Anatole France, who said that the poem lacked common sense, but indicated that he found it nevertheless an amusing work which did not need to have a meaning. Paterne Berrichon, Rimbaud's brother-in-law, was baffled by the possibility that the saint and mystic would have condescended to invent a colored alphabet and insisted that the sonnet was unworthy of Rimbaud. Among the more amusing speculations about the sonnet are those of C. A. Hackett and Colonel Godchot. The former, who has a psychoanalytic eye, considers the objects evoked in the sonnet to be sexual symbols, the *"golfe d'ombre"* of the very first line being an allusion to the maternal womb. The most comical explanation, however, is that of Colonel Godchot, who believes in a literal interpretation: he is willing to accept "A" as black and like a fly because this letter, if turned upside down on a period, does have the shape of a fly with its wings spread. Omega he also finds logical because the Greek letter forms the shape of an eyeglass through which the "rayon violet" may be seen. But Colonel Godchot is indignant that "E" should be white and "I" red: "Why," he protests, "is 'E' white? . . . Why is 'I' red? Mystery."[37] He also finds a contradiction between the first line, in which Rimbaud says that "O" is blue, and the last, where he says it is violet.

Three recent explanations of the famous sonnet are more ingenious. (1) According to Paul Reboux and an American, Van Roosebroeck, the sonnet is an example of the psychological phenomenon known as colored hearing which exists quite naturally in some people, chiefly adolescents, without the use of hashish. (2) Enid Starkie suggests that the poem may have alchemical significance, but because her work is primarily biographical, she does not work out the details of this explanation. (3) The solution which has finally gained the most favor among critics is that of Gaubert who says that Rimbaud associated the colors with the vowels he had seen in his spelling book. According to Gaubert, the illustrations which accompanied the vowels were: A — Abeille; E — Eau; I — Indien; U — Universe; O — Orgue and Oeil.[38] It is an ingenious explanation, but the objection which immediately arises is that in the list of objects which the poet evokes in connection with the color, not one of the words appears exactly as listed above. The accompanying table lists the image evoked along with a symbolic significance stemming from the object itself, which, when seen as a whole, give some clue as to what Rimbaud possibly meant in his poem.

VOWEL	*COLOR*	*IMAGES*	*SYMBOLIC MEANING*
A	Black	black corset	darkness which represses or restrains
		flies	bestiality
		stench	corruption and chaos
		dark abyss	depths of obscurity and ignorance
E	White	vapors, glaciers	lack of solidity and impermanent solidity, coldness
		tents, white kings	the Crusades (cf. "Alchimie du verbe": "I was dreaming of Crusades")
		shiver of umbels	frail and transient beauty weakness
I	Red	blood spat out	bloodshed in war
		laughter of beautiful lips	love, passion
		anger, drunkenness	violence, loss of control
U	Green	cycles, vibrations of green seas	states under hashish and absinth
		peace of the pastures, peace of wrinkles	two kinds of peace: that which arises from rustic life and that which comes from study
		alchemy	the subject of that study — alchemy, based on the so-called Emerald Tables of Hermes
O	Blue	supreme Claríon	sound which marks the end of the world and the completion of the alchemical process
		strident noise silence	reconciliation of the opposites — sound and silence
		Omega — violet ray	supreme unity of the end with the beginning, of sound and color

Taking into consideration the symbols used in the sonnet as a whole, it reads in this fashion: out of the darkness which represses, which is bestial, filthy and chaotic — an abyss of obscurity — emerges its opposite, a whiteness and purity which is, however, both cold and lacking in solidity ("vapeurs") or possesses a solidity which is impermanent and will not stand heat ("glaciers"). It is a whiteness which is fragile and delicate ("shiver of umbels") and which reminds the poet of the whiteness of the tents and kings of the Crusades. The next two colors, red and green, also form a pair of opposites; the former represents the passions of love and hate, which in their most intense form become "*ivresse*" or loss of rational control; green, on the other hand, represents peace and tranquility, originating from two sources: Nature ("peace of the pastures"), the quiet of country meadows and books in the absorbing study of the ancient wisdom of alchemy ("peace of the wrinkles which alchemy impresses upon large studious foreheads"). The poet mentions the study of alchemy in connection with the color green because the Hermetic wisdom was written down in the so-called "Emerald Tables." The "supreme Clarion" of the last stanza of "Voyelles" refers to the trumpet of the last judgment or to the end of the world when all will return to the original oneness and harmony from which it came — the pairs of opposites represented by loud sound ("*strideurs*") and silence, colors and sounds which will become one in "*le rayon violet*" which proceeds from the eyes of the deity ("*Ses Yeux*"), who is Alpha and Omega, the beginning and the end.

In this analysis of the imagery in the sonnet a definite progression from chaos and darkness into harmony and light is noted. Such is the Kabbalistic account of the emanation of the cosmos, beginning with black and white, passing through red and green, and ending with the last emanation, which is blue. The poet, however, makes a direct allusion in the poem to alchemy, but it is a well-attested fact among Illuminists that these two facets of ancient lore were intimately related. The alchemical process was supposed to be a reenactment of the creation of the world and also a symbol of the steps by which the regenerated man used to return to God: the cosmos which also emerged from darkness will return finally to harmony and light. Descriptions which alchemical writers give of the exact methods whereby they worked with the metals in an effort to change the baser metals into gold contain, as psychologist Jung points out, a hopeless mass of contradictions, since each writer tried to reveal and at the same time conceal the secret of the *Magnum Opus*, as the process was called.[39] From all these contradictions, however, the first three stages in this process have been clearly defined. Following the steps outlined by Jung, the first stage is one of blackness (*nigredo*) during which a union of contradictory principles takes place. Then disintegration or death takes place (*putrefactio, mortificatio, calcinatio*), after which comes the washing off (*ablutio*) which results in a whitening (*albedeo*) of the metal. It should be noted that the blackness with putrefaction and the flies are mentioned in Rimbaud's sonnet and that this is followed by whiteness. The next transformation in the alchemical process was a reddening (*rubedeo*) of the metals and Rimbaud mentions red as the third color, compared by the alchemists to blood (cf. Rimbaud's *"sang craché"*). Unfortunately, at this point Jung's list ceases, but following the Kabbalists, the union of red and white produced green, while blue, which was said to be the last emanation, corresponded with the philosopher's stone, necessary for the final transmutation into gold. According to both Serouya and Karppe, the tenth and last emanation was blue. Serouya writes: "The last Sephira, Kingdom, is a transparent sapphire which reflects all the colors. This Sephira condenses in itself the harmony of all the Sephiroth."[40] Karppe says: "The color sapphire includes all the colors and is the fundamental stone of the universe. . . . This sapphire . . . is the primordial point of everything."[41] M. Pattison Muir, in *The Story of Alchemy and the Beginnings of Chemistry,* says that the philosopher's stone was blue.[42] We have already noticed that Rimbaud used the color in connection with the thyrsus which was the symbol of initiation into the mysteries. Blue was the mystic color and it shall presently be seen that Rimbaud also used it to represent the mysteries.

The question arises from the analysis of the sonnet "Voyelles" as to what extent, if any, Rimbaud used the colors symbolically in other poems. Even if he did use them symbolically in many instances, it does not necessarily follow that he always used them in this way or that he is obligated to follow the rigid order set down in the sonnet. This the poet does not do, but he frequently uses them alone with the symbolic meaning set forth in the sonnet. With one exception, which Rimbaud himself qualifies in the poem, even the order of the colors and a similar imagery may be found in "Les Poètes de sept ans":

Second stanza: (black)	"black tics, the shadow of corridors, the coolness of latrines" (cf. the darkness, bestiality and "stench" of "Voyelles")

Third stanza: (white)	"was lighting up with moonlight . . . calcium, weak" (cf. the whiteness and frailty of the sonnet)
Fourth stanza: (red)	"Ravished liberty . . . red he was looking . . . dresses of Indians . . . the little brutal girl . . . the flavor of her skin" (cf. the passions — war and love — of the sonnet)
Fifth stanza: (green)	"A Bible with a cabbage-green edge . . . he was dreaming of the prairie" (cf. "peace of the pastures" of the sonnet)
Sixth stanza: (blue)	"the high and blue room . . . vertigo . . . in the sidereal woods" (aspiration toward the infinite)

Is it possible that Rimbaud saw in these same terms the five stages through which poetry had passed since the Golden Age of Greece, as he outlined them in the *Voyant* letters:

(1) Ennius to Theroldus: ("*les siècles barbares*") – Black – The Dark Ages
(2) Theroldus to Casimir Delavigne: – White – period of the Crusades, the Age of Faith
(3) The First Romantics: – Red – period of the passions in literature
(4) Second Generation Romantics: – Green – period of intellectual reaction against the passions in literature
(5) First Seer, Baudelaire: – Blue – the beginning of the period of visionary literature

Instead of following a rigid sequence of colors which would have been artificial and detrimental to his art, Rimbaud wrote certain poems in which a single color such as green or red predominates, or again in certain brief passages within a poem he used colors symbolically, as has been shown, for example, in the passage about the blue thyrsus. The color green is also used with the obvious symbolism of the sonnet "Voyelles" in the poem "Les Soeurs de la charité," which gives an account of a young man who, irritated and hurt by the ugliness of the world, turned to woman for comfort but found her anything but a creature of mercy or charity. As he was suffering greatly in her clutches: "Viennent la Muse verte et la Justice ardente / Le déchirer de leur auguste obsession."[43] The green Muse who comes to rescue him is Reason, the opposite of the passions and the irrational red. We shall examine next the symbolic use of red and white in "Barbare" and "Villes II," and finally the colors used in "Bateau ivre," which is generally considered Rimbaud's greatest masterpiece.

As the individual emerges from his own inner darkness and chaos to harmony and illumination, so within the universe itself a comparable struggle is taking place. It is the conflict of the positive and negative forces, of the masculine and feminine, the red and white principles. This cosmic struggle is depicted in the poem "Barbare," which is perhaps the most obscure of all *Les Illuminations*. Like "Eternité," it is filled with a vocabulary of opposites, but here the equilibrium has been broken. The first line of the poem indicates that its setting is apocryphal, that it is a cosmic struggle which occurs quite beyond space and time (*"Bien après les jours et les saisons, et les êtres et les pays"*). An age of great violence and destruction has come upon the earth, the final episode of which is presented here as a struggle of the forces of nature. A number of objects are listed in opposition to each other: a bloody banner is contrasted with the "silk of seas" and "arctic flowers"; "embers" with "gusts of hoarfrost"; fire with rain; "embers" with "foam"; and in the last paragraph, "gentleness" (*"douceur"*), "white tears," and the "feminine voice" with the "bloody banner."

Now if these objects listed above are categorized, we find a contrast of redness and heat ("the flag of bloody meat" and the "braziers") with whiteness and coldness ("foam," "white tears," and "ices"); an opposition of softness and gentleness ("silk" and "softness") with the bloody banner. Some of the words used here suggest a few which appear in "Eternité": *"braziers,"* for example, which occurs twice in "Barbare" is closely related to *"braise"* in "Eternité" and instead of the word *"soie"* in "Barbare" we find *"satin"* in "Eternité." In the last paragraph of "Barbare" a struggle between the red flag or banner and the feminine voice, terminates in the victory of force or violence, the red or active principle over the white or passive principle; of the masculine over the feminine. Thus the title of the poem becomes clear; if Eternity is represented by the poet as a synthesis of opposites or an equilibrium of the masculine-feminine principles, then barbarity or a return to an original chaos occurs when, in the course of human events, the masculine or force-principle triumphs over the feminine. It is clear from poems such as "Guerre," "Démocratie," and others that Rimbaud considered the modern era in particular to be one of violence.

The interior landscape, created by Rimbaud and later developed by Laforgue, is elaborately constructed in "Villes II." As architect of his dreams the poet has built an entire city and populated it with mythological as well as ordinary inhabitants. The fabulous world of "Après le déluge" and "Enfance" appears again in this poem: giants and centauresses, the goddesses Diana and Venus, and Rolands sounding their horns in gorges. "Villes II" was doubtless fashioned as a contrast with the city of everyday life depicted in "Ville I." This modern city, thick with "eternal coal smoke" and built without taste is further described as a place where death, crime, and desperate love lurk everywhere. By contrast with this, "Villes II" is a city of crystal chalets which move magically on "invisible pulleys." In Rimbaud's interior landscape nothing is stationary, even the houses of his dream world are mobile. A day of public festivity is being celebrated in honor of love (*"les fêtes amoureuses"*), a series of red objects rises up in the poet's fancy: fires and oriflammes; copper palm trees (in alchemy copper is the metal which corresponds with the planet Venus); and finally, "Processions of Mabs in red dresses like opals climb the ravines." The reference to Mab serves as a further indication that it is a dream city which the poet is describing, for Mab was the queen of English fairies who presided over the birth of dreams. This dream city is also the city of the future, of the new Fourierist society which Rimbaud hoped would come about, for its citizens are celebrating, in addition to the birth of Venus, "the joy of new work." Fourier taught as a cardinal principle the importance of the passions and particularly the doctrine that workers would produce much more if they were assigned to the kind of jobs for which they were best suited. A general atmosphere of happiness pervades the poem as a whole along with an unrestrained expression of the emotions on the part of everyone: "the Bacchantes who sob in the suburbs" and the "savages who dance in a storm of fury." Just as Fourier encouraged artists to "sing the ideas of the people," Rimbaud says that "groups of belfries are singing the ideas of the people." "Ville II" ends with the poet's regret that he will be unable to retrieve his dream city once it has vanished.

No sea poem in the French language approaches the "Bateau ivre" in verve and originality or communicates such real feeling for the sea. When applied to this poem, superlatives such as these are not excessive, especially if one thinks of "Bateau ivre" in comparison with Baudelaire's sea poem, "Le Voyage," which, fine though it is, does not equal this one; nor could any of Hugo's sea poems be summoned to match it in poetic intensity. Written by a boy of sixteen who had never seen the sea, and used by him to make his debut into Parisian literary society, the poem stands as one of the great masterpieces of the language. Scrutiny of the creative technique which Rimbaud used to produce it reveals the very process he had advocated in the *Voyant* letters: the magical union of subject and object. For not only does the poet effect a fusion of sea and sky ("*la mer mêlée avec le soleil*"), but also a union of man and his boat with the background.[44] As man loses his identity and becomes fused with the elements, the sea, by contrast, becomes a living breathing creature with a rhythmic pulsation of its own. This is apparent in the metaphors of the fourth stanza, when the poet compares himself to a piece of cork on the water ("lighter than a cork I danced on the waves") and in the seventh and tenth stanzas, when he mentions the rhythm and circulation of the sea ("the circulation of unheard of sap"). Put into practice in this poem, the esthetic ideal of the fusion of subject and object advocated in the *Voyant* letters produces the exact results which the Impressionists later sought: the destruction of the plastic, of lines which differentiate objects from each other and people from their environment. In addition to being a great sea poem, therefore, "Bateau ivre" may also be called the first truly Impressionist poem in the French language. As a painter with words, Rimbaud uses the richest and most varied colors of his palette to unleash the splendor of the tempest, the brilliance of sun and wave or the quiet pools of submarine life. "Bateau ivre" is a veritable symphony of colors in which the poet returns constantly to the theme color, green, while other colors are subtly mingled with the green and used symbolically as well as literally.

The drunken boat of the poem should be contrasted with two other uses which Rimbaud makes of the boat image: (1) the "motionless canoe" ("*le canot immobile*") of the poem "Mémoire" and with the "rescue ship" ("*le navire sauveur*") of *Une Saison en enfer* which is discussed in the last section of this chapter. In stanza eighteen of "Bateau ivre" the poet identifies himself with his boat ("Now I, a lost boat . . ."); a similar identity is implied though not stated in the last two stanzas of "Mémoire" with its delicately drawn pictures of the poet's childhood beside the Meuse with his two sisters. The boat mentioned there is a small rowboat or canoe which the poet and his brother, Frederick, had probably been allowed to use sometimes on the river, but which was significantly described as "always fixed" and kept in this immovable state by a chain. The flowers which the child-poet wants cannot be attained because they are out of his reach and the boat is chained. He is therefore frustrated by the restrained boat and identifies himself with it: was he not also chained like the boat, to his mother and to his dull life in Charleville? On the other hand, the drunken boat is a symbol of release from restraint; it is the boat of his freedom, first from the "impassible rivers," from the heavy cargoes with which it has been laden, and finally from everything which impedes his escape. For ten nights the drunken boat is tossed by the tempest but it has a glimpse of marvels in the deep which the *"canot immobile"* would never have been able to see. Like his *"bateau ivre,"* the poet is also drunk, as the lines in which he says that he has been "devouring green azures" and feeling rhythms which are "stronger than alcohol" would seem to indicate. The green liquor producing an effect stronger than alcohol is absinth, which the poet himself mentions having taken in "La Comédie de la soif." Therefore, when he says that the "green water penetrated my pine shell," he is probably using it in a double sense: to refer to the water of his sea of absinth as well as to the actual sea of his *"bateau ivre."* As the drink arouses his passions, he begins to blend the color red with the green in the line: "The bitter rednesses of love ferment!" Like hashish, absinth also opens the doors upon the mysteries for the poet, who begins to paint that world in violet, as he does in the sonnet "Voyelles." Here he sees the "mystic horrors" of the setting sun "illuminating with long violet settings." Not only is there music in these colors of the sea, as the poet suggests in the phrases about "singing phosphorescences" and "singing fish," but there are also "dark perfumes" in its depths. In the "Bateau ivre," as in many other poems, Rimbaud makes a constant appeal to all the senses and not merely to the visual sense as the critic Guy Michaud maintains.[45]

The submarine landscape having wonders of all sorts is presented by the poet in stanzas twelve through seventeen. It is the world of Jules Verne's *Vingt mille lieues sous la mer*: submarine islands and glaciers, uprooted trees and giant serpents, flowers of foam among which he fancies he sees "panther's eyes" and "rainbows stretched like bridles controlling the glaucous herds beneath the sea's horizon." Verne's work, which appeared in time for a New Year's gift in 1870, also contains an account of mountains under the sea and of the "singing phosphorescences." Rimbaud uses the word *"lactescent"* to describe the foam on the sea, while Verne employs the adjective *"lactifiée."* Whatever borrowings the young poet may have made, they have all been transformed into a work which is uniquely his own.

From these submarine visions the poet is suddenly transported by a maelstrom into the islands of the sky and its "sidereal archipelagoes." Thus, just as he had previously discovered the sky within the sea in the lines, "And afterwards I bathed myself in the Poem / Of the Sea, milky and infused with stars," so he also finds the sea in the sky with "a million golden birds." He has been tossed to such heights that it seems to him that he is near enough to the sky to be able to bore a hole in it as if it were a wall ("*Moi qui trouais le ciel rougeoyant comme un mur . . .*"). In such a way the poet succeeds in dissolving the distinctions between sea and sky; each blends into the other while the sky and man are brought nearer to each other. The sea becomes a living creature when the maelstrom is compared with an animal in heat ("*Le rut des Béhémots et les Maelstroms épais*"). A similar metaphor may be found in this passage from Hugo's novel, *Les Travailleurs de la mer*:

> For those who are familiar with the sea, its appearance during these times is strange; one would say that it desires and fears the cyclone. Certain marriages moreover which Nature wills are welcomed in this fashion. The lioness in heat flees before the lion. The sea also is in heat. For this reason it trembles. The immense marriage is about to take place.[46]

After the episode of the maelstrom, the poet begins to long for "Europe with its ancient parapets," but he is so exhausted from the tempest that he wishes instead for his own destruction ("*O que ma quille éclate! O que j'aille à la mer!*"). The death wish which the poet expresses here may have resulted from the depressing effects of absinth, as suggested when he says that he is "swollen with drunken torpors." The end supports this interpretation, for the poet says that if he does reach European waters, he wants only a modest pond where at sunset a child may be seen sailing a toy boat "frail as a May butterfly." He wants no more voyages in the drunken boat, however marvelous this experience may have been. The reason for this is perhaps that absinth had an injurious effect upon him since he denounces it in more direct terms in "La Comédie de la soif," where he first calls the drink by name — "Absinth with its green columns" — and then says:

Et si je redeviens	And if I become again
Le voyageur ancien,	The ancient traveler,
Jamais l'auberge verte	Never can the green inn
Ne peut bien m'être ouverte.[47]	Be open to me again.

The Vision of the Golden Ship

Traditional criticism of the "Bateau ivre" has pointed to the fact that the voyage of the boat symbolized the poet's life in that he returned at last, like his ship, to the religion of his childhood, and also, at the end of his life, to European waters. Although the latter part of this statement is correct (the first can be shown by evidence from the *Saison* to be untrue), another comparison between the poet and his drunken boat coincides more accurately with the events: while exploring submarine wonders in his drunken boat, and in the depths of his own unconscious by means of hashish and absinth, the poet is lashed by a maelstrom and is buffeted by the unleashed fury of the animal instincts within the unconscious. But as the maelstrom tosses him into "sidereal archipelagoes," so does his inner storm or season in hell lift him to a different spiritual landscape. In a passage from the *Saison* the poet relates that his boat was shipwrecked and he was rescued at last by the *"navire sauveur"*:

> The reasonable song of the angels rises from the rescue ship ["le navire sauveur"]: it is divine love. . . . You are choosing me from among the shipwrecked ones; are not those who remain my friends? Save them! Reason was born to me. . . . God is my strength and I praise God.[48]

At this point we have reached the fourth and last season or phase in the poet's spiritual metamorphosis, where the inevitable and tantalizing question arises which every reader as well as critic of Rimbaud must always ask and answer in one way or another: Why did this precocious poet, this "meteor" in the world of French letters, as Mallarmé so aptly called him, suddenly decide to renounce literature completely, just before his nineteenth birthday, and take no further interest in it, even when, during the 1880's, his name became famous in Paris? Not once in all the letters from Abyssinia, where he worked as a merchant, does he ever refer to his writing or give the slightest clue as to what his intimate thoughts were during all those years. His silence about himself was total. The answer to such a question is by no means simple enough to be stated in a single sentence, for no person renounces abruptly what has been the center of his existence without great inner struggle and complex reasons. Rimbaud lists a number of reasons in the *Saison*: that his health was menaced; that he would fall into a sleep of several days duration, and when he got up the dreams would continue. He had reached the outer limits of sanity and feared madness. None of these, however, are reasons for ceasing to write poetry, but rather for giving up a harmful drug (and for renouncing Verlaine). After all, he had written excellent poetry before he began taking hashish. What then was his real reason for renouncing literature? To answer this adequately requires that we evaluate Rimbaud's experience as a whole, weighing as accurately as possible certain other statements of the *Saison*.

Rare is the person, especially in the twentieth century, who is able to give himself wholly to anything or to pursue a particular experience to the very end as this boy was able to do. We are too cynical, too sophisticated; most of all we lack his idealism and conviction. Everywhere in the *Saison* he deplores his lost purity; yet where can purer devotion be found than in him? He gave himself totally, not merely to his art but to truth itself in the Socratic sense. He was willing to destroy himself completely for the sake of truth, and would undoubtedly have done so except for the fact that he was rescued from destruction by that very truth which he loved so devotedly. This is the secret of his constant appeal to every generation, the reason why so many have felt the urge to write and then rewrite their books about him, for in spite of the errors into which he fell his basic and fundamental authenticity attracts like a magnet the idealism within his readers. If such a person began to feel that a conflict existed between his art and truth, he would, after a certain struggle, choose the latter, and this is exactly what Rimbaud did. The second sentence of the *Saison* begins: "One evening I sat Beauty upon my knees and I found her bitter" and ends with the statement that he is contented, after much spiritual struggle, to bury his imagination and his art. He considers that he has won a victory ("*la victoire m'est acquise*"), for henceforth he will be "free to possess truth in one soul and one body." Thus we may conclude that it is truth rather than art to which Rimbaud felt the deeper devotion. In this conflict which he felt to exist between art and truth there is a certain similarity to the dilemma which Balzac perceived between art and Swedenborgian mysticism, when Louis Lambert, his philosopher-self, says to the poet, his alter ego: "It is I who must die, but you who will live."[49] Confronted with a similar conflict, Balzac chose art, but at one time during his youth he also experienced an inner struggle over the two. The question with which we must finally deal is this: Why did Rimbaud believe that a conflict existed between his art and the truth which he was seeking? We are finally forced to ask Pilate's ancient question, in slightly different words: What does he mean by truth, and for what, in somewhat more specific terms, was he searching?

The chapter "L'Impossible" of the *Saison* should be read carefully, for it contains the real clue to Rimbaud's decision. Here the poet recapitulates his past deeds, weighing them in his own mind and pointing out wherein he considers that he was right and on what points he believes he fell into error. The fact that Rimbaud took prompt action following this self-appraisal proves the authenticity of his confessions here, for it is characteristic of neurotic confessors that they often indulge in confessing for histrionic effect and to enhance their own self-importance. Since such persons seldom take any action or change their conduct in any way, we may conclude that their repentance is insincere. But such was not the case with Rimbaud's confession. The vision which he had of the *"navire sauveur,"* cited in the above passage from the *Saison,* would indeed seem at first glance to mean that the poet intended to return to his Catholic faith. However, still using his nautical metaphors, the poet denies this emphatically in two other passages — in one which follows briefly upon the vision of the *"navire sauveur"* and again in the chapter "L'Impossible." In the first he says: "I do not intend embarking on a wedding with Jesus Christ as a father-in-law,"[50] meaning that he is not contemplating union with the church. In other words, it is God and not the church to whom he is turning, and this becomes increasingly evident in "L'Impossible." Appraising his past deeds, the poet considers his revolt and disdain justified on the grounds that he was trying to escape something: "I was right in all my disdain, since I am freeing myself (*"je m'évade"*). In the paragraphs which follow, he says that what he was trying to escape was the hypocrisy not only of Christianity but of the whole of Western culture. "We cultivate fog!" he says, and "Charity is unknown to us." One of the chief sources of Western self-deception and self-righteous mediocrity is Christianity (meaning the social institution), for "M. Prudhomme was born with Christ." In order to escape what Rimbaud calls the "Occidental swamps" and to find something purer and less hypocritical he decided to turn to the Orient, "the primitive country" and the birthplace of "the first and eternal wisdom." He therefore calls Christianity "the source of all my spiritual vagrancies." This is true since he now considers his belief that he could find something purer in the Orient to be an error, because what he really sought was Eden or a perfect society, which of course does not exist. Furthermore, one does not escape so easily one's background and formation, however great the desire to do so ("I am the slave of my baptism"). Nor have those philosophers who imagine that they have penetrated Eastern thought really been able to throw off their Western background (is Rimbaud perhaps thinking of Illuminists like Lévi and Delaage?): "Philosophers, you are of your Occident."

The realization of the futility of his search for the absolute in the Orient of Illuminist thought was the real reason for Rimbaud's renunciation of his art. In a moment of spiritual awakening he saw at last that he had been seeking his absolute in the wrong direction and by the wrong means. He believed that through the wisdom of the ancient Magi and Egyptians, together with the modern discovery of Mesmerism, he could acquire supernatural powers to change human life into something better ("I thought I had acquired supernatural powers").[51] It was the discoveries of Mesmer which had made such claims as voyance and communication with the dead seem plausible to so many during the nineteenth century. It was this belief that he could become a seer which had inspired his whole esthetic doctrine, and when he ceased to believe it possible for him to become a seer and discover the unknown, he no longer cared to pursue his art. It is true that he had written poetry before formulating his doctrine, but to renounce his very goal, the one which he had sought with such singleness of purpose, was too much. One may object that the poet did not have anything better to take the place of the literature which he renounced, but that he gave up a talent which did in fact bring him fame in less than ten years from the time of the composition of the *Saison,* even without any further effort on his part, a fame which might have come much sooner had he not run away to Abyssinia to become a merchant. When we are adding up the balance sheet of truth and error, however, to require that what we have left be a pleasing figure is not a demand made by those who seek truth.

As a matter of fact the poet was by no means left with an empty spirit, for he was given, in what he calls a "flash" ("*L'Eclair*"), a vision of the whole of the mystical experience. Significantly, he refers to this as his "moment of awakening" while his season in hell he called "sleeping." Here again, as was shown in Chapter 1, the mystic vision is described in metaphors which are the opposite of those used to describe the vision proceeding from the unconscious. Rimbaud's season in hell was a sleep in a double sense — (1) in that he had been exploring the region of sleep and the unconscious, and (2) in the sense that any person under twenty years of age may be said to be asleep, having not yet come into full possession of his rational powers. In the passage from the *Saison* about his awakening, the poet gives further evidence that the desire for truth was his chief passion:

> But I perceive that my spirit is asleep. If it were wide awake, from that moment on we would soon arrive at Truth, which may even now surround us with her weeping angels. . . . If it had been awake . . . I should never have yielded to my deleterious instincts. . . . If it had always been awake, I should be under full sail on the high sea of wisdom! . . . It is this moment of awakening that has given me the vision of purity! Through the Spirit we go to God![52]

Although Rimbaud rejects the church, all the elements of the mystical experience may be found in the account of his "awakening." The first indication of this may be noticed in his sense of the oppression of things and his desire to be rid of everything which is cluttering up his life. This urge to be rid of the nonessential, to reduce oneself to the minimum which the mystic believes to be the only reality is generally described by mystic writers as the beginning of the desire for purgation. Such a feeling of surfeit is apparent in two poems near the end of *Les Illuminations,* "Départ" and "Solde." The terse lines of "Départ" express the poet's satiety with all that he experienced during his plunge into the unconscious:

> Seen enough . . . .
> Had enough . . . .
> Known enough . . . .
> Departure in affection and new noise![53]

The natural reaction to this state of spirit is to take definite measures against the oppressive excess. The poet therefore prepares an itemized list of all these things, both material and spiritual, and offers them for sale to any interested person. Although the tone of "Solde," in which the items appear, is bitter and ironical, it nevertheless expresses the poet's determination to be rid of what he considers false. It is moving to observe that one who knew so few material comforts even lists some of these, but first on his list are the illusions which he has pursued and all those things which do not exist: "For sale what Jews have not sold, what neither nobility nor crime have tasted, what censured love and the infernal probity of the masses do not know; what neither time nor science need recognize."[54]

Purgation, which is a process of self-emptying and the first step toward purification, must precede anything of a positive nature in mystical experience, because it is believed that the human spirit must empty itself before it can be filled with God. After the self-emptying comes a strong urge for purity and a loathing of dissolute actions which the poet feels so intensely that he would offer to any divine image his *"élans vers la perfection."*[55] The frequent mention of purity in the *Saison* has caused many critics with a psychoanalytic orientation to consider this as further evidence of the poet's homosexuality. To say this, however, is to tear his statements from their context – unless evidence can be produced to show that the mystical experience itself attracts homosexuals and that many of the great mystics of the past have been homosexuals. But this is obviously impossible. The urge for purity and perfection which Rimbaud expresses is accompanied by the desire for God and the belief that "divine love alone controls the keys of knowledge." This is evident in the well-known lines, "I await God with great appetite" and "By the Spirit one goes to God." At this point he is moved by a desire to pray and meditate upon the idea of saintliness:

> If only God would grant me celestial, aerial calm, prayer – like the saints of old – Saints! They are the strong ones! Anchorites are artists of the sort which aren't wanted any more.[56]

The exact moment of Rimbaud's spiritual awakening comes only with his intuition of charity and his inner conviction that charity is the key to the mysteries and even to life itself ("Charity is that key").[57] It is only then that he has a vision of the *"navire sauveur"* with the angels on board and is rescued from the shipwreck of his drunken boat.

Whether Rimbaud pursued the knowledge which came to him in his moment of awakening is not known, since the last season of his life is veiled in silence. We should not assume that his final silence was that of the mystic. It is possible that, as he lay dying in 1891 in the hospital at Marseille, after having his leg amputated, he disclosed this hidden part of his life to his sister, Isabelle, who was his companion until his death, and that this was the reason why she insisted upon depicting her brother as a mystic and a saint. But this is merely conjecture and, certainly, the Rimbaud of the Parisian literary world was no mystic or saint. All we can know for a fact is that the poet finally received a glimpse of the path to truth which undoubtedly comes to the pure in heart, even when they pursue it in the wrong direction.

In one last vision, recorded in the final chapter of the *Saison*, appropriately entitled "Adieu," Rimbaud sees in the sky a large golden ship ("*Un grand vaisseau d'or*") with its multicolored banners floating on the morning breeze. As the marvelous ship sails among the islands of the sky, he sees "beaches filled with white nations in joy."[58] This was undoubtedly his "*navire sauveur*" with the angels on board, which had come to carry him away to that more perfect society of which he had dreamed and in which he would undoubtedly feel more at home.

Appendix A
Text of the Voyant Letters

To George Izambard
27, Abbaye-des-Champs Street,
Douai (North)

Charleville, May 13, 1871

Dear Sir!

There you are acting the professor again. One owes oneself to Society, you told me; you are a member of the teaching profession; you move in the beaten tracks. – I too, follow the principle: I cynically have myself *kept*: I unearth the old boys from the school: all the stupidity, filth, evil I can invent in action and in works, I give them: They pay me in glasses of beer and bottles of wine. *Stat mater dolorosa, dum pendet filius.*

– I owe myself to Society, that's fair, and I'm right.

– You too, you are right, at least for today. At bottom you see in your principle only subjective poetry: your persistence in returning to the university fold – pardon me – proves it. But you will always end up a satisfied person who has done nothing, not having wanted to do anything. Without taking into account that your subjective poetry will always be horribly insipid. Some day, I hope, – many others hope the same thing, – I shall see objective poetry in your principle, I shall see it more sincerely than you would! – I shall be a worker: This is the idea which holds me back when foolish fits of anger push me toward the battle of Paris, – where so many workers are still dying at the same time that I am writing you! To work now, never, never; I am on strike.

Now, I am debauching myself as much as possible. Why? I want to be a poet, and I am working to make myself a *seer;* you won't understand at all, and I can scarcely explain it to you. It is a question of arriving at the unknown by a disordering of *all the senses.* The sufferings are enormous, but one must be strong, must be born a poet, and I have recognized myself to be a poet. It isn't my fault at all. It is false to say: I think. One should say: I am thought. Pardon this play on words.

"I" is another. So much the worse for the wood which finds itself a violin, and insolently braves the unconscious ones who split hairs over matters of which they are entirely unaware!

You aren't *teaching* insofar as I am concerned. I give you this: Is it satire, as you would say? Is it poetry? It's fantasy, in any case. – But I beg of you, don't underline with a pencil, nor with too much thought:

Le Coeur supplicié [translated on page 160]

That doesn't mean a thing.
ANSWER ME: C/O Mr. Deverrière, for A. R.
Hearty greetings,

Arth. Rimbaud.

TO PAUL DEMENY
Douai

Charleville, May 15, 1871

I have decided to give you an hour of new literature. I am beginning consecutively with a psalm of present-day interest:

Chant de Guerre Parisien [discussed on pp. 163-165]

– Here is prose about the future of poetry: –

All ancient poetry ends with Greek poetry, harmonious Life. – From Greece to the Romantic Movement, – Middle Ages, – there are scholars, – versifiers. From Ennius to Theroldus, from Theroldus to Casimir Delavigne, everything is rhymed prose, a game, intellectual impotence and the glory of innumerable generations of idiots: Racine is the pure, the powerful, the great. – Even if his rhymes had been breathed over, his hemistiches confused, the Divine Fool would still be as unknown as any author of *Origins* you might chance on. – After Racine, the game became stale. It has lasted two thousand years!

No joking nor paradox. Reason inspires me with more certainties on the subject than a Young-France ever had bursts of anger. Besides, the *new ones* are free to execrate their forbears: one is within one's rights and one has the time.

Romanticism has never been very well judged. Who would have judged it? The Critics! The Romantics? who prove so well that the song is so seldom the work, that is, the song sung and understood by the singer.

For "I" is another. If the brass instrument wakens as clarion, that is not its fault. That is evident to me: I am present at the blossoming of my thought: I look at it, I listen to it: I give a stroke of the bow: the symphony makes its stir in the depths or comes with a bound on the scene.

If the old imbeciles hadn't found out anything about the Self except its false meaning, we shouldn't have to sweep out these millions of skeletons which, for an infinite time past have accumulated the products of their one-eyed intelligence, proclaiming themselves the author.

In Greece, I said, verse and lyres give rhythm to Action. Afterwards, music and rhymes are games, diversions. The study of this past charms the curious: Some people take pleasure in reviving these antiquities: Let them have them. The universal intelligence has always scattered its ideas naturally; men picked up a part of these fruits of the brain: they acted by, they wrote books from them: in such a way went the advance, without men straining, not being yet awakened, or yet in the fullness of the great dream. Officials, writers: author, creator, poet, this man has never existed!

The first study for the man who wants to be a poet is knowledge of himself, completely. He searches his soul, he inspects it, he tries it, he learns it. As soon as he knows it, he must cultivate it! That seems simple: in every brain a natural development is accomplished; so many *egotists* proclaim themselves to be authors; there are many others who attribute to themselves their intellectual progress! – But what is required is to make the soul monstrous: on the model of the *comprachicos,* what! Imagine a man planting warts on his face and cultivating them.

I say that one must be a *seer,* one must make oneself a *seer.*

The poet becomes a seer by a long, immense and calculated *disordering* of *all his senses.* All the forms of love, of suffering, of madness; he himself looks for, he exhausts in himself all the poisons, in order to keep only their quintessences. Ineffable torture in which he has need of all faith, of all superhuman strength, in which he becomes the great sick man, the great criminal, the great wretch of them all – and the supreme Savant! – For he arrives at the *Unknown!*

Since he has cultivated his soul, already rich more than anyone else's! He arrives at the unknown, and even if, driven mad, he should end by losing an understanding of his visions, he has seen them! Let him perish in his leaping by means of things unheard and unnameable: other horrible workers will come; they will begin with the horizons where the other collapsed.

— The continuation in six minutes —

Here I insert a second psalm *out of text*: please lend a sympathetic ear, — and everyone will be charmed. I have the bow in hand, I begin:

Mes Petites Amoureuses [discussed on pp. 158-159]

There you are. And note too that if I were not afraid of making you spend more than 60 c. postage — I a poor bewildered one who for seven months has not held a single centime in his hand! — I would deliver to you as well my *Amants de Paris,* a hundred hexameters, Sir, and my *Mort de Paris,* two hundred hexameters!

— I continue:

The poet is therefore really a stealer of fire.

He is in charge of humanity, even of the animals; he must make his inventions felt, touched, listened to; if what he reports from *down there* has form, he gives form; if it is without form, he gives formlessness. To find a language; — Besides, every word being idea, the time of a universal language will come! One must be an academician — deader than a fossil, — to complete a dictionary of any language whatsoever. Weak creatures who could plunge quickly into madness, would begin *to think* about the first letter of the alphabet!

This language will be soul for the soul, summarizing everything, perfumes, sounds, colors, thought hooking thought and pulling. The poet would define the amount of the unknown which becomes awakened in his time in the universal soul: he would give more — than the formula of his thought, than the inventory *of his advance toward Progress!* Enormity becoming the norm, absorbed by all, he would be truly a *multiplier of progress!*

This future will be materialistic, you see. — Always full of *Number* and of *Harmony,* these poems will be made to last. Essentially it would be something like Greek poetry again.

Eternal art would have its functions, just as poets are citizens. Poetry will no longer give rhythm to action; it *will be out ahead.*

These poets will be! When the endless servitude of woman has been broken, when she lives for herself and by herself, man, — up to this time abominable, — having given her her discharge, she will be a poet too! Woman will find the unknown! Will her worlds of ideas differ from ours? — She will find strange things, unfathomable, repulsive, delightful; we shall take them, we shall understand them.

While we are waiting, let us ask of the *poet* something *new,* — ideas and forms. All the clever ones would soon believe that they have satisfied this demand: — it isn't that!

The first Romantics were *seers* without being too well aware of it: the cultivation of their soul began with accidents: abandoned, but burning locomotives, which the rails take for a while.

— Lamartine is sometimes a seer, but stifled by the old form: Hugo, *too pigheaded,* certainly has the SEEN in his last volumes: *Les Misérables* is a real poem. I have *Les Châtiments* close at hand: "Stella" pretty well gives the measure of Hugo's *sight.* Too much Belmontet and Lamennais, of Jehovahs and of columns, old broken down monstrosities.

Musset is fourteen times execrable to us, doleful generations, seized with visions, — whom his angelic idleness has insulted! Oh! the stories and the insipid proverbs! Oh the *Nuits!* Oh *Rolla,* Oh *Namouna,* Oh *La Coupe!* All these are French, that is odious to a supreme degree; French, not Parisian! Still another work of this loathsome genius which inspired Rabelais, Voltaire, Jean La Fontaine, commented upon by M. Taine! Vernal, the spirit of Musset! Charming, his love! There you have it, painting in enamel, substantial poetry! *French* poetry will be relished for a long time, but in France. Every grocery boy is getting ready to unwind a Rollaesque apostrophe, every seminarist bears off the five hundred rhymes in the recesses of his notebook. At the age of fifteen, these bursts of passion put the young in heat; at sixteen they are already happy to recite them with *emotion;* at eighteen, at seventeen even, every collegian who has the means acts the Rolla, writes a Rolla! Some are still perhaps dying of it. Musset couldn't do anything: there were visions behind the gauze of the curtains: he shut his eyes. A Frenchman, in a mess, dragged from the tavern to the college desk, this beautiful youth is dead, henceforth let us no longer even take the trouble to reawaken him with our curses!

The second Romantics are very *seeing*: Théophile Gautier, Leconte de Lisle, Théodore de Banville. But to inspect the invisible and to hear the unheard being something other than to recapture the spirit of dead things, Baudelaire is the first seer, the king of poets, *a real God.* Yet he lived in too artistic a milieu; and the form so much praised by him is shabby. The inventions of the unknown demand new forms.

Experienced in the old forms, — among the innocent, A. Renaud, — he wrote his Rolla; — L. Grandet, — he wrote his Rolla; — the Gauls and the Mussets, G. Lafenestre, Coran, Cl. Popelin, Soulary, L. Salles; the schoolboys, Marc, Aicard, Theuriet; the dead and the imbeciles, Autran, Barbier, L. Picart, Lemoyne, the Deschamps, the Essarts; the journalists, L. Cladel, Robert Luzarches, X. de Ricard; the fantasists, C. Mendès; the bohemians; the women; the talented ones, Léon Dierx and Sully-Prudhomme, Coppée; — the new school, called Parnassian, has two seers, Albert Mérat and Paul Verlaine, a true poet. There you are.

Thus I work to make myself a *seer*. — And let's finish with a pious chant:

Accroupissements [discussed on pp. 161-162]

You would be execrable not to answer: quickly, for in a week I shall be in Paris, perhaps.

Until then,

A. Rimbaud.

Appendix B
Symbolism of the Hebrew Alphabet

THE FIRST TEN LETTERS of the Hebrew alphabet will be sufficient to illustrate what was meant by the correspondence of the letters and numbers in Kabbalistic thought and also to indicate the nature of their symbolic significance. The first ten letters represented the first ten emanations in the process of the creation of the world. (This chart has been compiled from information found in the several works on Kabbalism mentioned in the Bibliography.)

No.	*Letter*	*Emanation*	*SYMBOLIC SIGNIFICANCE*
One	Aleph	Crown	Unity, the Absolute, the Macrocosm; the masculine or active principle; in alchemy, the King.
Two	Beth	Wisdom	Duality, the feminine or passive principle; Isis the veiled virgin-mother; in alchemy, the Queen.
Three	Gimmel	Intelligence	Multiplicity, the Word, the sacred Trinity The Word calls into being the letters, numbers, and colors — and the entire material universe.
Four	Daleth	Beauty	The Cosmos or the material universe: the four elements, the four seasons, the four points of the compass; the sacred Tetragrammaton represented in the form of a cross.
Five	He	Love	The Microcosm, the seer whose visions can perceive beyond the material universe; the five pointed star or pentagram was sometimes represented on the Tetragrammaton, signifying the one on the cross, or the Macrocosm having descended to the Microcosm; the deity having become humanity.
Six	Vau	Justice	Equilibrium, the harmony of opposites or "astral light," the spiritual medium by which the *mage* is able to have visions.
Seven	Dzain	Foundation	Correspondence: the doctrine that everything on earth has its spiritual counterpart, the mysterious, hidden aspect of Nature which the *mage* can penetrate by means of second sight. Seven represents the *mage* in control of nature.
Eight	Cheth	Triumph	Realization of the spiritual world; an awareness of the "astral" or spirit self, growing comprehension by man that he is made in the image of God. The *mage* is able to perceive the "aura" or radiation of the "astral bodies" of others.
Nine	Teth	Splendor	Initiation into the higher mysteries of the *mage* who has mastered the symbols and allegories and has achieved control over himself. (It is interesting to note that in Mozart's *Magic Flute* nine priests on each side of the temple of Isis blow nine times on their trumpets to herald the initiation of Tamino.)
Ten	Jod	Kingdom	The Macrocosm: creation as a whole, the work and the mirror of God.

It should be noted that from one to five we have moved from the Macrocosm to the Microcosm, that is, from God to God made man; from five to ten we have moved from the Microcosm back to the Macrocosm, that is, from God made man to man who has returned to God. The circle which has thus been completed represents the beginning which contains within itself the end and the end which is also a beginning (cf. "I am Alpha and Omega, the beginning and the end"). The Hebrew letter Jod appears on all Masonic rings, signifying the idea of God in man and man in God.

Appendix C
List of Parnassians

With the single exception of Joseph Autran, the names of the Parnassians appearing at the end of the Demeny letter may be found in the *Parnasse contemporain* of 1869. It seems possible that Rimbaud had the review on hand and glanced at its table of contents as he wrote the letter. The authors mentioned have been listed and classified in a manner significant for what it reveals about the literary judgment of the poet. The classification shows that before the liaison with Verlaine, Rimbaud had already recognized him as a more gifted poet than Banville, editor of the first *Parnasse contemporain* (1866). It was not until twenty years later that Verlaine had such recognition from more renowned literary critics. Leconte de Lisle and Gautier, both of whom were considered by the generation of 1870 to be greater poets than Baudelaire, were assigned a lower rank by Rimbaud, and any critic of today would agree with this. The most astute classification, however, is the one made of Sully-Prudhomme, Léon Dierx, and Coppée whom Rimbaud calls "les talents." And with what exactness! But it should be remembered that at the time of Rimbaud's letter these were the great names, particularly Sully-Prudhomme. The evaluation of the poets of one's own time concurring with the critics of a hundred years later is evidence of remarkable insight – the more so when the critic is only sixteen years old. The chief weakness, or rather oversight, in Rimbaud's classification consists in his failure to mention Mallarmé's "Hérodiade," which was certainly the best of the contributions.

A glance at the list of Parnassians (with a thought to biographical details) explains two of Rimbaud's sarcastic remarks in the body of the Demeny letter. One is: "There you have it, painting in enamel, substantial poetry" ("*la poésie solide*"). Four of the poets listed – Coran, Popelin, Soulary, and Silvestre, were students of the plastic arts. Popelin acquired his first celebrity as a painter in enamel, having published a technical work on that subject, *L'Art de l'émail.* Soulary's volume of poetry, *Les Figulines,* also bears witness to his interest in the plastic arts. Armand Silvestre's interest in this field led to his appointment as *Inspecteur des Beaux-Arts.* The second scornful remark in the Demeny letter which this biographical data explains is the poet's reference to officials who have become writers: "Des fonctionnaires, des écrivains . . . !" Ten of the group of Parnassians listed here were either holding or had held minor government posts and were, therefore, in Rimbaud's opinion, bourgeois and unworthy of being called poets. Such an attitude was not mere childishness, but was the general attitude of the literary world of the period just prior to the war of 1870; the government of Napoleon III had taken harsh measures against writers, and in return the literary world turned its hate upon the government. Critic Ernest Raynaud in *La Bohème sous le second Empire* gives this as an explanation for the Bohemianism of the writers of this generation: "Bohemianism is not always the daughter of caprice and fantasy," he states, adding that in this case it was a total rejection by writers of the growing materialism of the end of the century.

Some explanation should be given here for Rimbaud's addition of the name of Joseph Autran, whose poems do not appear in this issue of the *Parnasse.* Autran was a member of the group of Parnassians known as the *Vilains bonhommes,* which held meetings in the *Hôtel des Etrangers* at the corner of the Rue Racine and the Boulevard Saint-Michel. Verlaine, Charles Cros, Mérat, Banville, Hérédia, Valade, Coppée, Germain Nouveau and others, as well as Rimbaud, frequented this group, which later came to be known as *Zutistes* (those who said "zut" to bourgeois materialism). There was also the fact that Autran had recently been elected to the French Academy (1868), and perhaps for this reason Rimbaud adds his name in order to attack him; in the classification he is listed by implication as an *"imbécile."* What seems more probable, however, is that the future author of "Bateau ivre" had read Autran's volume of sea poems, *Les Poèmes de la mer* (1852), and had considered them inferior in their conception and unworthy of a recently elected member of the Academy. Certainly, not one of Autran's sea poems may be compared with Rimbaud's "Bateau ivre."

Rimbaud divided the Parnassians into ten groups. In the case of two — the "Bohemians" and the "Women" — no names are mentioned; but one has only to look at the table of contents of the *Parnasse contemporain* (1869) to fill in the blanks:

(1) *The Innocents.* "Those experienced in the old forms": Armand Renaud and Léon Grandet. "Each of these wrote his 'Rolla' " Rimbaud says with contempt.

ARMAND RENAUD (1836-1894) contributed to all three issues of the *Parnasse contemporain,* but was perhaps best known as the author of *Les Nuits persanes* (1870). (Rimbaud mentions this collection in a letter of July, 1871 to Izambard: "Do you like *Les Nuits persanes?* A title which can attract attention even among bargain books.") His "Rolla" may be found in the collection *Pensées tristes* (1865), in the poem "La Science amère," the story of a young *débauché* who falls in love with a very young girl and who finally kills both himself and her. In this collection of poems, Renaud precedes Coppée in the "genre populaire," whose artistic theory he attempts to justify in the Preface of his later work, *Les Nuits persanes.* He felt constrained, he says, to write about the material misery of people even at the risk of incurring the anger of *"les artistes épris d'art pur."* Like many other Parnassians, Renaud held a government post, attaining the rank of inspector in chief of fine arts of the prefecture of the Seine and custodian of historical works of Paris.

LÉON GRANDET (pseudonym Léon Barracand) was a mediocre poet and novelist who contributed only to the 1869 *Parnasse* and is not discussed by Schaffer or other Parnassian critics. His "Rolla" is the long poem *Donaniel* (1866), whose hero, the son of Don Juan, spends many alexandrines regretting the *"siècle sordide"* in which he was born.

(2) *The Gauls and the Mussets.* Georges Lafenestre, Charles Coran, Claudius Popelin, Josephin Soulary, Louis Salles. In using the term Gaul, Rimbaud seems to have in mind the *"esprit gaulois"* as exemplified by Rabelais and La Fontaine (examples given by Rimbaud himself), and perhaps, by extension, all those poets for whom poetry, in his opinion, was a game. By "Mussets," he means those who wrote in a lush sentimental style.

GEORGES LAFENESTRE (1837-1919). Again Rimbaud shows remarkable insight as a literary critic, for modern critic Schaffer also cites Lafenestre for his extraordinary similarity to Musset and as an example to refute the error that Parnassians were all "impassibles." Lafenestre served for many years as conservator of the Louvre and also as professor at the Ecole du Louvre. At the time of the Demeny letter, Lafenestre had written only one volume of verse, *Les Espérances* (1863).

CHARLES CORAN (1814-1901), author of two volumes of anacreontic verse, *Onyx* (1840) and *Rimes galantes* (1847), for which he received the title, "un Parisien hellénisé." Because of the large number of rich rhymes in his poems, Schaffer says that he belongs among those Parnassians to whom versifying was largely a game. It was no doubt for this reason that Rimbaud classified him as *"gaulois."* Before his marriage, Coran was an art student, as the imagery of his poetry would suggest.

CLAUDIUS POPELIN (1825-1892) acquired his first celebrity as a painter in enamel and as author of a work on that subject, *L'Art de l'émail* (1868). Like Coran, Popelin was an Anacreontic poet and sonneteer, whose works suffer from banality. A meticulous workman, Popelin is called by Schaffer an "émailleur" in verse.

JOSEPHIN SOULARY (1815-1891), another of the painter-poets of Parnasse, whom Sainte-Beuve describes as: *"Un Gautier plus rare, mais qui a des idées."* "Les Figulines," one of the nine sonnet cycles in his *Sonnets humoristiques* (1858), bears a close resemblance to the *Emaux et Camées* of Gautier. Soulary, the leader of a group of Lyonese poets, was older than the three founders of the Parnassian mouvement — Leconte de Lisle, Banville, and Baudelaire.

LOUIS SALLES, although the author of three volumes of poetry and of three poems in the *Parnasse* of 1869, is almost entirely unknown according to Schaffer. One volume of his verse, *Les Amours de Pierre et de Léa* (1869), which had appeared by the time of Rimbaud's letter, earned for Salles the title of "the Parnassian Petrarch." This work consists of a cycle of passionate love sonnets which reveal that the poet had widely read the Romanticists.

(3) *The Schoolboys.* Gabriel Marc, Jean Aicard, André Theuriet. Although the artificiality and immaturity of the verses of these three poets would seem to justify their classification as *"écoliers"* by Rimbaud, one cannot help smiling both at the irony of a

sixteen-year-old boy who calls those older than himself "schoolboys" and also at the confidence which Rimbaud felt in his own genius. Still, these were the youngest of the contributors to this issue of the *Parnasse contemporain.*

GABRIEL MARC (1840-1900) was a cousin of Théodore de Banville, who doubtless introduced him to the Parnassians. Twenty-one years old at the time of the *Parnasse contemporain* of 1869, Marc contributed four poems, which do not show outstanding talent. His first volume of poems, *Soleils d'octobre,* which also appeared in 1869, contains a dedicatory poem to his uncle, Théodore, "le phare éblouissant qui brûle dans la nuit." For the most part, it is a collection of regional verse written in a Banvillesque style. Marc was another of the Parnassians who held a government post.

JEAN AICARD (1848-1921), only nineteen years old when he wrote his first volume of poetry, *Les Jeunes croyances* (1867), was the most precocious of the contributors to the *Parnasse contemporain.* Aicard established his reputation first in Provence as a sort of local troubadour, and his charm in reading his verses no doubt did much to add to their popularity. He appears with Rimbaud and Verlaine in the painting "Le Coin de la Table" by Fantin-Latour. Although in his youth a republican and a *révolté,* by the time of World War I Aicard had become an arch-conservative.

ANDRÉ THEURIET (1833-1907), who in his youth wanted to be Lamartine or nothing, strove more for musical than for pictorial effects in his verse. His first volume, *Le Chemin des bois* (1867), established him as primarily a nature poet who wrote about Lorraine. His biographer, Besson, says of him: *"Il a le sentiment, l'émotion et surtout ce don essentiel de la poésie: le rêve."* Theuriet later became known as an author of rustic novels written in the idyllic style of George Sand. He is another of the Parnassians who held a government post.

(4) *The Dead and the Imbeciles.* Autran, Barbier, Laurent-Pichat, Lemoyne, the Deschamps brothers, Des Essarts. Since the Deschamps brothers were the only ones of this group who were actually deceased, we may assume that Rimbaud considers the others to be imbeciles.

JOSEPH AUTRAN (1813-1877) achieved a rapid success when he wrote an ode to Lamartine at the time of the latter's departure for the East. This ode was followed by several others later collected in the volumes *La Mer* (1835) and *Les Poèmes de la mer* (1852). His tragedy, *La Fille d'Eschyle,* was presented at the Odéon in 1848, when it shared the honors of the Academy with Emile Augier's play, *Gabrielle.* Autran wrote several other volumes of poetry and was elected to the Academy in 1868.

AUGUSTE BARBIER (1805-1882) was famous at the age of twenty-six as the author of *Iambes,* and although he lived fifty-one years longer and brought out eight more volumes, he was still known as *"le poète des Iambes."* This collection contains a protest against the Napoleonic legend. Barbier was a law student before he began his literary career, and was elected to the Academy in 1869.

LEON LAURENT-PICHAT (1823-1886) came into possession of a fortune at the age of eighteen. In the company of Henri Chevreau, he traveled through Italy, Greece, and the East, publishing his first volume of poetry, *Les Voyageuses* (1844), in collaboration with his friend. Later he became a collaborator on the newspaper *Progrès de l'Aube* with Louis Ulbach, together with whom the publication *La Revue de Paris* was later shared with Maxime du Camp until its suppression in 1858. Elected representative of the Seine in 1871, Laurent-Pichat took part in some of the most important discussions of the National Assembly, his political sympathies belonging to the extreme left. By the time of the Demeny letter, he had written three volumes of poetry: *Libres paroles* (1847), *La Chronique rimée,* and *Avant le jour* (1870).

ANDRE LEMOYNE (1822-1907), a lawyer who, after having been admitted to the bar, had to take a job as typesetter and proofreader because of financial reverses which overtook his family during and after the revolution of 1848. He became finally a librarian in the *Ecole des arts décoratifs,* which perhaps accounts for the quality of his verse as Schaffer describes it: "meticulously chiseled word-cameos." Lemoyne contributed to each issue of the *Parnasse contemporain,* and of his nine volumes of poetry, four received the honors of the Academy. Two of these, *Les Roses d'antan* and *Les Charmeuses,* had appeared by 1871. *"Le poète de courte haleine,"* Schaffer calls him because of the brevity and restricted subject-matter of his poetry.

EMILE DESCHAMPS (1791-1871) and *ANTONI DESCHAMPS* (1800-1869) belong both in time and activity to the Romantic rather than to the Parnassian movement. Both were active in the early

Romantic *cénacle,* Emile having been one of the founders of "La Muse française," in which he wrote articles (signed "le jeune moraliste") collected in 1826 into a volume, *Le Jeune Moraliste.* His *Etudes françaises et étrangères* (1828) contains a Preface comparable to Hugo's famous Preface to *Cromwell.* Emile made his literary debut with a poem which won the compliments of Napoleon, "La Paix conquise" (1812). He took a government post in the ministry of finance, where he remained until his retirement. Antoni, brother of Emile, was not nearly so active nor so productive. He went to Italy and translated the *Divine Comedy* into French verse (1829). Stricken with a nervous malady, he had to retire to a sanatorium. His two volumes of verse, *Trois satires politiques* (1831) and *Résignation* (1839), were personal and melancholy in tone.

EMMANUEL DES ESSARTS (1839-1909) of the Ecole Normale, who held the chair of French literature first at Clermont and then at Dijon, was primarily a scholar and literary critic and only secondarily a poet. Among his critical works were three lectures presented to the faculties of Clermont and Dijon: *Du Génie de Chateaubriand* and *Les Prédecesseurs de Milton,* presented in Clermont; and *Origines de la poésie lyrique en France au XVIe siècle,* given at Dijon. His thesis for the *doctorat-ès-lettres* in 1871 was *Du Type d'Hercule dans la littérature grecque, depuis les origines jusqu'au siècle des Antonins.* In addition to these, he did critical studies on the theater of Musset and Marivaux and translated with annotations Erasmus' *Praise of Folly.* Much later he wrote an article on the Parnassian school for *La Revue bleue* (1902). As a poet, he was not nearly so prolific, even though he did contribute to all three issues of the *Parnasse contemporain.* The only volume of verse which his critics mention is *Poésies Parisiennes,* published by Poulet-Malassis in 1862. These love poems in an Anacreontic vein reveal his neopaganism as well as his cleverness as a versifier. The long pedantic poem, "Les Amants de la liberté," which he contributed to the *Parnasse contemporain* of 1869, is both banal and bombastic and would make Rimbaud's harsh classification of Des Essarts among the "dead" and the "imbeciles" seem somewhat justified.

(5) *The Journalists.* Léon Cladel, Robert Luzarches, and Louis Xavier de Ricard.

LÉON CLADEL (1835-1892), born at Montauban, is best known as a novelist who depicted scenes and rural mores of Quercy. Baudelaire wrote a preface to his first novel, *Les Martyres ridicules* (1862); his second, *Pierre Patient,* the story of a schoolmaster, was published *en feuilleton* in the review *L'Europe.* His third novel, *Une Maudite,* cost him a month in prison. At first a lawyer's clerk, journalist of *Les Petits cahiers,* Cladel was finally employed in the prefecture of the Seine.

ROBERT LUZARCHES (1848-1870), son of publisher and bibliophile Victor Luzarches, founded in 1867 the *Gazette rimée,* a review which served as one of the chief organs of Parnasse, but survived only six months. He was author of a small volume of verse published posthumously, *Les Excommuniés,* written when he was only nineteen. The work reflects the emotions of an adolescent at war with society, his ideal rebel being Agrippa d'Aubigné. The second part of the volume reflects chiefly the influence of Baudelaire, the themes of Satanism, spleen, and love of the city predominating.

LOUIS XAVIER DE RICARD (1843-1911) was coeditor with Catulle Mendès of the first *Parnasse contemporain* (1866). Prior to this he had been editor of two other reviews: *Revue de progrès* (1863), of brief duration because its editors were prosecuted on charges of atheism; and *L'Art,* which formulated Parnassian doctrines and first won for them the title, *"les impassibles."* In his poetic expression, he is classified as a philosophic lyricist, his work being particularly characterized by a passion for ideas. His first volume, *Chants de l'aube* (1862), is a sort of hymn to progress, in which he maintains that genuine poets are *"conduits par le progrès."* In the poem "Aphrodite Anadyomène" (which suggests Rimbaud's poem by the title "Venus anadyomène") in his second volume, *Ciel, rue et foyer* (1866), Xavier de Ricard flaunts his atheism in a verse which is suggestive of Rimbaud: *"L'homme est le dieu qui crée incessamment; l'homme est Dieu."* A radical in politics and religion, Xavier de Ricard was exiled for his attacks on the Second Empire and, on one occasion, served a term in prison for atheism.

(6) *The Fantasist.* Catulle Mendès.

CATULLE MENDÈS (1841-1909), at the age of nineteen was founder and editor of "La Revue fantaisiste" and coeditor with Louis-Xavier de Ricard of the first *Parnasse contemporain.* An extremely versatile person, Mendès was poet, novelist, playwright, critic, editor, and a sort of Maecenas to less fortunate poets. His own versatility, plus the fact that he was the son-in-law of Théophile Gautier, brought him a place in the limelight of French letters far beyond his real ability as a poet. *Philoméla,* his first volume, reveals his facility, mastery of technique, and pleasure in experimenting with traditional forms. *Pagode,* his second volume, shows his wide reading of Hindu literature.

(7) *The Bohemians.* Glatigny, Armand Silvestre, and Charles Cros. Although their names are not mentioned by Rimbaud in the Demeny letter, these three were by far the most bohemian of those in the table of contents. All were frequenters of the salon of Nina de Callias and the *Vilains bonhommes,* and were therefore acquainted with both Verlaine and Rimbaud.

ALBERT GLATIGNY (1839-1873) lived a vagabond existence and came from humble origins. The son of a carpenter at Bernay, he was apprenticed to be a court usher (*hussier*), but left this and became apprenticed as a printer at Pont-Audemer. There he wrote a play in three acts for a local theater, a feat which he accomplished in only four days, so great was his gift for improvisation. His ability to write with such facility proved to be no great blessing, however, for his work suffered as a result of it. At seventeen he departed with a troup of comedians and, in Brussels, met publisher Poulet-Malassis, who acquainted him with the *Odes funambulesques* of Banville. This was a revelation which led him to publish, a few months later, his *Vignes folles* (1857). He continued to live a vagabond existence and to write until he became a colleague and collaborator with Catulle Mendès during the 1860's. He published, among other works, *Les Flèches d'or* (1864), *Nouveaux châtiments* (1871), and *Le Fer rouge.* These last two volumes were mentioned in a letter of April 17, 1871 from Rimbaud to Demeny.

ARMAND SILVESTRE (1837-1901), one of the most prolific writers of his time, studied at the Ecole Polytechnique and entered government service in the ministry of finance, rising to the post of inspector. Under the patronage of George Sand, he made his debut into the world of letters and — although he wrote many plays, librettos for operas by such eminent composers as Gounod and in Saint Saens, much art criticism and a volume of memoirs, *Au pays des souvenirs: mes maîtres et mes maîtresses* — he seems to have had no illusions about his originality as a writer. He was noted among his contemporaries for his scatological works, and when he joined the staff of *Gil Blas* in 1879, he contributed to it many of his *contes grivois*. His interest in the plastic arts led to his appointment as inspector of fine arts, a post which he held until his death. Along with Glatigny, Silvestre was one of the chief disciples of Banville.

CHARLES CROS (1842-1888), scientist as well as poet — who taught Hebrew and Sanskrit at the age of sixteen, studied chemistry and medicine, and invented the phonograph at the same time as Edison and color photography twenty-four years before Lippmann — was nevertheless so unstable in his character and so incapable of completing the task begun that success always escaped him at the last moment. To console himself for his brilliant failures Cros took refuge in alcohol and absinth, singing the praises of the "Green Hour" in his volume of poems, *Le Coffret de santal*. His mood in this volume is one of smiling mockery, which was the mask behind which he hid the real misery of his unstable destiny. He was particularly friendly with Verlaine and originated the group which called itself the "Zutistes" — those who said "zut" to everything bourgeois — which it was fashionable to hate with great violence. Cros accompanied Verlaine to the station to meet Rimbaud whom the latter had summoned from Charleville.

(8) *The Women*. Nina de Callias, Madame Blanchecotte, Louise Colet, Louisa Seifert, and Madame Auguste Penquer. Again, Rimbaud does not list these by name, but there were five women who contributed to this issue of the *Parnasse contemporain*. Another of the feminine contributors to the other two issues of the review, Madame Ackermann, whose work does not appear in the 1869 issue, is generally acknowledged to have been the most talented. Following her in talent was Louisa Seifert, whose work does appear in the issue under discussion.

NINA DE CALLIAS (1846-1884) held many social gatherings of Parnassian litterati in her salon — *"l'atelier de détraquage cérébral,"* it was called in the journal of the Goncourt brothers. *La Maison de la vieille,* Nina de Callias' scandalous *roman à clef,* reveals to what an extent the lives of the Parnassians were closely knit. Charles Cros dedicated his *Coffret de santal* to her, and critic Pierre Calmettes names her as *"la grande passion d'Anatole France,"* in a book by that title. Her poems were published posthumously in a volume entitled *Feuillets parisiens.*

MADAME BLANCHECOTTE (1830-1897), cited by Sainte-Beuve for her volume, *Rêves et réalités* (1855), was awarded a prize of one thousand francs by the French Academy. Madame Blanchecotte progressed in her poetry from a lacrymose to a more stoical outlook in her later work, *Les Militantes.* In Schaffer's opinion she has a more valid claim to be numbered among the Parnassian than have Madame Colet and Madame Penquer.

LOUISE COLET (1810-1876), *"la dixième muse,"* was as famous for her salon, a rendezvous for the Forty Immortals, as for her friendship with Flaubert. In point of time, as well as in her verse, she belongs to the Romantic movement and has little claim to being included among the *"impassibles."* It should be added that Madame Colet kept up her literary ambitions to the very end, since she was fifty-nine years old at the time of the third *Parnasse,* to which she contributed only a short time before her death.

LOUISA SEIFERT (1845-1877), a very popular, successful poet of the Lyonese school and protégée of Josephin Soulary, published in 1868 *Rayons perdus,* which was praised by Banville, Sainte-Beuve, Leconte de Lisle and Coppée. In a letter to Izambard (Aug. 25, 1870), Rimbaud says that he would like to know her and quotes one of her poems, "Marguerite," from the collection *Rayons perdus.*

MADAME AUGUSTE PENQUER (1817-1889) lacked the social connections of Nina de Callias and the talent of Louisa Seifert and Madame Ackermann. Her volume, *Chants du foyer,* written in the style of Lamartine, is almost pure imitation. Schaffer says that the more Hugo praised her, the more emotional she became.

(9) *Les Talents*: Léon Dierx, Sully-Prudhomme, and Coppée.

LÉON DIERX (1838-1912), student of Leconte de Lisle and born on the island of Réunion, even resembled his teacher in appearance. He took a position with the Ministry of Public Education and, in 1864, published *Poèmes et poésies,* which he dedicated to Leconte de Lisle. His poetry possessed some of the same general qualities as that of his teacher but lacked its intensity. In spite of this, Dierx was one of the more talented of the Parnassians, and succeeded Mallarmé to the Academy in 1898.

SULLY-PRUDHOMME (1839-1907) tried himself out in three different professions before becoming a writer. He began as an engineer, studied law, and later became a notary's clerk. His first volume, *Stances et poèmes* (1864), revealed a precision of expression for the most delicate nuances. His second volume, *Les Epreuves* (1866), is mentioned scornfully by Rimbaud in a letter of August 25, 1870, to Izambard. By 1869, with *Les Solitudes* and his translation of the *De Rerum Natura,* Sully-Prudhomme's work became increasingly philosophic. One of the half-dozen best-known poets of his time, Sully-Prudhomme won the Nobel prize for poetry in 1901.

FRANCOIS COPPÉE (1842-1908) is liberally represented in each of the issues of the *Parnasse contemporain.* Introduced to Leconte de Lisle by Catulle Mendès, he became, after the brilliant success of his poetic drama, *Le Passant* (1869), the most highly respected of the younger Parnassians. Before the time of the Demeny letter, Coppée had published three volumes of poetry: *Le Réliquaire* (1866), *Intimitées* (1868), and *Les Poèmes modernes* (1869). The title *"le poète des humbles"* was given to him because he began about 1868 to specialize in depicting the social evils against the poor. For this reason, a break finally took place between his section of the Parnassians and that of Leconte de Lisle. Rimbaud wrote seven poems, "Vieux Coppées," which are pastiches on the style and subject matter of *"la poésie des humbles."*

(10) *The Seers.* Albert Mérat, Paul Verlaine.

ALBERT MÉRAT (1840-1909) published his first work, *Avril, mai, juin* (1863), jointly with his friend, Léon Valade. Although this volume was largely descriptive and, like most of his works, chiefly concerned with externals, his second collection, *Les Chimères* (1866), is described by Schaffer as showing "a brief reaching for the Infinite." This probably accounts for Rimbaud's classification of Mérat as a seer. In 1868, Mérat translated the *Intermezzo* of Heinrich Heine, again in collaboration with Valade. *Les Villes de marbre* and *L'Idole* appeared in 1869, the latter containing his famous *"sonnet du ventre."* Both Mérat and Valade were employed in the prefecture of the Seine, Mérat finally becoming Librarian of the Senate, a post which he retained until his death by suicide in 1909.

PAUL VERLAINE (1844-1896), although he later became leader of the decadent wing of the Symbolist movement, was at the outset of his career a Parnassian and author of the first volume of Parnassian poetry to be published by Lemerre, *Poèmes saturniens* (1866). An account of his role in the movement has been given by his biographer and contemporary, Edmond Lepelletier. Rimbaud's remark about Verlaine's first three volumes was: *"C'est fort bizarre, très drôle et vraiment c'est adorable!"* Encouraged by his friend Charles Bretagne, Rimbaud wrote to Verlaine, and in September 1871 received the reply: *"Venez, cher grande âme, on vous appelle, on vous attend,"* which marked the beginning of the liaison. The relationship lasted with some interruptions until Verlaine's imprisonment for shooting Rimbaud at Brussels in 1873; Verlaine joined him again in Stuttgart after being released in 1875. Three volumes of Verlaine's poetry contain individual poems which treat this relationship: *Romances sans paroles* (1872-1873), *Jadis et naguère* (1885) and *Parallèlement* (1889).

Notes

PREFACE

1. Honoré de Balzac, *La Comédie humaine,* Editions de la Pléiade, (Paris: Gallimard, 1950), X, 1149.
2. F. S. C. Northrop, *The Meeting of East and West* (New York: Macmillan, 1946), pp. 335-336.

CHAPTER 1

1. The word *vātes* is thought to be of Italo-Celtic origin; cf. *devins.* Ernout and Meillet in their *Dictionnaire de la langue latine* write: "When *poeta* became generalized, *vātes* acquired a pejorative meaning."
2. *The Dialogues of Plato,* trans. B. Jowett, in *Great Books of the Western World* (Chicago: Encyclopaedia Britannica, 1952), VII, 144.
3. Plotinus, *The Enneads,* trans. Stephen MacKenna and B. S. Page (London: Medici Society, 1930), Bk. VI, pp. 9-10.
4. Plotinus, *The Enneads,* trans. Stephen MacKenna (London: Faber & Faber, 1930), Bk. V, pp. 3-17.
5. Carl Gustav Jung, *Modern Man in Search of a Soul* (New York: Harcourt, Brace & World, 1933), pp. 175-199.
6. Aldous Huxley, *The Doors of Perception* (London: Chatto & Windus, 1954), p. 52.
7. D. H. S. Nicholson and A. H. E. Lee, *The Oxford Book of Mystical Verse* (Oxford: Clarendon Press, 1917), pp. 63-64.
8. *Escritos de Santa Teresa,* añadidos por Don Vicente de la Fuente, Biblioteca de Autores Españoles (Madrid: M. Rivadeneyra, 1877), I, 59. The quotation in the paragraph which follows is from the same source, p. 60.
9. Novalis, *Fragmente* (Dresden: Wolfgang Jess Verlag, 1929), p. 263.
10. Guy Michaud, *Le Message poétique du symbolisme* (Paris: Librairie Nizet, 1947), II, 418-419.
11. Charles Morice, *La Littérature de tout à l'heure* (Paris: Perrin, 1889), p. 35. The quotation which follows is from the same source, pp. 65-66.
12. Rémy de Gourmont in Jules Huret, *Enquête sur l'évolution littéraire* (Paris: Charpentier, 1891), p. 141; Vielé-Griffin, cited by Jean de Cours, *François Vielé-Griffin, son oeuvre, sa pensée, son art* (Paris: Champion, 1930), pp. 16-17; Saint-Pôl-Roux, *Enquête sur l'évolution littéraire,* pp. 148-149.
13. Stéphane Mallarmé, *Oeuvres complètes,* Editions de la Pléiade, (Paris: Gallimard, 1945), p. 340.
14. Jules Laforgue, *Mélanges posthumes* (Paris: Mercure de France, 1909), p. 306.
15. Anatole France, "Préface," *Traité élémentaire de science occulte* of Papus (Paris: G. Carré, 1888), p. 10.
16. Raymond Queneau, *Communiqué,* No. 3 (13 avril, 1925).

17. Antonin Artaud, *A la grande Nuit ou Le Bluff surréaliste,* cited in Maurice Nadeau, *Documents surréalistes,* (Paris: Gallimard, 1948), p. 115.
18. Paul Eluard, *Donner à voir* (Paris: Gallimard, 1939), p. 147.
19. André Breton, *Les Vases communicants* (Paris: Cahiers Libres, 1932), p. 171.
20. Breton, *Les Pas perdus* (Paris: N. R. F., 1924), p. 185.
21. Breton, *Second manifeste, Les Manifestes du surréalisme* (Paris: Éditions Jean-Jacques Pauvert, 1946), p. 45. See also *Qu'est-ce que le surréalisme?* (Bruxelles: R. Henriquez, 1934), p. 17.
22. Breton, *Les Pas perdus,* p. 185.
23. Eluard, *Donner à voir,* p. 147.
24. Jung, *Modern Man,* pp. 175-199.
25. Gérard de Nerval, *Aurélia* (Bordeaux: Delmas, 1950), pp. 71, 96, 98, 113, 135, 141.
26. Nerval, *Oeuvres complètes,* Editions de la Pléiade, (Paris: Gallimard, 1952), pp. 311-324.
27. *Ibid.,* p. 103.
28. *Ibid.,* p. 71.
29. *Ibid.,* p. 185; Jean-Arthur Rimbaud, *Oeuvres complètes,* Editions de la Pléiade (Paris: Gallimard, 1946), pp. 212-213.
30. Charles Baudelaire, *Les Paradis artificiels* (Lausanne: Clairefontaine, 1947), pp. 188-189. The three quotations which follow are from the same source, appearing respectively on pp. 92 and 223, 158, and 160.
31. Nerval, *Aurélia,* p. 82.
32. Jung, *The Integration of Personality,* trans. Stanley Dell (London: Routledge and Kegan Paul, 1940), p. 67.
33. Baudelaire, *Les Paradis artificiels,* p. 222.
34. *Ibid.,* p. 221.
35. *Ibid.,* p. 158.
36. Thomas De Quincey, *The Confessions of an English Opium-Eater,* (London: J. M. Dent, 1952), p. 235.
37. Arthur Rimbaud, *Les Illuminations,* Edition de la Pléiade (Paris: Gallimard, 1946), p. 168.
38. Baudelaire, *Les Paradis artificiels,* pp. 170, 176, 194.
39. *Ibid.,* p. 190.
40. *Ibid.,* p. 187.
41. Nerval, *Aurélia,* p. 87.
42. *Ibid.,* p. 84.
43. *Ibid.,* pp. 84 and 184. The quote which follows is from the same source, p. 137.
44. Rimbaud, *Les Illuminations,* p. 178.
45. Baudelaire, *Curiosités esthétiques, Oeuvres complètes,* Editions J. Crépet (Paris: Conard, 1923), pp. 273 and 333.
46. Baudelaire, *Correspondance, Oeuvres complètes,* Editions J. Crépet, (Paris: Conard, 1947), I, 322.
47. Baudelaire, *Les Paradis artificiels,* p. 77.
48. *Ibid.,* p. 77.
49. Baudelaire, *Les Journaux intimes* (Lausanne: Clairefontaine, 1947), p. 252.
50. Rimbaud, *Une Saison en enfer,* Edition de la Pléiade (Paris: Gallimard, 1946), pp. 206, 209.
51. Nerval, *Aurélia,* p. 97.
52. Baudelaire, *Les Paradis artificiels,* p. 84.

53. Huxley, *The Doors of Perception,* p. 31.
54. Baudelaire, *Les Paradis artificiels,* p. 103. The quotation which follows is from the same source, p. 95.
55. Baudelaire, *L'Art romantique,* Editions d'art (Genève: Skira, 1945), p. 397.
56. Baudelaire, *Les Paradis artificiels,* p. 214.
57. Baudelaire, *Les Journaux intimes,* p. 237.
58. Baudelaire, *Les Fleurs du mal,* Editions Crépet et Blin (Paris: Librairie José Corti, 1942), pp. 197, 198.
59. Baudelaire, *Les Paradis artificiels,* p. 53.
60. Baudelaire, *L'Art romantique,* p. 212.
61. Rimbaud, *Une Saison en enfer,* p. 207.
62. Nerval, *Aurélia,* p. 135.
63. *Ibid.,* p. 112.
64. Baudelaire, *Journaux intimes,* p. 258.
65. Nerval, *Aurélia,* p. 80.
66. Rimbaud, *Une Saison en enfer,* p. 223.
67. Théophile Gautier, *Histoire du romantisme* (Paris: Flammarion, n.d.), pp. 129-130.
68. *"Maintenant je puis dire que l'art est une sottise."* Rimbaud, *Une Saison en enfer,* p. 235.
69. Rimbaud, *Une Saison en enfer,* p. 230.

CHAPTER 2

1. Court de Gébelin, *Le Monde primitif* (1772), I, 68. The statements made in this paragraph and the next constitute essential points of Vol. I. For the expression quoted, "Tout est allégorie," see p. 65.
2. Gébelin, *Le Monde primitif,* p. 12.
3. Jean-Silvain Bailly, *Lettres sur l'origine des sciences et sur celles des peuples d'Asie* (Paris et Londres: Debure, 1777), pp. 56-64, 232; Pierre-Simon Ballanche, *Palingénésie sociale, Oeuvres* (Genève: Barbézat, Paris: 1832), p. 252; Jean Reynaud, *Terre et ciel* (Paris: Furne, 1854), p. 221; Antoine Fabre d'Olivet, *Histoire du genre humain* in *Gnostiques de la révolution* (Paris: Egloff, 1946).
4. Jacques Roos, *Aspects littéraires du mysticisme philosophique* (Strasbourg: P. H. Heitz, 1951), Chapts. I-IV.
5. Henri Serouya, *La Kabbale* (Paris: Bernard Grasset, 1947), p. 54.
6. *Encyclopaedia Britannica,* "Kabbala."
7. See Jung's study of the symbolism of alchemy in *Psychology and Alchemy,* trans. R. F. C. Hull, Bollingen Series, V, 12, (New York: Pantheon Books, 1953); for briefer treatment of the subject, see Jung's chapter, "The Idea of Redemption in Alchemy," *The Integration of the Personality* (London: Routledge & Kegan Paul, 1940), pp. 205-280.
8. Menéndez y Pelayo, *Enciclopedia universal ilustrada,* Vol. 28, "Iluminados ('Alumbrados')".
9. *Grande Encyclopédie,* "Molinos."
10. Cf. Sanskrit *Veda* (I know), historically the perfect tense of the root *vid-,* therefore "I have seen."
11. Auguste Viatte, *Les Sources occultes du romantisme* (Paris: Champion, 1928), I, 181-182, 130.
12. Mme. Germaine de Staël, *De L'Allemagne* (Paris: Firmin Didot, 1893), pp. 561-562.

13. Novalis, *Fragmente* (Dresden: Wolfgang Jess Verlag, 1929), p. 539.
14. Benjamin Constant, *Journaux intimes* (Paris: Gallimard, 1952), p. 10.
15. Mme. de Staël, *De L'Allemagne,* p. 562.
16. *Encyclopaedia Britannica,* "Rosicrucianism."
17. Thomas De Quincey, *London Magazine* (Jan.-Feb., 1824), article on Rosicrucianism. Although there is no connection today between Freemasonry and Rosicrucianism, many of their rites as well as beliefs are similar, indicating a historical connection. The farther back one traces them, the more difficult it becomes to distinguish between the two. Certainly at the time of the Congress of Wilhelmsbad they greatly resembled each other.
18. Paracelsus, cited by R. Swinburne Clymer in *The Book of Rosicruciae* (Quakertown, Pa.: Beverly Hall Corp., 1946), Vol. II.
19. E. Spenlé, *Novalis* (Paris: Hachette, 1903), pp. 248-249.
20. Viatte, *Les Sources,* I, 147; and Mme. de Staël, *De L'Allemagne,* p. 563. Joseph de Maistre's remark is cited by Viatte, p. 149.
21. Spenlé, *Novalis,* p. 211. The names listed by Spenlé are: Lessing, Herder, Goethe, Fichte, Pestalozzi, G. H. von Schubert, and Ritter. The others are listed by Fernand Runkel in *Geschichte der Freimauerei in Deutschland* (Berlin: Verlag von Reimar Hobbing, n.d.).
22. *Ibid.*, p. 2.
23. R. Jasinski, *Histoire de la littérature française* (Paris: Boivin, 1947), II, 124.
24. The information about Swedenborg's life was taken from Signe Toksvig's biography, *Emmanuel Swedenborg* (New Haven: Yale University Press, 1950), and from George Trowbridge, *The Life of Emmanuel Swedenborg* (London: Swedenborg Society, 1945).
25. Emmanuel Swedenborg, *Heaven and Hell* (London: Swedenborg Society, 1937), p. 54.
26. Alfred Action, *Swedenborg and the Egyptian Hieroglyphics* (reprinted from a publication of the Swedenborgian Society, *New Church Life,* Sept., 1939). Action quotes from Swedenborg's appendix to the treatise on the White Horse: "It is well-known that in Egypt there were hieroglyphics and these were inscribed on the columns and walls of temples . . . They were nothing else than the correspondences of natural things with spiritual to which the Egyptians at that time gave their study more than any other peoples in Asia and according to which the oldest authors in Greece wrote their fables. This and no other was the most ancient style of writing. From that time the science of correspondences was so greatly obliterated that at this day it is hardly known that it ever existed."
27. Swedenborg, *Doctrines of the New Jerusalem (1758)* trans. from Latin (Boston: Otis Clapp, 1835), p. 59.
28. Swedenborg, *Heaven and Hell,* p. 147.
29. Swedenborg, *Dictionary of Correspondences* (Boston: New Church Union, 1899), p. 191.
30. Swedenborg, *Heaven and Hell,* p. 150. The quotation which follows is from the same source, p. 151.
31. Immanuel Kant, *Sämtliche Werke,* ed. G. Hartenstein (Leipzig: Voss, 1867), II, 29-34, 381.
32. Spenlé, *Novalis,* p. 76.
33. Jean-Paul Richter, *Sämtliche Werke, Die Unsichtbare Loge* (Berlin: G. Reimer, 1826), p. 190.
34. Johann Hamann, *Briefwechsel mit Friederich Henrich Jacobi,* letters of Nov. 2 and Nov. 14, 1784 (Gotha: Friederich Andreas Perthes, 1868),

pp. 7, 15.
35. Hamann, *Sämtliche Werke* (Wien: Thomas-Morus-Presse, Im Verlag Herder, 1951), III, 32; II, 197; I, 6-10.
36. In Chapters 2 and 3 all statements of the theme of the poet as seer have been underlined for emphasis.
37. Hamann, *Sämtliche Werke,* p. 241.
38. Hamann, *Briefwechsel mit Jacobi* (letter of June 8, 1786), p. 351.
39. Hamann, *Sämtliche Werke,* p. 164.
40. Viatte, *Les Sources,* I, 178.
41. Georg Gessner, *Lavaters Lebensbeschreibung* (Zurich: Winterthur, 1802) III, 24.
42. Johann Lavater, *Ausgewahlte Schriften, Handibliothek* (Zurich: Verlag Fr. Schulthess, 1844), VIII, 218.
43. G. H. Lewes, *The Life of Goethe* (New York: Dutton, 1908) pp. 64, 65, 68.
44. Wolfgang Goethe, *Wisdom and Experience,* trans. and ed. Herman J. Weigand (New York: Pantheon, 1949), p. 205.
45. Friederich Schiller, *Das Verschleierte Bild* (Berlin: G. Grotesche Verlag, 1875), pp. 263, 265.
46. Novalis, *Die Lehrlinge zu Saïs* (Paris: Aubier, 1947), p. 189; and on p. 257: "Einem gelang es—er hob den Schleier der Göttin zu Saïs—Aber was sah er? Er sah—Wunder des Wunders—sich selbst."
47. Friederich Wilhelm Schelling, *Essais,* trans. and intro. S. Jankelévitch (Paris: Aubier, 1946), p. 86.
48. Novalis, *Die Lehrlinge,* pp. 231, 247. The quotation which follows is from the same source, p. 179, and the reference to higher-than-human beings appears on p. 229.
49. Novalis, *Fragmente,* pp. 261, 596. The quotations which follow are from the same source, p. 714.
50. *Ibid.,* p. 665.
51. *Ibid.,* p. 389.
52. *Ibid.,* p. 98.
53. Novalis, *Fragmente,* p. 227. The quotation which follows is from the same source, p. 661.
54. *Ibid.,* p. 598.
55. Arthur Rimbaud, *Une Saison en enfer,* Edition de la Pléiade (Paris: Gallimard, 1946), p. 216. The quotations which follow are from Novalis, *Fragmente,* p. 257 and Rimbaud, *Les Illuminations,* Edition de la Pléiade (Paris: Gallimard, 1946).
56. Ludwig Achim von Arnim, *Sämtliche Werke, Novellen,* ed. Wilhelm Grimm (Berlin: Veit, 1839-1842).
57. Arnim, *Kronenwächter* (Berlin: Veit, 1840), I, 5. The quotations which follow are from the same source, pp. 6-7 and 5-6, respectively.
58. *Ibid.,* p. 8.
59. Edward Dent, *Mozart's Operas* (London: Oxford Univ. Press, 1947), pp. 224-225. (Schikaneder and Mozart were both members.)
60. Mme. de Staël, *De L'Allemagne,* p. 302.
61. Karl Goedeke, *Grundriss zur Geschichte der deutschen Literatur* (Dresden, 1895), p. 93.
62. Zacharias Werner, *Die Söhne des Tales* (Wien: Leopold Grund, 1818), p. 249.
63. Werner, *Briefe des Dichters Friederich Ludwig Zacharias Werner,* intro. and ed. by Dr. Oswald Floeck, (München: George Müller, 1914), I, 254.

64. This idea may also be found in Novalis, *Fragmente,* p. 192.
65. This work was translated into French under the title, *Enseignements secrets de Martinez de Pasqually.*
66. Franz von Baader, *Die Weltalter* (Leipzig: Besold, 1868), pp. 374, 377.
67. *Ibid.,* pp. 375-376, 378.
68. Baader, *Sämtliche Werke* (Leipzig: Hermann Bethmann, 1853), IV, 138.
69. J. W. Ritter, *Fragmente aus dem Nachlass eines Jungen Physikers (1810)* (Heidelberg: Mohr und Zimmer, 1870), p. 83ff.
70. Heinrich Steffens, *Schriften* (Breslau: Josef Max, 1821), II, 138.
71. Johann-Carl Passavant, *Untersuchungen über den Lebensmagnetismus und das Hellsehen* (Frankfurt: H. L. Broner, 1821), p. 173.
72. Cf. Balzac's statement in *Louis Lambert,* "The sciences are one and you have divided them."
73. G. H. von Schubert, *Ansichten von der Nachtseite der Naturwissenschaft,* (Dresden: Arnoldischen Buchhandlung, 1818), pp. 115, 301, 311, 357.
74. Schubert, *Die Symbolik des Traumes* (Leipzig: F. A. Brockhaus, 1862), pp. 6, 16, 24, 30, 33.
75. E. T. A. Hoffmann, *Lebensansichten des Katers Murr* (Hamburg: Alfred Jannsen, 1912), p. 146.
76. Hoffmann, *Sämtliche Werke* (Leipzig: Max Hess, 1905), p. 139ff.
77. *Ibid.,* pp. 83, 90.
78. *Ibid.,* p. 54. The quotations which follow are from the same source, p. 251.
79. *Ibid.,* p. 15. The quotations which follow are from the same source, p. 83.
80. Hoffmann, *Kreisleriana,* trans. Albert Béguin (Paris: Gallimard, 1949), p. 86.
81. Mme. de Staël, *De L'Allemagne,* p. 459.
82. Sir Walter Scott, "Du Merveilleux dans le roman," *La Revue de Paris* (1829). The episodes mentioned here may be found in *Walter Scott contre Hoffmann, les épisodes d'une rivalité littéraire en France* (Paris: Nizet, 1950).
83. Sainte-Beuve, *Oeuvres, Premiers lundis,* Edition de la Pléiade (Paris: Gallimard, 1949), p. 384.
84. This may be compared with the storm scene in *The Golden Pot.*
85. P. Lévy, "Les Romantiques français et la langue allemande," *Revue Germanique,* XXIX (1938), 225-252.
86. Xavier Marmier, "Notice sur Hoffmann" in *Contes fantastiques,* ed. Fasquelle (Paris: Charpentier, n.d.), p. 1.
87. *Ibid.*
88. Quotation cited by Taine in *Les Philosophiques du XIXe siècle,* (Paris: Hachette, 1923), p. 140.

CHAPTER 3

1. Auguste Viatte, *Les Sources occultes du romantisme* (Paris: Champion, 1928), I, 18, 47, 186.
2. Martinez de Pasqually, *Traité de la réintégration des êtres* (Paris: Chacornac, 1899), pp. 150, 295, 373.
3. "Coëns" is the French form of the Hebrew word for priest, hence the term "Elus Coëns" would mean "chosen priests."
4. Papus, *Martinésisme, willermosisme, martinisme et Franco-Maçonnerie* (Paris: Chamuel, 1899), pp. 7-8.
5. E. Caro, *Essai sur la vie et la doctrine de Saint-Martin* (Paris: Hachette, 1852), p. 33. In the preface to this work, Caro calls Saint-Martin, "un

illuminé."

6. Critic André Tanner, however, deplores this characteristic of Saint-Martin, since the *"philosophe inconnu"* was not enough a man of action, and calls this equilibrium "a lack of tension in his genius." See introduction to *Gnostiques de la révolution: Claude de Saint-Martin* (Paris: Egloff, 1946), p. 46.
7. Claude de Saint-Martin, *L'Homme de désir,* cited in *Gnostiques de la révolution: Claude de Saint-Martin,* pp. 228, 233.
8. Honoré de Balzac, *Séraphita, La Comédie humaine,* Edition de la Pléiade (Paris: Gallimard, 1950), X, 505.
9. Saint-Martin, *Oeuvres posthumes* (Tours: Letourny, 1807), II, 316. The quotation which follows is from the same source, p. 307.
10. Antoine Fabre d'Olivet, *La Langue hébraïque restituée* in *Gnostiques de la révolution* (Paris: Egloff, 1946), pp. 19-63.
11. Fabre d'Olivet, *Histoire philosophique du genre humain* in *Gnostiques de la révolution,* pp. 201-212.
12. Fabre d'Olivet, Introduction to *Les Vers dorés de Pythagore,* in *Gnostiques de la révolution,* p. 159.
13. Sainte-Beuve, *Portraits contemporains* (Paris: Michel-Lévy, 1870), II, 35.
14. Joseph Bédier and Paul Hazard, *Littérature française* (Paris: Librairie Larousse, 1949), II, 195.
15. Pierre-Simon Ballanche, *Palingénésie sociale, Oeuvres,* (Genève: Barbézat, 1830), p. 11.
16. Viatte, *Les Sources occultes,* II, p. 217.
17. Ballanche, *La Ville des expiations* (Paris: H. Faloue, 1907), p. 20. The quotation which follows is from the same source, p. 84.
18. Henri-Marie Delaage, *Le Monde occulte* (Paris: E. Dentu, 1856). In the Introduction to this book, Lacordaire affirms his faith in "animal magnetism," which he discussed before his audience at Notre Dame during the winter of 1846. (Cf. p. 6.)
19. Gérard de Nerval, *Oeuvres complètes* (Paris: Champion, 1929), V, 338-339.
20. Jean Larat, *Nodier, La Tradition et l'exotisme dans l'oeuvre de Charles Nodier* (Paris: Champion, 1923), p. 15.
21. Charles Nodier, *Oeuvres* (Paris: Renduel, 1832), Preface to *Smarra.*
22. Viatte, *Les Sources occultes,* II, 164-165.
23. *Ibid.,* p. 23.
24. Nodier, *Contes et nouvelles, Oeuvres choisies* (Bordeaux: Delmas, 1953), p. 249.
25. *Ibid.,* p. 188.
26. Nodier, *Lydie ou la résurrection* (Stuttgart: Eduard Hallberger, 1850), p. 88.
27. Claude-Henri de Saint-Simon, *Oeuvres choisies* (Bruxelles: Fr. Van Meenen, 1859), I, 40.
28. Saint-Simon, article in *Le Globe* (Jan. 3, 1832) cited by S. Charléty in *Essai sur l'histoire du Saint-Simonisme* (Paris: Hachette, 1896), p. 140.
29. Saint-Simon, *Oeuvres choisies,* I, 52. The quotation which follows is from the same source, p. 201.
30. E. Barrault, *Aux Artistes du passé et de l'avenir des Beaux-Arts,* (Paris: A. Mesnier, 1830), p. 76. The quotation which follows is from the same source, p. 84.
31. Jean de Lamennais, *Esquisse d'une philosophie* (Paris: Pagnerre, 1840), III, 272.

32. George Sand, *Consuélo* (Bruxelles: Société Belge de Librairie, 1842-1843), V, 151. The quotation which follows is from the same source, p. 255.
33. *La Phalange* (Paris: Imprimerie Lange Lévy et Cie., Aux Bureaux de *La Phalange,* 1845), I, 9.
34. *Ibid.,* article by Hugh Doherty, "De la Mission de l'art et du rôle de l'artiste," I, 260.
35. Charles Fourier, cited by Flora Tristan on frontispiece of *L'Emancipation de la femme* (Paris: La Vérité, 1845).
36. Fourier, *L'Harmonie universelle* (Paris: Librairie phalanstérienne, 1849), II, 92-93.
37. Fourier, *Publication des manuscrits de Charles Fourier* (Paris: Librairie phalanstérienne, 1851-1858), II, 51.
38. Flora Tristan, *L'Emancipation de la femme* (Paris: La Vérité, 1845), p. 116. See also Eliphas Lévi's *L'Assomption de la femme* (Paris: Gallois, 1841), pp. 75-79.
39. Tristan, *Méphis* (Paris: L'Advocat, 1838), p. 171. For further details about the life of Flora Tristan, see Jules J. Peuch, *La Vie et l'oeuvre de Flora Tristan* (Paris: Rivière, 1925).
40. Tristan, *L'Emancipation de la femme,* pp. 74, 111. The quotations which follow are from the same source, pp. 111, 81, 57, and 71, respectively.
41. Nerval, *Le Voyage en orient* (Paris: Le Livre du Divan, 1927), II, 328.
42. *Ibid.,* pp. 380-381.
43. *Ibid.,* III, 128-309.
44. *Ibid.,* II, 304.
45. Nerval, *Les Chimères* (Lille: Librairie Giard, 1949).
46. Philarète Chasles, article on Balzac in the Introduction to *Etudes philosophiques, La Comédie humaine,* Vol. XIV, 1842 ed.
47. Balzac, *Louis Lambert, La Comédie humaine,* X, 415-416.
48. *Ibid.,* pp. 400-401.
49. Balzac, *Falthurne,* manuscrit de l'Abbé Savonati (Paris: José Corti, 1950), pp. xxi, 147.
50. Balzac, *Le Centenaire, Oeuvres de Jeunesse* (Paris: Marescq, 1858), p. 61.
51. Balzac, *Avant-Propos de La Comédie humaine,* Edition de 1842 (Paris: J. Hetzel), I, 25.
52. Balzac, *La Peau de chagrin, La Comédie humaine,* Edition de la Pléiade, IX, 92.
53. Balzac, *Louis Lambert,* X, 451.
54. *Ibid.,* p. 393.
55. "O métamorphose mystique / De tous mes sens fondus en un!" Charles Baudelaire, *Les Fleurs du mal,* Edition par Crépet et Blin (Paris: José Corti, 1942), p. 44.
56. Anton Friederich Mesmer, *Aphorismes* (Paris: Collection magnétique, 1785), IX, 44.
57. Balzac, *Le Cousin Pons* (Paris: Classiques Garnier, 1950), p. 122.
58. Balzac, *Séraphita,* Edition de la Pléiade (Paris: Gallimard, 1950), X, 524.
59. Balzac, *Le Lys dans la vallée* (Paris: Nelson Editeurs, 1952), pp. 14-15.
60. Balzac, *Oeuvres posthumes, Lettres à l'Etrangère* (Paris: Calmann-Lévy, 1899), I, 403. The quotation which follows is from the same source. For other expressions of the same idea, p. 336.
61. André Billy, *Vie de Balzac* (Paris; Flammarion, 1944), I, 99-102.
62. Balzac, *Lettres à l'Etrangère* (July, 1837), I, 418.
63. Balzac, *Le Lys dans la vallée,* p. 64.

64. Balzac, *Louis Lambert,* p. 401.
65. Balzac, *La Vieille Fille* (Paris: Edition André Martel, 1951), p. 169.
66. Balzac, *Avant-Propos de la Comédie humaine,* p. 24.
67. Balzac, *Séraphita,* p. 458.
68. *Ibid.,* p. 554.
69. Balzac, *Les Proscrits,* Edition de la Pléiade (Paris: Gallimard, 1950), p. 355.
70. Victor Hugo, Preface to *Lucrèce Borgia, Oeuvres complètes,* Edition Ollendorf (Paris: Albin-Michel, 1908), II, 443.
71. Hugo, Preface to *Littérature et philosophie mêlées, Oeuvres complètes,* Edition Ollendorf (Paris: Albin-Michel, 1934), p. 15. The second quotation comes from the preface of *Lucrèce Borgia.*
72. Hugo, *Correspondance, Oeuvres complètes* (Paris: Ollendorf, 1947), I, letter of July 25, 1833.
73. Hugo, *Les Voix intérieures,* Collection Minerve (Paris: Classiques Garnier, 1950), p. 119:

    comme un prêtre à l'église,
    Je rêve à l'art qui charme, à l'art que civilise,
    Qui change l'homme un peu,
    Et qui, comme un semeur qui jette au loin sa graine,
    En semant la nature à travers l'âme humaine,
    Y fera germer Dieu.

74. Hugo, *Littérature et philosophie mêlées,* p. 90.
75. Hugo, *Oeuvres posthumes, Choses vues* (Paris: Edition J. Hetzel, 1897), p. 257.
76. Delaage, *Le Monde occulte,* pp. 104-105.
77. Paul Chacornac, *Eliphas Lévi* (Paris: Chacornac Frères, 1926), pp. 36, 131-132.
78. Eliphas Lévi, *Histoire de la magie* (Paris: Germer-Ballière, 1960), Introduction.
79. Chacornac, *Eliphas Lévi,* pp. 200-201.
80. *Ibid.,* p. 278.
81. Lévi, *Dogme et rituel de la haute magie* (Paris: Editions Niclaus, 1948), pp. 9-13.
82. *Encyclopaedia Britannica,* "Spiritualism."
83. Gustave Simon, *Les Tables tournantes de Jersey, Procès-verbaux,* (Paris: Conard, 1923), pp. 30-35.
84. Paul Berret, *Victor Hugo* (Paris: Garnier, 1927), p. 103.
85. Simon, *Les Tables,* p. 76.
86. *Ibid.,* p. 97. Hugo was present at the first session with Chénier, but not at the second (p. 97). Simon insists that the verses dictated by Chénier cannot be found in any of Hugo's works (p. 83).
87. *Ibid.,* p. 146.
88. *Ibid.,* p. 310. See also pp. 306-309.
89. *Ibid.,* p. 322.
90. Viatte, *Victor Hugo et les illuminés de son temps* (Montreal: Les Editions de l'arbre, 1942), pp. 140, 145.
91. Hugo, *William Shakespeare* (Paris: Nelson Editeurs, n.d.), p. 39.
92. *Ibid.,* pp. 278-280.
93. *Ibid.,* p. 156.
94. *Ibid.,* p. 298.
95. *Ibid.,* pp. 40-41.

96. *Ibid.*, p. 42.
97. Hugo, *Post-Scriptum de ma vie* (Paris: Calmann-Lévy, 1901), pp. 115, 117.
98. Hugo, *William Shakespeare*, p. 160.
99. Joseph Vianey, *Editions critiques des Contemplations* (Paris: Hachette, 1922), pp. lxi-lxiv.
100. Henri Serouya, *La Kabbale* (Paris: Bernard Grasset, 1947), p. 279.
101. *Ibid.*, p. 279; see also Karppe, *Etude sur l'origine du Zohar* (Paris, 1901), p. 343.
102. Serouya, *La Kabbale*, pp. 256-261; see also Eliphas Lévi, *Dogme et rituel de la haute magie*, Chapts. I-X, for the correspondence of the numbers and letters.
103. S. Karppe, *Etude sur l'origine du Zohar*, p. 378. The "Word" is discussed on p. 392.
104. Hugo, *Les Contemplations*, (Paris: Nelson Editeurs, 1949), p. 344.

    Ecoutez. Je suis Jean. J'ai vu des choses sombres,
    J'ai vu l'ombre infinie où se perdent les nombres.

105. Hugo, "Ce que dit la Bouche d'ombre" in *Les Contemplations*.

    T'imaginais-tu donc l'univers autrement?
    Crois-tu que Dieu, par qui la forme sort du nombre,
    Aurait fait à jamais la forêt sombre?

106. Hugo, *Les Contemplations*, pp. 462-463.

    La clarté montera dans tout comme une sève. . . .
    Les douleurs finiront dans toute l'ombre; un ange
    Criéra: Commencement!

107. Hugo, *Dieu et la fin de Satan* (Paris: Nelson Editeurs, n.d.), p. 18.
108. *Ibid.*, pp. 218-219.
109. *Ibid.*, p. 214.

    Il est X, élément du rayonnement, nombre
    De l'infini, clarté formidable de l'ombre,
    Lueur sur le koran comme sur le missel. . . .
    Dieu, c'est la flamme aimante au fond de toutes choses. . . .
    La clarté s'arrête, comme tout éblouie,
    Je m'évanouissais, et vue et l'ouie,
    Et jusqu'aux battements du coeur s'interrompant,
    S'en allaient hors de moi comme une eau se répand.

    Balzac also refers to this *X* in *Louis Lambert*: "il est en l'homme un phénomène primitif et dominateur qui ne souffre aucune analyse . . . . Cet X est la Parole, dont la communication brûle et dévore ceux qui ne sont pas préparés à la recevoir. Elle engendre incessamment la substance" (p. 449).

110. Hugo, *Dieu et la fin de Satan*, p. 228.

    Veux-tu, flèche tremblante, atteindre enfin la cible?
    Veux-tu toucher le but, regarder l'invisible,
    L'innommé, l'idéal, le réel, l'inoui;
    Comprendre, déchiffrer, lire? être un ébloui?
    Le veux-tu? Réponds.

111. Hugo, *Les Contemplations,* "Ce que dit la Bouche d'ombre," p. 455.
112. *Ibid.,* p. 456.
113. Jean-Paul Sartre, *L'Etre et le Néant* (Paris: Gallimard, 1948), p. 53.
114. Hugo, *Les Contemplations,* p. 440.
115. *Ibid.,* p. 368.
116. *Ibid.,* p. 365.

> Dans l'éternité, gouffre où se vide la tombe,
> L'homme coule sans fin, sombre fleuve qui tombe
> Dans une sombre mer.

117. *Ibid.,* p. 346.

> Nous sommes le néant; nos vertus tiendraient toutes
> Dans le creux de la pierre où vient boire l'oiseau.
> Le bien que nous faisons est spectre comme nous.

118. *Ibid.,* p. 400.

> Nous sommes le gouffre agité
> Nous sommes les flocons de la neige éternelle
> Dans l'éternelle obscurité.

119. *Ibid.,* p. 394.

> Dieu pour le penseur attristé
> Ouvre toujours dans les ténèbres
> De brusques gouffres de clartés.

Ibid., p. 426.

> Le grand caché de la Nature
> Vient hors de l'antre à leur appel
> A leur voix l'ombre symbolique
> Parle; le mystère s'explique.

120. *Ibid.,* p. 349.

> L'Etre éternellement montre sa face double
> Mal et bien, glace et feu;
> L'homme sent à la fois âme pure et chair sombre
> Et le baiser de Dieu.

121. *Ibid.,* p. 442.

> Dieu, soleil dans l'azur, dans le cendre étincelle,
> N'est hors de rien, étant la fin universelle,
> L'éclair est son regard, autant que le rayon.

122. *Ibid.,* p. 443.

> Crois-tu que cette vie énorme, remplissant
> De souffles le feuillage et de lueurs la tête,
> Qui va du roc à l'arbre et de l'arbre à la bête,
> Et de la pierre à toi monte insensiblement,
> S'arrête sur l'abîme à l'homme, escarpement?

Non, elle continue, invincible, admirable,
Entre dans l'invisible et dans l'impondérable,
Y disparaît pour toi, chair vile, emplit l'azur
D'un monde éblouissant, *miroir d'un monde obscure,*
D'êtres purs, de voyants dont les splendeurs témoignent
D'anges faits de rayons comme l'homme d'instincts;
Elle plonge à travers les cieux jamais atteints,
Sublime ascension d'échelles étoilées,
Des démons enchainés monte aux âmes ailées,
Fait toucher le front sombre au radieux orteil,
Rattache l'astre esprit à l'archange soleil,
Relie, en traversant des millions de lieues,
Les groupes constellés et les légions bleues,
Peuple le haut, le bas, les bords et le milieu,
Et dans les profondeurs s'évanouit en Dieu.

123. Emmanuel Swedenborg, *Dictionary of Correspondences* (Boston: New-Church Union, 1899).
124. Hugo, *Les Contemplations,* p. 369.

L'arbre Eternité vit sans faîte et sans racines;
Ses branches sont partout, proches du ver, voisine
Du grand astre doré;
L'espace voit sans fin croître la branche Nombre
Et la branche Destin, végétation sombre,
Emplit l'homme effaré.

125. Serouya, *La Kabbale,* p. 351.
126. Hugo, *Les Contemplations,* pp. 411, 443.
127. Swedenborg, *Heaven and Hell* (London: Swedenborg Society, 1937), p. 56.
128. Hugo, *Les Contemplations,* p. 342.

Pourquoi cacher ces lois profondes?
Rien n'est muré.
Dans vos flammes et dans vos ondes
Je passerai;
J'irai lire la grande bible;
J'entrerai nu
Jusqu'au tabernacle terrible
De l'inconnu.

129. *Ibid.,* p. 340.

L'homme en cette époque agitée,
Sombre océan,
Doit faire comme Prométhée
Et comme Adam.
Il doit ravir au ciel austère
L'éternel feu;
Conquérir son propre mystère,
Et voler Dieu.

CHAPTER 4

1. L. Aragon and André Breton, *Une Coeur sous une soutane* (Paris: Ronald Davis, 1942). Not published until after the death of Paterne Berrichon. See also Rimbaud, *Oeuvres Complètes,* Edition de la Pléiade (Paris: Gallimard, 1946), pp. 686-687.
2. Paul Claudel in Ernest Friche, *Etudes claudéliennes* (Perrentruy, 1943), p. 84.
3. Claudel, Preface to *Oeuvres d'Arthur Rimbaud,* publiées par Berrichon (Paris: Mercure de France, 1912).
4. Claudel, *Pages de prose* (Paris: Gallimard, 1944), p. 280.
5. Jacques Rivière, *Rimbaud* (Paris: Kra, 1930), pp. 45, 280.
6. Jean-Marie Carré, *La Vie aventureuse de Jean-Arthur Rimbaud,* Nouvelle Edition, 1939 (Paris: Plon, 1926). In the edition of 1926 Professor Carré said this had been withdrawn from the Bibliothèque Nationale and also from the library of the University of Strasbourg. Another critic, however, has also taken note of this statement: Pierre Debray, *Rimbaud, le magicien désabusé* (Paris: Juillard, 1949), p. 12.
7. C. A. Hackett, *Le Lyrisme de Rimbaud* (Paris: Nizet et Bastard, 1938), p. 69.
8. Colonel Godchot, *La Voyance de Rimbaud* (Paris: La Guiterne, 1935), p. 22.
9. Stéphane Mallarmé, *Oeuvres complètes,* Edition de la Pléiade (Paris: Gallimard, 1945), p. 513.
10. *Ibid.,* p. 512.
11. André Gide, *Journaux (1889-1939),* Edition de la Pléiade (Paris: Gallimard, 1939), p. 185.
12. Breton, *Les Pas perdus* (Paris: N. R. F., 1924), pp. 80, 185.
13. Guy Michaud, *Le Message poétique du symbolisme* (Paris: Librairie Nizet, 1947), Chap. IV, I, 127.
14. Breton, *Flagrant délit,* (Thésée, 1949), p. 8.
15. Jules Mouquet, *Lettre du baron Petdechèvre* (Pierre Gailler, 1949).
16. Henry de Bouillane de Lacoste, *Rimbaud et le problème des Illuminations* (Paris: Mercure de France, 1949), pp. 31, 136.
17. Ernest Delahaye, *Souvenirs familiers à propos de Rimbaud, Verlaine, Germain Nouveau* (Messein, 1925), p. 146.
18. Enid Starkie, *Arthur Rimbaud,* Rev. Ed. (New York: W. W. Norton, 1947), p. 174.
19. Breton, *Flagrant Délit,* p. 43.
20. Delahaye, *Rimbaud, l'artiste et l'être morale* (Paris: Messein, 1942), p. 32.
21. Arthur Rimbaud, *Oeuvres complètes,* Edition de la Pléiade (Paris: Gallimard, 1946), p. 77.
22. *Ibid.,* p. 77.
23. Mouquet, *Arthur Rimbaud, Vers de collège* (Paris: Mercure de France, 1942), pp. 68-69.
24. Rimbaud, *Oeuvres complètes,* pp. 521-522.
25. Mouquet, *Arthur Rimbaud, Vers de collège,* p. 29.
26. *Ibid.,* p. 57.
27. Rimbaud, *Oeuvres complètes,* p. 100.
28. Mouquet, *Arthur Rimbaud,* pp. 45, 47, 49, 51.
29. *Ibid.,* pp. 24-25.

30. Rimbaud, *Oeuvres complètes,* p. 389.
31. *Ibid.,* pp. 491-492.
32. Mouquet, *Arthur Rimbaud,* p. 28.
33. *Ibid.,* p. 34.
34. Rimbaud, *Oeuvres complètes,* p. 4.
35. *Ibid.,* p. 263.
36. Delahaye, *Souvenirs familiers,* p. 105.
37. Starkie, *Arthur Rimbaud,* p. 53; also, Rimbaud, *Oeuvres complètes,* p. 248.
38. Rimbaud, *Oeuvres complètes,* p. 65.
39. *Ibid.,* p. 68.
40. Starkie, *Arthur Rimbaud,* p. 54.
41. Rimbaud, *Oeuvres complètes,* p. 76.
42. Starkie, *Arthur Rimbaud,* p. 56.
43. Delahaye, *Souvenirs familiers,* pp. 102-146.
44. Rimbaud, *Oeuvres complètes,* pp. 241, 243, 249-250.
45. Delahaye, *Souvenirs familiers,* pp. 102-146.
46. Paul Verlaine, *Les Poètes maudits,* p. 40.
47. Delahaye, *Souvenirs familiers,* p. 22.
48. Rimbaud, *Oeuvres complètes,* p. 74.
49. *Ibid.,* pp. 74-75.
50. *Ibid.,* p. 75.
51. *Ibid.,* pp. 74-75.
52. *Ibid.,* p. 80.
53. *Ibid.,* p. 491.
54. *Ibid.,* p. 92.
55. *Ibid.,* p. 72.
56. *Ibid.,* p. 76.
57. *Ibid.,* p. 77.
58. *Ibid.,* p. 73.
59. *Ibid.,* pp. 73, 74.
60. Starkie, *Arthur Rimbaud,* p. 87.

CHAPTER 5

1. Arthur Rimbaud, *Oeuvres complètes,* Edition de la Pléiade (Paris: Gallimard, 1946), p. 255. From this point references to these two letters are not given in the footnotes.
2. Charles Fourier, *Oeuvres choisies* (Paris: Recueil Sirey, 1932), p. 9.
3. Thomas Love Peacock, *The Works of Thomas Peacock* (London: Constable, 1924). The quotation that follows is from the same source, III, 9.
4. Johann-Gottfried Herder, *Sämtliche Werke* (Stuttgart: T. P. Cotts'chen, 1829), XVI, 7-8.
5. *Ibid.,* pp. 11-12.
6. Edgar Quinet, *Histoire de la poésie, Oeuvres de E. Quinet* (Paris: Pagnerre, 1857), IX, 283.
7. *Ibid.,* p. 281.
8. *Ibid.,* p. 311. The quotation that follows is from the same source, p. 293.
9. *Ibid.,* pp. 293, 302. The quotation that follows is from the same source, p. 321.
10. *Ibid.,* p. 314.
11. *Ibid.,* p. 345.
12. *Ibid.,* pp. 336-337.

13. *Ibid.*, p. 365.
14. Leconte de Lisle, *Derniers Poèmes* (Paris: Alphonse Lemerre, 1895), p. 216.
15. *Ibid.*, p. 218.
16. Théophile Gautier, *Souvenirs romantiques,* ed. Adolphe Boschot (Paris: Garnier, 1929), p. 95.
17. Victor Hugo, *Les Châtiments* (Paris: Hachette, 1932), II, 563-564.
18. *Ibid.*, p. 563.
19. Gautier, *Souvenirs romantiques,* p. 94.
20. *Ibid.*, p. 191.
21. Leconte de Lisle, *Derniers Poèmes,* (Paris: Alphonse Lemerre, 1895), pp. 245-250.
22. Gautier, *Histoire du romantisme* (Paris: Flammarion, n.d.), p. 259.
23. Hippolyte Taine, *La Fontaine et ses fables* (Paris: Hachette, n.d.), p. 55.
24. Charles Baudelaire, *L'Art romantique* (Geneva: Albert Skira, 1945), p. 156.
25. *Ibid.*, p. 364.
26. Gautier, *Emaux et Camées,* (Paris: Charpentier, 1863), p. 6.
27. Henriette Emilie Velthuis, *Théophile Gautier* (Netherlande: Gröningen, 1924), p. 42.
28. Baudelaire, *L'Art romantique,* p. 171.
29. Leconte de Lisle, *Poèmes barbares* (Paris: Alphonse Lemerre, 1878), p. 1.
30. Baudelaire, *L'Art romantique,* p. 352.
31. *Ibid.*, p. 347.
32. *Ibid.*, p. 348.
33. Gautier, *Souvenirs romantiques,* p. 300.
34. Baudelaire, *L'Art romantique,* p. 166.
35. Leconte de Lisle, *Préface, Poèmes antiques* (Paris: Lemerre, n.d.), p. 218. The quotation that follows is from the same source, p. 219.
36. Leconte de Lisle, *Préface, Poèmes barbares* (Paris: Lemerre, 1878).
37. Sully-Prudhomme, *Oeuvres, Préface à Lucrèce: De la Nature des choses, Ier Livre,* (Paris: Lemerre, 1925), p. 49.
38. F. W. Schelling, *Système de l'Idéalisme transcendental, Essais de Schelling,* trans. S. Jankelévitch (Paris: Aubier, 1946), p. 161.
39. Sully-Prudhomme, *Oeuvres,* p. 72.
40. *Ibid.*, pp. 72, 93.
41. G. W. F. Hegel, *The Philosophy of History* in *Modern Student's Library,* ed. J. Loewenberg (New York: Scribner's, 1929), p. 423.
42. *Ibid.*, pp. 376-377.
43. D. D. Rosca, *L'Influence de Hegel sur Taine théoricien de la connaissance et de l'art* (Paris: J. Gamber, 1928), p. 407.
44. Taine, *Histoire de la littérature anglaise* (Paris: Hachette, 1863), V, 312-313.
45. *Ibid.*, p. 45.
46. Taine, *Les Philosophes classiques du XIXe siècle en France* (Paris: Hachette, 1923), p. 370.
47. Court de Gébelin, *Le Monde primitif* (Paris: 1772), I, 151.
48. Eliphas Lévi, *Dogme et rituel de la haute magie,* Edition Niclaus (Paris: 1947), I, 65, 90.
49. *Ibid.*, II, 91-92.
50. *Ibid.*, pp. 168, 170.
51. Lévi, *Histoire de la magie* (Paris: Germer Baillière, 1860), p. 8.
52. *Ibid.*, I, pp. 53, 108.
53. *Ibid.*, I, 114.

54. Gautier, *Souvenirs romantiques,* p. 304.
55. Lévi, *Histoire de le magie,* I, 363.
56. *Ibid.,* pp. 338-339, 345-354.
57. See Appendix B.
58. Baudelaire, *Les Paradis artificiels* (Lausanne: Clairefontaine, 1947), p. 221.
59. *Ibid.,* p. 86.
60. Rimbaud, *Oeuvres complètes,* p. 176.
61. *Ibid.*
62. Baudelaire, *Les Paradis artificiels,* p. 109.
63. *Ibid.,* p. 67.
64. Rimbaud, *Une Saison en enfer,* Editions de la Pléiade (Paris: Gallimard, 1946), p. 213. For Baudelaire's description of his "*fantasmagorie intérieure,*" see pp. 76 and 157 of *Les Paradis artificiels.*
65. Baudelaire, *Les Paradis artificiels,* pp. 218-219.
66. *Ibid.,* p. 88.
67. *Ibid.,* p. 103.
68. Rimbaud, *Une Saison en enfer,* p. 224.
69. Baudelaire, *Les Paradis artificiels,* pp. 64, 66, 72, 77, 92, 223.
70. Rimbaud, *Une Saison en enfer,* p. 224.
71. Baudelaire, *Les Paradis artificiels,* pp. 59-60, 66.
72. *Ibid.,* p. 83.
73. *Ibid.,* p. 139.
74. Baudelaire also mentions that hashish arouses the sense of smell: *Les Paradis artificiels,* pp. 76, 224.
75. *Ibid.,* p. 103.
76. *Ibid.,* pp. 221 and 74, respectively.
77. *Ibid.,* p. 73.
78. Rimbaud, *Une Saison en enfer,* p. 219.
79. Emmanuel Swedenborg, *Dictionary of Correspondences* (Boston: New-Church Union, 1899), p. 212.
80. Novalis, *Die Lehrlinge zu Saïs* in *Kleine Schriften* (Paris: Aubier, 1947), p. 248.
81. Court de Gébelin, *Le Monde primitif,* III, 277.
82. Lévi, *Dogme et rituel de la haute magie,* II, 337-339. Lévi gives credit to Court de Gébelin for the discovery of this "key."
83. *Ibid.,* pp. 332-333.
84. *Ibid.,* pp. 338, 339.
85. Lévi, *Histoire de la magie* (Paris: Germer Baillière, 1860), p. 541. See also the *Jewish Encyclopedia,* p. 448.
86. Rimbaud, *Une Saison en enfer,* p. 213.
87. Gérard de Nerval, *Aurélia* (Bordeaux: Delmas, 1950), p. 113.
88. *Le Globe* (Jan. 26, 1831).
89. *La Phalange,* (Paris: Imprimerie Lange Lévy & Cie., 1845), I, 245, 260.
90. Hugo, *William Shakespeare* (Paris: Nelson, n.d.), p. 276.
91. Fourier, *Pages choisies, L'Harmonie universelle* (Paris: Recueil Sirey, 1932), II, 93.
92. Lévi, *L'Assomption de la femme* (Paris: Gallois, 1841), p. 45.

CHAPTER 6

1. Arthur Rimbaud, *Oeuvres complètes,* Edition de la Pléiade (Paris: Gallimard, 1946), p. 213.

2. Albert Camus, *Le Mythe de Sisyphe* (Paris: Gallimard, 1942), Chapt. I.
3. Rimbaud, *Oeuvres complètes,* p. 193.
4. John Read, *Prelude to Chemistry* (New York: Macmillan, 1937), p. 275.
5. Eliphas Lévi, *Histoire de la magie* (Paris: Germer Baillière, 1860), p. 5. For Lévi's chapter on Alchemy, see p. 344 of his *Histoire.*
6. Rimbaud, *Oeuvres complètes,* p. 218.
7. Charles Baudelaire, *Les Paradis artificiels,* (Lausanne: Clairefontaine, 1947), p. 223.
8. Rimbaud, *Oeuvres complètes,* p. 170.
9. Baudelaire, *Les Paradis artificiels,* p. 81.
10. *Ibid.,* p. 158.
11. *Ibid.,* p. 222.
12. *Ibid.,* p. 160.
13. *Ibid.,* p. 161. The quotations that follow are from the same source, pp. 161-162 and p. 163, respectively.
14. Rimbaud, *Oeuvres complètes,* p. 174.
15. Rimbaud, *Oeuvres complètes,* p. 235: see also p. 224.
16. Rimbaud, *Oeuvres complètes,* p. 205.
17. Rimbaud, *Oeuvres complètes,* p. 99.
18. Baudelaire, *Les petits Poèmes en prose,* (Genève: Editions d'Art Albert Skira, 1943), p. 102.
19. Rimbaud, *Oeuvres complètes,* p. 132.
20. Read, *Prelude to Chemistry,* p. 133. The quotations that follow are from the same source, pp. 131 and 133 respectively.
21. Manly P. Hall, *An Encyclopedic Outline of Masonic, Hermetic, Cabbalistic and Rosicrucian Philosophy* (San Francisco: H. S. Crocker, 1928), p. 118.
22. Lévi, *La Clef des grands mystères* (Paris: Librairie Chacornac, n.d.), p. 218. The quotation that follows is from the same source.
23. Rimbaud, *Oeuvres complètes,* p. 222.
24. Henri Delaage, *Doctrines des sociétés secrètes* (Paris: E. Dentu, 1852), p. 51.
25. *Ibid.,* p. 32.
26. Delaage, *Le Monde occulte* (Paris: E. Dentu, 1856), p. 92.
27. Rimbaud, *Oeuvres complètes,* p. 139; *Une Saison en enfer,* p. 224.
28. Rimbaud, *Oeuvres complètes,* p. 134.
29. Gershom Scholem, *Major Trends in Jewish Mysticism,* trans. (in part) George Lichtheim (New York: Jewish Institute of Religion, 1946), pp. 44, 61, 77.
30. Rimbaud, *Oeuvres complètes,* p. 134.
31. Rimbaud, *Oeuvres complètes,* p. 220-221.
32. Baudelaire, *Les Paradis artificiels,* p. 221.
33. Aldous Huxley, *The Doors of Perception* (London: Chatto & Windus, 1954), p. 20.
34. Henri Serouya, *La Kabbale* (Paris: Grasset, 1947), pp. 264-265.
35. Delaage, *Doctrines des sociétés secrètes,* p. 54.
36. Serouya, *La Kabbale,* p. 263.
37. Colonel Godchot, *Arthur Rimbaud ne varietur* (Nice: chez l'auteur, 1936-1937).
38. E. Gaubert, *Une Explication nouvelle du Sonnet des Voyelles* (Paris: Mercure de France, 1904), pp. 551-553.
39. Carl Gustave Jung, *The Integration of the Personality,* trans. Stanley Dell (London: Routledge & Kegan Paul, 1940), pp. 206, 208.
40. Serouya, *La Kabbale,* p. 263.

41. S. Karppe, *Etude sur les origines du Zohar* (Paris: Mercure de France, 1901), p. 441.
42. M. Pattison Muir, *The Story of Alchemy and the Beginnings of Chemistry* (London: George Newnes, 1902).
43. Rimbaud, *Oeuvres complètes,* pp. 85-86.
44. A. R. Chisholm, *The Art of Arthur Rimbaud* (Melbourne: University Press, 1930), Chapt. II.
45. Guy Michaud, *Le Message poétique du symbolisme* (Paris: Nizet, 1947), p. 127.
46. Victor Hugo, *Les Travailleurs de la mer* (Paris: J. Hetzel, n.d.), Chapt. III, p. 112.
47. Rimbaud, *Oeuvres complètes,* p. 128.
48. Rimbaud, *Oeuvres complètes,* p. 210.
49. Honoré de Balzac, *Louis Lambert, La Comédie humaine,* Edition de la Pléiade (Paris: Gallimard, 1950), p. 401.
50. Rimbaud, *Oeuvres complètes,* p. 211. The quotations that follow are from the same source, pp. 212, 225, 226.
51. *Ibid.,* p. 229.
52. *Ibid.,* pp. 226-227.
53. Rimbaud, *Oeuvres complètes,* p. 175.
54. *Ibid.,* p. 200.
55. Rimbaud, *Oeuvres complètes,* p. 208. The quotation that follows is from the same source, p. 207.
56. *Ibid.,* p. 211.
57. *Ibid.,* p. 205.
58. *Ibid.,* p. 229.

Bibliography

ACHIM VON ARNIM, LUDWIG. *Kronenwächter.* Berlin: Veit, 1840.

BAADER, FRANZ. *Sämtliche Werke.* Vol. IV. Leipzig: Verlag von Hermann Bethmann, 1853.

BALLANCHE, PIERRE-SIMON. *Palingénésie sociale, Oeuvres.* Vol. III. Genève: Barbézat, 1830.

BALZAC, HONORÉ DE. *La Comédie humaine.* Vols. IX, X. Editions de la Pléiade. Paris: Gallimard, 1950.

BAUDELAIRE, CHARLES. *L'Art romantique.* Editions d'art. Genève: Albert Skira, 1945.

———. *Les Paradis artificiels.* Lausanne: Clairefontaine, 1947.

BÉGUIN, ALBERT. *L'Ame romantique et le rêve.* Paris: José Corti, 1946.

BOUILLANE DE LACOSTE, HENRY DE. *Rimbaud et le problème des Illuminations.* Paris: Mercure de France, 1949.

BRETON, ANDRÉ. *Flagrant Délit.* Paris: Thésée, 1949.

CARRÉ, JEAN-MARIE. *La Vie aventureuse de Jean-Arthur Rimbaud.* Paris: Plon, 1939.

DEBRAY, PIERRE. *Rimbaud, le magicien désabusé.* Paris: Juillard, 1949.

DELAAGE, HENRI. *Le Monde occulte.* Paris: E. Dentu, 1856.

DELAHAYE, ERNEST. *Souvenirs familiers à propos de Rimbaud, Verlaine, Germain Nouveau.* Paris: Messein, 1925.

ETIEMBLE ET Y. GAUCLÈRE. *Rimbaud.* Paris: Gallimard, 1950.

GAUTIER, THÉOPHILE. *Souvenirs romantiques.* Paris: Garnier Frères, 1929.

———. *Histoire du romantisme.* Paris: Flammarion, n.d.

GÉBELIN, COURT DE. *Le Monde primitif.* Vol. I. 1772.

GENGOUX, JACQUES. *La Symbolique de Rimbaud.* Paris: La Colombe, 1947.

———. *La Pensée poétique de Rimbaud.* Paris: Librairie Nizet, 1950.

GODCHOT, COLONEL. *La Voyance de Rimbaud.* Paris: La Guiterne, 1935.

HACKETT, C. A. *Le Lyrisme de Rimbaud.* Paris: Nizet et Bastard, 1938.

———. *Rimbaud, l'Enfant.* Paris: José Corti, 1948. Contains a useful bibliography of books and articles on Rimbaud.

HAMANN, JOHANN. *Sämtliche Werke.* Vols. I, II, III. Wien: Thomas-Morus-Presse, Im Verlag Herder, 1951.

HOFFMANN, E. T. A. *Kreisleriana.* Trans. Albert Béguin. Paris: Gallimard, 1949.

———. *Sämtliche Werke.* Leipzig: Max Hesses Verlag, 1905.

HUGO, VICTOR. *William Shakespeare.* Paris: Nelson Editeurs, n.d.

———. *Dieu et la fin de Satan.* Paris: Nelson Editeurs, n.d.

———. *Les Contemplations.* Paris: Collection Nelson, 1949.

HUXLEY, ALDOUS. *The Doors of Perception.* London: Chatto & Windus, 1954.

JUNG, CARL-GUSTAV. *Modern Man in Search of a Soul.* New York: Harcourt Brace & World, 1933.

———. *The Integration of Personality.* Trans. Stanley Dell. London: Routledge & Kegan Paul, 1940.

KANT, IMMANUEL. *Sämtliche Werke* in chronologischer Reihenfolge. Ed. G. Hartenstein. Vol. II. Leipzig: Voss, 1867.

KARPPE, S. *Etude sur les origines du Zohar.* Paris, 1901.

LECONTE DE LISLE. "Préface des poèmes antiques" in *Derniers poèmes.* Paris: Alphonse Lemerre, 1895.

LÉVI, ELIPHAS. *Dogme et rituel de la haute magie,* Vols. I and II. Paris: Editions Niclaus, 1947.

MICHAUD, GUY. *Le Message Poétique du symbolisme.* Paris: Nizet, 1947.

MOUQUET, JULES. *Arthur Rimbaud, Vers de collège.* Paris: Mercure de France, 1942.

NADEAU, MAURICE. *Documents surréalistes.* Paris: Editions du Seuil, 1948.

NERVAL, GÉRARD DE. *Aurélia.* Bordeaux: Delmas, 1950.

NODIER, CHARLES. *Contes et Nouvelles.* Bordeaux: Delmas, 1953.

———. *Oeuvres,* Vol. III. Paris: Renduel, 1929.

NOVALIS. *Heinrich von Ofterdingen,* Trans. Marcel Camus. Paris: Aubier, 1947.

———. *Kleine Schriften.* Trans. Geneviève Bianquis. Paris: Aubier, 1947.

———. *Fragmente.* Dresden: Wolfgang Jess Verlag, 1929.

PASQUALLY, MARTINES DE. *Traité de la réintegration des êtres.* Paris: Chacornac, 1899.

———. *La Phalange.* Paris: Imprimerie Lange Lévy et Cie., Aux Bureaux de la Phalange, 1845.

QUINET, EDGAR. *Histoire de la poésie, Oeuvres,* Vol. IX. Paris: Pagnerre, 1857.

RIMBAUD, ARTHUR. *Oeuvres complètes.* Edition de la Pléiade. Paris: Gallimard, 1946.

RIVIÈRE, JACQUES. *Rimbaud.* Paris: Editions Kra, 1930.

SAINT-MARTIN, CLAUDE DE. *Oeuvres posthumes.* Tours: Letourmy, 1807.

SAINT-SIMON. *Oeuvres choisies.* Bruxelles: Fr. Van Meeren, 1859.

SCHUBERT, G. H. VON. *Die Symbolik des Traumes.* Leipzig: F. A. Brockhaus, 1862.

SEROUYA, HENRI. *La Kabbale.* Paris: Grasset, 1947.

SIMON, GUSTAVE. *Les Tables tournantes de Jersey, Procès-verbaux.* Paris: Conard, 1923.

SPENLÉ, E. *Novalis.* Paris: Hachette, 1903.

STAEL, MADAME GERMAINE DE. *De l'Allemagne.* Paris: Firmin-Didot, 1893.

STARKIE, ENID. *Arthur Rimbaud.* New York: W. W. Norton & Co., 1947.

SULLY-PRUDHOMME. *Oeuvres, Préface* au *De Rerum Natura* de Lucrèce. Paris: Alphonse Lemerre, 1925.

SWEDENBORG, EMMANUEL. *Heaven and Hell.* London: Swedenborg Society, 1937.

TANNER, ANDRÉ. *Gnostiques de la révolution: Fabre d'Olivet.* Paris: Egloff, 1946.

———. *Gnostiques de la révolution: Claude de Saint-Martin.* Paris: Egloff, 1946.

Tristan, Flora. *L'Emancipation de la femme.* Paris: La Vérité, 1845.
Viatte, Auguste. *Les Sources occultes du romantisme.* Librairie Ancienne Honoré. Paris: Champion, 1928.
Werner, Zacharias. *Die Söhne des Tales.* Wien: Léopold Grund, 1818.

Acknowledgments

In addition to my heavy indebtedness to all those minds of the last century whose works I have so freely used, conspicuous debts of gratitude are due to certain contemporaries who inspired this study and made it possible: to Professor Henri Peyre who introduced me to Rimbaud, encouraged me to attempt textual analyses of the enigmatic poems, and directed the dissertation on which this book is based; to the late Professor Andrew Morehouse for his deep insight into human nature and the inspiration of his saintliness; and to Professor Kenneth Douglas for his keen grasp of philosophical problems.

Grateful acknowledgment is also made to Professor Jacques Voisine and to the late Professor Jean-Marie Carré of the Sorbonne for advice and fruitful suggestions; to the librarians of the University of Strasbourg; and to M. Taute, librarian of Charleville, for his hospitality and for valuable discussions of the ideas of various other Rimbaud scholars who have visited that city.

Thanks are also due my husband for his indefatigable patience in proofreading and to Ingrid Schwab, Mary Cowgill, and Mildred Caldwell for their skill in the preparation of this manuscript.

A particular acknowledgment should go to the Fulbright Commission, whose generous grant made it possible for me to spend some years in France and Germany, and to the Ford Foundation for its contribution to the publication of this work.

Finally, I should like to express my gratitude to the following publishers for granting me permission to reprint or translate copyrighted material:

Albert Langen Georg Müller Verlag for a quotation from Zacharias Werner, *Briefe des Dichters Friederich Ludwig Zacharias Werner,* edited by Oswald Floeck, copyright 1914.

Charles Scribner's Sons for a quotation from G. W. F. Hegel, *The Philosophy of History,* edited by J. Loewenberg, copyright 1929.

Editions Bernard Grasset for quotations from Henri Serouya, *La Kabbale,* copyright 1947.

Editions Conard-Lambert for quotations from Gustave Simon, *Les tables tournantes de Jersey,* copyright 1923.

Faber and Faber Ltd. for quotations from Plotinus, *Enneads,* trans. by Stephen MacKenna, copyright 1930.
The Hogarth Press Ltd. for a quotation from Rainer Maria Rilke, *Sonnets to Orpheus,* trans. J. B. Leishman, copyright 1946.
Librairie A. Hatier for a quotation from R. Jasinski, *Histoire de la Littérature française,* copyright 1947.
Librairie Gallimard for quotations from Stephen Mallarmé, Lettre à M. Harrison Rhodes in *Medaillons et portraits,* © Editions Gallimard, 1945; André Breton, *Les Pas perdus,* © Editions Gallimard, 1924; André Gide, *Les Journaux,* © Editions Gallimard, 1952; Jean-Paul Sartre, *L'Etre et le Néant,* © Editions Gallimard, 1948; Benjamin Constant, *Journaux Intimes,* © Editions Gallimard, 1957; E. T. A. Hoffmann, *Kreisleriana,* trans. A. Béguin, © Editions Gallimard, 1949; Paul Claudel, *Pages de Prose:* un lettre à Jacques Rivière, © Editions Gallimard, 1944; Paul Eluard, *Donner à voir,* © Editions Gallimard, 1939.
New Directions for a quotation from *Remember to Remember* by Henry Miller. Copyright 1947 by New Directions. Reprinted by permission of New Directions, Publishers.
Routledge & Kegan Paul Ltd. for quotations from C. G. Jung, *The Integration of Personality,* trans. Stanley Dell, copyright 1940.

Index